THE INTERNATIONAL RACING ANNUAL

HAZLETON PUBLISHING, RICHMOND, SURREY

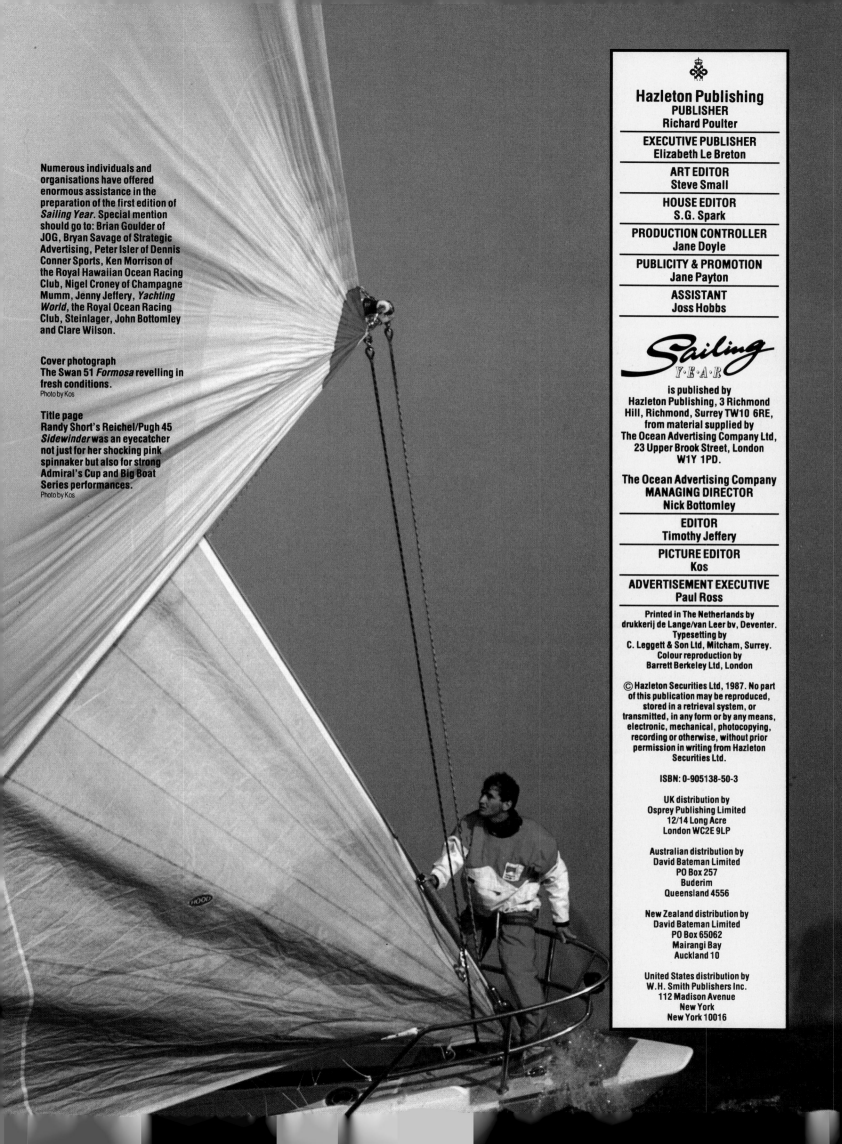

Numerous individuals and organisations have offered enormous assistance in the preparation of the first edition of *Sailing Year*. Special mention should go to: Brian Goulder of JOG, Bryan Savage of Strategic Advertising, Peter Isler of Dennis Conner Sports, Ken Morrison of the Royal Hawaiian Ocean Racing Club, Nigel Croney of Champagne Mumm, Jenny Jeffery, *Yachting World*, the Royal Ocean Racing Club, Steinlager, John Bottomley and Clare Wilson.

Cover photograph
The Swan 51 *Formosa* revelling in fresh conditions.
Photo by Kos

Title page
Randy Short's Reichel/Pugh 45 *Sidewinder* was an eyecatcher not just for her shocking pink spinnaker but also for strong Admiral's Cup and Big Boat Series performances.
Photo by Kos

✧

Hazleton Publishing
PUBLISHER
Richard Poulter

EXECUTIVE PUBLISHER
Elizabeth Le Breton

ART EDITOR
Steve Small

HOUSE EDITOR
S. G. Spark

PRODUCTION CONTROLLER
Jane Doyle

PUBLICITY & PROMOTION
Jane Payton

ASSISTANT
Joss Hobbs

Sailing Y·E·A·R

is published by Hazleton Publishing, 3 Richmond Hill, Richmond, Surrey TW10 6RE, from material supplied by The Ocean Advertising Company Ltd, 23 Upper Brook Street, London W1Y 1PD.

The Ocean Advertising Company
MANAGING DIRECTOR
Nick Bottomley

EDITOR
Timothy Jeffery

PICTURE EDITOR
Kos

ADVERTISEMENT EXECUTIVE
Paul Ross

Printed in The Netherlands by drukkerij de Lange/van Leer bv, Deventer. Typesetting by C. Leggett & Son Ltd, Mitcham, Surrey. Colour reproduction by Barrett Berkeley Ltd, London

ISBN: 0-905138-50-3

UK distribution by
Osprey Publishing Limited
12/14 Long Acre
London WC2E 9LP

Australian distribution by
David Bateman Limited
PO Box 257
Buderim
Queensland 4556

New Zealand distribution by
David Bateman Limited
PO Box 65062
Mairangi Bay
Auckland 10

United States distribution by
W. H. Smith Publishers Inc.
112 Madison Avenue
New York
New York 10016

Foreword

by DENNIS CONNER

I spent some time recently with my America's Cup navigator, Peter Isler, reflecting on my past in sailing and how the sport is shaping up for the future. With events being so full during the run-in to and after our Cup win in Fremantle, there has been little opportunity to take stock, but I thought the readers of the inaugural issue of *Sailing Year* might like to share my thoughts.

The biggest change that I can see has to be in the entry level to our sport. When I started sailing, as a kid in San Diego, there were no organised Junior sailing programmes. Today, the training available to young sailors in the States is enormous. Programmes teach thousands of kids how to race every year. The level of instruction continues to improve.

In the Olympic classes and collegiate sailing, which is really strong in the US, use is beginning to be made of professional coaches. Such methods and techniques are sure to trickle down to sailing instructors at all levels.

I have also noticed that entry level boats are better today. They are easier to maintain and more exciting to sail. Again, that will help keep kids involved in our sport. The bottom line of all these changes is that we see more good sailors today than ever before. They may never reach the America's Cup level, for various reasons, but the level of competition in the sport has definitely improved thanks to the training our youngsters are receiving. Nor is this something which is only happening in the States: worldwide, youngsters are getting better.

The second major change in the sport is in the area of technology.

Obviously, the use of new materials in all parts of the sailboat has had a profound effect and, I think, a *good* effect, for sailing cannot stand still.

A more subtle development has been in the level of commitment people make to the sport. Thanks to this, the quality of sailing has improved, something that has been helped along by the greater numbers sailing now than when I started out. More people are aware of the sport, and more are aware that sailing is an activity that they, too, can enjoy.

All this is evident in the America's Cup. When I sailed my first Cup in 1974 the level of commitment was of a different order. You would start sailing in the early part of the summer and sail intensively through the Cup, although even that was nowhere near the level we sail today. In Newport in '74, we had just 15 members on the *Courageous* team – a far cry from operating a multi-million dollar syndicate half-way around the world in Australia!

The people in Cup sailing have changed, too. Today, every crew member has earned his or her position based upon ability. When I started sailing, there were people aboard 12-metres because of their money. Moreover, the modern America's Cup campaign requires more attention to the non-sailing aspects of the competition. Organisation, leadership, motivation, logistics, technology – all play a much fuller role than they did in the early Seventies.

The most significant of these developments in Cup sailing has been increased visibility for the sport as a whole. Wherever I go today people

recognise me. Yet I am no better a sailor than when I won the Star Worlds in 1977, but the Cup has made me famous – well-known to the general public, not just among other sailors.

The Cup has played its own part in improving the sport, too. Many of the techniques developed aboard the 12-metres have filtered down to the everyday sailor. The dip-pole gybe was first used aboard the Twelves and is now the standard for gybing larger boats. Spinnaker changes where the bowman rides out to the end of the pole with the new sail on a spare halyard was also seen first on 12-metres. So were moveable jib leads, the use of hydraulics . . . the list goes on and on.

Yet, despite all this technology and technique, the most important contribution made by the Cup is a human one. America's Cup sailors sail with and teach other people. Information about new ways to make a sailboat go faster is disseminated by an ever-broadening base of sailors trained aboard 12-metres.

The 1974 America's Cup summer holds many memories for me. I sailed aboard *Mariner* with Ted Turner, and it was my first exposure to a Cup summer in Newport. Another highlight was my first SORC (Southern Ocean Racing Conference) victory in 1975 where I sailed my own boat, *Stinger*. And of course I am very proud of my Olympic medal in the Tempest Class in 1976.

Having been involved so heavily with the Cup you might be surprised to know that my proudest successes have come not in 12-metres but in another class. My first international victory was

particularly sweet. It was the Star World Championship in 1971 where I sailed against many of the modern day heroes of sailboat racing.

But perhaps my biggest victory, the one I am most proud of, is the 1977 Star World Championship in Kiel, West Germany. There were 89 boats and we won the regatta with a perfect score, straight 1sts, in the most competitive class in the world.

Then, of course, there was the Cup again. In 1980 I was involved in all aspects of the successful *Freedom* campaign. That was followed, in 1983, by the loss which is painted indelibly in every sailor's mind, including mine, and finally by the winning back of the Cup in 1987. It is quite a store of memories.

So what of the future? Sailing is enjoying a banner year thanks to the recent America's Cup and is enjoying greater popularity than ever before. I see this continuing. Glassfibre technology is improving still further, so that boats should last longer. Entry level boats such as a daysailer are quite reasonably priced; there are now many ways to enter and participate in sailing. Chartering, sailing clubs and so on all bring new people into the sport. Even a cheap, secondhand sailboard can provide as much fun as we had in winning the America's Cup.

These new participants will tell their friends, and word of mouth is the most effective marketing method there is. So the more people who sail, the more people will hear about it.

Sailing is just starting to flower. I, for one, will be excited to see just where our sport is heading.

Introduction

Sailing has always been one of the great sports. In a rare and heady mix it combines physical demands with mental stimulation; it provides appreciation of the outdoor world in its fairest and foulest of moods; and it permits a unique opportunity for the beginner to compete in the same races as the most accomplished experts. This is quite apart from the spectacle of it all which can be appreciated by participants and spectators alike, and the endless enjoyment which sailing can bring ashore.

Sailing Year's debut cannot have come at a more exciting time. Against the background of sailing's traditional image, some parts of the sport have quickened the pace of change by joining the razzmatazz world of professional sport.

For better or worse, sailing at its highest levels will increasingly become the preserve of full-time sailors. The complexities of fast and flighty multihulls, inhospitable International Offshore Rule ocean racers and idiosyncratic 12-metres will mean that those good enough to crew them will be those able to devote their working life to them.

In the process, some of our top sailors will enjoy more than fame alone. Dennis Conner is, perhaps, the epitome of the new super sailors, a man whose modest business was close to decay not so long ago. In those days, he knew to the nearest cent how much loose change he had in his pocket, but today he doesn't need to care.

Virtuoso amateurs will have to find their sport in other levels and other classes. If weekend sailors can be left to compete in the events and classes they want, away from the money-propelled super classes, so much the better. The majority will then be able to enjoy sport among themselves and yet be able to follow the goings-on of the Grand Prix circus.

What is even clearer is that there will be more events added to an already crowded world sailing calendar. They range from local clubs organising new events such as inter-club or shorthanded races, to more ambitious courses such as the trans-ocean Atlantic Rally for Cruisers to exotic venues. The latter will have been prompted by the interest now being shown by sponsors, television concerns and major promoters such as Mark McCormack's International Management Group and Bernie Ecclestone, a leading figure in Formula 1 motor racing. Such men have already changed the face of tennis, golf and Formula 1 motor racing; now they are turning their attention to yachting.

When the idea for *Sailing Year* was being developed, it became clear just how valuable the annual would be for sailing enthusiasts, yacht clubs and race organisers. Although there has never been so much published and broadcast about sailing, an accurate record of key events, a compendium of their results and a selection of the finest photographs has not existed . . . until now.

But we don't want *Sailing Year* to be collected simply because it has brought so much together in one book; rather, we hope it will appeal because it contains the best in journalism, photography and graphic design.

Y·E·A·R

1
Dennis Conner
2
Philippe Jeantot
3
Stuart Childerley
4
Bruce Farr
5
Iain Murray
6
Philippe Poupon
7
Michael Fay
8
James Hatfield
9
Jim Kilroy
10
Philippe Monnet

Top Ten People

1 Dennis Conner

The America's Cup is now more firmly linked to Dennis Conner's name than to any of his illustrious forebears – Schuyler, Barr, Herreshoff, Lipton, Vanderbilt, Stephens and Lexcen included.

By winning back the Cup he'd lost in 1983 he secured more than just a place in the annals of yachting. If there is one name in sailing alone known the world over it is Conner's – the man given a tickertape welcome in New York and received by President Reagan at the White House. Conner has become the first sailor to be a sporting superstar with the earning power of a golfer, footballer or tennis player.

All this has been achieved through sheer dogged determination. He may have sailed more hours in 12-metres than any other sailor (some 10,000 hours) but the vast majority of those have been the drudgery of sail testing and tuning. For his 1987 Cup win, he may have surrounded himself by more able intellects in the realms of administration, design and technical innovation, but Conner was still the lynch pin. He made the endless 'smile and dial' fund-raising telephone calls, the public appearances and the begging boardroom presentations. Then he went out and sailed a 12-metre better than anyone else had done before.

DENNIS CONNER – photo by KOS

2 Philippe Jeantot

Philippe Jeantot wins his place in the Top Ten for not only winning the longest (27,000 miles) and toughest single-handed yacht race there is but for having done so twice.

His second victory in the BOC Challenge was a much finer one than his first as the competition was appreciably stiffer. He was racing against several boats which were as fast as his own *Credit Agricole III* and the intensity of the race was such that Jeantot clipped 25 days off his previous best to set a new race record of 134d 5h 46m 45s.

It was the first BOC which brought this Marseilles-based diver to notice. He proved his exceptional abilities subsequently with the *Credit Agricole II* catamaran in which he rattled off 514 miles in 24 hours during the 1984 Quebec–St Malo Race. When the big cat was dismasted in the Route de la Decouverte race, Jeantot used his diving skills successfully to salvage the boat. Less than six weeks later he set a new record in Martinique, sailing at 27.08 knots over a one-mile course.

A superb athlete, he is a joy to watch on a boat. Both nimble and powerfully built, he is, above all, a very determined sailor. When *Credit Agricole III*'s genoa tore on the first leg of the BOC Race, he spent nearly four weeks sewing the heavy sail back together by hand because his machine had broken down.

But for this sail damage, his win in the race might have been even more emphatic.

PHILIPPE JEANTOT – photo by François Richard

3 Stuart Childerley

Though the Olympic sailing classes fail to attract the attention they used to, the level of achievement in the eight classes is still outstanding.

This year, the finest performance of all in the five-ring circus was put up by a 21-year-old Englishman, Stuart Childerley. A former member of Britain's Youth Squad and coached by Jim Saltonstall, Childerley sailed the Laser class when the Squad won the World Youth Championships in 1985.

From the Laser, he switched to the Finn class and has not stopped winning. In securing six championship wins in one season, Childerley has put up what is considered to be the best performance the class has ever known. Childerley won his titles at Palamos (Spain), Genoa (Italy), Cannes (France), Garda (Italy) and, most significantly, at the European Championship in Rungsted (Denmark) and the pre-Olympic regatta in Pusan (S. Korea). He also clocked up three 3rds in other championships; his 13th in the World Championships at Kiel (plagued by light winds and an illness) can be counted as his only real failure.

Moreover, all the victories have been in 40-plus boat fleets and Childerley has met and beaten all the top Finn sailors likely to be in the running for next year's Olympic gold medal, especially those from the USA and Eastern Bloc where there is great strength in the Finn fleets.

4 Bruce Farr

Yacht design is a precarious business, especially in the racing field where the competition is cut-throat.

While yacht design has really opened up in the last five years with more designers active than ever, New Zealander Bruce Farr has achieved a dominant share of success.

He played a leading role in the creation of the New Zealand 12-metres, both in hull form and their glassfibre construction. It surprised few that when Michael Fay unveiled his 90 ft waterline boat challenge, the commission to design the boat went to Farr and not to other members of the original Kiwi challenge design team.

Other successes logged during the year included *Nakiri Daio*'s win of the Melbourne–Osaka two-handed race and *Propaganda*'s top-yacht performance in the Admiral's Cup. A version of the now-famous Farr 40 design, Crown Prince Harald's *Fram X*, won the One Ton Cup, so giving Farr wins in the two most important and most competitive IOR events of the year.

The Farr 40 design has been on top for an unusually long time. Race boat designs are not normally longlived yet the Farr 40 first appeared in 1982 in the guise of *Pacific Sundance* and *Exador*, and the developed design is still winning six seasons later. *Sundance* and *Exador* marked Farr's return to the IOR big time, having been legislated out of it in the late Seventies, which left him thoroughly disenchanted as a consequence. He has been able to continue massaging the shapes to keep them competitive and for the 1987 season made a special effort to concentrate crew weight amidships around the radius of gyration rather than pursue the usual bow-down trim/crew weight aft route favoured by most designers.

With such a grasp on the IOR fleet it is not surprising that Farr has four maxis to design for the next Whitbread Round the World Race.

5 Iain Murray

Sadly for Iain Murray he will be remembered as the man who failed to keep the America's Cup in Australia after Alan Bond had won it in 1983.

This is an unfair penalty for being the loser, especially as it overshadows what had been a magnificent America's Cup for Murray – until he met Conner.

Of all the skippers in the Cup, none took on such a wide role as Murray. True, Conner was the pivotal figure in his syndicate, but did he design his own yachts? Murray did. The young Sydneysider also recruited the 100-strong team and set up the boatbuilding and in-house spar- and sail-making facilities which made the Taskforce syndicate the most self-sufficient in Fremantle. Murray's strategy was responsible for the *Kookaburras* being the most technically advanced of the 12-metres in computing terms, and that allowed him to beat the Bond camp's 12 years of Cup expertise.

And Murray won the respect of all his group by being no different from them. His down-to-earth character has no side and he gets on with the business in hand. He also has great poise and a laconic sense of humour which stood him in good stead when facing the combined barrage of the world's media ashore and *Stars & Stripes '87* afloat.

In the last race against Conner, with the Cup as good as lost, a bomb threat was taken seriously enough by the police for a committee boat to rush alongside *Kookaburra III* to see if Murray wanted to pull out of the race. When told about the possibility of a bomb being aboard, he said: 'We checked through our option list and said "what's the bad news?".'

The Cup behind him, Murray skippered Peter Kurts's *Madeline's Daughter* in the Aussie Admiral's Cup team. It says much about the man that, after the Fastnet Race, he was sponging out the bilges of the yacht together with the owner and crew. There was no lording it ashore while others worked, as was the case with some famous skippers.

You can be sure, Murray's time will come again soon – just as it did when he designed and sailed six successive 18 ft skiff championship winners.

6 Philippe Poupon

For several years now, 33-year-old Philippe Poupon has been at the top of the tree in the sponsored multihull racing world sailing a fleet of *Fleury Michons*. His association with his sponsor Fleury Michon (a meat products manufacturer) has been a textbook example of how a sailor and commercial backer can work together. Since 1985, Bristol-based multihull designer Nigel Irens and leading French builder Jeanneau have also willingly entangled themselves in Poupon's web, with all four parties enjoying considerable success.

During the TAG Round Europe Race, Poupon was racing the 75 ft (22.9 m) *Fleury Michon VIII*, the ultimate downwind trimaran, with which in 1986 Poupon won the prestigious single-handed race from St Malo to Guadeloupe, the Route de Rhum. However, on two occasions during the TAG race, he had to pass the helm over to his brother Luc in order to fly off to race his equally successful *Fleury Michon* Formula 40 at Grands Prix at Southampton, England, and Nieuwpoort, Belgium. By the time of the seventh Grand Prix, the boat was 1st-equal in the International Formula 40 Championship. Not many sailors are provided with two new boats to race in one season!

Poupon's biggest success in 1987, however, was breaking the fully crewed west–east transatlantic record from New York to the Lizard, setting a new time of 7d 12h 50m at an average of 17.3 knots.

Poupon, like so many well-known French multihull racers, served his apprenticeship under Eric Tabarly, with whom he sailed the 1977/78 Whitbread Round the World Race aboard *Pen Duick VI* and on *Pen Duick II* in the first St Malo–Point à Pitre Race.

Nigel Irens, now a close friend, summed up the secret of Poupon's success: 'Philou at every level is a good, shrewd decision-maker. His success is due to skill and a nose for surrounding himself with good people.'

For 1988 there is to be yet another new *Fleury Michon* trimaran, this time a 60 ft (18.3 m) Nigel Irens design for the Carlsberg Singlehanded Transatlantic race. In 1984, Poupon reached Newport in 1st place but unfortunately lost the race on a time correction to rival Yvon Fauconnier. Poupon is looking to set the record straight.

7 Michael Fay

In the America's Cup arena, New Zealand's Michael Fay is either seen as the villain of the piece or some kind of hero. His detractors dislike his assertive manner and the way in which he does not let convention stand in his way.

To our eyes, these are the very characteristics which make him such good news for sailing. Although a newcomer to sailing and to the America's Cup, Fay's arrival on the scene has certainly gingered things up. His talent for communication ensured that the Kiwis were never in danger of losing the 'Glassgate' squabble over their glassfibre boats, while his astute business brain has turned the Kiwi campaign into a money-spinner.

Just like Alan Bond and Peter de Savary, Fay used the America's Cup to launch himself on the worldwide stage. A trained lawyer, Michael Fay was just a salaried employee, until he founded his own merchant bank along with partner David Richwhite in 1975. The Fay, Richwhite bank now operates in Sydney and London as well as in New Zealand; Fay has achieved national and international prominence.

The sheer audacity of a 90 ft waterline challenge to the San Diego YC for an America's Cup to be fought between just the Kiwis and the US in 1988 is typical of the man. Tipped off that the Deed of Gift had a loophole big enough to sail a 120 ft yacht through, he lodged his challenge. It is a means to an end because it short-cuts the America's Cup multi-challenger elimination procedure and improves the odds for winning the Cup . . . and making a financial killing in staging a defence in New Zealand.

Whether or not the grand smash-and-grab plan succeeds or fails, Michael Fay has put some real zip into the America's Cup and forced the lawyers to get their paperwork sorted out. To his credit, he has backed many other aspects of Kiwi yachting, including their winning 1986 Kenwood Cup and a crew training scheme at the Royal New Zealand Yacht Squadron.

Just like Bond and de Savary, Fay is a larger-than-life figure. As a sport, sailing is none the worse for it.

MICHAEL FAY – photo by Barry Pickthall

JAMES HATFIELD – photo by Eyeline

8 James Hatfield

In May 1984 a 24 ft (7.3 m), gaff-rigged Cornish Crabber called *British Heart II* set out from Penzance, England, on a round-the-world voyage. More than three years later, in September 1987, a 29 ft (8.8 m) sloop called *British Heart III* sailed into Penzance to complete the circumnavigation by her lone skipper, James Hatfield.

Apart from the unusual aspect of changing boats half-way round, this voyage was unique in that James Hatfield, now 31 years old, was born with a hole in his heart and was given only three days to live. After a series of ten operations over the course of his very active life, James decided to undertake the west–east voyage both for his own satisfaction and to raise money for a body scanner to be used at Papworth Hospital, one of Britain's leading heart hospitals. By the end of his voyage he had raised £23,000.

The circumnavigation was full of incidents and near-disasters, but Hatfield survived them all. Bad weather forced him to put into Brazil and he had to sail 700 miles of the passage to Cape Town without a rudder. From South Africa he sailed to Australia, where he spent four to five months held up by bad weather and various engine problems, but all this was nothing compared to the disaster that awaited him beyond New Zealand. In a position some 1700 miles off the coast his boat sank, leaving him to be rescued by a Belgian container ship. Undeterred, James Hatfield used insurance money to buy a 29 ft replacement boat, sailing on from Panama to Florida, then north to Boston and back across the Atlantic to England.

It was a truly courageous circumnavigation. Although sailing around the world is not the rare achievement it used to be, Hatfield's voyage was rather special.

9 Jim Kilroy

Jim Kilroy has been racing maxis for 25 years and now, more than ever, he is the man to beat. His latest *Kialoa V* (Polynesian for 'long white canoe'), is the fifth in a famous line and is the 1987 World Champion maxi. She won the International Class A Yacht Association's Championship which was split between regattas in Newport, Rhode Island, and Porto Cervo, Sardinia – an achievement all the more remarkable because the class has become even more competitive of late.

Jim Kilroy is also one of the diminishing breed of owners who steer their own yachts and his involvement is total. 'It's more than a hobby,' says skipper Alan Prior about *Kialoa V*'s owner, 'it's a way of life for him now. He likes sailing, he likes winning and if something doesn't work he's willing to change it and experiment.'

Jim Kilroy himself declines to accept personal responsibility for the *Kialoa* success story. He pays tribute to Alan Prior, mate Alex Wadson and the 50 or so who sail aboard in any given year. 'It's not an individualistic effort. We have so much input from everyone', he says. Yet, without Jim Kilroy, his five *Kialoa*'s would not have been the dominant big boats for so long – a record few can equal.

JIM KILROY – photo by KOS

PHILIPPE MONNET – photo by Christian Février

10 Philippe Monnet

There is nothing unusual in a French sailor pulling off yet another sailing stunt, for there can be few stretches of water remaining which have not been crossed by anything from a sailboard to a maxi multihull.

But when 26-year-old Philippe Monnet sailed into Brest on 19 April he confounded all manner of sceptics. For Monnet had just sailed around the world non-stop, single-handed in the 65 ft trimaran *Kriter Brut de Brut*, setting a remarkably quick time of 129d 19h 27m.

Monnet's aim had been to beat the non-stop single-handed time set by American Dodge Morgan in *American Promise* as well as the long-standing solo multihull record set by Alain Colas in *Manureva*.

His chance of the non-stop record was missed when Monnet had to stop for 67 hours on the outward leg to attend to forestay repairs. He needed assistance with the work, which ruled him out of reckoning for the record.

The circumnavigation was not without its dramas. The tri was repeatedly swept by seas, making for a very wet five months for the Frenchman. He also had a lucky escape when he fell from the top of the mast as his safety line broke. He was able to save himself by grabbing a halyard on the way down, but the rope burns to his hands were severe.

In a yacht without the relative comforts of BOC Race monohulls and with the capsize potential of a multihull, Monnet's trip was concluded through sheer gritty courage.

Sailing Y·E·A·R

Top Ten Boats

1 Stars & Stripes '87

Without *Stars & Stripes '87* Dennis Conner would not have made his mercurial America's Cup come back. Yet, for a time, she was a boat he did not believe he needed and his syndicate did not have the money to fund. But as the last 12-metre to be built for the America's Cup she proved to be the best for the job.

Stars & Stripes '87 was the product not only of an incredible design team but of a development process that was unprecedented in its scope. It took four other 12-metres to get *Stars & Stripes '87* right. First there was *Liberty*, the humbled 1983 defender which was the yardstick. Then there were *Stars & Stripes '83*, the old S&S-designed *Spirit of America* which was rebuilt on *Australia II* lines, and *Stars & Stripes '85*, which was a smaller derivative. By floating up the big boat and sinking the small one, the length *v* sail area options were bracketed. These were combined with a radical bulb bow concept tried on *Stars & Stripes '86* which explored wave-making reduction theories.

Of all of them, Conner heavily favoured '85 despite a light-air weakness. But the design team had seen enough of '86's features to press for one more boat, a synthesis of all that had been learnt – a true breakthrough boat.

The resulting '87 was a deceptively normal-looking boat at first sight. But those who studied her noted the full bow and stern which featured an unfashionably big bustle. This pushing of volume distribution to the ends was quite radical. It cut down wave-making drag and dampened motion.

As a result, *Stars & Stripes '87* could point high upwind, reach fast by pushing her stern wave right aft, and run downwind at deep angles. She was a true all-rounder, optimised to shine in the 15-knot-plus conditions found in Gage Roads. What she lacked was manoeuvrability but, since Conner wanted speed first and nimbleness second, she was the best of all the Fremantle Twelves.

2 Propaganda

The name was going to be used for a racehorse but backers Adrian Burr, Peter Tatham and Bevan Woolley decided to build a boat instead.

Just six months before becoming the top yacht in the Champagne Mumm Admiral's Cup with an impressive 19-1-1-5-4 record, *Propaganda* looked to be everything but a winner. Launched just before the New Zealand AC trials, the boat had all sorts of rating problems. Instead of rating on the one ton level of 30.55, *Propaganda* was classified 31.2 ft IOR.

The boat's RM (Righting Moment) was way below design, so 600 mm was lopped off the keel. The removal of some 1000 lb (450 kg) of lead lost enough stability to get the rating down to 30.6 ft and the boat sailed her way into the Kiwi team.

In an attempt to get the rating right, the Farr office advised that some 660 lb (300 kg) be put back on the keel. To their surprise, no rating increase occurred other than a small CGF (Centre of Gravity Factor), which was removed for a final rating of 30.58 ft.

Clearly the boat was very sensitive to inclines at measurement. But, with that behind them, her crew set about a winning campaign. They had bought well in choosing Cookson Brothers as their builder for the advanced carbon fibre, Kevlar and Nomex honeycomb boat. Then, mindful of past Kiwi campaigns coming unstuck as their local masts fell down, they procured a Sparcraft 6000 series mast from England. They also copied the top European one tonners by adding titanium metalwork fittings from Ian Terry Engineering in Lymington, England.

Sails came from North in Auckland, though local Windward and overseas Sobstad and Diamond sails were bought as quality/speed checks.

After the trials, Bevan Woolley reorganised the crew. Initially, Brad Butterworth (*KZ-7*'s tactician) had helmed and called the tactics, but Woolley brought in Peter Lester from the failed triallist *Fair Share* to steer the boat so that both helmsman and tactician could concentrate 100 per cent on their departments.

While the rest of the crew are not yet household names such is the depth of Kiwi talent now that they can count Whitbread races, an America's Cup and a 12-metre Worlds series on their sailing CVs.

The sum of all these factors was that *Propaganda* had the speed, tactical strength and slick crewing to turn in a winning performance. *Propaganda* was certainly the quickest one tonner upwind in the whole fleet by some margin and was better than average in other departments.

3 Credit Agricole III

All yachts are designed for a purpose, yet those of the BOC Challenge Singlehanded Around Alone race have to meet both tougher and more varied requirements than most.

Paris-based designer Guy Ribadeau-Dumas has the unusual distinction of having designed both Philippe Jeantot's winners of this tough singlehanded round the world race. With *Credit Agricole III*, Ribadeau-Dumas developed ideas from the first boat much further. The boat had everything to make sailing a big, powerful 60-footer easy for one man.

The cockpit, for instance, was like a ring of winches (some 14 self-tailers in all), the primaries powered by a coffee grinder pedestal. Everything could be handled from there apart from the jib and spinnaker halyards which were bounced at the mast.

Then the decks were covered with light but very effective cork TBS deck covering, a clue to Jeantot's highly refined sense of seamanship. And the rig, a massive section Marechal mast with internal sleeving, looked like a spar designed to withstand the worst the oceans could throw at it. In the light of rig problems which plagued other entries, the conservative approach paid dividends.

Massive wire standing rigging was fitted instead of rod because its greater stretch reduced the onset of fatigue.

And, of course, the big genoa was set on a roller furler, though smaller jibs were hanked on to a normal forestay in the conventional manner.

But it was the hull design which was particularly clever. Compared with the earlier boat, Ribadeau-Dumas flattened out the sections to make the yacht much beamier. This extra form stability was supplemented by internal tanks into which 1.5 tons of sea water could be flooded. Combined with a plumb stem which gave a 6 ft (2 m) longer waterline than *CA 1* and a much bigger rig, the whole boat was a real powerhouse in comparison.

Not surprisingly, Jeantot knocked some 25 days off his earlier circumnavigation, while the boat was able to hit sustained (20 minutes) speeds of just under 20 knots.

The novel hull form was tank tested, with assistance from Ribadeau-Dumas's brother, Eric. Twin rudders were fitted. These had the same drag as the single rudder and daggerboard configuration used on the earlier boat, but they were more efficient and offered in-built emergency steering. And the heavily tumblehomed topsides not only saved weight but were designed with a view to reducing inverse stability should the yacht be capsized 180 degrees.

In all, a singularly successful yacht built for a specific purpose.

4 Biscuits Cantreau

Seeing Jean le Cam's original *Biscuits Cantreau* racing at the Southampton Grand Prix in 1986 was quite an eye-opener. Part of his technique in sailing the foil-assisted trimaran involved pushing her so hard that even the main hull was just clear of the water, thereby reducing wetted surface area. One of the fundamental problems with this, though, was that if the main hull was airborne, so was the rudder. For the new 1987 *Biscuits* her Paris-based designers, Marc van Peteghem and Vincent Lauriot Prevost, came up with a simple solution: three rudders, one on each transom.

Apart from this basic curiosity, *Biscuits II* is a most revolutionary design. With three rudders came three helming positions which did away with the need for a cockpit in her central hull. This hull is as a consequence only marginally larger than the floats, which in turn were also greatly inflated, as those on the first *Biscuits* would bury when the tri was sailed flat-out. The elliptical carbon/epoxy beams of the new boat were also

extended and, at 35 ft 5 in. (10.8 m), were very much larger in comparison to her predecessor's 28 ft 7 in. (8.7 m) beam. Conceptually, *Biscuits Cantreau II* is a catamaran with a centre hull.

After the success of Randy Smyth and Serge Madec in catamaran Formula 40s in 1986, le Cam and his colleagues at CDK Composites in Port la Fôret, France, were the only ones to build a new trimaran for the 1987 season. This decision paid off, as by the time of the seventh Grand Prix on Lake Garda in Italy, *Biscuits II* had won the Grands Prix at Cherbourg, Southampton, Lake Geneva and Lake Garda and was well on her way to winning the F-40 championship.

Biscuits Cantreau II performed best in light airs, especially on the wind, which gave her a big advantage on the lakes, but the extra beam over her catamaran opponents allowed her to keep the pressure on in the strong conditions too. It should be interesting to see how many *Biscuits Cantreau II* clones will be racing in 1988.

5 KZ-7

Call her *KZ-7*, Kiwi Magic, Plastic Fantastic or what you will, the boat which carried New Zealand's torch in their first America's Cup achieved a remarkable record.

That she failed to win the Cup itself and was crushed by Dennis Conner and *Stars & Stripes '87* in the Louis Vuitton Challengers' finals does not detract from *KZ-7*'s stunning record. That she won 38 of her 43 America's Cup races is one of the great achievements in yachting.

Designers Bruce Farr (and, crucially,

his engineering partner Russell Bowler), Ron Holland and Laurie Davidson made what now seem very simple choices in creating *KZ-7*. Given anticipated Fremantle conditions they placed a high emphasis on stability and went for a low centre of gravity. In choosing glassfibre construction they literally broke the mould of 12-metre construction. Not only were *KZ-3* and *KZ-5* the world's first glassfibre 12-metres but they were an extremely expedient means of catching up with the more experienced 12-metre cam-

paigners by allowing their designs invaluable full-scale testing. Thus *KZ-7* found the right mark. Moreover, glassfibre construction enabled a much stiffer boat to be constructed than had been achieved before, allowing the rig to be loaded up more and the boat to point high.

There is little doubt that if *KZ-7* had not come up against Conner's straight line drag racer, she would have been the challenger. And we know from Michael Fay's unprecedented decision to help the defending Taskforce syndi-

cate prior to Murray's clash with Conner that *KZ-7* was more than a match for *Kookaburra III*.

To prove the versatility of *KZ-7*, she went on to win the 12-metre World Championships in Porto Cervo six months after the America's Cup. After some minor tinkering with her ballast and sail plan, she was fully competitive in conditions a full 10–15 knots down from Fremantle.

KZ-7 was, and remains, a remarkable all-round performer.

6 Whirlwind XII

In concert with the new levels of awareness of sailing, has been the boom in certain aspects of the sport and industry. This is no more true than in the super-luxury market where yachts cost millions, take thousands of hours to build and can be measured in hundreds of feet.

Of the small handful of 100 ft-plus sailing yachts which have slipped into the water, none are finer than *Whirlwind XII*, built for Englishman Noel Lister. Designed by Ron Holland, the Irish-based New Zealander, *Whirlwind XII* was constructed by the world-renowned Royal Huisman Shipyard, close by the IJsselmeer at Wolenhove in the Netherlands.

Although $3.5 million may seem an extraordinarily high sum to pay for a yacht, *Whirlwind XII* is not just an object to be appreciated but an appreciating object. Just a year after her launch, she would have cost half as much to build again.

Her fairness of construction, depth of gloss of her topside finish, the engineering and installation of her machinery and systems, and the beautifully worked joinery all stand as testament to her Dutch builders. To give but one example, the saloon table took 1000 man-hours to complete, its intricate necklace of marquetry work showing the history of sail in beautifully worked inlays.

But the Peter Sijm-designed interior is more than amply matched by the sailing qualities of the hull. As one of the new generation of super-sloops, a towering 110 ft rig is tamed by use of in-mast mainsail and headsail hydraulic roller furling. *Whirlwind XII* marks a new level of achievement in combining power with convenience.

While other big yachts were launched in the last 12 months, perhaps more ritzy in their styling or more technically innovative, the sheer quality of the execution of the yacht-builder's art makes *Whirlwind XII* the definitive super-cruiser.

François Richard

7 Jet Services V

The most recent *Jet Services* catamaran was the scourge of the 1987 TAG Round Europe Race in July and August, in which out of eight legs she won six. Her remarkable performance in this race can partly be attributed to her designer, Gilles Ollier, who has opened up a new avenue in maxi-multihull design.

The 38-year-old naval architect also designed the previous 60 ft (18 m) and 85 ft (26 m) *Jet Services* catamarans for their original skipper, Patrick Morvan, and currently leads the field in maxi-catamaran design. With the new *Jet*, however, Ollier has broken new ground. Bearing a strong resemblance to a scaled-up Formula 40, in particular Ollier's *Jet 40* design for Serge Madec, she is equipped with a powerful 2700 ft^2 (250 m^2) North mainsail, a comparatively small 750 ft^2 (70 m^2) jib and a tall 103 ft (31 m) wingmast. In comparison to the wingmast on *Elf Aquitaine*, which Ollier also constructed, *Jet*'s is very slender – more like Barry Noble's mast for *Apricot* – and has a chord of 2 ft 3 in. (700 mm), a surface area of 240 ft^2 (22 m^2) and even has hydraulic spreaders to ensure mast bend. Each of *Jet*'s hulls has its own cockpit with duplicated sail controls. *Jet* was built by Multiplast, Ollier's shipbuilding yard in Vannes, France, which is owned by Jet Services and specialises in the building of high-tech racing multihulls. Such is their know-how that they claim to be flexible enough to take on work for the aerospace industry.

Jet's entire construction was in carbon fibre and the exotic recipe for her cylindrical beams and wingmast was the use of pre-impregnated composites which were then baked in a specially made oven, at 180°C for the beams and at 120°C for the wingmast. The whole boat was built in sections, and can still be disassembled for transportation if necessary as her 44 ft (13 m) crossbeams sit in cradles that are secured to the hulls by enormous bolts and carbon braces.

Capable of reaching at a steady 30 knots, Ollier's latest design was assessed by Eric Tabarly: 'in comparison with *Jet Services*, all our boats are obsolete' – an accolade indeed.

8 Il Moro di Venezia III

Buenos Aires-based German Frers Jnr has established himself as *the* maxi designer with the lion's share of commissions in the 80 ft class. The sheer expense of a new maxi – say $1.5 million to get one launched and ready for campaigning – has tended to act against owners experimenting with design and designer, unlike the situation in the smaller classes. Frers' maxis have thus developed steadily through *Bumblebee IV*, *Helisara*, *Xargo IV* and *Boomerang* to *Kialoa V* and *Ondine VII*.

Just when it seemed another designer might come and give the maxi fleet a shake-up, German Frers has done it himself with the new *Il Moro di Venezia III*. She was built for Italian industrialist Raoul Gardini, backer of the *Italia* 12-metre in Fremantle, major shareholder in Italy's biggest chemical company and owner of two previous successful Frers boats.

German Frers has plumped for a complicated four-spreader fractional rig in a class where masthead rigs are almost *de rigueur*. Even the new Bruce Farr-designed maxi now building for the Spanish Navy is masthead rigged. *Il Moro*'s spar and rig control, such as a circular vang track, use much of the knowledge gained in 12-metres.

Even more surprising was that *Il Moro* was fast straight out of the box. She won her first series in Palma, and in the second half of the Maxi Worlds in Porto Cervo was beaten only by *Kialoa V* among the 70 raters. The new boat looks particularly strong reaching and running.

B.V. Int

Franco Pace

9 Phocea

At 242 ft (74 m) long, *Phocea* is not the largest private yacht ever built. Past leviathans such as Marjorie Hutton's *Sea Cloud* at 308 ft (94 m) or *Valhalla* which is a mere 1 ft 5 in. (450 mm) longer than *Phocea* can lay claim to the title.

But why be pedantic? *Phocea* is by far the largest yacht of recent times. She began life as the monster *Club Méditerranée* and was sailed by the late Alain Colas in the 1976 Observer Singlehanded Transatlantic Race having been built by the Arsenal de Toulon. After the race she sailed in the Pacific between Papeete, Bora-Bora and Moorea, and was finally bought in a sorry state by industrialist Bernard Tapie.

A massive rebuilding programme has completely transformed the yacht. Paris-based designer Jacques Pierrejean was called in to style the interior. Accustomed to designing aircraft interiors, he must have been familiar with the problems posed by a long and narrow space. But ten cabins have been fitted, quite apart from the general, crew and owner's cabins.

Bernard Tapie has chosen to keep the interior largely secret and will not have its splendours, including a number of very valuable paintings, photographed. But he is delighted to show off the yacht's exterior: features such as the long, lean liner-like deckworks, which were rebuilt twice until the aesthetics pleased him; or the four-masthead rig. Any assumption that such a large yacht would be unwieldy would be mistaken. Although she can enter few harbours or ports, lying regally outside them with her tenders to-ing and fro-ing as if she were a cruise ship, the rig itself is child's play.

Instead of using conventional sheets, each boom is a braced girder to which an electrically operated hydraulic ram is attached. By using a tiny joystick control on a wandering lead, it's possible to trim all four rigs by the movement of two fingers. Speeds of 15 knots in just 15 knots of wind have been achieved close reaching.

Phocea is undoubtedly a truly remarkable vessel in a sailing world full of yachts no larger than one of her tenders . . .

10 Vagrant

It may seem a contradiction to choose a yacht built in 1910 as one of the most outstanding of 1987. Nevertheless, Peter de Savary's *Vagrant* must rank among the finest restoration projects of recent times. Combine this with *Vagrant*'s original blue-blood pedigree and you have a superb yacht indeed.

Vagrant was built by the famous American Herreshoff yard in Bristol, Rhode Island, for the Vanderbilt family, who presented the 106 ft gaff schooner to Harold Vanderbilt as a graduation present.

Nathaniel Greene Herreshoff is, rightly, regarded as a prince among designers, and the aesthetics of *Vagrant* must make her one of his finest efforts. From all angles, there is not a line on *Vagrant* which does not look sweet. Above all else, she sails beautifully. Her wake is clean and she creates a remarkably flat waveform.

In the past, these characteristics allowed her to win many a race. Harold Vanderbilt took her to the Bermuda Race straight after her hand-over, and

won. She changed hands but continued to race on the US East Coast, winning many races under her new name, *Queen Mab*. After the Second World War she went to the West Coast and raced in nine consecutive Transpacs and never finished worse than 12th in any of them.

She fell on hard times, though, and eventually ended up in Antigua in a poor state. Her condition deteriorated when she was dismasted and nearly lost. At this point (1985), British America's Cup tycoon Peter de Savary bought her. Extensive structural work was carried out, including a completely new rig from the legendary Spencers of Cowes. Top interior stylist Terry Disdale was brought in too, to assist in the restoration of the interior to her Herreshoff-designed glory – a stained glass window in the saloon, exotic woods in the panelling and everywhere the Herreshoff detailing which set his yachts apart.

That is as true today as it was in 1910.

THE ROLEX CUP
MAXI YACHT WORLD CHAMPIONSHIP 1987, PORTO CERVO

Manoeuvring the 80 feet long, 100 feet high Maxis takes the concerted effort of at least 20 crew.

Maxis are to yachts what Rolex are to watches.

The élite of ocean racers, Maxis are the biggest and fastest yachts racing under the International Offshore Rule.

A Maxi's mast towers over 100 feet high, yet is so spindly that a complex of highly-loaded staying systems are needed to support it and control the rig's power.

Maxi boat crews have to be the best, to tame these highly-strung machines. Many have been around the world many times, sailed in the America's Cup, or competed in Grand Prix regattas such as the Sardinia Cup, or Admiral's Cup.

Some crew members will have flown in especially for the Porto Cervo Rolex Cup, at the skipper's invitation. Others will have sailed their yachts to the Mediterranean from the previous regatta, arriving early to make the vital pre-race preparations that could mean all the difference between winning and just competing.

Every piece of deck gear will have been overhauled, lubricated and replaced. Every sail laid out and checked over, inch by inch.

The navigator will be checking his charts and complex instrumentation and computer systems.

Around the race course, the Maxis unleash their strength, powering upwind and striding out downwind under the colossal spinnakers. Close-quarters manoeuvring is combative and precise, the object to gain the initiative.

The International Class A Maxi series is hosted by the Yacht Club Costa Smeralda. Six days of inshore and offshore racing in the azure waters off Sardinia.

The series will be the second half of the Class A title fight; the early rounds contested on the other side of the Atlantic at Newport, Rhode Island. At the series' conclusion, the Class A World Champion will be named. The finest Maxi there is.

The choice of a Rolex watch is the obvious one for crews and owners. Designed to be watertight, built to take any amount of rough treatment, no other watch is more superbly equipped to stand up to the rigours of a life at sea.

For everyone in the Maxi championship, and for Rolex of Geneva, second best is simply not good enough.

The Rolex Submariner Date Chronometer and the Rolex Lady-Datejust Chronometer both in steel and 18ct. gold with matching Oyster bracelets.

The Industry

by DAVID GLENN

Stories of takeovers, mergers and the ramifications of Big Bang haven't been restricted to the financial institutions and well-known multinationals during 1987.

Flagging business in the sailboat market worldwide has forced rationalisation among some of the leading companies. This has led to a number of significant 'marriages' forming powerful partnerships which are now in good shape to face the increasing levels of sponsorship and sophisticated commercialism of the 1990s, which already demand aggressive marketing.

John Burton's monopolistic, English-based winch manufacturing company Lewmar, for instance, having already joined forces with the American hydraulics concern Navtec, saw a natural progression into integrated, automated sailing systems when the chance arose to link with instrument manufacturers Brookes & Gatehouse.

Another powerful business cocktail involves the winch manufacturers Barient and the all-conquering race mast builders Sparcraft, who together are linked with no fewer than five other winch and hardware companies – Barlow, Gibb, Kenyon and Penguin in America and the giant French production boat spar manufacturers Francespar.

In America, blockmakers Harken have acquired the Italian winch manufacturers Barbarossa so that they can combine their marketing and engineering strengths. Harken's growth in the deck gear market has been very strong in the last five years. The cash-rich company run by brothers Peter and Olaf Harken was particularly keen to expand into new areas. Pooling the best elements of some of the world's leading brands will surely herald a more efficient future.

Like the world of motor racing, research and development at the Grand Prix level of yachting is designed to filter through eventually to production line manufacturing, and in no country more than France is this apparent.

Between them, Bénéteau and Jeanneau, the world's biggest production boatbuilders, had no fewer than five boats (*Pro-motion*, *Xeryus*, *Corum*, *CGI* and *Port du Crouesty*) competing in this year's Champagne Mumm Admiral's Cup – not bad for the producers of fast cruising yachts and motor boats for the family. The knowledge gained in the Cup campaigns will soon be benefiting their 'bread and butter' customers.

Bénéteau Développement is a new division charged with testing new materials on the race courses of the world. Composite materials expert, Australian Chris O'Nial is running the unit and yachts such as *Corum* and *Port du Crouesty* have been the immediate results.

This investment is designed to keep Bénéteau at the very forefront of yacht production technology. Their new American plant in South Carolina, USA, can produce 700 craft a year and the intention is to take on the US domestic industry and to expand from sixth to first in the American boat building league. Aggressive promotion through association with important race meets like the Liberty Cup match race series sailed in New York harbour is part of Bénéteau's move towards global dominance in the sailboat market.

Even though Bénéteau earned 42 per cent of its astonishing FF558 million turnover from home market sales in 1986 (65 per cent of that was from sailboats), it recognises that the only areas of major expansion are overseas. With other European countries well infiltrated and business moving fast in the United States and on the Canadian Great Lakes, smaller corners of the world like Hong Kong haven't been ignored.

But Jeanneau isn't far behind. The company has had to divert its efforts towards the powerboat field as the world boom in that sector continues, but that hasn't handicapped the sailboat effort. A state-assisted employee buyout of the company from owners Lear Siegler, recently gave Jeanneau a new lease of life and with Admiral's Cuppers (*CGI* for instance) and the supply of Jeanneau Sélections to events such as the Tour de France à la Voile and the prize-monied Grundig World Cup match race series, technical and marketing advances have been rapid.

A high-tech prototype department, which was responsible for Philippe Poupon's enormous 74 ft (22.8 m) trimaran, which won last year's Route du Rhum, and for numerous Nigel Irens-designed catamarans in the fast-growing Formula 40 class, has kept the company neck and neck with Bénéteau on the world's race courses.

Gibert Marine through their Gib'Sea range have also tried to follow Jeanneau and Bénéteau down the race boat route, producing the one-off Joubert/Nivelt one tonner *Torquoise*.

But this level of commitment to the latest in building and design techniques hasn't always been reflected in the runaway success.

Going against all trends is the Danish yard of X Yachts where Niels Jeppeson is both the designer and chief executive. Though relatively small, X Yachts is Denmark's biggest exporter and one of the few companies in the world to hit consistent success building production IOR designs.

It all began with the X-102, a three-quarter tonner which won the 1981 Three-Quarter Ton Cup (with an iron keel!) and went on to dominate the class for six seasons. This was backed up by the X-1 Ton which made its debut at La Trinité in 1984, was top inshore yacht (in the shape of *Euro*) in the 1985 Champagne Mumm Admiral's Cup and the 1986 One Ton Cup winner as *Andelstanken*. Latest from Niels Jeppeson's board is the X-2 Ton, a 34 rater. The first boat, *Original Beckmann*, was a top performer in the 1987 CMAC, proving that boats built in normal female moulds can take on and beat the fancy one-off custom boats.

This success is ably supported by cruiser-racer versions of the race boats (the newest is the 452 version of the 34 rater) and one-designs such as the X-77 and X-99. The conclusion is that while the giants get bigger, so the opportunities increase for the smaller, more individualistic companies.

Although there is little to match the size of Bénéteau and Jeanneau in any other European country, small specialist builders have enjoyed a significant level of success in Grand Prix series.

In Britain, for instance, Neville Hutton (*Mean Machine*), Adrian Thompson (*Juno*, *Centurion* (ex-*Jade*)), Rob Lipsett and Killian Bushe (*Jameson Whiskey*) are among a growing number of specialist one-off builders who can produce world-beaters. However, these and the many which exist in America and Australasia may well feel threatened by the racing divisions of the giant builders.

But the Grand Prix scene has shown signs of outpricing itself and if it wasn't for the injection of money from sponsors there would be too few owners left in IOR racing. Sadly, the once happy-go-lucky atmosphere among crews is less evident as it is being replaced by an altogether more grim-faced brigade. It's not everybody's cup of tea.

This has led to the increasing demand for one-design racing which, although restricted in development and controlled in price, has diverted considerable attention from the 'Formula 1' divisions. Oyster Marine's Carl Schumacher-designed Lightwave 395s were racing at Sandhurst Cowes Week and could form the basis of a new California-designed ULDB high-speed fleet in Europe.

The boat beat the new David Thomas-designed Sigma 38 on to the water, the yacht eventually chosen by the Royal Ocean Racing Club and the Royal Thames Yacht Club as the inter-club racer intended to promote cheaper one-design racing in UK waters.

The 38's public debut was delayed, which is not the way to face up to the ever-threatening developments on the Continent. Marine Projects of Plymouth, builders of Sigma Yachts, were running flat-out in 1986/7 constructing motor yachts which did not make the introduction of a new sailing yacht easy. Nevertheless, the Thomas design promises the desired combination of being a manageable racing boat and a capable cruiser, although some critics were expecting a racier looking craft. More than 30 orders for the Sigma 38 were placed when the decision was announced by the RORC to adopt the design and it is hoped it will sell strongly throughout Europe.

While Sigma are still enjoying astonishing success with their first one-design cruiser-racer to be sold in any great numbers (the Sigma 33 has sold over 300 units), other companies are showing similar strengths.

Westerly Yachts, who have been very successful in establishing an export foothold in America, have supplied the Westerly Sea School Fulmar fleet for events like the Lymington Cup match racing series. This Ed Dubois design performs well and successfully combines the cruiser-racer elements.

Returning to yacht equipment; to be able to dominate the world in any single aspect of the sport is quite a claim. It is fair to say that Sparcraft and Lewmar, and to a slightly lesser extent North Sails, have done just that. Many eyes will be on North now that Tom Whidden is the new president. Having been closely associated with Conner's America's Cup campaigns, Whidden has done more than anyone to make Sobstad a serious threat to North, now that he has switched allegiance.

The market for specialist racing

Tim Jeffery

Danish X I-Ton. *Stockbroker Leif Jensen* sailing in the Admiral's Cup.

Tim Jeffery

Bénéteau one tonner *Xeryus* in the French Admiral's Cup team.

Philippe Poupon's Jeanneau-built Formula 40 *Fleury Michon*.

Corum, the joint venture between French boatbuilding giant Bénéteau and Swiss watchmaker Corum.

Tim Jeffery

23

Whirlwind XII, the 102 ft Ron Holland-designed sloop by the Royal Huisman Shipyard.

Inset: **Sumptuous dining area of Whirlwind XII.**

masts is understandably small on a global basis, but to be able to claim 30 of this year's Admiral's Cup fleet is outstanding. The precisely engineered 6000 and 7000 series spars dominate one ton yachts, and the use of ultra-light but very strong titanium fittings combined with cobalt rod rigging has produced the ultimate racing spars. By linking with production spar manufacturers like Francespar, Sparcraft are not dependent on the specialist racing market.

Lewmar claimed 28 of the 42 Admiral's Cuppers this year and were dominant among the 12-metre fleet in Perth last winter. Having cornered such a large part of the market there has been money available to spend on such complex units as their computer-controlled, electro-hydraulic Commander system, designed for large cruising boats.

Capable of driving sheet winches, hydraulic furling gear for headsails and mainsails, the Commander is used on the ever-growing number of sailing super-yachts now being launched, themselves a product of technology which makes sloop-rigged 100-footers feasible. The company's latest piece of equipment, the Lewmar Line Management system, automatically sheets headsails and outhauls (in or out) under full load. This can even be linked to Brookes & Gatehouse's Hercules 390 sail instrumentation package and by a further coupling to an autopilot . . . and so one has an automatic yacht.

Brookes & Gatehouse have further developed a computer system for handling the complex navigation systems for 12-metres. Using Sailmath, software developed by Dr Graeme Wynn for the British, New Zealand and Italian syndicates, as well as the expertise of Derek Clark, *Kookaburra III*'s tactician, the system will eventually be transferred to the 'ordinary' yacht with information displayed on the traditional B & G readouts or on their new Deckman screens.

Still within the rapidly changing world of electronic navigation, an American company, Laser Plot Inc., have discovered how to digitise an Admiralty Chart (including all the colours), transfer the information onto a disc (just like a compact disc) and then have it displayed on screen. Superimposed on the chart can be the yacht's position, track and intended course via waypoints. Interfaced with the almost obligatory satellite or Decca

position fixing aid of one's choice, one can watch the yacht move across the chart and guide her past all hazards by activating the autopilot.

Navstar have the rights to manufacture the equipment in the UK but British Admiralty copyright is proving a major obstacle to its adoption.

The system is but the latest example of electronic navigation. In France, particularly, the MacSea system has proved popular in the BOC Challenge Race and in the big multihulls as an almanac, pilot and chart database and full tactical computer.

Outstanding race boat designer of the year must be Bruce Farr who, with the CMAC top boat in *Propaganda*, four Whitbread maxis commissioned and a 90 ft LWL America's Cup mega-maxi for Michael Fay, has expanded his operation by opening a

second office in Newport, Rhode Island. Phil Stegall is running this base.

While Ed Dubois enjoyed some revived success in IOR with *Irish Independent/Full Pelt* and *Swan Premium 1*, he and the likes of Ron Holland have found a lucrative and developing market in really large sailing yachts.

The Royal Huisman yard in Vollenhove, Netherlands, is unquestionably a world leader in large one-off projects, such as *Whirlwind XII*, and a big rebuilding programme at the yard now enables Wolter Huisman to complete two or three yachts in excess of 120 ft (36 m) at the same time undercover.

The 112 ft Holland/Jon Bannenberg sloop *Archarné* has recently been launched and sailed across the Atlantic

and now Huisman is concentrating on completing *Endeavour*, Sir T.O.M. Sopwith's 1934 J class yacht which was deprived of an America's Cup by the skill of defending skipper Harold Vanderbilt. *Endeavour* has now been completely replated in the UK and her new owner, New England millionairess Elizabeth Meyer, is having the yacht fitted out below in the finest Edwardian club style. *Endeavour* will sail again in 1989, it is hoped, and a series against *Astra* (a former 23 m class) and *Quadrafoglio* (ex-*Shamrock*) is promised. What a prospect . . .

David Glenn is the Deputy Editor of Yachting World. As such he has close links with the industry the world over.

OVERVIEW: THE INDUSTRY

Made exclusively in the USA but worn by leading yachtsmen around the world.

The Sport

by BOB FISHER

The past year will be remembered as a year of truth, a pivotal point in the sport at its highest level and one in which the zeniths and nadirs were wider apart than ever before. Yachting became more of a public property, through the medium of television, and in the same year the sport was dragged through the slough of public criticism following the revelation of cheating in an event of the highest order. Yachting will survive both assaults, although its character has suffered some bruising.

The greatest exposure came, inevitably, with the America's Cup. Taken from the mists and fickle winds of Newport to a place almost exactly on the opposite side of the world in almost exactly opposite weather conditions, America's Cup racing changed. The result was nothing short of spectacular. Regular strong winds and sunshine converted the America's Cup from an esoteric event of consequence only to a handful of dedicated aficionados to a sporting event of public importance exceeded only by the Olympic Games and the World Cup. The transformation was complete and wonderful.

All the doubts that the Cup would diminish in stature in consequence of its transfer to Australia were blown like the flies into the desert by the Fremantle Doctor (that essential ingredient) when 13 syndicates fought for the right to challenge the best of the four defence syndicates. It was almost double the number involved three and half years earlier. The Cup had grown; more significantly, it had matured.

As part of that maturing process, the need for dedication became all the more important and those who demonstrated it were the ones who triumphed. The greater the dedication, the greater the triumph.

There were upsets, certainly, but the ultimate destiny of the Cup was obvious from the outset. The New Zealanders provided the side issue. In a manner which has become typical of the Kiwis, they were resourceful, innovative and very motivated in the campaign. The results were impressive – 36 wins from 37 races – but there was no progressive improvement in their boat as there was in almost every other syndicate. It was only a matter of time, therefore, before one of the other 12 challengers had to be better.

Characteristically, it was Dennis Conner who nailed the lie of New Zealand's invincibility. He was the only skipper to beat Chris Dickson in the round robins and, when push came

to shove, in the challenger selection final, there was never any real doubt as to the outcome.

The Kiwis proved, in an act of ANZAC collaboration which syndicate head, Michael Fay, may live to regret, that they were the second-fastest 12-metre in Fremantle. By electing to bypass tradition and assist the challenger in the final preparation for the Cup, Fay may well have established an enemy in the San Diego Yacht Club, although Dickson, after KZ-7 had sailed against Kookaburra III, was said to have told Conner that he would have no worry with her.

The dedication of the Australians, and their complete professionalism, to defending the Cup had a sense of self-destruction surrounding it. They had seen the way in which the challengers had finally succeeded in wresting the Cup from the New York Yacht Club – by competitive improvement – but had failed to see how the Americans had kept it for years – by collective co-operation. It was, for example, only when the Sydney syndicate chanced upon the shape of the wings of Kookaburra and built a keel of that type for Steak 'n Kidney that the Peter Cole-designed Twelve began to be anything but ordinary. Had the Australians fully realised the potential of that boat, the next Cup series might well have been held in the fresh winds of the Fremantle Doctor rather than the vaguest zephyrs off Point Loma, California.

Four syndicates, one with a budget reputed to exceed A$26m, had co-operated very little (indeed, the animosity between the two major syndicate heads became very public), and the Australian effort was weakened because of it. That has already been recognised and plans for an Australian challenge to regain the America's Cup are placing great store by the need to amalgamate effort, if for no other reason than to ensure the necessary budget for research and development.

That was where Dennis Conner scored. His research and development, co-ordinated by John Marshall, explored every possible avenue in the search for speed. Two-tenths of a knot of windward advantage provided him with a vehicle which totally destroyed the Australians. His campaign was superlative; his victory comprehensive; his joy unbounded.

So too was that of the Kiwis six months later, but this time at the Admiral's Cup. Never was a demon-

stration of sailing as a team so evident as that of the three New Zealand boats. They had the inspiration of a string of earlier successes from home in a number of regattas worldwide but the ultimate prize of their offshore sailors had always eluded them. This time it was to fall into their hands like a ripe pear.

Everything was right about the New Zealand challenge: they had learned from previous expeditions across the world and used each lesson properly. To them the choice of boats within the minimum aggregate rating introduced this year by the RORC was obvious, as it was to most, two one tonners and a 34.4 ft rater to take advantage of the extra crew member allowed. Mad Max, a Davidson one tonner which changed her name for commercial expediency to Goldcorp, had already proved her speed and she was systematically improved before the New Zealand trials, as befitted a boat which was close to two years old and had been raced hard. Mal Canning picked up the bills while Rick Dodson provided the generalship. Propaganda was a new Farr 40 complete with all the guile of seasoned campaigner Bevan Woolley and the steering skills of Peter Lester, while Kiwi, the big boat, was a Farr 43 built especially for the Admiral's Cup by Peter Walker, a Farr associate from way back.

Julius Caesar would have been proud of the way in which the Kiwis came, saw and conquered but might have been saddened at the way in which the British team (winners of the Southern Cross and Sardinia Cups) presented the invaders with their spoils. Graham Walker's Indulgence made the first of the strategic errors, in the opening race in the Solent, by leaving the fleet to sail her own course in light airs and lost a dozen places in consequence. It wasn't an act of percentage sailing and that is quintessential for success in this event.

Worse was to happen in the third inshore race, before which Britain led by a single point, where there was one very obvious strategy facing the British team. With the heavy points loading of the Fastnet and a confidence in their ability to beat the Kiwis offshore, the three British boats should have made the decision to 'match race' their opposite numbers in the New Zealand team. From earlier results, both in the Cup and races prior to it, the pairing of Jamarella with Propaganda and Juno with Goldcorp was outstandingly

obvious and it might have been expected that the team captain would have given that order when the skippers met that morning. If he had, there was no heed paid, although Indulgence did make an effort to stay with Kiwi. The other two British boats however, simply ignored their rivals on the first beat and went out, in company with Indulgence, to the right-hand side of the course and there they suffered.

That side of the course was paying early on but when the two one tonners had found themselves advantaged, they should have sailed towards their rivals to ensure that they finished in relatively close proximity. But no. The wind shifted and the three British boats were all well behind their Kiwi opponents. As the race wore on, matters went from bad to worse and the Cup was thrown way beyond their reach. One of the two British one tonner skippers said afterwards that each time he tried to tack for the left he found a bigger boat parked on his wind and quite often it was the one from his own team. That was in complete contrast to the way the Kiwis sailed and the New Zealanders were among the first, and most vehement, to decry other competitors' tactics.

In a card room the cry of 'cheat' would bring all proceedings to a halt and cause the guilty party to be banished from the company for ever; there seems little reason why the same should not hold true for yachting, if the degree of cheating alleged to have taken place during the Champagne Mumm Admiral's Cup were correct. The Kiwis, and their Australian ANZAC partners, aware of a confession by an Australian crew member of the Austrian I-Punkt, suggested that other boats, including all three members of the British team, were also lightened off wind by having their water tanks pumped dry.

The Austrian boat, whose skipper Hubert Raudaschl walked off when he learned of what had been going on, took on up to 200 litres of water in portable containers which were stowed on the upper weather bunk when going to windward. That is equivalent to having three extra men on the weather rail in a boat where the crew is limited to nine. The Kiwis say that I-Punkt

Peter Gilmour in **Kookaburra III** (right) **peels off Colin Beashel in** Australia IV **on the committee boat during the America's Cup Defenders' Final.**

displayed uncharacteristic speed at times and they also say that this was true of *Indulgence* and *Jamarella* in the Channel Race and of *Juno* in the Fastnet.

These are grave allegations, and ones whose seriousness has been recognised by the Royal Ocean Racing Club. Each crew member of every boat was contacted by the RORC and asked to provide information of any known cheating on board their own or other boats and the Club has stated that it is to hold an official inquiry from which action will have to be taken. Some of yacht racing's rules are difficult, if not impossible, to police, but adherence to them is essential – especially so now that the sport is turning increasingly professional.

That move was as inevitable as the daily sunrise. Every other major sport has undergone this transformation, although yachting is only at the point reached by tennis 35 years ago. 'Shamateurism' is proving to be less and less acceptable to either side, so the American proposal of three types of regatta – the professional, the pro-am and the strictly amateur – would appear to be a sensible way of accepting the change and protecting the majority of sailors from the minority who spoil their enjoyment of yacht racing as a recreation. It is either that or the International Yacht Racing Union will lose control of the sport.

The IYRU's interest in the amateur sport culminates in the Olympics and it has more than its fair share of problems to face before the Games are held. The pre-Olympic regatta was hardly exemplary of good organisation but its results showed a return of British dominance in the small dinghies. Cathy Foster displayed her talents at the last Olympics; racing now in the Women's Division she has, with Jackie Patton, shown that she can take gold. So too did her crew from Long Beach, Peter Newlands, currently on the wire of the 470 with Nigel Buckley, but the outstanding British dinghy sailor of 1987 was undoubtedly Stuart Childerley. His performance in the Finn class marks him as being the best prospect, anywhere in the world, for a gold at Pusan in 1988. Winner of the pre-Olympic gold and the European Championship as well as of three other major European regattas, Childerley shows all the unrealised Olympic promise of Chris Law in 1980.

The grass roots of the sport are strengthening in Britain, as record

turn-outs at Cowes Week and in many other regattas have indicated, but there are massive changes underfoot. The death of the IOR is not imminent, despite many cries to that effect, but its place in offshore racing is altering. Shortly it will become, essentially, the Grand Prix formula only, but used elsewhere for those boats which are slightly outdated although considered the leading edge by their owners.

That trend became clear in 1987 with huge locally handicapped and Channel Handicap System fleets in evidence from Loch Fyne in the north to Cowes in the south, and from Burnham in the east to Torquay in the west. There was also, of course, a proliferation in one-designs. Sigmas and Contessas were everywhere and the indication is that there are more to come; the Lightwave 395 ULDB one-design showed early promise at Cowes and Burnham.

The influx of ultra-lights will continue. Many senior yachtsmen have

made the change and their lead will act as an incentive to others. What the Californians understood ten years ago is now being comprehended by the Europeans: 1987 showed that it is worth sacrificing a fraction of upwind performance for sparkling downwind slides.

One other change also marked the end of an era. Britain did not send a team to the Southern Cross Cup, for the first time since the inception of the Australian offshore series. Lack of supporting finance was blamed but the real cause was the anticlimactic aftertaste of the Admiral's Cup and One Ton Cups. The financial drain of both had been heavy for the owners. Britain's 2nd place at Cowes earned the team considerable (£50,000) travel sponsorship for the Kenwood Cup in Hawaii in August 1988, which must also have contributed to the unwillingness to go to Sydney.

Others were extending their horizons. The International 14s held their

Below: **Thomas Friese (in cap) was disqualified retrospectively from the Admiral's Cup after investigations into illegal use of water ballast aboard *I-Punkt* in the Admiral's Cup and the One Ton Cup.**

Bottom: **The acceptable faces of yachting – Brad Butterworth (left), Bevan Woolley (middle) and Peter Lester (right) masterminded *Propaganda*'s success in the Admiral's Cup, a vital element in the Kiwis' win.**

first World Championship in Japan, and that was also to be the scene of the last of the year's international match racing series, for the Nippon Cup. Perhaps influenced by the exposure of the America's Cup, match racing has begun to fire many imaginations, and competitions have begun to be established at club level. The pinnacle of these was the Viyella Cup which saw a win for the establishment, Iain Macdonald-Smith representing the Royal Thames YC.

The 12-metre World Championship may have threatened to kill match racing for ever with its extreme tedium in the virtually windless Mediterranean off Porto Cervo, but the other major international events countered that by their closeness of competition. Eddie Warden-Owen followed in the footsteps of Harold Cudmore by winning the Congressional Cup but he couldn't do the same at Lymington, going down in the final to Peter Gilmour. The Australian became tactician for his America's Cup skipper once again at Cannes, France, when Iain Murray won his first-ever match race series – and with it the US$100,000 prize at the Grundig Cup. Gilmour won again at the Liberty Cup, the first of the qualifiers for the World Cup at Long Beach, August 1988.

The huge cash prize at the French event marked one of the turning points of the sport. Naturally, it proved attractive to the skippers and it certainly gave the non-sailing public a reason for interest. It was certainly far above the pittance which the IYRU allows skippers to race for and maintain their amateur status, but the money could be 'laundered' through their national authorities. The IYRU's hypocrisy was exposed for all to see.

The wind of change, in attitude, began to reach gale force in 1987. New parameters were openly discussed wherever sailors met, and, if the international authority refuses to accept the problems and to endeavour to find suitable solutions, it faces anarchy and yachting, in general, will suffer. The bruising needs to be nursed back to health.

Bob Fisher is probably the best-known and most-travelled yachting journalist in the world. Here he uses his experience to put the past twelve months' sailing into perspective.

OVERVIEW: THE SPORT

Berthon
Experience in action

Mari-Cha A 70-foot fast ocean-cruising yacht built by Berthon Boat Company with interior styling by Terence Disdale. Mari-Cha is typical of the cruising yachts offered by Berthon International, who are recognised as one of the finest yacht brokers in the world.

The Berthon 80 First in a range of custom-built motor yachts designed by Laurent Giles for Berthon. Built in aluminium and fitted out to the highest standard by Berthon's craftsmen.

This truly international business is backed by our office in Palma. We have yachts listed and a client base worldwide.

Juno Launched in '87, designed by Rob Humphreys and winner of '87 Fastnet Trophy as a member of the British Admirals Cup team, Juno is for sale through the Race Boat section of Berthon International. This section is staffed by active racing sailors who know and are known on the racing circuits of the world.

Kenneth Thelwall, built for the RNLI, is an Arun 52 lifeboat, one of a series of Arun class boats built at Berthon. The high standards demanded for a lifeboat are the standards which we apply to all our work, whether new building or in our substantial refit and service operation.

Lymington Marina adds the final touch to the complete service which The Berthon Group can offer our clients.

Listed below are the addresses and contact names in each company.
Take advantage of our wealth of experience.

Berthon International
Contact Robin Campbell on 0590 79222

The Berthon Boat Company
Contact John Day on 0590 73312

Lymington Marina
Contact Carole Gaute on 0590 73312

The Berthon Group
The Shipyard, Lymington, Hampshire SO41 9YL.
Tel 0590 73312 Telex: 477831 BERTHN G Fax: 0590 79811

Steinlager Challenge

by DAVID PARDON

An artist's impression of Peter Blake's 60 ft (18.28 m) Round Australia trimaran, *Steinlager 1.*

Some people believe Peter Blake should have been an astronaut, not a yachtsman. He's been around the world so many times he knows North America, North Africa and Northern Australia almost as well as he knows his home in North Auckland.

And each time round is a little faster than the time before.

For the tall 38-year-old New Zealander, life means being constantly on the move. Even reference to 'home' is misleading. It's home only in the sense that Auckland's North Shore is where he was born, raised, learned to sail and where his parents still live. Home for Peter, wife Pippa and their two young children is a seaside house in England, an apartment in Auckland, a hotel room in Sydney, San Francisco, Suez, or wherever the next port of call happens to be.

And they wouldn't have it any other way.

Blake does admit, however, that after completing the 1985/86 Whitbread Round the World Race in the Ron Holland-designed maxi, *Lion New Zealand,* he'd had enough of that particular circumnavigational route. 'Those long, hard slogs on the wind all the way up the Atlantic get to be so boring. Four Whitbreads are enough for anyone.'

He wanted something new, more excitement, a fresh challenge.

As far back as 1982, when he spent time in England selling *Ceramco New Zealand,* his Bruce Farr-designed aluminium round-the-world yacht, he had his first real taste of sailing big multihulls. It came mainly through his friendship with a young English designer, David Alan-Williams, whom Blake had first met when the pair joined the crew of Leslie Williams's *Burton Cutter* for the very first Whitbread Race in 1973. They kept in touch and came together yet again on *Heath's Condor* in the second Round the World Race four years later. Both those ventures ended prematurely, the first when *Burton Cutter* began to ship water, the second when *Heath's Condor* lost her experimental carbon-fibre mast.

Throughout the third and fourth Whitbreads aboard his own *Ceramco* and *Lion New Zealand,* Blake nursed the idea of entering the next race in a multihull, much as Chay Blyth had

tried to do with the 80 ft (24.4 m) Derek Kelsall-designed *Great Britain III* in 1977, and he is among those who have argued strongly, but so far in vain, for the admission of multihulls to the Whitbread.

So, bored with the Whitbread, Blake finally decided on an all-out attempt to demolish as many as possible of the world's sailing records, including an attempt to circumnavigate in 80 days . . . what he now calls his 'Jules Verne Project'. Alan-Williams's ideas, and especially his success with the Alien 35 inshore catamaran design and, more recently, his modifications to the 60 ft (18.3 m) Adrian Thompson-designed offshore tri, *Paragon,* impressed Blake, who asked him for the lines of a multihull capable of cracking all existing records.

The result was an outline proposal for a 75 ft (22.86 m) trimaran that would be lighter, stronger and faster than anything yet built, but still within the multihull racing size limit. With it Blake could challenge all comers over any distance and on any course anywhere in the world.

Armed with Alan-Williams's drawings and calculations, Blake called on 48-year-old A.D. (Douglas) Myers, managing director of Lion Corporation and the man who had backed his 1985/86 Whitbread challenge in *Lion New Zealand.* 'Douglas was sold on the idea from the word go', recalls Blake. However, he hadn't expected the brewery boss to add, 'We've got to do the Whitbread too, of course. There's no way we'll miss out on that.'

Lion had indeed shown a healthy commercial return on their backing of

the 1985/86 challenge, increasing domestic sales of Lion beer through a period in which not only the sales of their competitors but of beer generally had declined throughout the country. That brand-awareness was directly attributed by Myers's marketing experts to the association with *Lion New Zealand.*

Blake suggested that, in view of the expense involved in the trimaran project, they should build a smaller boat for the Whitbread. 'I thought perhaps a crack at the small-boat trophy with something that would keep the brewery's name in the race headlines but would be less expensive and technically demanding than a maxi. But Douglas wouldn't listen. He said "We're going for the Big One again; we want a maxi and we want the best!".'

By now Blake had decided that the new Whitbread course, taking in Australia and the US and leaving out South Africa, would not be so bad after all. 'Lots of fast reaching . . . a new ball game. If it had been the old course there's no way I would have made a fifth attempt. Now I'm keener than ever to knock this thing off.'

Certainly Myers wanted action . . . and wanted it quickly. Lion's Steinlager brand was enjoying spectacular growth in popularity in New Zealand and the company was about to launch it internationally in an all-out bid to gain recognition as one of the world's leading lager beers. It was a bold step into markets in which it is difficult and expensive to achieve a profile, particularly for a small country not recognised as a producer of beer. 'The *Steinlager Challengers* and the young Kiwis who race them will be floating billboards . . . high-profile examples of the quality of what New Zealand produces. Let's see how we can take on the world and beat them, on the water and in the marketplace', declared Myers.

There was a problem, however: time. The new Whitbread maxi would not be in the water before the end of 1988; the big tri would have to wait until that was out of the building shed and Blake's Whitbread campaign was over. It would not star on the international publicity stage before mid to late 1990 at the earliest.

From this need to 'get the show on

The Challenge has placed what is believed to be the world's largest single sail order – for 75 sails worth NZ$1.5m – with North Sails' Auckland loft. Of these, 20 are for *Steinlager 1*, 30 for the Whitbread maxi, and the remaining 25 for the second, and larger, of the David Alan-Williams-designed multihulls in which Blake will attempt an 80-day circumnavigation of the world. Blake (seated) is pictured handing over his order to North's loft manager Tom Schnackenberg (left). Standing centre is Tom Dodson, also from the North loft, and at right, Steinlager Challenge business manager Paul Kennedy.

Carbon fibre being applied to the hull of *Steinlager 1*.

the road' the 60 ft (18.2 m) trimaran and Two-Man Round Australia plan was hatched. After another meeting and discussion when the pair met at the New Zealand America's Cup camp in Fremantle, Myers agreed to put his company behind all three Steinlager yachts, inaugurating a six-year continuous project underwritten to a minimum of NZ$2m a year.

'What we are seeking to achieve is the opportunity for New Zealanders to continue to display their sailing prowess against all comers by linking their achievements with a co-ordinated and orchestrated export drive that will be of enormous benefit to the country and to the companies that take part', said Myers when the overall plan was revealed in Auckland.

All three yachts are being built at Mairangi Bay, Auckland, by a team under Tim Gurr, who was responsible for *Lion New Zealand*. Full use is being made of the latest composite construction materials and techniques supplied by Healing Industries, Auckland, who developed and manufactured the resins used for *Lion New Zealand* as well as for the New Zealand America's Cup 12-metres. Earlier this year Healing entered into an agreement to act as New Zealand stockists of high-tech materials supplied by SP Systems of England for use in conjunction with their own specialist resins.

All three craft involve the vacuum-bag epoxy pre-preg lay-up system cured at 75°C in a 90 ft (27.43 m) oven built along one wall of the shed. The trimarans are building in sections (main hull, floats, crossbeams, etc.) and the expandable oven is doubled in width to accommodate the Bruce Farr-designed Whitbread maxi monohull.

First out will be the 60 ft (18.28 m) wing-masted trimaran *Steinlager 1*. This was scheduled for launching on 1 December 1987 and will undergo trials on Auckland's Waitemata Harbour before being sailed across the Tasman for the start of the Sydney–Auckland Two-Handed Race on 28 February 1988. It will then take part in the Auckland–Mooloolaba (Queensland) Two-Handed Race commencing 18 March, returning to Auckland to prepare for the Round Australia Race which starts in August 1988.

As part of the planned programme, the trimaran will then return to New Zealand (its sixth Tasman crossing) and, with the Whitbread maxi *Steinlager 2*, which is due to be launched in

November 1988, will make a publicity tour of all the major ports of New Zealand in January/February 1989.

In March/April 1989, both yachts will be shipped to England where the trimaran will take on a public relations role while Blake prepares his maxi for the start of the fifth Whitbread Round the World Race in September 1989.

Coinciding with the Whitbread start will be construction of *Steinlager 3*, the 75 ft (22.86 m) – it may yet be even bigger – trimaran with which Blake will attack the sailing speed records. That is due to be launched in August 1990 and all three Steinlager craft are due to be present at the America's Cup series in San Diego in 1991.

Blake expects to begin his round-the-world-in-80-days attempt in December 1991 and to return the yacht to Auckland for refitting and probable sale in June/August 1992.

Peter Blake is probably New Zealand's best-known yachtsman, having competed in all four Whitbread Races so far. Racing and cruising, he has covered more than 350,000 ocean miles, including five Sydney–Hobart races, five Fastnets (he skippered *Condor of Bermuda* to win the tragic 1979 race), the Round Britain Two-Handed Race, three trans-Tasmans (Hobart to Auckland), a transatlantic, the Cape Town–Rio, two Auckland–Suva races, the Miami–Jamaica, Antigua–Newport and Buenos Aires–Rio events.

The son of a commercial artist, he was born and raised on Auckland's North Shore, learned to sail and row the family dinghy, and at the age of eight was given his own boat, a 7 ft (2.13 m) plywood P-class dinghy designed more than 60 years ago by Harry Highet and still the most geographically widespread and popular trainer in New Zealand. He graduated through various other local one- and two-handed dinghy classes before building his own keelboat, a 23 ft 4 in. (7.10 m) *Yachting World* Buccaneer in a lean-to shed next to the garage of his parent's home.

Trained in Auckland as an engineer, he sailed his first ocean race, the Auckland–Suva, before he was 20, and in 1970 sold his own boat to finance a trip to England. There he met Robin Knox-Johnston and Leslie Williams, joined them aboard the 70 ft (21.3 m) ketch *Ocean Spirit* for a Malta–Cape Town delivery trip, and began his career as a full-time yachtsman.

Far left: **With the hull in place, the oven doors are slotted back into position in preparation for curing at 75°C. The prefabricated oven is 90 ft (27.4 m) long and will be doubled in width to take the hull of the Whitbread maxi once the first trimaran has left the shed.**

Building the mould for the 86 ft (26.21 m) wing mast, which has a maximum chord length of 5 ft (1.5 m) tapering top and bottom, and is constructed of Nomex honeycomb stiffened with carbon fibre *(centre).*

Left: **The curved carbon-fibre traveller track base is upside-down while being laid up. The circular discs, which will be underneath the topside of the structure, are tapped washers, or pads, into which go bolts securing the alloy track.**

Below: **The main hull, with carbon fibre in place. Up to 26 layers have been applied, the orientation of the fibres being of critical importance in relation to hull stresses and loadings.**

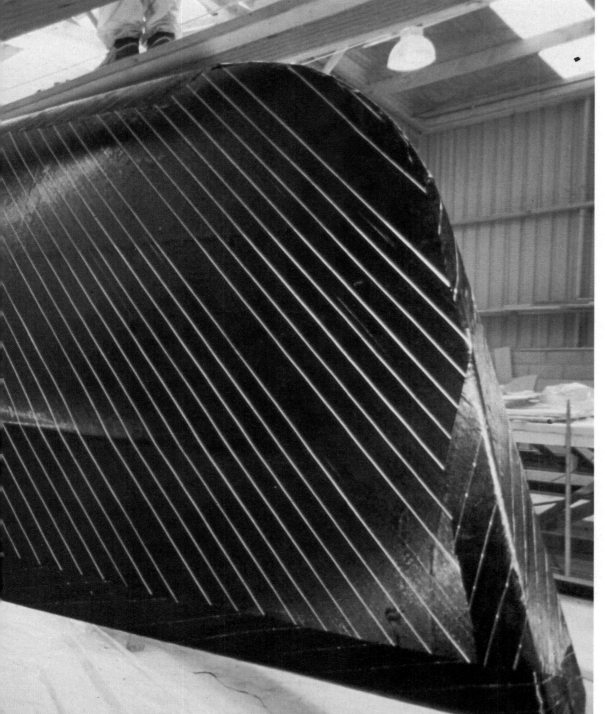

Blake met his wife, Pippa, in England and they married in 1980. They have a daughter, Sarah-Jane, and a son, James. Peter was awarded the MBE in 1983 for his services to yachting and has co-authored three books.

His partner in the two-handed Round Australia Race will be 34-year-old sailmaker Mike Quilter, who was navigator aboard *KZ-7* during the 1986/87 America's Cup campaign off Fremantle.

Quilter was also born in Auckland, began sailing Moths, but graduated to keelboats at the age of 14. He was a watch captain for Peter Blake aboard *Lion New Zealand*, has competed in two Admiral's Cup challenges, three Clipper Cups, two Southern Cross Cups as well as races from New Zealand to Fiji, New Caledonia, Raratonga and the New Hebrides.

Educated at Auckland Grammar School, Quilter completed a BSc in Zoology at Auckland University but began work with the North sail loft, where he became involved with Tom Schnackenberg in designing sails for the 1983 America's Cup winner, *Australia II.*

Designer Alan-Williams says the first trimaran, *Steinlager 1*, is conservative, aimed at minimum weight in a boat that will be seaworthy and easily handled in the heavy seas around the south of Australia. 'If it was purely an inshore boat I believe it could be a bit more extreme. Even so, the way we are building it and the materials we are using mean it will be lighter than anything previously achieved with a boat of this size.'

The design shows long, high-buoyancy floats and an 86 ft (26.2 m) free-rotating wing mast of Nomex-cored carbon fibre. Load cells fitted under the mast and side stays give a continuous readout of compression loads, etc., and are linked to alarms pre-set for critical loadings.

Top speed is estimated to be more than 30 knots.

A full technical and administrative back-up team, including a weather-forecasting unit, will follow the trimaran around Australia by land in two four-wheel-drive vehicles.

'I'm really looking forward to racing a multihull', says Blake. 'At last I won't have to keep worrying about ratings!'

Record Year

by PETER JOHNSON

Since the end of 1986, there has existed an internationally authorised list of sailing records on major races and routes. This fascinating list is issued by the international body for ocean racing, the Offshore Racing Council, and approval is given by the World Sailing Speed Record Committee of the International Yacht Racing Union. The ORC had promulgated such a list for seven years previously, but only in the last year or so has the WSSRC put on its stamp of approval. The latter committee is best known, of course, for the control and ratification of the half-kilometre sailing record, but passage times are also speed records, though of a rather different sort.

The primary figure for an offshore passage is a time rather than a speed, though the latter can be averaged over distance. Ah! The distance: great circle? rhumb line? And how close to those rocks does one measure the turning point which may occur on an offshore race? So far, times from record to record have not been small enough for minutiae like the exact startline position to cause any worry. The records of the ORC are based on the course laid down by the organisers (of the Bermuda race, or Fastnet, or Round Hawaii or any of the others) and this is coupled with the record time. An average speed is calculated from the rhumb line distance usually, but not necessarily, as given by the organisers. When work was being done on the records, it was found that the Island Sailing Club had for many years given the distance on the front of its Round the Island race programme as 60 miles; yet the course sailed is really a little under 50!

The increased interest in accurate and acclaimed records has arisen from the regular campaigning of maxi ocean racers (that is, a boat to the maximum allowed IOR rating of 70·0 ft) and very fast offshore multihulls. After all, it can make more sense to beat predecessors of equal size than smaller boats in the same race. A maxi may win a regular race, but she is more likely to be well down the list on corrected time, once time allowances are applied.

Where records are concerned, it should be noted, corrected times mean nothing, as rating rules and time allowance systems change. Corrected time is only there to give a race result and order.

Although most of the offshore records concern regular courses, there are several classic routes which are seldom raced. The most famous of these is the North Atlantic route from west to east – in particular, starting at Sandy Hook outside New York harbour and finishing at Lizard Point, the southernmost point of the English mainland. It is 2925 miles, and a record by the 185 ft American schooner *Atlantic* of 12d 4h 1m stood until 1980, when the famous French sailor Eric Tabarly in *Paul Ricard*, a foil trimaran, crossed with two companions in 10d 5h 14m. Since then the record has been broken four times by French multihulls, the most recent being in 1987.

The other passages outside racing which are sought by the record breakers are the various round the world routes. These may be single-handed or fully manned and are usually differentiated by the number of stops (in other words, calls at ports). So there are records for round the world non-stop, crewed and alone, as well as records for a circumnavigation stopping at, say, three ports (like the Whitbread Round the World Race), in which case the total sailing time is added together. There is also a record for sailing around with only one stop, although the record keepers have to put some hold on the acknowledged variations.

Dominating the most difficult and sensational routes at present are the French sailors and their multihulls. They seem able to find the massive sponsorship necessary, but, more importantly, possess the qualities of seamanship and daring for such feats. Sadly, there are also casualties: Loic Caradec from *Royale* and Daniel Gilard from *Jet Services V* were lost, to become the latest in the commemorative roll of honour of ocean sailors.

Records of 1987

The fastest passage across an ocean ever recorded is the new record for the Sandy Hook to Lizard Point by Philippe Poupon (France) and his crew on the 75 ft trimaran *Fleury Michon VIII*. She crossed in 7d 12h 50m, finishing off the Lizard at 06·52 GMT on 20 June 1987. Poupon claims that on 16-17 June, the vessel made a 24-hour run of 520 nautical miles, which means an average of 21·67 knots. His average for the full passage works out at 15·49 knots, but he logged 3126 miles, which is rather longer than the nominal distance. This was not in a race, but the latest in a long line of attempts on this record since the late '70s. Five of them, including the latest, proved successful, while at least two boats have sunk, though crews were rescued.

The completion of another BOC Challenge Around Alone race from Newport and back around the world this year saw a new record established for a monohull single-handed with three stops. *Credit Agricole III*, sailed by Philippe Jeantot of France, arrived in Newport on 7 May 1987 after sailing for 134d 5h 23m 56s.

Another single-handed record was achieved by Bruno Peyron (France) in the catamaran *Ericsson* on the Sandy Hook to Lizard Point route. Previous records are sparse as this route is traditionally fully manned, but on 19 April he arrived having completed the course in 11d 11h 46m.

Second to none among all these feats by French multihull sailors is the single-handed voyage around the world by Philippe Monet, aged 26. He resolutely left Brest on 10 December 1986 in the 77 ft trimaran *Kriter Brut de Brut*, intending a non-stop passage around the world. Forty-two days later he lost his forestay off the African coast and had to put into Cape Town for repairs. There he spent two days, but he never stopped again and arrived back in Brest after 129d 19h 17m at sea. His stated best day's run was 328 miles and his maximum speed 33 knots. It is a new record for a single-hander with one stop, previously held by the late Alain Colas. The fastest round the world voyage non-stop remains that of American Dodge Morgan, who sailed in his well-equipped 60 ft (18·2 m) monohull, *American Promise*, from Bermuda to Bermuda between November 1985 and April 1986.

In regular ocean racing courses, 1987 has not been a notable year for records, the Sydney–Hobart run remaining untouched and, in British waters, many of the races of the RORC including spells of very light weather. *Nirvana*, Marvin Green's beautiful maxi from the USA, sailed the Fastnet once again but had no opportunity to break her 1985 record. She remains unique in continuing to hold the records for both the Fastnet course and the Newport–Bermuda (1982), which is of about the same length. Like many another maxi owner, Green continues to look for records to break. She did have one success this year, however, in breaking *Midnight Sun*'s record for the Gotland Rundt.

Some official offshore records from before 1987 (*see table opposite*)

It is remarkable how many records have been achieved in the last three or four years – a pointer to actual boat speed improvement in ocean racing yachts, whether monohull, multihull or single-handed yachts.

Sir Peter Johnson Bt, is the Offshore Racing Council's official keeper of records.

Christian Février

NOTABLE EXISTING RECORDS

Regular race courses

Race or course	Distance (miles)	Time	Date	Yacht name	Length (ft)	Skipper (nationality)	Av. speed (knots)
Newport–Bermuda	635	2d 14h 29m	Jun 1982	*Nirvana*	80	Marvin Green (US)	10·16
Fastnet	605	2d 12h 41m 15s	Aug 1985	*Nirvana*	80	Marvin Green (US)	9·97
Sydney–Hobart	630	2d 14h 36m 56s	Jan 1975	*Kialoa*	79	John B. Kilroy (US)	10·06
Transpac (Los Angeles–Honolulu)	2225	7d 7h 30m	Jul 1983	*Double Bullet*	65	Bob Hanel (US)	12·70
Round the Island race (Isle of Wight)	50	3h 55m 28s	Jun 1986	*Paragon*	60	Mike Whipp (GB)	13·50
Round Britain and Ireland	1950	8d 15h 3m 10s	Jul 1982	*Colt Cars GB*	60	Rob James (GB)	9·42

Long routes

Race or course	Distance (miles)	Time	Date	Yacht name	Length (ft)	Skipper (nationality)	Av. speed (knots)
Transatlantic east to west (Plymouth–Newport): single-handed	3000	16d 11h 55m	Jul 1984	*Fleury Michon VIII*	60	Philippe Poupon (F)	7·75
Round the world: non-stop, single-handed	25500	150d 6h 1m	Nov 1985–Apr 1986	*American Promise*	60	Dodge Morgan (US)	7·07
Round the world: three stops, fully crewed	27430	117d 14h 32m	Sep 1985–Apr 1986	*UBS Switzerland*	80	Pierre Fehlmann (CH)	9·32

RECORD YEAR

Sailing is not only about
blown spinnakers or aerial
views of yachts powering upwind.
Sailing Year's 'Year in Camera'
portfolio chooses the more
unusual and striking images
of the past season.

*It may be one of the world's most
famous yacht races, but the Fastnet
goes largely unrecorded by the
Admiral's Cup press corps. Standing
a few miles off the south-western tip of
Ireland, the Rock is one
of the most revered turning marks
in yachting.*

PHOTO: KAORU SOEHATA

There can be few places left in the
world not yet reached by a French-
organised yacht race. The more
obscure the destination, the greater
seems the appeal to Gallic sailors.
During a race from Lorient and back,
Eric Tabarly's maxi, Côte d'Or, is
dwarfed by the pack ice off
Newfoundland.

PHOTO: CHRISTIAN FÉVRIER

*Going for broke: the Irish Admiral's
Cup team member, Jameson
Whiskey, is pinned down by a severe
gust after tacking.*

PHOTO: RICK TOMLINSON

*Looking at you – it's not often that
18 ft Skiff sailors get a chance to look
around and enjoy the view. It is a full
time job keeping these highly strung
boats on their feet.*

PHOTO: KOS

*The Champagne Mumm Admiral's
Cup attracted the world's press, who
used as their base the Press Office in
the restored Ancasta Marina building.
For one photographer, the office was
more than just a place of work as it
provided a subject for a picture.*

PHOTO: CARLO BORLENGHI

Photographers loved the America's
Cup for the exciting opportunities
created by the Fremantle Doctor – and
also for the quality of light in Western
Australia. French Kiss sails on a blue
sea turned white by the low sun.

*Put your hand in the hand of the one
you trust. In this case Full Pelt's
bowman Paul Standbridge uses a very
light Mylar headsail to guide him back
to the cockpit.*

PHOTO: KOS

*Even the best foredeck men sometimes
get down on their knees and try some
gentle praying, especially on a
12-metre where the foredeck is very
narrow and very exposed.*

*The most extraordinary
monohulls in the world, the 40 ft Class
Libera Lake Garda racers give photographers
the chance to capture such curious
sights as these ten men attached to
the boat by just their toes and
a trapeze wire.*

PHOTO: CARLO BORLENGHI

Kialoa V's owner Jim Kilroy
(white hair) and North Sails president
Tom Whidden (in peaked cap)
conduct a dockside conversation in
Monaco. A special filter
transforms an ordinary scene into an
extraordinary image.

PHOTO: KOS

*Fly past. Philippe Poupon's Atlantic
record-breaking trimaran* Fleury
Michon *hisses across the ocean.*

PHOTO: CHRISTIAN FÉVRIER

*A run in the sun – Buddy Melges in
Heart of America chases Marc
Pajot's French Kiss during the
Challenger Round Robins of the last
America's Cup.*

PHOTO: FRANCO PACE

*Quayside artists work to
capture the atmosphere of St Tropez,
the picture-perfect port on France's
Côte d'Azur.*

Spinnakers are the classic subject for any sailing photographer and, despite the familiarity of the image, can still provide a colourful and dramatic spectacle. The yacht pictured here is Blade Runner.

PHOTO: GUY GURNEY

BOC Challenge

by TIM JEFFERY

François Richard

François Richard

Philippe Jeantot celebrated his 35th birthday a few hours early. With arms raised in triumph, the Frenchman sailed back into Newport, Rhode Island, having won the BOC single-handed around the world race for the second time. Enough reason, surely, to shower himself and the throng of press and well-wishers with great jets of champagne?

This former deep-sea diver from Marseilles made his mark when he won the inaugural 'Le BOC' in 1982/83 with *Credit Agricole 1*, and since then he has become one of the finer endurance sailors in France's burgeoning ranks.

Asked which of his two victories he found the more satisfying, Jeantot declared: 'This one because there was far more competition. But I enjoyed the first race more. There was more time to enjoy what I was doing, more time to enjoy the human experience. This race, there was no time for that; someone was always right behind you and we all wanted to win.'

A measure of the intense competitiveness in the second BOC is that the first six finishers in Class I beat Jeantot's previous elapsed time, as did Mike Plant's *Airco Distributor*, the

Class II winner. Jeantot himself slashed his own previous best for the 26,000-mile marathon by 25 days in setting a new time of 134 days 5h 23m 56s.

The welcome the sailors received in Newport was as tremendous as their send-off some nine months earlier on Saturday 30 August 1986. It was that start which encapsulated so much of what has made the BOC an absorbing race. On the sponsorship front, the British-based BOC industrial and medical gases multinational had thrown an enormous New England clam bake party for competitors, officials and employees, topped off with a fireworks display which could have been twenty traditional Cowes Week pyrotechnic finales rolled into one.

In the dock over the preceding few days, the varied specialist yachts which had gathered proved the race to be a forcing ground in monohull design and equipment development. Perhaps more than anything else, the competitors themselves set this race apart from all others. Even though they ranged from sponsored superstars to mildly eccentric corinthians, an overwhelming fraternal bond existed between them all.

Many sages thought that 26-year-old Brazilian Edourdo de Almeida was unlikely to finish even the first leg to Cape Town because his former IOR one tonner (*Carro Chefe*) was too trim-sensitive to make a sensible single-handed yacht, yet that did not stop one competitor leaving a $100 note on the saloon table to help eke out the Brazilian's meagre funds for provisioning. This spirit ran deep throughout the race. On leg 4 from Rio de Janeiro, Frenchman Jean Luc van den Heede rendezvoused with Finn Pentti Salmi to hand over injectible antibiotics to combat blood poisoning and gangrene which had developed from a minor thumb infection.

Perhaps the most tangible expression of goodwill appeared in a telex sent to the Falkland Islands where the race's youngest competitor had put in to step a new mast. Canadian John Hughes had lost the spar on his *Joseph Young* deep in the Southern Ocean, yet had managed to make a jury rig with two spinnaker poles and sail the 4400 miles to the Falklands, including rounding the Horn in 50 knots of breeze. Not only did Hughes make what is probably the longest jury-rigged passage on record, but also, by spending just five

and a half hours off Rio de Janeiro instead of the six-week stop enjoyed by the Class I front runners, he managed to make the awards banquet in Newport at the race's end.

Even Philippe Jeantot enjoyed his fellow competitors' generous spirit when he failed to meet the pre-start qualification and inspection deadline. Although a small time penalty was applied for this inspection violation, the other was waived in favour of an 'I am sorry I'm late party' thrown by Jeantot on the dock at Goat Island marina, Newport.

The distance from Newport to the first stop, Cape Town, is about 6700 miles and there was plenty in store for the 25 yachts which crossed the line. Indeed, for Warren Luhrs, sailing the novel and ultra-light *Thursday's Child*, the excitement began ten minutes before the start. French author and artist Titouan Lamazou aboard *Ecureuil d'Aquitaine* collided with Luhrs in the mêlée created by a thousand spectator craft jammed into the harbour entrance start area. The collision damaged *Thursday's Child*'s articulated rudder gantry. This device permits the small rudder blade to remain vertical no matter how much the yacht heels, so

allowing a small wetted surface area/ low steering effort rudder blade to be carried. South African seaman John Martin, whose 1981 Angelo Lavronos-designed *Tuna Marine Voortrekkar* was one of the oldest yachts in the race, collided with a spectator craft and upset her crew into the sea. Martin barely looked behind, but forged ahead into the ocean and, ultimately, into Cape Town first.

Jeantot was denied the charmed progress normally enjoyed by the race favourite. One hour after the start his genoa shredded and within sight of Newport he had to heave-to, strip it off the Profurl headstay gear and return to the race. With his sewing machine out of action, the Frenchman took a whole month to hand-sew the genoa back into a useable sail.

Elsewhere in the fleet, boats dropped out fast. Dick Cross's beautiful wooden Art Paine-designed *Air Force* struck a container and sank. Kiwi Richard McBride had a promising-looking yacht (designed by Bruce Farr), but eleventh-hour sponsorship failed to make her any the more ready for sea. The complicated fractional rig on *Neptune's Express* came down on the Equator, so McBride headed for

Brazil and out of the race.

John Biddlecombe must have felt doomed, having lost his first *ACI Crusader* before the race on a reef. His new *ACI Crusader* proved far too tender and went into Bermuda for lengthy alterations, extra lead being added to the keel as the first gale had laid her flat, mast in the water. Clearly, this wasn't meant to be Biddlecombe's race, for he had put into Bermuda once before for medical attention after falling through the deck hatch and severely straining his groin.

Whatever *ACI*'s failing, she did have one of the more elegant water ballast systems – an idea which had been proved by Jeantot in the previous race. Race regulations stipulated that the ballast must be restricted to an amount which would heel the yacht no more than 10 degrees in static trim: *Biscuits Lu* and *UAP-Pour Médecins sans Frontières* required tanks holding as much as two tons. Engine-driven, electric and manual pumps, large-bore transfer pipes and rapid-dump valves were common in the fleet. But *ACI*'s system was simply a refinement of the dinghy self-bailer principle in which water could be scooped up, distributed to either tank and exhausted by one

retractable tube. To prove how tender *ACI* was, Biddlecombe flooded her weather ballast tank in 6 knots of breeze and triple-reefed the mainsail by the time 18 knots of wind had piped up.

Autopilot and wind vane gear troubled nearly every competitor at some stage, but worst affected must have been Titouan Lamazou who had to hand steer for 20 hours a day during the last five weeks of the opening leg. And in the final run into Cape Town, Lamazou's boom broke from constant gybing, forcing him to fashion another from his spinnaker poles. 'It was not an enjoyable trip', commented the Frenchman.

Capsizes and rudder trouble also put out Mac Smith's *Qauilo*, Takao Shimada's *Madonna* and Edourdo Louro de Almeida's *Miss Global*.

In Leg 2, Jeantot in *Credit Agricole III*, Lamazou in *Ecureuil d'Aquitaine* and Jean-Yves Terlain in the bright yellow *UAP-Pour Médecins sans Frontières* headed further south than the rest of the fleet and enjoyed more favourable conditions. All three yachts were equipped with Macsea computers which not only co-ordinated inputs from their navigational equipment,

Skioern IV's skipper, Jacques de Roux, was lost during the race *(above)*.

UAP-Pour Médecins sans Frontières showing her beamy hull and satcom dome *(main picture)*.

Far left: Credit Agricole III, showing how all controls lead to the cockpit where there are protected watch-keeping seats.

BOC CHALLENGE

51

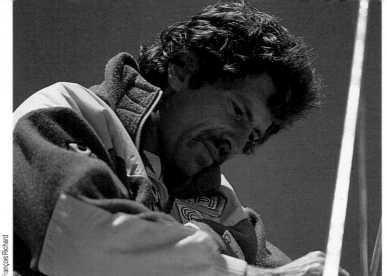

Philippe Jeantot.

François Richard

François Richard

François Richard

**Guy Bernadin's Joubert/Nivelt-designed
Biscuits Lu (top).**

**Bank of self-tailing winches aboard *UAP-Pour
Médecins sans Frontières* (above).**

François Richard

Credit Agricole III under spinnaker showing her flared hull sections and tumblehome.

Right: **Titouan Lamazou reefing the fully battened mainsail of *Ecureuil d'Aquitaine* heading towards Cape Town.**

but also contained an electronic database of charts and pilots. Most telling of all, though, was the ability for each yacht's back-up team in France to communicate directly with the computer to determine optimum routings.

The Southern Ocean between Africa and Australia did provide the fleet with Roaring Forties conditions. Using the ham radio network which monitored the fleet around the globe, Jeantot relayed to race headquarters that *Credit Agricole* was surfing downwind at 22 knots through driving rain, fog and freezing temperatures. Concern arose about Lamazou's condition when the Argos satellite plotting system showed a sudden loss of speed from 12 knots to just 1-2 knots and that was with the set of the current too. It was known that *Ecureuil d'Aquitaine* had been laid flat twice and had broken both spinnaker poles, but in this case it turned out that Lamazou's Argos transponder had been washed overboard. As for Lamazou, he maintained an astonishing pace during the middle of the leg, logging 230 miles a day.

But with steady gale force winds whistling along at 65 knots combined with enormous seas, the fleet took a battering. Eleven of the nineteen yachts were flattened or rolled a full 360 degrees. A terrible toll was taken of gear and sails. And, sadly, a life was lost in this, the toughest and most dangerous of all sailing events.

Jacques de Roux in *Skioern IV* had set a tremendous pace in Leg 1 to have won Class II even though he spent much of the time competing with the larger Class I yachts. De Roux had that quiet confidence that comes from being fully familiar with his yacht, a Dominique Presles design which had been built specially for the event. It was part of the tragedy that de Roux nearly lost his life in the last race during Leg 3 when *Skioern III* was pitch-poled just about as far from land as you can get in the empty wastes of the Southern Ocean. He was saved from his sinking yacht by fellow competitor Richard Broadhead. A former submariner, de Roux spent the time between races running an Indonesian fishery to raise the funds for his new *Skioern* and to 'rectify my failure in the last race'.

De Roux lost his life just 250 miles from Sydney, off Gabo Island on the Victorian coast. He was heading the Class II fleet; Guy Bernadin aboard *Biscuits Lu* said that de Roux had told him on the radio that he was pressing

the boat hard in tough conditions and was exhausted. He had been without navigational aids for the previous two weeks and getting just three to four hours sleep a day.

A search was called when de Roux failed to keep three radio schedules and when *Skioern IV*'s Argos plot slowed and showed an erratic course. Bernadin, who had just finished at Sydney joined the search along with Titouan Lamazou aboard naval vessels. They found *Skioern IV* rudderless and de Roux's safety line and oilskins hanging below. The former submarine commander had, presumably, gone on deck briefly and then fallen or been washed overboard.

Philippe Jeantot arrived just 40 minutes behind Lamazou in the van of the fleet, and that after 6000 miles and 28 days at sea. Jeantot's problems did not go away. His Guy Ribadeau-Dumas-designed yacht leaked badly, causing Jeantot to pump out 175 gallons (800 litres) of water a day while the keel was working. But it said something about the design of the BOC boats that Jeantot sailed into Sydney with the Whitbread race maxi *Atlantic Privateer*, some 20 ft longer and with a crew of 22. Both were under spinnaker and Jeantot, with autopilot set, pulled away from the IOR maxi . . .

Elsewhere in the fleet, South African veteran Bertie Reed suffered diesel poisoning whilst repairing the generator of *Stabilo Boss* (ex-*Disque d'Or III*), and Warren Luhrs lost the Lars Bergstrom rig on *Thursday's Child*. Harry Harkimo aboard the Swan 51 *Colt-Rettig*, one of the heaviest yachts in the fleet, had been rolled many times. He had even been washed overboard but was saved by his harness.

Despite being the longest in the race at 8200 miles, Leg 3 from Sydney to Rio de Janeiro was much less demanding. Instead of heading as far as 54 degrees south to find tailwinds as in Leg 2, the strategy was to stay further north to avoid headwinds. Guy Bernadin reported wearing shorts and a tee-shirt one night, although the Southern Ocean summer is bleak by most standards.

When faced with a high-pressure area, the Macsea users – Terlain, Lamazou and Jeantot – headed south to find more breeze and more of a lead. At one stage, the three were racing boat for boat, close enough to photograph each other. It made a spectacle which Terlain was able to relay to France via

his satcom telephone system. The enormous dome on *UAP-PMSF*'s stern looked quite incongruous. Indeed the 221 lb (96 kg) dome is normally fitted to ships and large motor yachts, and it gave Terlain special problems with its power requirements and stabilising the gyro-controlled antenna. But it did allow him broadcast quality communications and to publicise the work of Pour Médecins sans Frontières, a worldwide flying doctor service best known for reaching Mexico City just ten hours after the recent earthquake.

Publicity almost got the front runners into difficulty at the Horn, the crossroads of the oceans and sailing's most significant landmark. Jeantot rounded first, just 3h 10m ahead of Lamazou and was asked to drop his spinnaker by a French photographic boat which was lying in wait. Jeantot indulged their request briefly. The photographers then asked Lamazou to close in on the bluff Cape, which he did – only to strike a rock. 'There could have been a rock on chart,' said Lamazou, 'but I am not the best navigator.' Lamazou was forced to pump *Ecureuil d'Aquitaine* all the way to the finish, tightening the keel bolts each time he tacked.

Three thousand miles from Chile, John Hughes lost the mast of *Joseph Young* just above the gooseneck and it made a sizeable hole in the deck before he was able to cut away the mess. His jury rig, with the spinnaker poles stepped on the gunwales in food cans stuffed with rags, and his subsequent passage round the Horn was a most remarkable act of seamanship. A professional seaman, Hughes was determined not to call for outside assistance while he felt able to solve the problems himself. Friends at home, meanwhile, raised money to buy a new mast and persuaded the Royal Canadian Air Force and British armed forces to have it ready in Port Stanley.

Jeantot won the race to Rio and moved into the overall lead of Class I. With the loss of de Roux, Class II's front runners were French maths teacher Jean Luc van den Heede in his narrow-beam, low-freeboard *Let's Go*, and American Mike Plant in *Airco Distributor*.

Carnival time in Rio gave those who arrived in time a real chance to relax, Jeantot joining the parade wearing a Louis XIV costume.

Despite being one of the shorter legs at 5300 miles, Leg 4 back to Newport was expected to be slow due to the

Doldrums. But the near absence of light airs in these latitudes meant that the fleet made fast pace towards the finish line.

As others had suffered before him, Jeantot faced rigging problems, something which seemed almost inconceivable given the enormous gauge of *Credit Agricole*'s wire shrouds and their wide staying base. But the intermediates supporting the massive 81 ft Marechal mast were stranding, and Jeantot was concerned he would have to ease off the pace. He put into Recife, Brazil, where his support team met him and reinforced the rig. Jeantot spent just five and a half hours in port, but the deviation from course put him in

François Richard

different weather from arch-rival Lamazou. Jeantot's three-day lead was now far from secure for Lamazou had pulled out a 135-mile advantage.

It was John Martin, however, who led the charge back into Newport just as he had headed the fleet out. But for rig and steering problems on Legs 2 and 3, his successes might have been greater. Likewise, Lamazou lost three and a half days in the opening leg with autopilot and boom failure, a margin he managed to claw back from Jeantot.

Even though he crossed the finish line 3rd, Jeantot could count four good, solid performances and, with the differences so small between the boats, that was the telling factor.

Jean-Yves Terlain inside *UAP-Pour Médecins sans Frontières'* futuristic doghouse *(left)*.

BOC CHALLENGE

Photo finish at the end of a day-long duel
between *Roter Baron* (foreground) and *Oyster
Lady* who crossed the finishing line within two
seconds of each other.

Gran Canaria—Barbados

ARC Race

November–December 1986

by JIMMY CORNELL

A better finale to the first Atlantic Race for Cruisers could not have been anticipated as the last of the 204 yachts sailed into Bridgetown less than one hour before the presentation party on 1 January. Not even the first arrival received such an impressive reception as David Shipton who spent 33 days single-handing his 24 ft (7.3 m) *Dunkers* the 2700 miles from Gran Canaria and found most of the participants assembled in Barbados to greet him.

One of the main aims of this race for cruising boats was to bring all the boats and crews safely across the Atlantic without the tragic losses that have marred some other ocean races. Another objective pursued by the ARC was to return to the amateur spirit of early transatlantic races. One way to ensure that only genuine cruising boats entered the ARC was not to allow any sponsorship of individual boats or advertising by the competitors. That the time was ripe for such a race became apparent as soon as the idea was launched and hundreds of enquiries began flooding in from all parts of the world. Four months before the start, over 250 yachts had registered and the list of entries had to be closed. Eventually, 209 yachts from 24 nations lined up for the start on Saturday, 29 November 1986, making the ARC the largest trans-ocean race ever staged.

For many of the participants, the atmosphere of the race began long before the start in Las Palmas, as they sailed from Northern Europe, the English Channel, the Mediterranean and even from the east coast of the United States, meeting other competitors in anchorages and marinas along the way. By the time they reached Gran Canaria, many already knew each other, and if not, soon did in the congenial atmosphere of Las Palmas. Fiestas, folklore concerts and fireworks were just some of the entertainments put on by the municipal council of Las Palmas, which helped to coalesce the ARC participants into one large family.

It was a moving moment when the Barbados flag was hoisted by special permission on the Spanish naval ship *Villa de Bilbao*, and the President of the Canary Islands, Señor Jeronimo Saavedra, gave the signal for the start. As the yachts jostled for best positions along the mile-long start line it was evident that the racing bug had already bitten many of the cruisers, few of whom had taken part in a race before. The bay of Las Palmas filled with hundreds of sails sparkling in the sunshine as the boats fanned out and sped on their way. An uncommon southerly wind turned the planned downwind start into an upwind leg, which caused the fleet to split into two, some choosing to sail round the north of Gran Canaria instead of the usual route south.

It was only 13 days 22 hours later that Larry Pollock brought his 54 ft (16.4 m) trimaran *Running Cloud* across the finishing line in Bridgetown, followed just five hours later by Michael Gluck's *Moonshadow. Moonshadow*'s time was excellent by any standards as the 62 ft (18.9 m) cruising monohull almost outperformed the much faster trimaran on the mostly downwind run. The secret of *Moonshadow*'s success lay in the perfect teamwork provided by the crew assembled by Michael Gluck, which included some veteran US East Coast sailors such as Harvey Levine, Martin Halpern and Emanuel Greene, as well as the Englishman Phil Wade, former watch leader on *Drum*.

Moonshadow's achievement was almost overshadowed by that of *Albatros* which sailed in at midnight to a rousing welcome, with just two crew aboard. Determined from the start to put in a fast passage, circumnavigators Manfred Kerstan and Vera Schmidt were deeply disappointed to lose their spinnaker only one day out of Las Palmas. Undeterred, they got the best out of *Albatros* by handsteering almost the entire 2700 miles and their victory in Class A and the Prime Minister's Trophy were fully deserved.

By Sunday noon, the whole of Barbados had warmed up to the race and a steel band had been provided by the Board of Tourism to welcome the arrivals in a special area of the port which had been set aside for the ARC. A huge shed had been cleared of

The ARC fleet in Las Palmas.

containers which were then used to block off the entire area from the rest of the harbour. The Barbados Port Authority had arranged a reception area in which all facilities were provided for the ARC yachts: customs, immigration and health officers, bank, telephone, tourist information, bar, restaurant, mail delivery, showers, toilets and plenty of fresh water on the dock. Everything possible was done to welcome the participants and Mount Gay Distilleries, who sponsored all ARC events in Barbados, had someone on hand day and night to greet the crews with delicious cold rum punches and a presentation pack which included even more Mount Gay rum!

The first boat in Class B to cross the finishing line was Tim Aitken's *Airwave*, a Centurion 47 sailed efficiently by a keen crew. Although recording excellent fast passages, the first four boats had all been expected to do well, but it took everyone by surprise when Pål Stiansen sailed the 41 ft (12.5 m) *Aquarion* into Bridgetown only 19 minutes after *Airwave* to complete the crossing in 15 days 11 hours. Pål had made the decision to take the more northerly great circle route instead of sailing south to pick up the tradewinds and his gamble had paid off. Fellow Norwegian Ernst Torp, in radio contact with *Aquarion*, had started off by sailing his larger 49 ft (15 m) *Her Ladyship* along the same route, but later steered further south, a decision he paid for by coming in 5 hours after John Green's *Rebound* and almost 21 hours after *Aquarion*.

After fifteen days, the frequency of arrivals accelerated, 9 boats completing the passage in sixteen days, 14 in seventeen days and 22 in eighteen days. The order of arrivals, however, continued to surprise everyone, with small boats and shorthanded crews often appearing before much larger boats with bigger crews. Outstanding were Stuart Feinblatt who sailed his 33 ft (10 m) *Desire* across the line in seventeen days and Erkki Lempiainen, who also took the great circle route to astonish everyone by bringing his 26 ft (8 m) *Alfa* across the Atlantic in eighteen days.

As the number of arrivals gained momentum, the group of local sailing enthusiasts keeping watch 24 hours a day off the finishing line were treated to some exciting finishes. The most spectacular finale was between two well-matched boats, *Oyster Lady* and *Roter Baron*. For the last fifty miles they

Left: **The crew of 49 ft Norwegian yacht *Her Ladyship*, whose skipper Ernst Torp joined the ARC Race despite crippling multiple sclerosis.**

Below left: **Alex Plummer, the youngest participant, with his parents Lyn and Brian Plummer of the New Zealand yacht *Bounder*.**

had engaged in a nail-biting duel which continued right up to the end, when Gerd Seubert sailed *Roter Baron* across the finishing line only a few feet and two seconds before Chris Vale's *Oyster Lady*. The following day 41 ft (12.5 m) *Shearwater* and 40 ft (12.2 m) *Ziggurat*, both 20-year-old boats crewed by couples on their own, provided another exciting finish, Marcia and Moore Davock sailing *Shearwater* over the line only one minute ahead of Alice and Howard Wright's *Ziggurat*.

The ARC also attracted a large number of multihulls, most of them cruising catamarans. Loaded with provisions and cruising gear, their performance was evenly matched to that of the monohulls. *Kuralu* and *Vertige IV* were the first catamarans to arrive within minutes of each other on Day 16, although the overall prize for best multihull performance on handicap went to the much smaller 26 ft (8 m) *Twinsum*, which crossed in 22 days 19 hours.

The ten singlehanders had a keen competition among themselves and, to everyone's surprise – herself included – the first to arrive was Noelle Corbett, the only woman among them. More than three-quarters of the ARC yachts had women on board and the high level of female participation must be unprecedented for an ocean race. The winner of the ARC on handicap, the Finnish yacht *Molla III*, was also sailed by a family crew. Kari Hynninen, an electrician from Helsinki, had fitted out the 30 ft (9 m) hull himself and was making a circuit of the north Atlantic with his wife Mariella and eight-year-old son Toni. For their overall win, the crew of *Molla III* received the Jimmy Cornell Trophy, an original bronze sculpture, as well as an Avon Redcrest dinghy (donated by Avon Inflatables) and the use of a car for a week (contributed by Sunset Crest Motors from Barbados).

A major attraction of the ARC was the chance it gave owners of standard cruising boats, as well as those of older racing yachts, to compete on equal terms in a transatlantic race. The fast times achieved by most participants showed that cruising people know how to race their boats when the opportunity arises. Several long-term cruising sailors stressed after the race that they had put in a much greater effort than they would normally have done on an ocean passage. Many of the boats were sailed hard by their crews and the average time taken for the crossing was

considerably lower than the usual number of days.

Although promoted as a fun race across the Atlantic, the fun was very much restricted to the time spent in port, for the safety aspect was taken very seriously both by organisers and participants alike. One of the few rules for the event stipulated that every yacht must be in the possession of an EPIRB (Emergency Position Indicating Radio Beacon) and liferaft. As many people appeared to have joined the ARC for the safety in numbers it provided, it was decided to operate a VHF emergency net during the race. All participants were required to listen to Channel 16 from 11.00 to 12.00 GMT and from 22.00 to 22.30 GMT. If anyone had a serious emergency for which outside assistance was necessary, a message could be relayed by VHF until a yacht was reached that was equipped with long-range radio and could pass it on to the outside world. The few emergencies that did occur were dealt with promptly within the net, which had the advantage of being able to consult one of several doctors who sailed in the ARC.

The VHF net was doubled up by a more far-ranging net run by the forty amateur radio operators sailing in the ARC. As well as keeping in contact with several amateur radio nets, Peter Rodenburgh of *Blyss II* and Zeke Holland on *Ace of Hearts* ran an informal net for all the boats heading west, which, recalling the cattle drives of the past, they named the 'Rawhide Net'. It proved a great success and relieved the monotony of the long passage for many of the participants as well as adding to the overall safety.

Although the safety aspect was uppermost in the minds of the organisers when the ARC was conceived, it was also hoped to add some zest to the long passage. This was achieved by arousing a competitive spirit that appears to be dormant in many cruisers. The greatest attraction of the ARC, however, was undoubtedly the framework it provided for people to meet each other and socialise, regardless of age, language, financial means or sailing experience. The docksides in Las Palmas and Bridgetown became a concrete example of what cruising is all about as crews made friends not only among fellow participants but also among local people.

The reception extended to the ARC fleet both in Gran Canaria and Barbados greatly contributed to the friendly atmosphere as local authorities, yacht clubs and people generally went out of their way to make the visiting sailors welcome. Fiestas were organised in Las Palmas by the Municipal Council, the Tourist Promotion Board put on a magnificent fireworks display on the eve of departure, while the Port Authority presented each competitor with an engraved silver plate commemorating the first ARC. This kind of welcoming was repeated in Barbados, where a local family invited all 34 children who had taken part in the ARC to a Christmas party, complete with Santa Claus and presents for everyone. Steel bands and carol singing choirs came to the waterfront to entertain the ARC fleet, while after Christmas the more racing-minded sailors took part in the Mount Gay Regatta. The three-day event was dominated by forty ARC yachts who

provided stiff competition for local yachtsmen and walked off with most of the magnificent prizes.

The fun aspect of the ARC was evident at the prize-giving ceremony when the merits of some boats and crews were recognised that had nothing to do with speed. The most appreciated prizes were those awarded to people like Chuck Hoffman of *Schussboomer*, for being the most helpful skipper, or to Ernst Torp, the skipper of *Her Ladyship*, for his help in computerising the ARC lists in Las Palmas, but primarily in recognition of his determination to continue sailing undeterred by the onset of multiple sclerosis.

Among the special prizes, one that was hotly contested was that for the oldest competitor, as three were born in 1915 and the dates in their passports had to checked to see who was the oldest. David Ward of *Seannine*, who celebrated his 71st birthday in Barbados, beat Emanuel Green of *Moonshadow* and Arthur Watchorn of *Canada Goose* by a whisker to carry off the special Barbados Board of Tourism Trophy. At least there was no dispute over the youngest competitor as he was known all along. Alex Plummer joined the crew of New Zealand yacht *Bounder* only two months before the race and is probably one of the youngest babies to cross the Atlantic in a sailing yacht.

There were many other prizes which reflected the less-serious side of this genuine amateur race. The prolonged cheers at the end of the prize-giving ceremony when participants were reminded that the ARC had tried to be a true reflection of the Olympic spirit showed that this aim had been achieved against all odds. It was symbolic that the only Spanish competitor, Jorge Brosa of *Ave Phoenix*, flew the Olympic flag, not only because he came from Barcelona (the 1992 venue), but also because he was a firm believer in the Olympic principle. The maxim that to take part is more important than to win remains the true ARC philosophy as the scene is set for the coming of the second ARC.

Jimmy Cornell is a former BBC World Service radio journalist. He has already sailed around the world with his family in their yacht Aventura. *In between planning the next ARC Race and writing articles and books on world cruising, he is building a new yacht for his second circumnavigation.*

CONRAD RITBLAT

Round the Island Race

by BOB FISHER

If Ratty's theory that 'there is nothing – absolutely nothing – half as much worth doing as simply messing about in boats' is ever borne out in reality, it is annually in June when the Island Sailing Club holds its race around the Isle of Wight. The support which the race receives justifiably confirms that riverbank sage of *Wind in the Willows*.

Boats which never race at any other time are there as the early morning mists clear for the series of starts from the Island Sailing Club's line. There is a clearing of mists of other kinds – many of the competitors will have met the previous evening for a lengthy session in the ISC or the Royal Corinthian and few of them are used to rising this early. The aim is to send the boats off with a fair tide to the Needles, generally a beat in the prevailing south-westerly, and to see them with a fair tide again from St Catherine's Point. Of course, with such a diversity of boats no-one has the same chance of making the tidal 'gates', but that is another of the charms of this race.

The tide dictated that the first start should be at 06.00 with the numerous classes sent off in seven starts at ten-minute intervals. For many, this meant clambering out of sleeping bags and into sailing kit at 03.00, with reluctant brains catching up some hours later with bodies on autodrive.

The race originated in 1931, the brainchild of Major Cyril Windeler. At that time one newspaper correspondent expressed surprise that as many as 77 boats would take part in what he described as 'the largest yacht race in the world'. That event was won by a converted fishing boat. The following year a 6-metre took the Gold Roman Bowl – but not the same trophy as the one competed for in 1931. Major Windeler was appalled that the Bowl he had presented was 'only' silver gilt, and he replaced it for the second year by the present 9 carat version. It took him until 1939 to win it with his 7 tonner, *Kalliste*.

Early records of the race are well kept although there is some doubt expressed about the time taken by *Dolly Varden*, Tom Ratsey's gaff cutter in the first race. It is recorded that she took 5h 51m 24s, but that is out of place with all the other times for the day. If that was indeed the correct time, she still holds the monohull record for the race, but the current holder is generally taken to be Bill Whitehouse-Vaux's *Mistress Quickly*. In 1979 the Ben Lexcen-designed 73 footer (22 m), with Harold Cudmore calling the shots, took 5h 57m 15s. Seven years later the 45 ft (14 m) *Barracuda of Tarrant* took only ten minutes longer on the day when Mike Whipp's 60 ft (18 m) trimaran *Paragon* claimed the multihull record with 3h 55m 15s.

The list of the 51 winners of the Gold Roman Bowl, now the 'Grand Prix' class prize, for the IOR boats reads something like a Who's Who of Yachting. The most successful has been the Rt Hon. Edward Heath who has won it on four occasions (three times in a row) with three different *Morning Clouds*; the most notable absentee is the club's Admiral, Sir Owen Aisher, who has probably competed in more Round the Island races than any man alive, although his son Robin took it home in 1985. But it is not winning which most competitors consider when they enter for this race; for them there is a much more Coubertinesque appeal – they are there simply to take part.

By 1952, when 134 boats took part, *Yachting World* was referring to it as 'a kind of barometer by which to judge the general well-being of sailing'. By that yardstick, sailing is very healthy indeed as the 1987 Round the Island Race attracted no less than 1362 entries of many shapes and sizes. Although there is no official record of crew numbers, it seems quite likely that some 7000 made the annual 60-mile pilgrimage and felt to the full the race's 'charm' and the vagaries of the winds and currents around the Isle of Wight.

For a change, the start was in a northerly light breeze, eliminating those heart-stopping moments early in the race when a call for water along the island shore can result in most of the fleet having to tack. This time the important factor was to gain clear air as early as possible and make as much use as possible of the strongest of the tidal stream. The further the fleet progressed towards the Needles, the more the wind went towards the west and it was only a few who were able to fetch the Archibald Reid buoy (where the old Palm buoy used to be laid, to keep the boats clear of the wreck of the *Varvassi* off the Needles) without having to tack.

The early boats around did have an advantage: that of not being caught in the inevitable log jam as boats began to turn into the unfavourable stream from the south side of the island. In order to dodge this tide it becomes increasingly necessary to head straight for the cliffs

Main picture: **a sight familiar to all Round the Island competitors as the fleet starts off Cowes in the early morning light.** *Right:* **fresher winds round the back of the Island helped speed yachts home back towards Cowes.**

ROUND THE ISLAND RACE

A solitary Scampi intrudes among the Sigma 33 fleet shortly after rounding the Needles.

and into Freshwater Bay, and when any boat bore off through 140 degrees it seemed to come almost to a halt. But this was one of the critical parts of the race and there was the overwhelming feeling that with the wind backing all the while there would be a stronger breeze coming in from the sea.

Catch 22 – how appropriate this year! Those who did best were those who were prepared to bite the bullet and go all the way into the shore, gybing in and out to avoid the rocks and cheat the foul tide. Those who hung out, waiting for the early sea breeze, were those who perished – competitively, at least. It wasn't until the leaders were well round St Catherine's Point that the breeze did fill in from the expected direction.

The great joy of the Round the Island Race, sponsored for the first time in its history, is that there's a multitude of races within the event. As ever, there was a healthy contingent of chartered surveyors racing for their 'own' prize, the Shepherds Trophy. Of the 24 boats which contested it this year, Paul Gatrill's *Scorpio II* took the IOR honours and D.S. Browning's *Leda* won the CHS event. Apart from 30 divisions there are the personal races on which perhaps no more than a pint of beer will change hands, and much silverware to give encouragement to race hard.

It was just after St Catherine's that the real fun began, with boats trying to cheat the last of the foul tide, carefully avoiding Church Rocks and the snares provided by the lobster fishermen who don't seem to know how sharply their pot lines can impede the progress of a sailboat. As the breeze began to fill in gradually and the tide to turn, the pot watchers were able to provide even greater input than simply spotting them for avoidance plans. The tide turns quite rapidly and those who saw the change the earliest gained those extra seconds that make the difference between winning and losing.

By Bembridge Ledge on the eastern tip of the island, the larger boats which had started later in the high-rated Channel Handicap and IOR classes

started to edge through the smaller handicap and class yachts. In all, there were just over 200 IOR yachts competing, but the CHS division proved more popular with 284 entries.

The speediest part of the race was the shy spinnaker reach from Bembridge Ledge to the Forts, and it was there that the very earliest boats were 'parked' waiting for the southerly breeze to overtake the earlier northerly. When it arrived it provided a fetch to the finish.

First home was the trimaran *Triple Fantasy*, but this year it was not to be the best elapsed time. Robin Aisher's Farr 50 *Yeoman XXVII* took 13 minutes less, for 8h 4m 57s, and it was already obvious that the small boats were going to do well in every division. The Gold Roman Bowl went to John Allenby's *Catch*, a Briand-designed quarter tonner, beating Paul Gatrill's Humphreys-designed half tonner *Scorpio II* by two minutes.

But not all competitors race Round the Island at ten-tenths. For many it is a cruise in company, a jolly, or more simply a good day's sailing. Everyone who enters gets something to take home for the mantlepiece, with the Island SC offering a tankard to each entrant. Above all, it is a very long day and even with the early morning start some yachts just did not complete the course by the 20.30 time limit. The Old Gaffers did make it, however, their presence an essential ingredient in the varied mix of boats racing.

Most old scores were settled for a year but there was an invitation issued with the results. Each sheet gave the date of the 52nd Round the Island Race – 25 June 1988.

Bob Fisher is one of the best-known yachtsmen and yachting writers as well as an author and broadcaster. He is a regular visitor to the top events and has sailed in many of them. He competed in the Conrad Ritblat Round the Island race in his own 45 ft Tony Castro-designed Barracuda of Tarrant.

ROUND THE ISLAND RACE

Roger Lean-Vercoe

The new Corolla GT-i 16. Now fast doesn't have to mear

The hatchback is no longer the ill-mannered handful, the clutch-jumping urban tearaway.

It is the new Corolla GT-i 16.

It combines speed with responsiveness, firm chassis control with fluid handling. All characteristics common to its larger Toyota stable-mates.

The Corolla is a well-mannered car, designed around a well-mannered engine, the 16V 1600 Si.

This sixteen valve, 1600cc fuel injected twin cam unit has graduated from arguably the finest school of multivalve

engineering there is. Matured on the race tracks of Europe, it powered Toyota's British Touring Car Champion to victory along the way.

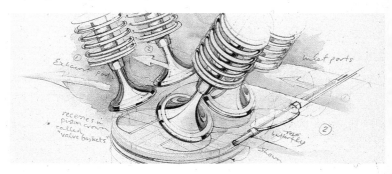

urious.

Multivalve technology means it breathes more easily, operates more efficiently, which is why it can touch 122 mph without screaming about it.

(As Motor Magazine says . . . "The Golf GTI is left trailing in the Corolla's performance wake.")

In fact so quiet is the car both under the bonnet and inside the compartment, that our Super Red paintwork is possibly the loudest thing about the Corolla.

The days when a hot-hatchback was more wrestling than driving are also at an end, with Toyota's power

steering and improved chassis and suspension systems.

Motor Magazine agrees: "The Corolla's superior ride is obvious . . . it's predictable, controllable . . . inspirational."

The very nature of the Corolla's contours point to a car that is truly well-rounded in every department.

Leave the adolescents behind and test drive a more refined hatchback.

The new Corolla GT-i 16.

TOYOTA
MULTI-VALVE TECHNOLOGY

America's

Main picture. **Kookaburra III** and her trial horse, **Kookaburra II**, leave Success Harbour, Fremantle, for the Cup course under the eyes of thousands of spectators and the world's television. Left. Iain Murray designed, skippered and masterminded the impressive Kookaburra campaign. Middle left. The Cup's stay in Australia may have been just three years but they were the most significant in its 136-year history. Middle right. **Stars & Stripes** flies the Stars and Stripes in victory. Right. Dennis Conner – from the despair of defeat to the glories and riches of triumph in three years.

Daniel Forster

Carlo Borlenghi

Cup

by BRUCE STANNARD

Right. **The highly fancied *America II* from the New York YC failed to shine. Like the other Twelves, she revelled in fresh Freo conditions.**

Iain Murray steering *Kookaburra III* (below) in the finals against Conner. The pre-starts were handled by Peter Gilmour whose liking for the red protest flag never diminished.

Carlo Borlenghi

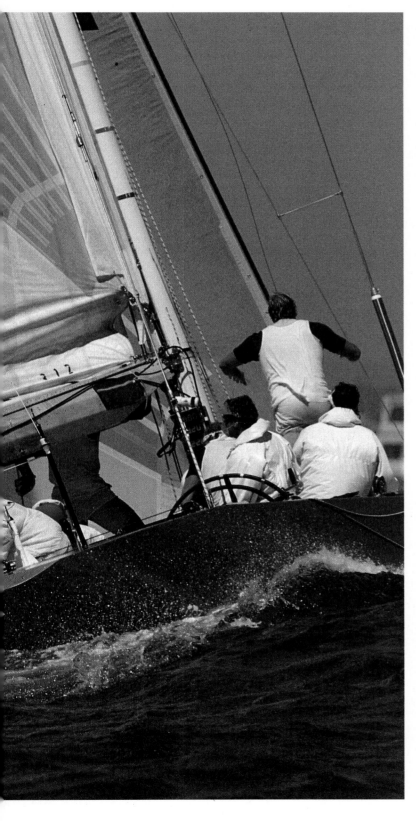

When *Liberty* lost the America's Cup in 1983, few could have imagined Dennis Conner's triumphant return in the summer of 1987. Conner went home to California unaware that *Australia II*'s historic win would act as a catalyst for what were to be an unprecedented thirteen international challengers. As far as Conner was concerned it was the superior technology of *Australia II*'s winged keel that had beaten him. Alone in those days he took it upon himself to drive that lesson home to the scientists in the aerospace industry who would be critical to his plan. The task required an organisation as far reaching in its scientific, technical and engineering skills as NASA, the National Aeronautics and Space Administration. Conner set up his own mini-NASA with three designers – Britton Chance, Bruce Nelson and David Pedrick. With the 12-metre veteran John Marshall co-ordinating their efforts, they set about creating the *Stars & Stripes* challenge. They purchased *Liberty* as a benchmark and with her came *Spirit of America*, one of Conner's early '83 discards. She was fitted with an experimental winged keel so that any improvements against *Liberty* could be measured. That in turn established the standard by which they could judge their first new boat, *Stars & Stripes '85*.

From the outset it was clear, in Conner's mind at least, that the 1987 America's Cup series was going to be a boat speed contest and not a contest of in-tight, close sailing. On Conner's insistence, the design team based its whole effort on producing a faster boat and they decamped to the relative seclusion of Hawaii where the northeast tradewinds could be relied upon to blow. In Hawaii they tested the radical failure, *Stars & Stripes '86*, before finally settling on the boat which was to become the ultimate Cup challenger, *Stars & Stripes '87*. Built very quickly at Bob Derecktor's yard at Mamaroneck, New York, she was sent briefly to Hawaii and then, with her tender *Betsy* and her trial horse *Stars & Stripes '85*, moved Down Under to Fremantle.

The Other Challengers

Ranged against *Stars & Stripes* in Fremantle were no less than five challengers from the United States

alone. Tommy Blackaller, of San Francisco Bay, was there with *USA*, the most innovative and daring of all the new breed of 12-metres. *USA*'s slender canoe body was not encumbered, as all the others were, with a variation of the revolutionary *Australia II* winged keel. Instead, suspended from a slender strut (like a cross between a fat cigar and a torpedo) was what was to become known as the 'geek', the brainchild of designers Gary Mull, Dr Heiner Meldner and Dr Alberto Calderon of the University of California. With so little lateral resistance in the 'geek', *USA*'s designers had added a forward fin which acted like a combination rudder and centreboard. *USA* looked as lean and mean as her skipper.

Buddy Melges was there too with his Gretsky/Graham & Schlagater-designed *Heart of America*, challenging on behalf of the Chicago Yacht Club. Melges has won just about every trophy there is in small boat sailing and yet this was to be his first crack at the 12-metre big time. Rod Davis, the Soling class gold medallist at the Los Angeles Olympics, was there in the battleship-grey *Eagle*, designed by the veteran Johan Valentijn, the creator of *Liberty* and sundry other America's Cup boats. Although she looked fast early on it was soon clear she was not going to make it.

Courageous, one of the most famous names in America's Cup history, was also there, at least in spirit. The Grand Old Lady was hardly recognisable as the magnificent yacht which won the cup back in 1974 and 1977 and came close to the hat-trick in 1983. She had been given an outrageous-looking bulbous winged keel by owner Leonard Greene, but was painfully slow and was soon withdrawn.

The last of *Stars & Stripes'* American rivals was believed likely to be the toughest. The America II syndicate from the New York Yacht Club had budgeted US$20 million, built three *America II*s and had been in Fremantle almost from the moment *Liberty* lost the Cup in '83. They had a very expensive and elaborate boatyard complete with impregnable underwater pens to protect their design secrets. In this compound, it seemed, money was no object, yet boat speed was not as abundant as cash. Even in October it

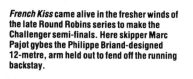

French Kiss came alive in the fresher winds of the late Round Robins series to make the Challenger semi-finals. Here skipper Marc Pajot gybes the Philippe Briand-designed 12-metre, arm held out to fend off the running backstay.

Overleaf: *Kookaburra III* chases *Australia IV* in the bloody defender trials. Chaos erupts aboard the trailing *Kooka III* as a late float spinnaker drop at the leeward mark sees flailing sheets and guys, the spinnaker pole overside and the genoa not sheeted home.

Carlo Borlenghi

was clear that *America II* could probably out-tack any boat in Fremantle. In anticipation of tight, in-fighting style match racing John Kolius and his crew had been practising tacking non-stop for three years, but the critical issue was simply speed. All through those practice months *America II* thought they had it whereas the truth was, as Buddy Melges correctly perceived, they had 'the fastest slow boats in Fremantle'.

The other international contestants in the series included two boats from France, two from Italy and one each from Britain, Canada and New Zealand. The Daniel Andrieu-designed *Challenge France* was unfortunately short of money and time, and although Yves Pajot and his young crew tried hard, theirs was largely a wasted effort. In *French Kiss*, Yves Pajot's brother Marc had teamed up with the brilliant young designer Philippe Briand to create a lovely pale grey boat whose blistering straightline speed had caused a sensation during the 1986 World Championships. *French Kiss* broke new ground, with her innovative design and the bold use of a name with obvious commercial connotations. She was sponsored by Kis France, the instant photo-processing and key-cutting company. Her success in retaining her name effectively broke the back of the International Yacht Racing Union's Rule 26.2 which had hitherto strictly forbidden advertising of commercial sponsorship and company logos on racing yachts.

The Italians were, as usual, long on style but short on sailing success. There were repeated changes in *Azzurra*'s crew early on and even the return of Mauro Pelaschier did not resolve matters. Worse still, the Andrea Vallicelli-designed boat was off the pace. Arch-rival *Italia* promised much better things. The sleek, gunmetal-grey hull and the combination of the red, white and green Gucci-clad crew made her look quite stunning. Prime sponsor Dr Maurizio Gucci would say before the summer was out that he would gladly trade all *Italia*'s style for just one-tenth of a knot more boat speed.

Canada II was in fact *Canada I*, the Bruce Kirby design revamped by him after the '83 campaign. She was good enough to beat her national rival, *True*

North, during a race off series sailed in California, and when she came to Fremantle in October there were plenty of pundits willing to predict a bright future for the red-and-white boat skippered by Finn sailor Terry Neilsen. Unfortunately, that early promise was not realised as the southern summer wore on.

The British had, of course, been involved with the America's Cup since 1851. It was, after all, their precious silver trophy that *America* had spirited away under Queen Victoria's gaze. Harold Cudmore had put together a fine team of top sailors and a potentially good design programme. He had two boats, one very radical, designed by David Hollom, and the other, conservative and conventional, designed by Ian Howlett. After what seemed a surprisingly short time for evaluation, Cudmore opted for the conventional boat, named *White Crusader*. Cudmore, the brilliant Irish skipper, happens to be one of the best match race helmsmen in the world and although at the start of the summer things looked so promising he was fated not to reach even the semi-finals.

New Zealand's *KZ-7* was the most sensational 12-metre in Fremantle. The Kiwis, in their first America's Cup challenge, sailed an almost flawless campaign. Led by aggressive Auckland merchant banker Michael Fay, they were the only ones to take on the task of producing glassfibre 12-metres to the scantlings laid down by the guardians of the 12-metre constructional integrity, Lloyd's Register of Shipping in London.

The Kiwis built two identical boats to a design by Bruce Farr, Ron Holland and Laurie Davidson, and these boats, *KZ-3* and *KZ-5*, were blooded in the boisterous World Championships in January – February 1986. The lessons learned from that exercise went into the design of *KZ-7*, nicknamed 'Kiwi Magic'. She was skippered by 25-year-old Chris Dickson, who, despite his youth, is one of the world's more experienced match racing helmsmen.

Dickson and his young crew, six of whom were veterans of the Whitbread Round the World Race, gave an excellent account of themselves, especially in strong winds and high seas. *KZ-7* was to carve a unique niche for herself in America's Cup history by

AMERICA'S CUP

Carlo Borlenghi

Right: **Italia** peels spinnakers – the Italians were stylish ashore but lacked speed afloat.

Far right: **Stars & Stripes** rounds the America's Cup bouy in Gage Roads. Fremantle's low and bright sun showed the Twelves off as yachts of beauty as never before.

The ritual dance of the duelling Twelves – here **Azzurra** and **White Crusader** thrust and parry in the pre-start, each trying to gain ascendancy (main picture).

winning 37 out of the 38 races leading up to the Louis Vuitton semi-finals.

The string of wins was not without controversy, however. A good part of the summer was dominated by claims and counter-claims concerning the composition of *KZ-7*'s glassfibre hull. Eventually, under pressure from the official Challenger of Record, the Yacht Club Costa Smeralda, the New Zealanders did subject their boat to ultrasonic testing which was conducted in an attempt to determine the weight and distribution and density within the glassfibre hull. Dennis Conner argued that core sampling was the only effective method of testing. The boat passed the ultrasound test, at least to the satisfaction of the International Measurement Committee. The issue was dropped and yet the controversy lingered for what was to be some of the best match racing of the entire Cup summer when *KZ-7* eventually faced *Stars & Stripes* in the challenger finals.

Elimination Races

One by one the challengers fell by the wayside and the vanquished hulls hung in their cradles, forlorn and lifeless along the Fremantle waterfront. By 28 December only four boats remained. The top points scorer, *KZ-7*, met the lowest points scorer, *French Kiss*, while the second-ranked boat, *Stars & Stripes* met the third best, *USA*. So far as the Conner's game-plan was concerned the draw could not have been better. What he and his crew needed more than anything was a good, hard series against his arch-rival, Tommy Blackaller. It was dangerous stuff. *USA* was fast and getting faster, and Blackaller alone among all the skippers in Fremantle had had a long history of sailing against Conner. Their rivalry, often bitter and always intense, stretched back over twenty years to the Star class in which they both won world championships. As for the Kiwis against *French Kiss*; well, the outcome of that match seemed all too predictable with *KZ-7* winning 4-0. *French Kiss* had only just made the semi-finals by coming alive in the windy third round robin, but she was no match for *KZ-7*'s all-round ability.

Before the start of the semi-finals Blackaller was, in Conner's own words, 'plenty fast'. But with such a radical keel shape and steering mechanism even Blackaller found it very hard to keep the boat tracking

properly. *USA* tended to go in fits and starts. Whenever the bow reared up in rough seas a substantial part of the forward fin/rudder was lifted clear of the water, lateral resistance went out of the window and *USA* lurched sideways, sometimes by as much as three or four feet at a time. On the eve of the semis Blackaller thought he had cured the problem after Lockheed aircraft engineers flew in from California and installed a new steering system. As *USA* was towed from the harbour for their first encounter, Blackaller, in an especially cocky mood, announced that he was ready to 'kick ass'.

That race, like the three that were to follow, went to *Stars & Stripes* in such convincing fashion that at the end of the semi-finals it was already obvious to members of the Conner camp that history would soon be made.

In the right to challenge for the America's Cup all the hopes and dreams of New Zealand's three and a half million population seemed to rest on the Kiwi champion. The New Zealand people were roused by the magnificent performance of their countrymen. Their boat enjoyed several names. She was *KZ-7*, she was 'Kiwi Magic', she was the 'Plastic Fantastic', but most of all she was 'New Zealand'. She had become the embodiment of the nation.

After all, she had done what no other foreign challenger had ever done. In a summer of racing she had lost only once . . . to *Stars & Stripes*.

KZ-7 put up a brave show. She won one race and showed that although Dickson and his crew may have been found wanting in terms of 12-metre experience, they lacked nothing when it came to sheer courage. *Stars & Stripes* was to face Australia's *Kookaburra III*, a boat that had shown herself superior in every sense to all the other would-be defenders.

The Australian Defenders

Australia II's victory over *Liberty* in September 1983 had brought with it a tremendous outpouring of Australia's nationalism and in its wake there came all manner of brave pledges to defend the hallowed silver pitcher. Only a handful of them were destined to get beyond the dream stage. Four defenders emerged and, of those, only two were ever really viable.

A Sydney syndicate headed by Syd Fischer commissioned designer Peter Cole, who came up with what was arguably the most interesting, innovative and potentially the fastest of all the Australian boats. She was named *Steak 'n Kidney* – rhyming slang for Sydney. *Steak* was plagued from the outset by all sorts of problems, not the least of which was a cash shortage which delayed construction and effectively ended her chances. Her crew lived from day to day. Helmsmen were changed three times and the boat, which showed tremendous promise after a keel change, was never able to stack up the points to survive under the elimination system organised by the Royal Perth Yacht Club.

The other also-ran was *South Australia*, the Ben Lexcen-designed boat which was developed directly from *Australia II*, for a syndicate headed by the vigneron and 12-metre veteran, Sir James Hardy. *South Australia*, had a cloud of sail which meant she was formidable in light air but not much good in anything else. Half-way through the trials she was abruptly withdrawn and sold to the Swedes.

Cup winner in 1983, Alan Bond commissioned Ben Lexcen to create *Australia III* (which was to become the 1986 World Champion) and later, *Australia IV*. *Australia III* lasted just a few weeks into the defence trials before the Bond camp concentrated all its efforts on *Australia IV*, sailed by Colin Beashel, Hugh Treharne and other key crewmen from 1983. But it was another Western Australian businessman, Kevin Parry, a self-made multimillionaire with interests in media, oil, gold mining and high-technology stocks, who came in with by far the most impressive outfit. His Taskforce '87 syndicate put together a three-pronged campaign, with boats all named Kookaburra after the Australian native bird. The Bond and Parry camps became great rivals.

From the outset it was reasoned that Bond had won the Cup and he was odds-on to defend it. Aiding the Kookas was seen to be akin to aiding the foreign challengers. That was a mistake. Early on there were dangerous incidents at sea in which boats very nearly collided. An embarrassed Royal Perth YC had to step in and separate the camps. With the benefit of hindsight, the failure of the Bond and Parry groups to co-operate signalled the end for the Australian defence. Carefully measured competition might have shown that neither camp really had anything special in terms of boat speed. Perhaps even at that late stage some-

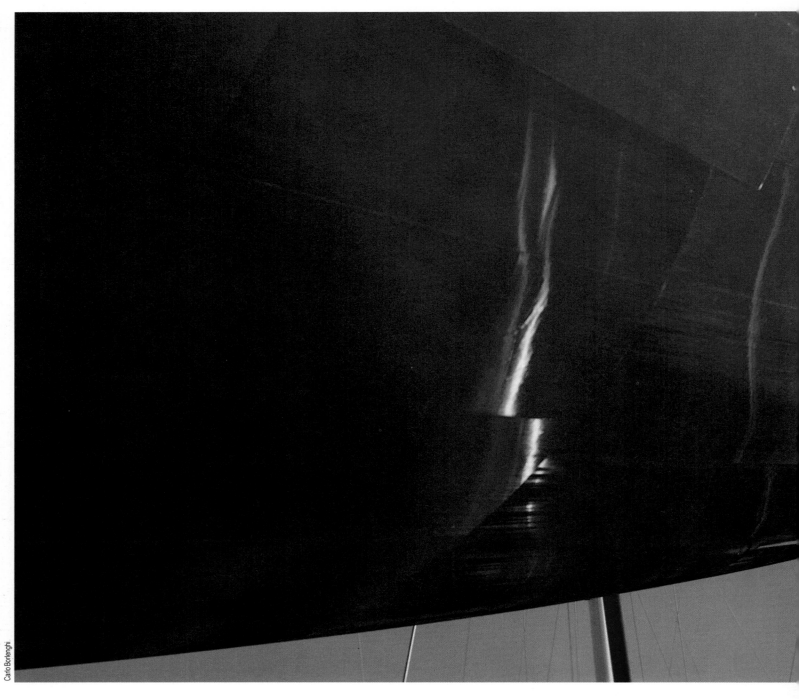

thing could have been done about it. They went their separate ways until it was too late.

In complete contrast, however, the Bond camp surprised many veteran Cup observers by its willingness to trial against the old foe, Dennis Conner, in *Stars & Stripes*. *Australia IV* and the boat that eventually became the Cup winner tossed out tradition and sailed against each other on many occasions. Throughout its long association with the America's Cup at no time had the New York Yacht Club ever allowed one of its defenders to come within a bull's roar of a foreign challenger. In breaking this tradition, the Australians perhaps unwittingly passed valuable information to the cup veterans aboard *Stars & Stripes*. The Australians got very little, if anything, in return.

The Kookaburras were supposed to be high-tech boats. Kevin Parry took a special pride in the enormous investment (some A$28 million) which in the end saw his defender, *Kookaburra III*, laden with the most sophisticated computer equipment ever carried

aboard a racing yacht. On the Cup course off Fremantle, however, boat speed was king and *Kookaburra III* just didn't have enough of it. *Stars & Stripes* did.

The Cup Match

The final of the America's Cup dawned hot and dry on 31 January. The day of the first race started out with a wild wind from the east. As strong as it was, it was to fade and confuse the sea breeze which later tried to blow from the south-west. The meteorological signs were not at all promising for *Stars & Stripes*.

There were those who expressed concern, but the Ockam computer expert, Richard McCurdy, predicted a favourable outcome for the gunsmoke-blue boat. The latest detailed computer analysis made possible when both boats were unveiled for measurement showed *Stars & Stripes* to be markedly superior to that of the Australian defender over a wide range – including light air, which was supposed to be *Kookaburra*'s forte.

Tens of thousands of fans had begun streaming down towards Fremantle waterfront since first light, clutching flags and bunting, shrill tin whistles and bassoon-like foghorns left over from New Year's Eve revelry. They perched in a colourful flock on every one of the jagged granite rocks which formed the long harbour breakwater. For once, Fremantle, whose decaying Victorian splendour had been spruced up for the Cup, looked like a crowded town. The crowd went crazy as the boats swept past the rocks, almost close enough to touch. Some people bounded around in boxing kangaroo suits while others dressed up like giant kookaburras complete with captain's caps. Mardi gras had come to Western Australia.

Both yachts elected to leave the mainsail choice until they arrived at the America's Cup buoy, eight nautical miles to the north-east. *Stars & Stripes* eventually chose a medium light air North mainsail which was then in the process of being purchased from the St Francis Yacht Club

syndicate. When the *Kookaburra III* crew saw the *Stars & Stripes*' choice they changed their main to match it.

The start was delayed twenty minutes because of shifting winds and when the ten-minute gun finally went off it was blowing around 15 knots. Conner had a non-engagement strategy firmly fixed in his mind's eye and he immediately took *Stars & Stripes* away from the line, running down into the crowd of enormous spectator boats in the so-called privilege fleet. *Kooka III* followed her with starting helmsman, 25-year-old Peter Gilmour, at the wheel. Conner was especially concerned about what he claimed was a very short starting line. He maintained it was half as long as the 400 yard line which had been regarded as standard in all the America's Cup races run by the NYYC.

After a perfectly judged start, *Stars & Stripes* found herself on a monumental lift and when the wind went round from 200 degrees to 170 that effectively meant an end to the race then and there. *Kookaburra III*

AMERICA'S CUP

Stars & Stripes' superiority was the result of many factors, among them the famous Scotchcal riblets made by 3-M, designed to modify boundary layer flow and reduce friction. Riblets proved their worth in the smooth water of the test tank, though full scale rough-water results were harder to assess.

Carlo Borlenghi

Crewman on *French Kiss* doing his bit for the crew-induced stability cause.

came back strongly in the second beat then the wind dropped to 8 knots. Half-way down the third leg the wind started to go back to the right, which meant that *Stars & Stripes* had the benefit of the reach using the genneker (the combination spinnaker-genoa they had copied from *Australia IV*).

The final margin was 1m 41s, in many ways the most significant of the Cup because it demolished at a stroke the notion that *Stars & Stripes* was purely a heavy air machine. In the hands of men like Dennis Conner and his all-star crew, half of whom had been in at least two Cups before, she looked invincible. Iain Murray offered no excuses but promised to go out and make it 1-1 the following day.

The second race was sailed in the conditions for which Fremantle had become famous: a wind of 23 knots with big, steep seas and white water everywhere. By the middle of this race the wind would be blowing at 31 knots true. Since 1958, when America's Cup racing moved into the 12-metre class, no Cup match had ever been held in

winds even remotely approaching this strength. Conner studiously avoided mixing it with Peter Gilmour in the pre-start manoeuvring, intent only in turning the start into a time-on-distance calculation which permitted him to begin at the buoy end on starboard tack. Immediately after the start, navigator Peter Isler was able to tell Dennis Conner that *Stars & Stripes* was almost a full boatlength ahead. Fifteen minutes after setting off on that long starboard leg, *Stars & Stripes* had stretched her lead to about 1.25 boat lengths. By the time she reached the port layline, Isler calculated the margin at 2.1 boat lengths. The final margin, 1m 10s, came as another decisive demonstration of *Stars & Stripes'* complete authority.

At two down in the best of seven series, Australia's grip on the Auld Mug was looking less than solid.

Perth newspapers reported that as many as 250,000 people were turning out to see the racing yachts on their voyages to and from the America's Cup battleground north-east of Fremantle.

AMERICA'S CUP

Tom Blackaller's *USA*, the radical twin-ruddered 12-metre designed by Heiner Meldner, Alberto Calderon and Gary Mull. To many she was the biggest design breakthrough seen in Fremantle.

Invariably, the boats were accompanied by an armada of spectator craft of all shapes and sizes. Cheeky windsurfers even braved the big winds and waves to skid in and out of the big motor yachts and cruise ships gathered around the America's Cup buoy anchored three miles off the coast. Many of the boats were flying red-white-and-blue balloons and ribbons for *Stars & Stripes* and green-and-gold streamers for *Kookaburra III*.

In the third race, the south-westerly sea breeze asserted itself at about 14 knots around midday and gave every indication of blowing much harder as the day wore on. Having crossed the starting line, *Kookaburra* was immediately in trouble with a jammed luff zipper in the main which Don McCracken went aloft to sort out. *Kookaburra III* was sailing very fast and when both boats came together for the first time with *Kooka III* having right of way on starboard, Conner chose to bear off and take their stern rather than tack underneath them. Now Iain Murray, who had resumed control of the helm, tried a slam dunk but Conner immediately tacked to starboard. Murray came about to cover after 45 seconds. For five minutes both boats straightlined on starboard and it was during this time that Conner's uncanny ability to pick wind shifts paid off. By the time he tacked back at *Kooka III*, *Stars & Stripes* found herself three-quarters of a boat length further upwind than the defender. That allowed *Stars & Stripes* to tack under *Kookaburra III* in a safe leeward position which eventually forced Murray to tack back to the right. *Stars & Stripes* and *Kookaburra III* stayed on diverging tacks for a few more minutes and then tacked back towards each other as before. As *Stars & Stripes* again tacked underneath *Kookaburra III*, Murray quickly tacked away and this time Conner followed about 15 seconds later.

Now, with both boats on port, Iain Murray was about to make one of his rare mistakes, a mistake which in retrospect probably cost him the race. He tacked back onto starboard too quickly and without sufficient time to build the speed necessary for an effective slam dunk. It was Peter Isler who suggested that Conner tried to break through with a duck around *Kooka*'s stern. While Conner hauled the helm hard over, tactician Tom Whidden cranked the trim tab hard over as well and *Stars & Stripes*

Fremantle's main shopping street was transformed by the Cup going Down Under. Premises were smartened up and some served as syndicate and public relations bases.

Below left. Enthusiastic supporters made their feelings known clearly. Even Dennis Conner received warm-hearted support.

managed a spectacularly sharp and sudden turn through 180 degrees. As *Kookaburra III* came about, *Stars & Stripes* came thundering through no more than a few feet underneath her to punch right through the defender's lee and out into clean air. Now *Stars & Stripes* had the upper hand, with the starboard tack advantage. That third win in succession put the America's Cup series almost beyond reach of the Australians. They had been beaten in light, heavy and now medium airs. There could be no excuses. On all three occasions they were outclassed by a superior boat handled by a superior crew.

The day of what was to be the final race dawned bright and cool. There was a very slight easterly, so light in fact that it barely ruffled the glassy surface of the harbour. Those who rose with the dawn that day were struck by the complete calm. Conditions like these almost certainly meant a gusty south-westerly sea breeze later.

By 9.0 a.m. the crowds had already swarmed over every vantage point on the harbour groins. People stood on roof tops and on car bonnets. Some even brought their own ladders to get a better view. The America's Cup had been in Australia for three years. With so much national euphoria generated by its historic journey Down Under there had been an expectation that the Aussies might be more than a little upset at its loss. In fact the crowds were there to cheer Dennis Conner and the crew of *Stars & Stripes* with just as much fervour as if they had been Australian national heroes. One particular placard held high in the crowd seemed to sum it up, 'Good on yer Dennis, you bastard!', it said.

At the ten-minute gun, *Stars & Stripes* entered from the port end while the *Kooka* came in from the committee boat side of the line. Once again, Conner headed down into the spectator boats with Peter Gilmour following him with all the grim determination of

a helmsman who knew that today he and his crew had to win. Either that or lose the America's Cup. After successfully wasting the best part of nine minutes, Conner got set to make his move towards the line.

In one of the most well judged starts, Conner put *Stars & Stripes* on the line at 8 knots precisely as the gun sounded. He turned round to see *Kookaburra III* in his wake, six seconds behind. The race was effectively over before it had even begun.

It was clear that much of the fight had gone out of the Australian defenders. They were, in Conner's own words, 'very docile, very well behaved'.

Media pundits who criticised *Kookaburra III* for not engaging *Stars & Stripes* in a tacking duel later in the race, failed to appreciate that it takes two to tango. Conner didn't have to sail anyone's race but his own. In match racing, boat speed is king!

When the committee boat cannon boomed its welcome, the final margin was 1m 59s. While a cacophony of sirens and horns and whistles and cheers rose up from the spectator fleet, on board *Stars & Stripes* there was a tremendous sense of elation. Dennis Conner took off his cap and saluted his crew: 'God damn, we did it,' he yelled, 'we did it guys!' Then, in perhaps the kindest words he had bestowed on them in three years of hard grind, he told them, 'You guys are the greatest. I'd sail with you anywhere'. It was all they needed to hear. For the men who had come so far with Conner, for all of them, who like him, had made the dreaded commitment, who had shared his obsession of rewinning the Cup, it was all suddenly worthwhile. There was a feeling among every man that they had all reached an historic milestone together – as individuals, certainly, but most importantly as a team. Of the thirteen international challengers and the four Australian defenders, only they had survived. They had won the America's Cup.

Bruce Stannard is one of Australia's foremost journalists and an acclaimed America's Cup author and broadcaster. He helped Dennis Conner write Comeback, *the story of* Stars & Stripes' *victory.*

AMERICA'S CUP

Kookaburra III (below) thanked Foster's Lager, one of her sponsors, by flying their spinnaker back into the harbour after the last race. The 1987 Cup will be remembered as the last where yachts' names and their sails were not allowed to be used for advertising whilst racing.

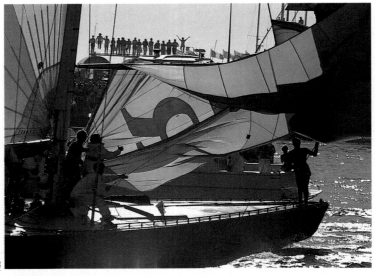

Kos

Kos

Above. No laurel garlands for Conner. Like all Cup sailors, he was given the ritual dunking by his crew.

Kaoru Soehata

AMERICA'S CUP

Left. **Just some of the back room boys supporting the *Stars & Stripes* and her crew — the high-speed chase boat and *Betsy*, her impressive tender.**

Below. **Enterprising Freo fishermen charged spectators A$50 for an *al fresco* grandstand view of *Stars & Stripes'* victorious homecoming to her dock.**

Daniel Forster

America's most potent symbols: 'Old Glory',
the Auld Mug, Dennis Conner and President
Reagan.

AMERICA'S CUP

THE WINCH THAT WON THE AMERICA'S CUP.

Out there in Fremantle, they've just proved - for the third America's Cup in succession — that there's only one winch brand seriously in the running at the highest levels of performance sailing.

Lewmar.

The latest America's Cup results leave no room for doubt. The two finalists were equipped with Lewmar winches — as were seven of the eight semi-finalists.

To gain victory, *Stars & Stripes* competed in hundreds of qualifying races and covered around 8000 nautical miles — not including the thousands during training.

Throughout, Dennis Conner and the other top skippers worked closely with Lewmar and Navtec engineers, testing, refining and pushing the equipment to its limits in a relentless pursuit of perfection.

The 12-metre contests provide the ultimate testbed for our technology, ensuring that the Lewmar and Navtec equipment you put on *your* boat is the most efficient and most reliable deck hardware you can buy. And what's more, Wavegrip™ self tailing and other major Lewmar innovations have sprung directly from our involvement in Grand Prix racing.

If you'd like more information on System Lewmar, see your nearest dealer. Or call us on Havant (0705) 471841-3.

System
LEWMAR

ARE YOU SURE YO

This idyllic scene is brought to you courtesy of the Volvo 740 Turbo Estate.

A sporting alternative to the sports car.

Its 2.3 litre, turbo-charged engine has a top speed of 125mph and a 0-60 time of 7.7 seconds.

Its road manners are equally impressive.

"Everyone at 'Motor' who drove the Volvo estate was impressed [with]…the ease with which the driver can deplo the shattering acceleration without any accompanying drama

Unlike most sports cars, there is no accompanying

ANT A SPORTS CAR?

comfort, either.

Power-assisted steering, electric windows, central locking,
ed glass and a leather/plush interior are all standard.

And when you fold down the back seat, you open up 75
bic feet of luggage space.

In the light of all this, it's difficult to see what a 2-seater
sports car has to offer by way of competition.

Except less leg room, a smaller boot, more noise, higher
insurance premiums . . .

THE VOLVO 740 TURBO ESTATE.

US Offshore

by ERIC SHARP

The Southern Ocean Racing Conference, along with the Champagne Mumm Admiral's Cup and Sardinia Cups, is one of the three most prestigious blue-water events in the world. And the 1987 version convinced the powers that be in the SORC that they had better make some major changes if they expect this Florida–Bahamas event to maintain its prestige, and perhaps even survive as a major offshore regatta.

The survival of the IOR as the top offshore class among American yachtsmen got another jolt last spring, a couple of months after the SORC, when only a dozen boats showed up at Newport, Rhode Island, for the Brenton Reef series to select the US Admiral's Cup team. Only six of the entrants were declared competitors for the three-boat team. Two years ago some 40 boats took part in the Brenton Reef event, 30 of them vying for berths on the three-yacht team. But as one experienced yachtsman commented, 'It might be an Admiral's Cup year, but you'd have to be crazy to build a new IOR boat without knowing if you'd even have an IOR fleet to compete in a couple of years from now. I think an awful lot of guys this year just decided to wait and see.'

The SORC is a six-race series that begins in St Petersburg, Florida, moves round the southern tip of the Florida peninsula to Fort Lauderdale and Miami, and ends in Nassau, the capital of the Bahamas. Sponsored by six yacht clubs, it is held over a four-week period with a seven- to ten-day break in the middle to allow crews and owners to make a quick trip home to take care of business. Traditionally in

this 60-year-old series, four of the races have been overnight events (ranging from 140 to 400 miles), and two have been 26- to 40-mile day races.

A few weeks before the 1987 series began at St Petersburg last February, SORC officials were confidently expecting 70 boats, perhaps as many as 80, mostly because of the implementation of the new International Measurement System class as an additional alternative to the traditional (and increasingly expensive) International Offshore Rule class. But when the sign-up deadline had passed just 60 yachts were enrolled, and even that number didn't give a true picture of the fleet. For while the lists said there were 37 IOR yachts and 24 IMS (the latter a disappointment for SORC officers, who had expected IMS to be the biggest fleet), several boats were competing only on the Florida west coast races, or didn't join the fleet until it reached Miami after the second race.

So the true number of starters in any given race was about 55, but Circuit officials were encouraged that it was an improvement over the 1985 fleet of only 47 yachts. Also, there were other heartening trends that bode well for a future SORC with yachts running in IMS, IOR-amateur and IOR-professional classes.

First, the maxi yacht fleet was the biggest ever. Ten boats competed in IOR Class I, six of them true maxis ranging from 79 to 81 ft (24·0–24·6 m) LOA. The other four were 68–70 ft mini-maxis, including the Italian-owned *Il Moro de Venezia*, a Frers 72 skippered by America's Cup victor Dennis Conner and including ten of his *Stars & Stripes* troops in its

twenty-man crew.

Second, there was close competition among the 11 boats in IOR Class 2, a gaggle of 50-footers that battled like dinghies. Eight of them rated between 40·0 and 40·6 ft, and the lowest rating among the other three was 38·76 ft.

But after those two classes, things started to get a bit thin. There were seven yachts entered in IOR Class 3, a group of 43-45 footers (13·1-13·7 m) that eventually produced the first-in-fleet boat, *Sprint*, a Joubert/Nivelt 42 owned by John Stevens. This class also boasted three of the top four in fleet. There was nothing unusual in that, though. Every year, the big boats win a couple of races and the little boats win a couple, but the 1st-in-fleet title nearly always goes to a boat in the 40 to 43 ft (12·2–13·1 m) LOA size range.

The shocker, though, was in IOR Class 4, the one tonners that in previous years had made up a third of the fleet. The 1987 SORC saw only five boats rating between 30·13 and 31·15 ft, and one of those entered the class only because it was the lesser of two evils (his rating in IOR was bad, but in IMS, where he had originally intended to sail, it was hopeless). That left only four little boats to comprise IOR Class 5: two 34 ft Dehler db2s, an X ¾ Tonner and a Farr 36. Despite winning 1st-in-fleet honours in two of the six races, the best that John Hughes's db2, *Kathryn*, could do on the final overall list was 9th.

The IMS fleet was broken into two divisions. IMS Class 1 included 10 yachts ranging from 42 to 61 ft (12·8–18·6 m), far too great a spread for any fair handicapping. IMS Class 2 looked a bit better on paper, with 13 boats

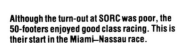

Although the turn-out at SORC was poor, the 50-footers enjoyed good class racing. This is their start in the Miami–Nassau race.

Main picture: **The SORC commences at elegant St Petersburg on the west coast of Florida before heading on to Miami and then Nassau.**

between 36 and 42 ft (10·9–12·8 m). But they ranged from Ted Hood's 12-year-old 36-footer, *Robin*, to *Pirate Twin*, a stripped-out, 37 ft Carl Schumacher boat built for this event.

Not surprisingly, when the smoke cleared at the end of six races the top two boats in IMS were IOR yachts less than three years old, and the third was a new J-35 – hardly a family cruiser. The best the older boats could manage was the 6th place scored by the IOR veteran, *Wassail III*. Despite one 1st-in-fleet (a freak event in which the wind filled in from behind while the front of the fleet was virtually becalmed), *Robin* could do no better than 9th overall; this with a skipper who is still one of the finest sailors in the world.

When the Circuit began this year, the IOR competition immediately shook down to a contest between Stevens's new *Sprint* and a year-old Farr 43, *Advantage*, skippered by John McBride. They finished 1st and 2nd in fleet in the opening 138-mile round trip between St Petersburg and Boca Grande on Florida's west coast. The second event, the 400-mile St Petersburg–Fort Lauderdale race, saw two maxis and a mini-maxi romp home 1st, 2nd and 3rd when the big boats were able to get around the corner at the 200-mile mark ahead of a breeze that died and left the smaller boats wallowing in their wakes.

The third race, the 40-mile, one-day Lipton Cup triangle between Fort Lauderdale and Miami, saw one of the strangest finishes in SORC history. Boats which had picked the right side of a wind shift and got around the first mark early, soon did a horizon job on the rest of the fleet. But about 10 miles from the finish the leaders ran out of wind. Mark Soverel, skippering the new 50 ft (15·2 m) *Locura* he designed for this event, was among those who got around early and was pleased to be doing well at last after two bad races. But when he looked back he saw a horizon abloom with spinnakers as the breeze filled-in from behind and blew the laggards right up to the front.

It was even worse for the race committee, with maxis and 33-raters finishing together in packs of eight to twelve. John Thompson, whose 50 ft (15·2 m) *Infinity* eventually finished

3rd overall in the IOR fleet, said he crossed the line with two maxis between him and the committee boat, 'and I don't know if the race committee even saw me. I don't know how they could have.'

The committee was as aware of the problem as the sailors, and an official finish list was delayed several hours while committee members tracked down the navigators of different boats, got the finish times from the navigators' watches and used crew recollections of who finished next to whom to work it all out.

The fortuitous breeze that hit the

US OFFSHORE

tail-enders first resulted in 34-footers taking the top three places in fleet. For the three final races, events of 140, 100 and 26 miles, the top fleet positions were split by maxis and minis, but the 33-raters managed to hang in there high enough to continue amassing good fleet points. And in the final race, while *Advantage* managed to beat *Sprint*, it was only by 20 seconds, and *Advantage* managed to put only two boats between her and her rival when she needed four.

So, once again, the SORC was won by a 33-rater, which experience has shown is the best size for the conditions that prevail. Little was ventured, less was learned. But when the fleet comes to the line for the start of the 1988 series in March, with separate classes for professionally sponsored yachts and a couple of changes in the race format, it may help American ocean racing sailors decide whether International Offshore Rule competition is worth supporting, or if something else is needed to help even wealthy owners keep up with the soaring costs of fielding an offshore sailing yacht.

Last spring, after watching entries decline steadily to fleets of 50 to 55 yachts from the 70- to 80-boat fleets of a decade ago, the race committe had adopted a number of changes.

The first big change, moving the start of the opening event in the six-race series from late January to late February, came about in 1987 and was dictated not by the SORC committee but by the America's Cup in Australia. Large numbers of skippers and crewmen, the quasi-professionals who form the backbone of the top SORC crews, were working for one of the six American syndicates campaigning for the Cup off Fremantle. And many yacht owners who would normally compete in the SORC had announced their intention to spend a good part of February Down Under taking in the sights.

While some people complained about changing the start for the benefit of a small number of professionals, it worked out well in the long run. Florida has pleasant winters but February is its coldest month, when the north-west cold fronts come racing out of the Arctic, and can still have a chill in them when they reach the Sunshine State. A very cold winter day in southern Florida is when the temperature drops to 50°F (10°C), but even that can have a real bite in it when helped along by a 30-knot breeze. And

in central Florida, where the first couple of SORC races start in St Petersburg, crews in overnight races can come on deck at 2.0 a.m. to find air temperatures hovering just above freezing point (32°F/0°C). The delayed start meant that most of the racing was in March and temperatures had risen sufficiently for even south Floridians to be in shirt-sleeves. An interesting phenomenon noticed on sunny days in the February races was when sailors from places such as Michigan and New England would be stripped down to bathing suits and diving off the boats between races into 70°F (20°C) water, watched with a mixture of horror and fascination by south Floridians who were still bundled up in foul weather gear and wouldn't dream of sticking a toe in the water until the water temperature reached 80°F (25°C). Virtually everyone polled agreed that this change made for more pleasant racing and should be continued.

The biggest change instituted for 1987 was the advent of the International Measurement System class: boats sailing under a measurement rule that, it was hoped, would give fast, family-sailed cruisers and over-the-hill IOR boats a chance to compete fairly in a class apart from the gold-platers. This was another of those best-laid plans that, in the opinion of some observers, went awry, although it will be given another year or so to prove that itself.

The IMS is a measurement rule, with all the vices and virtues which that implies. But the theory is that the IMS handicaps boat speed, rather than specifying a set of parameters and letting each designer do his best to create boat speed from them, as is the case with the IOR (or, in truth, find the loophole that gives the best combination of boat speed and rating).

Don Flitman, of Miami's Coral Reef Yacht Club and chairman of the SORC for 1988, thinks that, given a fair chance, the IMS will become the major blue-water sailing class.

'The IOR is getting so expensive only a handful of people can afford it. That's why so many of the boats in Europe are sponsored', Flitman declared. 'The IMS will give the true amateur a place to compete with a reasonable chance of winning . . . and he won't have to buy a new boat every two years.'

That would be nice – if the IMS doesn't fall prey to the same complaints and inequities that, seemingly, have

François Richard

hurt the International Offshore Rule.

Ted Hood established his reputation as a sailmaker, but he doesn't like provisions in the IMS that would allow such developments as fully battened mainsails or wing keels. Hood says that encouraging high-tech development will turn IMS into just another version of the IOR, where the winner will be the one who can afford to take advantage of loopholes.

As for the IMS's claim to handicap existing boats fairly, some say it had loopholes big enough to drive a maxi yacht through. Jack Goldberg bought *Jack Knife*, a J-41, when it looked like the boat would have a good IOR rating. But then the IOR changed a year later, penalising J-41s so seriously

that there was no way they could finish above the middle of any big fleet. So Goldberg decided to switch to IMS for 1987. He was disgusted when he got the IMS rating and found that it was even worse than the IOR. For example, he had to give 30 seconds a mile to the J-35s, boats that were demonstrably faster in most conditions on almost every point of sail.

'It didn't make a whole lot of sense, if they were trying to encourage people to join the new class', Goldberg said. 'I wanted to sail, so I decided to go back to IOR. At least there were fewer boats in my class.'

Both Flitman and his friend and former SORC chairman, W. Scott Piper III of Miami, have competed on

'We decided that if we couldn't get anyone else to define a professional, we'd let the professionals define themselves', Piper said. Flitman added, 'The idea was to protect the IMS from guys who'd build a new boat to the IMS rule every year. If you write the rule so that there's no advantage in that, then those guys will go over to the IOR where they belong.'

One way to accomplish that will be the institution of some local 'associated regulations' in 1988. One feature differentiating an IMS yacht from an IOR yacht is that the former supposedly has at least a minimal cruising interior, whereas the IOR boat can be a stripped-out shell. But it was obvious that using high-tech, ultra-light and highly expensive materials it would be possible to install a fairly extensive interior to a 40-footer without adding more than a couple of hundred pounds.

In 1987, the SORC didn't have associated regulations, so boats like *Lunatic* and *Pied Piper*, which were highly successful IOR boats only a couple of years ago, were able to compete in IMS with hastily installed interiors that made a mockery of the rule. Things will be different in 1988, though, where the IMS entrant will be required to have real cruising interiors, built of materials that most competitors can afford.

Something has to be done. Bill Ziegler, owner of the 49 ft Nelson/Marek, *Gem*, said one reason he went to the 50-footer class was that 'I figure we'll be able to sail these boats for a few years. We all got together and came up with a size that we could afford and still have a lot of fun with. Hell, we're all out there chasing each other around like one-designs.'

But Ziegler also noted that it costs about $500,000 to get into the 50-footer class, and that's with a used boat. A new boat costs from $750,000. Even for the smallest boats in the IOR division, a purchaser will need more than $100,000, and a skipper who expects to have a realistic chance to win must buy a new boat every other year.

That's where the SORC hopes the IMS will come in, and this experiment is being watched carefully by national yacht-racing bodies around the world.

their own IOR yachts for many years in the SORC and other events. Like Flitman, Piper thinks changes must be made to keep the SORC alive. And, again like Flitman, he sees the IMS as an intelligent alternative. But he's not so sure about another innovation that will be established in the 1987 circuit: professionally sponsored yachts.

'I'm afraid it will be like giving liquor to a drunk. At first it will seem great, but eventually it will be self-destructive', Piper prophesied. 'Sponsored yachts might sound good, but I just don't think there's enough sponsorship money available for 30 or 40 boats. In the end, I think you'll see a handful of very successful skippers grabbing most of the sponsorship money, and the result will be the same as it is today.'

Piper said that while he competes as an amateur, he is happy to pit himself against the likes of Dennis Conner and John Kolius for fleet honours.

'There's no way you're going to beat those guys consistently', admitted Piper. 'They're great sailors, and all they do is sail. But it is fun to go out there and beat the pros once in a while. I like sailing against the big boys. That's the way you find out how good you are, and if you *do* manage to beat them every now and then you can honestly feel good about it.'

Flitman and Piper found a neat way to get around the most perplexing problem of all – deciding who is a professional. Under Olympic standards, for example, top American skippers like Dennis Conner, Paul Cayard and Buddy Melges, all of whom spend most of their time sailing boats, building boats or building sails, are not considered professionals. They aren't paid specifically for helming boats, so technically they are amateurs.

Knowing they had little hope of getting an enforceable definition of a professional from the International or United States Yacht Racing Unions, the SORC committee simply said that anyone who entered a yacht in a specific division was a professional. Then they tailored the divisions so that the hot IOR yachts could only be entered in the pro classes.

U S OFFSHORE

89

BRENTON REEF SERIES

by GAIL SCOTT SLEEMAN

In 1985, when Newport's Brenton Reef Regatta was inaugurated as the selection series for the US Admiral's Cup team, 42 yachts competed in a series so hotly contested that one race day was consumed with nothing but starts and general recalls.

In 1987, eleven yachts raced the series. Of those, only six expressed interest in qualifying for the team. Of those, only three were considered contenders; not one was a one tonner.

Despite the United States Yacht Racing Union's intention of selecting a team of two yachts with ratings between 30.0 and 31.0 ft and a third rating between 33.0 and 36.0 ft, the selected yachts ranged from 34.22 to 35.18 ft. They were: Randy Short's Reichel/Pugh 45 *Sidewinder*, with John Bertrand as helmsman and Olympic gold medallist Robbie Haines, naval architect Jim Pugh and Ockam Instrument's Jim Marshall co-ordinating strategy; Nelson/Marek 45 *Insatiable*, co-owned by Fred Krehbiel and Deane Tank, whose braintrust included naval architect Bruce Nelson and racing wizard Gary Weisman; and finally Judel/Vrolijk 43 *Blue Yankee*, sailed by owner Robert C. Towse with a crew including former collegiate dinghy racing stars Steve Benjamin, Jonathan McKee and Tucker Edmundson.

The rising cost of racing in the Admiral's Cup was the most obvious factor in the disappointing turn-out at the 1987 Brenton Reef series. Efforts to find a commercial sponsor acceptable to USYRU failed. When potential team competitors were informed that the bill per team yacht owner would be at least $75,000, they stayed at home in droves.

Scuttlebutt grumbled about team organisation and the Brenton Reef race format, too. Among other things, after a disappointing 9th place for the US in the 1985 Admiral's Cup, critics had zeroed in on the lack of team effort. Yet, some complained, between the 1987 Brenton Reef Regatta (29 May – 7 June) and shipping to England, there was too little time for the US side to practise as a team. For competitors who had no intention of making the team, Brenton Reef's tough series of back-to-back day and distance races had minimal appeal.

As a result, the selection process will

change. The Brenton Reef series is off the list. The Ida Lewis Yacht Club will host the series independently, opening it to IOR and IMS rated yachts. US offshore team selection will once again be subjective, based on performance in a number of major events, according to E. Ben Mitchell, chairman of the USYRU Offshore Team Committee. Selection will also be made in advance of international team racing events and in good time to canvas sponsors.

Even before the 1987 Brenton Reef had properly got under way, the result seemed in no doubt. From the rolling upper deck of the Ida Lewis YC race committee's chartered yacht, the 67 ft (20 m) *Royal Reward*, US Admiral's Cup team managers Ken Morrison and Don Genitempo looked down on only five contenders in the fleet. And, illustrating the dwindling interest in the so-called 'small boats' in the US, none of the one tonners racing in the Brenton Reef series was really in the running.

Carl Vaughan's Bénéteau 40, *Tuff Enuff Texas Style*, initially entered as a team candidate, was withdrawn when John Kolius arrived in Newport with the news that he would not skipper the yacht in England. Scuttlebutt said Kolius considered the boat too slow for European competition, although Kolius was not so undiplomatic as to say so.

Peggy Comfort's Joubert/Nivelt 40, *Amazing Potato* (ex-*Innisfree*), was not (at that point at least) up to Admiral's Cup speed, and after the second race when a crew member suffered a crack from the spinnaker pole, was even less so.

David E. Marlow's new Graham & Schlagater one tonner, *Gunsmoke*, was delayed in shipping from builder Ian Franklin of Christchurch, New Zealand. Hoping that *Gunsmoke* could be shipped to England in time for team practice there, Marlow chartered the G&S 40 *Slip Sliding Away* for the Brenton Reef series. The plan was to qualify with *Slip Sliding* and then substitute *Gunsmoke*, despite a selection rule forbidding substitutions. In the end, Marlow didn't try to contest the rule. With 1985 Rolex Yachtsman of the Year and two-time J-24 World Champion Ken Read driving, *Slip Sliding* won the one ton slot in the team

with an 8th in the series, but *Gunsmoke* was still not ready. Rather than race the Admiral's Cup with an outdated design or chance chartering a yacht in England, Marlow withdrew his bid.

Although they raced the series, neither Bruce MacLeod, skipper/owner of Judel/Vrolijk 40 *Skye Hie* (ex-*Outsider*, 1985), nor Bill Corcoran, skipper/owner of Nelson/Marek 39 *Regardless*, could be persuaded to run for the team.

Bill Tripp III raced Steven Lever's Tripp 40 *Leverage* (ex-*Thumper*) in the Brenton Reef regatta, but Lever had other plans for the rest of the season, whilst Rod Johnstone raced revamped J-41 *Mad Max* as a warm-up for the Storm Trysail Club's Block Island Week.

Long-time Newport-area yacht racers Brendan and Pat Kelley and Alfred van Liew entered their less than state-of-the-art yachts (Joubert/Nivelt 40 *Full Tilt Boogie* and Peterson 42 *Fiddler*, respectively) because they enjoy racing and Ida Lewis can be counted on to run a good show. *Fiddler* raced only the first weekend.

That left the three big boats: *Insatiable*, *Sidewinder* and *Blue Yankee*.

'Well,' remarked one of the big-boat crew during the series, 'if it's a choice between three good big boats and two of us and one little boat that doesn't amount to a hill of beans, the outcome is obvious. There isn't a one tonner here that would do anything in Europe.'

From the first race, the fleet immediately settled into a pattern in the predominantly light to moderate south-easterlies of spring. *Insatiable* and *Sidewinder* led the day races, followed by *Blue Yankee* and then the smaller boats, scrapping for a place, usually behind *Tuff Enuff*. One tonners *Full Tilt Boogie* and *Skye Hie* each took a distance race.

Insatiable, designed by Bruce Nelson for the Admiral's Cup and built by Eric Goetz in neighbouring Bristol, Rhode Island, breezed to 1st place in day races one and two. Both races were sailed around set marks on Rhode Island Sound in light, hazy south-easterlies. Immediately after the second race, in the fading light of late afternoon, the race committee sent the fleet towards Long Island's Montauk Point for a

94-mile overnight race. The big boats finished the distance first as expected but not soon enough to save their time on the small boats. *Tuff Enuff* and *Full Tilt* traded places in the van of the one tonners throughout the race until, on the run home, *Full Tilt*, racing with skilful local sailors Bob Morton and David 'Moose' McClintock, ducked out of the tidal current. *Tuff Enuff* crossed the finish line seconds ahead of *Full Tilt* but *Full Tilt* had the corrected time win.

For race four, and theoretically reproducing Solent conditions, the race committee took the fleet north of the Newport Bridge where channel currents and land masses complicate racing. In this race, and in the equally light, shifty east-south-easterly winds of the following day race on the Sound, *Sidewinder* won her duel with *Insatiable*. It was *Insatiable*'s turn in the next day race, around Conanicut Island, but in the 110-mile race that started immediately after the fleet rounded the island, *Skye Hie* persevered to win. The distance race was interminable. The wind died. *Full Tilt* bagged it after drifting for hours the following morning. The rest hung on to finish. *Blue Yankee* crossed the line last with a corrected time of 29h 48m 04.57s.

When, at last, a gusty north-westerly powered the fleet around an Olympic course at the end of the regatta, the race order was once again *Insatiable*, *Sidewinder*, *Blue Yankee* and *Tuff Enuff*.

'It was a good, hard-sailed regatta', said Eric Schlagater at the end of the series. Schlagater raced with the *Slip Sliding* crew in their last-ditch effort to qualify Marlow's *Gunsmoke*. The crew was given the option, but, said Schlagater, 'we looked at the calendar and the schedule the builder had given us. There was no room for error. In my experience, under the circumstances there probably would be error. We couldn't tell these guys to spend thousands, depending on us to show up.'

Gail Sleeman is an American freelance journalist and photographer based in Massachusetts. Among the journals to which she contributes is Sail.

Bill Corcoran's one tonner *Regardless* competed in the Brenton Reef series but was unavailable for Admiral's Cup selection.

High Risk chases *Shockwave* past Alcatraz, one of San Francisco's most famous landmarks.

Guy Gurney

Big Boat Series

by CHRIS CASWELL

It's no secret that IOR racing is in decline in the United States, and that's certainly true in California, once a hotbed of offshore racing activity. Escalating costs, rapid design developments that make older boats obsolete, and the single-purpose use of modern ocean racers has forced many racing skippers into other forms of handicap racing that are less costly and more family orientated.

That's certainly the case at the St Francis Yacht Club's annual St Francis Perpetual Trophy Series, known throughout the sailing world as the Big Boat Series. Just a few years ago, this week-long regatta in mid-September drew 70 or more of the elite racing yachts from along the West Coast but, for the most recent event, a total of only 46 yachts competed. Of those, five were maxi-rater ULDB (Ultra Light Displacement Boat) 'sleds' designed purely for first-to-finish downwind racing and eight were Santa Cruz 50 ultra-lights racing as a class,

leaving only 33 true IOR yachts. But the depth in those three remaining classes was remarkable and nearly every yacht was a potential class winner, given a little luck and no mistakes.

The Big Boat Series is the centrepiece of racing activity on the breezy and tide-swept San Francisco Bay. Scheduled for mid-September when the afternoon breezes whistle under the Golden Gate Bridge, the regatta takes more than just boat speed and a good rating. Winners need a combination of weather savvy, local knowledge to play the swirling currents and enough sheer guts to set the big chute when all the other boats are spinning wildly out of control.

Some say that another reason for the declining popularity of IOR racing is that it requires a crew of so-called 'rock stars' to sail these sensitive yachts properly; with hundreds of thousands of dollars sunk into Kevlar sails, carbon-fibre hulls and slender masts,

most owners turn the helm over to a semi-professional sailor. In the entire fleet, there were only twelve owners at the helm, but the other skippers read like a 'Who's Who' of America's Cup racing.

Tom Blackaller was skippering a brand new Santa Cruz 70, *Mongoose*, and *America II* tactician John Bertrand was at the wheel of *Sidewinder*, freshly returned from the Champagne Mumm Admiral's Cup. Bertrand's former 12-metre skipper, John Kolius, was at the helm of the one tonner *Coyote*, while Blackaller's America's Cup tactician, Paul Cayard, was pitting *Jubilation* against *Locura*, skippered by Dennis Conner's navigator, Peter Isler, in the 40-rater class. There were sailmakers galore, including former International 470 champion Dave Ullman aboard *Quintessence* and Olympic Soling gold medallist Robbie Haines on *Lobo*.

Several ideas were introduced at this Big Boat Series, including the so-called 'Southern California' batten rule,

which allows longer battens than those permitted under the IOR regulations, to give the fragile Kevlar sails a longer life expectancy, particularly in the heavy San Francisco winds. The club also permitted the United States Yacht Racing Union's old-age allowance as an incentive to encourage some of the older (and therefore less competitive) ocean racing yachts to enter the regatta. For some, like the 1983 Frers 41 *Bondi Tram*, the difference was a real benefit. Because there were several entries from the fresh water Great Lakes area, the club officials also carefully checked the salinity factor on the rating certificates and recalculated those that were measured in fresh water. Finally, the club gave serious consideration to changing from their usual crew number limit (IOR crew plus two) to a crew weight limit, but decided at the last minute that it would be hard to enforce.

The first race of the series proved a disappointment to those who wanted to initiate newcomers into the wild San Francisco Bay, as light and shifty winds turned the usual gear-buster into a tactical race, but the next four races were sailed in the typical afternoon westerlies that satisfied photographers with blown spinnakers, white-knuckled crews rounding-up wildly out of control, and even a broken mast.

The largest boats sailed for the St Francis Perpetual Trophy, and these were all the new breed of ultra-light sleds. Tom Blackaller took a new ('It'll

be finished next week') flush-decked Santa Cruz 70, *Mongoose*, to five winner's guns in the fleet that generally staggered to windward and then rocketed downwind. *Mongoose*, with a deeper keel, had so much speed that she could choose to start at the wrong end of the line and still power away from the fleet. Except for the deck, Bill Wilson's *Citius* was her sister ship and sported a new Alan Andrews-designed elliptical rudder and bulb keel for improved closed-course performance, but still wound up 2nd in spite of the changes.

A fleet of Santa Cruz 50s, another ultra-light from the drawing board of Bill Lee, had asked the club for a class, and they had the City of San Francisco Perpetual Trophy all to themselves. Although they were theoretically identical, the owners agreed to minor handicap allowances to balance some of the quicker boats, but Kirke Erskine's *Earl of Mar* proved to be fastest both boat-for-boat and in the handicap standings as well.

The Atlantic Perpetual Trophy class attracted three of the new breed of 40-raters, yachts of about 50 ft LOA that had been competing on the Great Lakes in a level-rating regatta and were trucked 2000 miles for this event. Though the trio were almost the latest in IOR design thinking, it was Jack Jacobs's *Jubilation*, a Frers 53, that swept the class with four 1sts. With a longer waterline, *Jubilation* was able to break free of the fleet to sail in clear air,

Designer Bruce Nelson takes care to keep
Insatiable **in the groove in the boisterous San Francisco Bay conditions.**

94

Contractor, from Australia, joins the Big Boat
queue to round the leeward mark.

saving nearly enough time on a single
windward leg for the entire race, while
the others struggled along in dirty air.
The Soverel-designed *Locura* and
Wicktor Forss's Bénéteau 51, *Carat IV*,
wound up in mid-fleet and, to add
injury to insult, Jerry Schostak's Frers
50, *Fujimo* (which had won the Great
Lakes event) was dismasted in the third
race. It was a satisfying victory for
Jubilation on her third attempt. She
arrived late for the Big Boat Series two
years ago after being delayed by a police
officer in the American desert who
refused to allow the truck/trailer rig to
move over the weekend, and in 1986
the crew misread the sailing instructions and threw away a certain win.

In the Keefe-Kilborn Perpetual Trophy class, there were several 'if onlys'.
Sidewinder, Randy Short's Reichel/
Pugh-designed Admiral's Cupper,
would have been the class winner if her
crew hadn't fouled out at the start in
the second race. *Quintessence*, a
nearly-new Reichel/Pugh 42 that has
won every event since her spring
launching, had a three-point lead
going into the last race, but she fell in
the overall standings as a result of gear
failures (which included a turning
block that tore out, taking the deck
with it!) *Insatiable*, another Admiral's
Cupper, with designer Bruce Nelson at
the helm, took home the silverware in
spite of having the highest points of
any class winner. *Quintessence*, the
smallest boat in her class, attracted the
most attention at the regatta and

showed remarkable power in all wind
and sea conditions.

The Rheem Perpetual Trophy drew
the largest fleet and, with most of the
14-boat fleet rating within a few
decimal points of each other, was
essentially a one ton class. *Pendragon
III*, a Laurie Davidson one tonner with
ex-*Eagle* crew Kimo Worthington
steering, won the class by never
dropping below 3rd, proving that a
redesigned keel and rudder could make
a strong but ageing contender even
faster. At one start, *Pendragon* was
forced to decide between hitting
another boat and the starting buoy.
Choosing to tag the mark and then
round it again while the fleet sailed
away, *Pendragon* steadily ground down
the entire class to win the race!

Next year's Big Boat Series will be
the 25th anniversary of the event, and
everything indicates that it is going to
be an outstanding regatta. The St
Francis YC will be hosting the One
Ton Cup a few days before the series, so
there will be an international fleet of
level raters. Earlier in the summer, the
Kenwood Cup in Hawaii will be
hosting everyone from the winning
Admiral's Cup team to crews from
Down Under and the Orient, so most
of this fleet will also sail or ship by
barge to San Francisco to join the
festival. The maxis are due to return to
San Francisco for the final part of their
1988 championship, to make it truly a
Big Boat Series once again.

US OFFSHORE

San Francisco Bay provides a great natural amphitheatre for yacht racing.

391   43   46   53   59   61   651

THE WORLD'S PREMIER PRODUCTION YACHT

NAUTOR'S
Swan European Regatta

by DONALD J. McINTYRE

You've got your rock stars, your semi-pros, your factory teams. You've got hot-shots, Admiral's Cup alternates and light heavyweights. You've got hired guns.

And you've got your owners, like Richard Loftus aboard his Swan 65, *Desperado*, who plan accordingly.

'Look, we must do this right', he says earnestly as he plots final-race strategy with helmsman and navigator. His voice is loud above the reggae pouring from *Desperado*'s cockpit speakers. 'We don't want to tack too much. It interrupts the music.'

You've got perspective. Regardless of the talent shipped into Guernsey for the 1987 Swan European Regatta, a man's got to do what a man's got to do: party hard.

Since their inception at the 1980 World Cup in Sardinia, Swan regattas have become almost mandatory stops for anyone remotely connected to a Nautor yacht. Although the company was late to the 20-year game of manufacturers' regattas, they managed deftly to rewrite the rules when they stepped in. Big-time sponsorship and four choice venues from the Costa Smeralda to Southern California created an image that grants the events must-do status and guarantees participation regardless of racing skills. Many crews today remain strictly family affairs that rarely race beyond these gatherings, but everyone, from mom and pop to the sailmakers and Grand Prix skippers on loan to high-rolling owners, knows what the evenings can bring. A Swan regatta remains at heart a finely tuned marketing tool, feeding the next-boat syndrome, but the gloss is so high that no-one seems to notice or care.

The Swan European Regatta began in 1983 and is held biannually together with the Rolex Swan California

Regatta in Newport Beach (see separate report). Even-numbered years see the Rolex Swan World Cup in Porto Cervo, and the Rolex Swan Atlantic Regatta in Newport, Rhode Island. Cowes played host to the first and second European events, but this year the regatta moved to St Peter Port, Guernsey, in the Channel Islands. With the Guernsey Yacht Club as host and the States of Guernsey Tourist Board, Ruffino Wines and Jaguar Cars as sponsors, the regatta drew 41 boats from 12 nations.

No matter that the 25-square-mile island had to absorb more than six hundred Swan crew. The Guernsey tourist season runs at full steam in the third week of July, and what's another two-score boats for a week when 10,000 yachts visit annually? Midnight taxis were a challenge, but you probably should have been in bed by then anyway.

For those who didn't race to Guernsey from the Solent in the rough Martini Channel feeder, won by Clive King in his 371, *King of Hearts*, the competition began Monday 20 July and ran through to Friday 24. This year the organisers instituted a lay day, increasingly requested by owners, on Wednesday, and more importantly, implemented for the first time the Royal Ocean Racing Club's Channel Handicap System in place of IOR measurements. The IOR outgrew Swans a long time ago – or was it the other way around? – and CHS provides a more sensible alternative for similar boats. Despite the odd owner's predictable disagreement with his rating, it seemed to work relatively well.

If you like the food, you'll love the weather, a friend used to say of the British Isles, and Guernsey played true to form on the latter. Someone forgot to turn down the volume before we

arrived, giving conditions which Guernsey meteorologist Tim Millington had charmingly described at the skipper's ·briefing as 'settled in an unsettled way'. That translated to Force 5 to 6 north-westerlies, rain and two to three-foot slop to start, abating gradually throughout the week until Friday, when the sun finally appeared for good and the breeze fizzled out completely.

Monday morning's start of the Ruffino Medallion Race called for reefed mains, number threes and oilskins, and didn't really improve much from there. The Guernsey Yacht Club selected a 33-mile course from their booklet of 60 possible choices, sending the fleet to St Martin's Point at the south-east corner of Guernsey, east to round Sark from south to north, back to St Martin's and home.

From the beginning, interest focused on the 59 ft (18 m) *International*, the biggest of the three Guernsey entrants and the third-largest boat in the fleet. The well-travelled *International* had been chartered for the week by Guernseyman Derek Boyer, who had the boat's 'Colt' prefix deleted in accordance with Rule 26 and crewed her with mates from his quarter tonner.

Nor did they disappoint, scoring line honours in Race 1 and striking a psychological blow against the one entrant from Jersey, Simon Clarke's and Mark Lamy's chartered 65 ketch, *Beija Flor*. *Beija Flor* managed to save her time, however, finishing 5th in Standard Division I. *International*, the highest-rated boat in the fleet, ended 11th. This would not be the first unfortunate turn for Boyer's boys. In Division II, Gordon Walker's 43, *Pavlova II*, scored the first victory.

The shape of the regatta began to emerge by the end of Day 1, and it wasn't hard to see that the week's true

Above: Swan 65 *Desperado* leads smaller boats around the weather mark during an inshore race off Guernsey. *Left:* Serious partying is a hallmark of Swan events, even when fun is the theme at this Pirates party.

St Peter Port, in the shadow of Castle Cornet, played host to the Swans at the European Championship.

battles would be fought among the three 46s: Norman Brick's *Chastenet*, Keith Miller's *Crackerjack IX* and Joachim Silveira's *Mariposa II of Hamble*. In the tight final beat of that first race, *Crackerjack* squeaked by *Mariposa* by just four-hundredths of a second on corrected, for first in Division I, with *Chastenet* rolling in fourth. Attention was far less focused on the vintage blue 44 from West Germany, Haarold Baum's *Elan*, which finished a good quarter of an hour on elapsed after *Chastenet*, to take third overall. *Elan*, however, would prove difficult to ignore.

The fates sometimes smile on the misguided. Tuesday dawned sunny with a light to moderate north-westerly, providing recovery time from Monday night's Ruffino Italian party at the St Pierre Park Hotel. 'Why aren't you in bed with a hangover?', shouted a crewman in mid-race to the skipper's wife of a boat which shall remain nameless.

And maybe the Guernsey Yacht Club works in tandem with Fortune, as they managed to set a 29-mile, 9-leg course with just one beat. More than one genoa grinder was grateful.

Beija Flor moved out early, choosing the east side of the Little Russell Channel between Guernsey and Herm and capitalising on the fresher breeze. By the weather mark she had a good 10 minutes on the other 65 in the fleet, *Desperado*. There she stayed, out front, as the fleet reached and ran to the rocky and stunning Bec du Nez at the north end of Sark, around the outside to the southern tip, over to St Martin's Point, back to Sark and finally to the finish.

There was little kudos for the home team this day, however, as *International* met her match in an unfeathered propeller, resulting in last place in

The Guernsey regatta was sailed in typically grey English Channel conditions. Travel-brochure sunshine was noticeably absent.

Division I. Meanwhile, *Chastenet* tallied a 2nd, followed by *Elan*. Michael Spear's 41, *Moustique*, notched the win in Division II, while in the three-boat Modified Division, all 39s and one each from France, Spain and Ireland, Dirk Smith's *Stratus* scored its second win.

Each regatta sponsor hosts a day of racing and parties, and the optimistic Guernsey Tourist Board chose a beach barbecue on neighbouring Herm for Tuesday night. Three miles from St Peter Port by water taxi, the tiny island stretched its arms wide to accommodate a Swan population fifteen times greater than its own.

'WELCOME TO HERM – BARS IN EACH TENT' said the sign leading us to the striped marquees and our eventual downfall. So what if it rained cats and dogs? So what if an exuberant *Beija Flor* crew nearly got tossed for sliding down the marquee roof? So what if we and everyone else just had to try the island's only pub as well? Tomorrow was a lay day.

Champagne and smoked salmon breakfasts for owners in the hospitality tent on the quay, Guernsey Brewery Boat Races for crews (dinghies and drinking on the nearby model-boat pond), Alka-Seltzer all around . . . Wednesday gave sustenance for Thursday, when boats would begin consolidating their positions.

Sailed under leaden skies in 10- to 12-knot breezes, the Jaguar Trophy Race proved a test of patience, tight crew work and local knowledge and nerve. Set with a 22-mile series of triangles numbering ten legs in all – a fourth triangle was cancelled due to diminishing wind – crews contended with numerous hoists, gybes and drops. Local knowledge helped too, particularly where the tides normally rise some 30 ft (9 m) and streams flow fast to match. Under the direction of Guernsey rock experts, many boats stood well inshore on the beats from St Martin's to the Anfre marker near the harbour.

It didn't work for everyone, though. With true Gallic confidence, Jean-Pierre Peche's 47 *Gregal* rock-hopped the island shore until she found some Guernsey foundation the hard way – yet managed a 3rd in Division I regardless.

The solid, steady performance that *Elan* had been accumulating earlier in the week finally paid off on Thursday. Clear at the start and moving early to the right of the course, Baum and his crew picked a successful strategy and

sailed a clean race to take 1st in Division I. Michael Spear's *Moustique* looked a strong favourite to take Division II, but had to give way at the windward mark to Irishman Patrick Jameson and *Finndabar of Howth*, who eventually won on corrected time.

In the big boats, *International* restored some local pride with line honours and defeated *Beija Flor* into the bargain, but ended an unlucky 13th in Division I. In Modified, Spaniard Federico Garcia-German's *Flying Neleb* notched her first regatta victory, while the contest between the 46s saw Keith Miller triumphant in *Crackerjack*, eking out 4th in Division I just ahead of *Mariposa* and *Chastenet*.

If you want to throw a good party in the British Isles, make it fancy dress; it never fails. To make the party even better, get Jaguar to host it, give it a pirate theme and hold it in the ramparts of St Peter Port's Castle Cornet. Add wine for lubricant and lobster and roast beef for fuel. Stand back and watch captains of industry play Captain Kidd. Wield your trusty cutlass. Plan some late-night plunder and pillage. Find out your powder's no longer dry. Go down with the ship.

By the start of Nautor Day and the *Yachting World* Trophy Race, Haarold Baum's *Elan* was 10 points ahead of *Chastenet* on aggregate in Division I, and 12 ahead of *Crackerjack*. Division II was even closer; *Moustique* had only two points on both *Finndabar* and *Pavlova II*. *Stratus*, meanwhile, looked a clear favourite in Modified for an overall division win.

The day would have tried the most patient, and did, seeing four protests registered between eight boats before the course was radically shortened for lack of wind. What light breezes drove the fleet to the weather mark died to a whisper on the run down to St Martin's, calling for supreme dedication and willpower to keep boats moving effectively. By the time St Martin's had been rounded and the fleet made for the Hanois Buoy at Guernsey's south-west corner, concentration was dribbling away rapidly. Over on *Desperado*, the crew hauled a 3 ft Karaoke amplifier on deck, plugged in two mikes and crooned 'On A Slow Boat to China' to the rest of the fleet, interspersing their entertainment with well-aimed water balloons at *Finndabar* and the spectator boats.

Meanwhile, Keith Knowles's 391, *Shadow Of A Dream*, was quietly pulling together a week's consistent performance (7th, 11th and 2nd in Division I) and was primed to score a 1st when the race was finally terminated at the Hanois Buoy. Mike Atkins's 41, *Amadea of Wayde*, also a consistent performer for the week, took Division II, while *Stratus* once again swept the Modifieds. *Desperado*, sadly, came next-to-last in Division I, with no points awarded for amusement.

Elan, in turn, came a distant 10th, and that subject to protest, with the trio of 46s, *Mariposa*, *Chastenet* and *Crackerjack*, coming 5th, 6th and 8th. And so it was that the Swan European Challenge Trophy, for the overall winner in the combined standard divisions, would be decided in the protest room.

It was 9.31 p.m. and restlessness was running high in the regatta marquee. Fifty yards away in the Guernsey Yacht Club, the judges had just finished their deliberations. A number of crew had already headed off, and most of the prizes had been awarded. Keith Knowles, Mike Atkins and Dirk Smith had collected their *Yachting World* trophies, and Nautor Swan Trophies had been presented to *Stratus* and *Moustique*.

A selection of other awards had been presented as well: the Jaguar Prix d'Elegance to *Crackerjack IX*; the Ruffino Vintage Swan prize to Gem and Maureen Tetley's 19-year-old 36, *Carte Blanche*; the Lewmar Gold Winch for the best maintained boat to David Barham and his 38, *Xara*; the Sphere Drake Trophy for the most seamanlike Swan to Angus Newton's 38 ft *Kuutar*; and the Sebago Award for best-dressed crew to *Amadea of Wayde*. On it went.

Finally, Nautor agent Pat Lilley stepped up to the podium one last time. Haarold Baum had indeed taken overall honours, and with them the Swan European Challenge Trophy, the States of Guernsey Challenge Trophy, for lowest aggregate time, and the Nautor Swan Trophy for 1st in Division I. He needed his wife and son to help him carry away the silver.

Donald J. McIntyre is an American-based freelance boating writer. He has worked in England for a period and his travels have taken him to the northern countries of Africa.

SWAN EUROPEAN REGATTA

Main picture: **Even as fully fitted cruiser-racers, Swans are raced hard by their owners, as this start shows.** Right: **Californian-style Swan sailing means that even the committee boat crew wear bikinis.**

NAUTOR'S
Swan Californian Regatta

by CHRIS CASWELL

Daniel Forster

Daniel Forster

There are regattas and then there are *regattas*. The Nautor's Swan California Cup falls into the latter category as an unabashed weekend fling of good racing, superb partying and enjoyment of the camaraderie that comes from owning and sailing one of the world's finest yachts. In a sense, it is an elitist event but, in California, it's hard to be snobbish when everyone is wearing shorts. Somehow, the Californian lifestyle is a great equaliser.

Nevertheless, the California Swan Cup did attract a sophisticated group of sponsors, including Rolex, Rolls-Royce and Ruffino, not to mention the builder of Swan yachts, Nautor of Finland.

The base for this hedonistic weekend was the exclusive Balboa Bay Club on Newport Harbor, a wealthy enclave where the main thoroughfare is lined with luxury yacht brokers, restaurants and dealerships for Aston-Martin and Ferrari. Just as important as the venue was the weather, which was picture-perfect California, with warm temperatures, long Pacific swells and steady breezes.

There are always nay-sayers to any event that is supposed to be purely fun, and a few were heard to grumble that this was just 'furniture racing', a reference to the fine teak interiors of the Swans which contrast with the spartan IOR racing machines. And in years past there has been a certain truth to the contention that the skippers and

Daniel Forster

Main picture: **A text-book example of how not to drop the chute take-down.**

Above: **Not all Swan sailors get to wear co-ordinated crew clothing and sit at the back of the boat. For some, hard manual labour is involved.**

SWAN CALIFORNIAN REGATTA

Daniel Forster

Left: **The Balboa Bay YC in Newport Beach is one of the most exclusive areas in southern California.**

Below: **Sit-down dinners rate as highly as the racing for organisers and owners alike.**

crews were less than Grand Prix level. Sail handling and crew work *had* been rather rough at times, but everyone had a good time. You also have to understand that bringing a 'sleeper', such as a sailmaker or an Olympic sailor to steer your Swan, is considered bad form, although there were a few crew members whose names would be recognised nationally if not internationally. But, considering the prizes, you have to understand that this was not just another sailboat race.

Each of the three days of racing was sponsored by a separate company, each threw a posh party at the end of the day, and each offered a selection of their products to the lucky skippers and crews.

The long weekend started on Thursday with a welcoming party sponsored by Ruffino wines who gave the Ruffino Odyssey medallions – actually gold pieces of eight – to the owners who had travelled furthest to compete, as well as cases of their wines to ease the homeward journey.

Earlier that day, Rolls-Royce hosted their *Prix d'Elegance*, a concours for the already fine yachts, which brought the remarkable sight of Swan owners and crews on their knees using toothbrushes to polish every piece of metal that might catch the judges' eyes. The winner, Kevin Jaffe's Swan 46 *Bandit*, was already a gleaming black yacht when she arrived, but his crew deserved a 'wretched excess' award for actually buffing and waxing the bilges before the judges arrived! Rolls-Royce could not be enticed into donating a new Corniche convertible, but they did provide Sterling silver medallions.

The racing started on Friday, as did the judging for the best dressed crew, and both competitions were taken seriously. Winds were lightish for the first day of racing, sponsored by Rolls-Royce, although the following races brought stiffer breezes to give a good range to the regatta. A total of 30 Swans was involved, with 29 racing and a Swan motor sailer serving as the

race committee yacht (what would you expect?). Three classes were started, with A and B based on IOR handicaps whilst C was for non-spinnaker racers. At the trophy presentation and buffet that evening, the main ballroom was decorated with new and vintage Rolls-Royces and the daily winners received silver medals.

The second day of racing was fiercely contested, simply because it was the Rolex day and each class winner would go home with an engraved stainless steel Oyster Submariner watch. Realising that there would be more than a casual interest in the racing, Nautor had arranged to have a jury on hand for each day's racing, with former America's Cup skipper Bill Ficker leading a band of IYRU-certified international judges. To balance the ferocity of the sailing, the Rolex party that evening was a casual affair on a bayfront patio that took advantage of the pleasant weather.

The final day of racing was sponsored by Nautor which presented an array of trophies (including the Swan California Cup) that evening. Overall winner of the regatta was Ernie Townsend's *Trumpeter*, a Swan 46, and Townsend not only earned the perpetual trophy but both a stainless steel and a gold Rolex Submariner watch, suitably engraved, of course.

As the regatta ended and the owners drifted off into the warm California evening, there was a lot of talk about returning with a vengeance next year. Plans were made to start practising, new sails and gear were contemplated and mistakes were analysed. It had been an eclectic few days, with friendships made and renewed, families racing together and a social schedule that is absent at most regattas. Next year, it's going to be a lot tougher to win that Rolex watch!

Chris Caswell is based near San Francisco. A freelance journalist and photographer, he is the West Coast editor of Yachting.

JAGUAR

KINDRED SPIRIT.

Spend a few moments behind the wheel of the new XJ-S 3.6 and you'll soon discover why it's even more desirable.

Drawing on the technology applied to the XJR-8, the all powerful Jaguar that's just run away with the 1987 World Sports Car Championship, the whole feel of the XJ-S has been transformed.

We've added a rear anti-roll bar, uprated the springs, stiffened the dampers and fitted low profile tyres on 6½" alloy rims.

All of which makes handling extremely precise.

And does ample justice to the 221 bhp, all-alloy, 24 valve, electronically fuel injected engine.

Yet luxury is still assured. The cabin is finished with elm veneer. The new sports seats are a blend of tweed, and handstitched hide. Leather also binds the new thick rimmed steering wheel. There's air-conditioning, electronic stereo, heated mirrors. The choice of a 5 speed Getrag manual box, or an optional 4 speed ZF automatic.

A blend of equipment and excitement quite impossible to find elsewhere.

Especially when you consider Jaguar's final sporting gesture.

The price. Only £23,500.

XJS

THE NEW 3·6 SPORT

WORLD
SPORTSCAR
CHAMPIONS
1987

This is sailing Caribbean style, sailing in paradise — a fair breeze, blue skies, blue seas . . . will sailing at home ever be the same?

Caribbean

THE 1987 JOHNNIE WALKER MIAMI–MONTEGO BAY RACE

by ROGER LEAN-VERCOE

Of all the world's major ocean contests, the Miami to Montego Bay Race must rate near the top for pure crew enjoyment. Not only does it have all the usual requirements of a tough race, such as a long course with guaranteed wind and plenty of navigational difficulties, but also includes benefits not found in most races – enough sun to brown the knees of even the most hardened cold-water sailor, a scenically interesting course through the Bahama Islands and the Windward Passage, and at the finish an overdose of hospitality in the tropical paradise of Jamaica.

Despite all this, the race is actually one of the best kept secrets of the western world! In the Florida winter only a small number of racers can invest the three weeks that are needed to enjoy the event. From an expected turnout of 35, just 11 boats eventually crossed the Miami Beach startline. Still, as one competitor remarked, 'It isn't the size of the fleet that matters; the real challenge is in completing the course.'

The usual weather pattern experienced on the race gives an initial beat eastwards across the Gulf Stream to the Great Isaac Light that marks the north-west corner of the Bahamas Shoal, and on through the North-West Providence Channel to the northern tip of Eleuthera Island. That's about 250 miles dead to windward. From there it's often a close reach down past Cat Island, Long Island and Acklins Island, broadening as one closes with the Windward Passage, before the Trades supply the final run to Montego Bay. Like life, it's tough at the beginning but gets easier as you go on!

This year was different, with conditions in the early stages duplicating those of the 1971 race when the 73 ft (22 m) yawl *Windward Passage* sailed the course in 3 days 3 hours 40 minutes and 7 seconds, to set a record which still stands. At the start of the 1987 race, a cold front swept across from central USA towards Florida to provide a strong southerly breeze that slowly veered as the fleet reached under spinnaker across the Gulf Stream and down the Providence Channel in a sparkling 20 knots of breeze. Then, just at the right time, the front passed overhead and the Force 5 breeze swung sharply to the north-west as the leaders turned the corner of Eleuthera Island, giving them a continuation of their run.

Back in 1971 *Windward Passage* had, in the first two days, covered nearly 200 more miles than this year's scratch boat *Scaramouche of Warwick*, a Swan 48 owned by a syndicate from the NYYC and skippered by Arthur 'Bugs' Baer. However, a 48-footer is just not fast enough to keep pace with the average front, and *Scaramouche* suffered from lighter winds in its wake.

It was worse for those behind her, though. The rest of the fleet took the full brunt of the calm, and their speed

Main picture: **Concentration from the trimmers as scratch yacht *Scaramouche of Warwick*, a Swan 48, heads off the startline.**

Jamaica Race Week follows the Miami–Montego Bay race. Some sailors take part, others merely watch from the Sea Winds beach *(bottom left).*

often dropped to one knot or so. This opened up a large gap that gave *Scaramouche* the race by nearly 19 hours on corrected time, quite enough to win both the IMS class and the overall prize. Amazingly she had flown spinnakers for all but a couple of hours, and never tacked during the race!

Ugly Duckling, a Swan 391, was second to join the round of parties organised by the hospitable Montego Bay Yacht Club, taking the PHRF (Performance Handicap Rating Factor) class from a Cal 39, *Iroquois*. The 3rd place in PHRF was decided after one of the closest finishes in the 16-year history of the event. Despite the wildly different looks of *Nueva Vida*, a 48 ft (14 m) Cheoy Lee centre-cockpit cruising yacht that eventually took 3rd place, and *Spranzie*, a J-30 one-design that was placed 4th, they shared exactly the same PHRF handicap. After 811 miles, they crossed the line just over one minute apart. There can't be much wrong with a handicapping system that equates like that!

Next year will see yachts competing for the 'Windward Passage' Challenge Cup, a fabulous prize fashioned by the Crown Jewellers, Garrard, to be won outright by the first yacht to break the existing course record; the Johnnie Walker Cup for the overall winner; and the normal class prizes for IOR, IMS and PHRF classes. However, there will be more emphasis placed on an Inter-Club Team Trophy, an idea that was tentatively floated this year and won by the Royal Jamaica Yacht Club which was the only club to enter the required two yachts. In future, participation will be actively encouraged from clubs outside the US and Jamaica and, hopefully, made easy for them by a 'fly and charter' package.

For this particular sub-event the programme would be extended to include three or more inshore races during Jamaica Race Week which would immediately follow the offshore race. The 1988 start is off Miami Beach 5 February – why not be there?

Roger Lean-Vercoe is a former Royal Marines officer who has made a second career from writing and photographing sailing events around the world.

MIAMI–MONTEGO BAY

ANTIGUA SAILING WEEK

by JOLYON BYERLY

With the Caribbean to the west and the Atlantic to the east, the small island of Antigua lies a quarter of the way down the lazy crescent of islands known as the Lesser Antilles. It's a tropical venue that conjours up sunshine, rum punches, steel bands and a week-long regatta that, in the words of the late Jack Knights, 'could be Cowes Week after you have died and gone to Heaven'.

This little island was first settled by the Arawaks who paddled their dugout canoes from the jungles of Venezuela. Hard on their heels came the ravenous Caribs, in whose wake followed the great European naval fleets. Antigua's hidden and hurricane-proof harbour tickled the fancy of the British and one H. Nelson in particular. With considerable foresight they saw that the forts and quays of English Harbour would make a great setting for a regatta.

Antigua Sailing Week got underway 20 years ago. Some say that sailing was added in olden times because it was decided that it would be a great way to sell T-shirts. Antigua T-shirt Week was the unofficial title until it was realised that both males and females preferred to tan from the waist up.

This year the Trade Winds returned after a five-week absence to allow race officer Alan Green, on loan from the Royal Ocean Racing Club in London, to get the fleet away on schedule. In time-honoured Antiguan tradition, the slower boats were sent off first. This pleases spectators and photographers and also prevents boring processions as the boats bunch up again around the course. My uncle Albert, for instance, stopped for a nice cup of tea aboard his old gaffer at the gybe mark and somehow got inside a maxi's spinnaker sheet.

In the racing classes, the Bénéteau First Class 10s from the hot Caribbean

fleet have given the IOR boats a difficult time in the past. This year, however, veteran Puerto Rican yachtsman Tom Hill in *Titan IV* (ex-*Abracadabra*) climbed all over them. Hill was ably abetted in his campaign to stamp out the First Class 10s by Bill McAkteer's Farr 40 *Immigrant,* on charter to Englishman Chris Griffiths. The latter seems to make a habit of chartering boats for interesting regattas, having borrowed *Challenge 12* for the 1986 12-metre Worlds and *Marionette* for the 1985 Champagne Mumm Admiral's Cup.

Immigrant was lucky to be racing at all. In the course of her passage from the Rolex Regatta in St Thomas (see separate report on page 120) she met 40-knot winds and steep, square waves in the Anagada Passage. She fell into a 12 ft wave trough and began leaking badly. A May Day call brought help and she was towed into Antigua by the US Coast Guard twelve hours before the first start. Burning copious quantities of midnight oil, Griffiths and his all-star Canadian crew patched up the boat and went sailing in her for the first time with less than 30 minutes to spare.

Jim Kilroy raced his 'spare' maxi, the old Holland-designed *Kialoa IV,* and had things pretty much his own way in the big boat class, although every so often old grandma *Mistress Quickly* picked up her shawls and punched her torpedo hull form to windward with awesome effect.

Californian Carl Schumaker had his latest ULDB design in evidence in the form of *Eclipse,* a slender 40-footer with tubular sitting-out platforms which made her look a bit like a four-poster bed. Despite grumbles from traditionalists she was given a Caribbean Yacht Racing Rule (a simplified IOR) rating of just a few points lower than *Kialoa.* That she was allowed to race

and come 3rd behind a 'proper' maxi is all part of the Antigua Week fun.

The two big Swans, the 59 *Colt International* and the 57 *Bravo,* edged out the Martin Frances-designed cruising maxi *Speedy Gonzales* to give a well-rounded look to the top of the big class. Tom Hill won the Week back in 1975 in a little Cal 2/30 but since then his various *Titans* have not been able to repeat that success, though she did win Class 2 (around 40 ft), with *Immigrant* threatening more and more later in the regatta.

Growing interest in Venezuela brought two of their yachts over, the J-35 *Connie D* and a Frers 36 *Piolin.* They were rewarded with taking 3rd and 4th in Class 2 ahead of top Swan 46, Keith Millar's *Crackerjack.*

The real drama was in Class 3, with four First Class 10s slugging it out. The well-sailed *Reverie* from Martinique was top of the heap but the others were soundly thrashed by a previously unremarkable Pearson Flyer from St Thomas. Owner Rudy Thompson had recently modified *Cold Beer* with a chainsaw (believe it or not) and was the most popular runner-up in the whole regatta.

In the cruising classes, the former Argentinian two tonner *Sur* ruffled a few feathers, but the sweetheart of the regatta was the 80-year-old gaff-rigged Falmouth Quay Punt *Curlew* which was all-conquering in Cruising Class 3. Up wind and down, tanned topsails and all, she ate up the class – just the sort of thing Antigua Sailing Week loves.

Before leaving England for the Caribbean, Jolyon Byerly raced National 12s and Merlin Rockets. He has won Antigua Sailing Week three times and has been chairman of the race committee for many years.

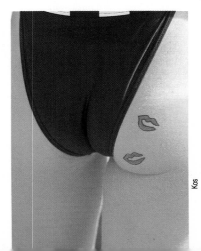

Left. **The cheek of it! Dressing up Antigua Sailing Week style places a premium on head-turning ability.**

Above. **Cruiser class 2 starts the fourth race at Curtain Bluff.**

ANTIGUA WEEK

Left. **Johnny le Bon watches *Kialoa IV*'s bowman peel spinnakers at the pole end during the Curtain Bluff race.**

Sailing Week's true colours come to light at the end of the first race. In Dickenson Bay, many small beach bars set up shop *(right).*

Above. **Peter de Savary's lovingly restored 1910 Herreshoff-designed gaff schooner, *Vagrant*, made her debut at Sailing Week.**

Left. **Watching the sun go down whilst drinking sundowners – who says Caribbean yachting is hard work?**

ANTIGUA SAILING WEEK

119

INTERNATIONAL ROLEX CUP REGATTA

by RICK TOMLINSON

The sailing waters around the Virgin Islands must be among the best in the world. Winds are a constant 15 knots and the sea and sky compete in their intensities of blue.

Racing in such conditions is most people's approximation of paradise. Certainly the competitors in the International Rolex Cup thought so, for 73 of them turned up in St Thomas for the regatta which is the high point of the CORT – the Caribbean Ocean Racing Triangle which brings in the Copa Valassco series off San Juan in March, followed by the BVI Spring Regatta in April and culminates in the Rolex Regatta.

An Easter weekend of sun, fun and sailing was promised and delivered. The event was hosted for the 14th year in succession by the St Thomas YC, which is perched on the eastern coast of St Thomas (one of the US Virgin Islands) looking over to the British Virgins.

The relatively low but abundantly lush volcanic islands sit at the top of the Caribbean chain and are a favourite stamping ground for yachts and yachtsmen escaping the northern winter. The Rolex Regatta drew in boats from neighbouring islands such as Tortola, Virgin Gorda, St John and San Juan, as well as those from the American mainland and Europe.

Enjoyment afloat is enhanced by the organisers keeping the races sensibly short, no more than four to five hours. Two of them are triangles with a passage race taking in the sights of the US and British islands. The PHRF system used in CORT makes the series open to all contestants, low-tech and high-tech, and gives most entrants a chance to win.

Often a few hot race boats turn up. This year the Joubert/Nivelt 1986 Southern Ocean Racing Conference winner *Abracadabra* appeared, under new ownership as *Titan IV*, as did the Britton Chance-designed ultra-light *Stuart Little*. The Swan 59 *Colt International* was one of the few big, expensive yachts, for this year there were no maxis.

Old scores among the skippers go back over many series, especially among the smaller boats in Classes C, D, E and F which make up the bulk of the fleet. Competition is strong between the local boats, for in the small-town world of the Caribbean rivals on the race course are friends, neighbours and working colleagues ashore. There are others, however, taking sabbaticals from the frenzied world of Grand Prix IOR sailing – men such as Burt Keenan whose current *Acadia* is a rather lovely cruising boat and Bill McAkteer from Annapolis who now races *Immigrant* in the Caribbean.

Once the racing was over, and occasionally before, the partying began in earnest. The St Thomas YC reverberated to steel bands, talk and laughter. Dancing, beach parties, conspicuous consumption of rum punches, and sizzling pork and steak barbeques were the order of the day.

In a completely different vein, there was also the Easter Sunday service. A 200-strong multi-denominational, multi-national congregation gathered under palm trees and sang and prayed with the waters of the Caribbean lapping around their feet. Music was courtesy of the Morman Tabernacle Choir and the Reverend Bazalay's ghetto blaster.

The finale was the prize-giving, a fabulous evening of Caribbean hospitality attended by Governor of the USVI, Alexander Farrally, and Rolex representative Walter Ammler. After a top class dinner there were nearly 100 awards to be presented. Master of Ceremonies Dick Johnson turned what could have been a monotonous affair into one of great style and humour with each award winner receiving unflagging applause. No applause was more enthusiastic than that for Peter Hollomberg and the crew of *Humbug*, a Metal Mast 30, who won the Rolex Cup Trophy, and for regatta chairman John Foster, who steered his stock J-27, *Hot Pursuit*, to the overall win of the CORT series.

Rick Tomlinson specialises in photographing the more glamorous yachting events. He helped to build, and then sailed aboard, Drum, during her incident-filled Fastnet Race and the Whitbread Round the World Race.

Left: **The party begins and the sound of the steel band drifts across the water as the rum punch begins to flow.**

Rick Tomlinson

The Bénéteau First Class 10 *Uncle Sam*, owned by Sam Laing, revels in the perfect sailing conditions on her way to the finish of the Jost van Dyke race in front of the St Thomas Yacht Club.

ROLEX CUP REGATTA

The balance of power and practicality.

Few cars inspire such confidence as the Honda Integra EX16. Even before you settle behind the wheel, the very look of the car seems unmistakably right.

The clean, unfussy lines with a low, sloping bonnet and retractable headlights not only give the Integra a cool, distinctive look, but also a drag coefficient of 0.33.

The long wheelbase helps make an apparently compact car remarkably airy and spacious for passengers and luggage.

The Integra is a five door hatchback with split folding rear seats, startling all round visibility and even a smoked glass sunroof.

Williams-Honda, powered by the Honda engine, captured the Formula One 1986 Constructors' Championship. This year Honda F1 engines are powering not only Williams but also Lotus, making life twice as difficult for every other team.

As you might expect from Honda other creature comforts include a four speaker stereo radio cassette, power steering and remote control tailgate and fuel lid, all fitted as standard.

Your sense of well being is sharpened into a feeling of sheer pleasure as you put the Integra through its paces.

You notice immediately the power and quick response of the four valve per cylinder DOHC 1.6 engine.

You say a blessing for Honda's involvement in Formula One as you feel the added punch and smoothness of the programmed fuel injection system (PGM FI), developed on the race track.

And, in your enthusiasm on the bends, you are grateful for slick, short-throw gear shift action and the positive, all round disc brakes.

In fact, if this is only a test drive, you'll be loathe to bring the car back at all.

But when you do and you weigh up everything the Integra has to offer, there's really only one decision to make.

Sign the cheque, get back inside and drive it away for good.

HONDA
INTEGRA EX16
Honda (UK) Ltd., 4 Power Road, Chiswick, London W4 5YT.

POWERED by HONDA

Guy Gurney

6-Metre World Championships

by LISA GOSSELIN

A certain amount of pride and emotion go into racing a 6-metre. In 1985 tears were shed aboard *St Francis IX* at the Worlds in Cannes, France. The Swiss sailor Philippe Durr had taken a flier on the last leg to tie with Tom Blackaller's San Francisco entry. It was only when the results had been broken down by a count-back and the number of 3rd places considered that the trophy was awarded. Durr was declared champion.

Then in 1986, when the Ferrari-red, bulb-keeled *Nivola* won the championship, the march from 'Aïda' echoed through the streets of Portofino (Italy). Handkerchiefs were waved from windows and women cried joyfully. The Bassani brothers had been victorious in their home waters.

But the finish of the last race in the 1987 series on 5 October was strangely quiet. A small but impressive fleet of spectator craft bobbed on the waters of Long Island Sound as the autumn haze shut out the distant Manhattan skyline. It was a sedate crowd which had issued forth from the Seawanahaka Corinthian YC and the surrounding mansion-rimmed inlets of Oyster Bay to toot their horns tentatively for the winner.

Publishing magnate Nelson Doubleday had his recent acquisition, the large Alden motor sailer formerly known as *Scotch Mist*, on hand. Mrs Harry Morgan, a long-time Six sailor and daughter-in-law of financier J.P. Morgan, steered her classic *Djinn* around the course. *Black Knight*, committee boat to numerous America's Cups staged off Newport, sailed with a charter party aboard, whilst Bill Whitehouse-Vaux watched the progress of his 6-metre from aboard his comfortable maxi racer *Mistress Quickly*.

This blue-chip spectator fleet had come to watch what had been billed, by virtue of the close competition throughout the week, as a showdown of yachts, yachtsman and yacht designs, taking in 23 entries from seven nations. It was clear that the Sixes are now very much in business and their popularity set to soar once more. Since the early '80s, the world's top designers and sailors have flocked back to the 81-year-old class and it has become something of a testing ground for 12-metre research and a laboratory for keel design.

By the fifth of the six races, a radical new Peter Norlin boat named *Notorious*, sporting a conventional keel *sans* trim tab, held a one-point lead which any one of four boats could snatch from her. In 2nd and 3rd places were two Pelle Petterson designs, the 1985 *St Francis IX* sailed by Blackaller's nemesis and America's Cup tactician Paul Cayard, followed by *Scoundrel* which featured a new Ron Holland-designed keel based on his *KZ-7* 12-metre experience. Norlin himself had a solid lock on 4th place with his own sponsored entry which had been renamed *Joe Cool* in this strictly amateur event. John Prentice's *Battlecry*, and *Thisbe* sailed by Peter Bateman (holding a surprise genniker in her sail quiver), lurked close behind to give the top places a nicely rounded Swedish/American/British flavour.

Over the week, those who had sought an easy answer to the perennial 6-metre question (perennial since 1983, that is) 'wings or no wings?' were disappointed. Long Island Sound is a normally placid stretch of water beginning in New York City and running 60 miles between the Long Island peninsula and the Connecticut shore, but during the series it amazed even the locals. Breezes ranged from a gentle 8 to 10 knots on balmy days to a gruelling 25. When 45 knot winds blasted through and snow fell inland, a day of racing was cancelled.

As a result, a different yacht won each race. Nor did the adage 'wings in a wind' hold true if one went by results alone. *Notorious* had thrived in the 25 knot breezes and won the race; *Battlecry*, a 1983 Ian Howlett design with an '87 wing keel grafted on, took the honours in a medium-air race. There were no simple answers.

So when the prevailing 10–15 knot south-westerly kicked in on the last day of the World Cup, no-one hazarded a guess at the outcome. As the fleet rounded the first weather mark with the leaders locked in mid-fleet, any prediction would have been a gamble. Paul Cayard and his crew drawn from the USA 12-metre were deep down in 10th with no jib up at the leeward mark, but one flier to the north later had moved up to 2nd with Peter Norlin right on his tail. In the ensuing tacking duel, Norlin forced Cayard out to the south side of the course while *Notorious* and the others held to the north. An accusation by Cayard that the Swede team-raced went unheeded. 'Of course we team-raced,' Norlin later admitted, his eyes lit with businessman's savvy, 'I wanted *Notorious* to win.'

It was only after *St Francis IX* continued miles to the south of the rest of the fleet and spectators gasped in horror as Cayard's Six ricocheted back across the Sound that it became clear that Norlin's tactic had backfired. Tacking on the port layline, *St Francis IX* sailed on her own lift to finish 1st, well ahead of the previous leader *Thisbe*.

But the San Francisco crew were unusually reserved as they crossed the line. A protest flag flying from their yacht's shrouds meant the final results were not yet firm. While the protest committee deliberated about the incident (a mark rounding where Cayard squeezed inside the Swedish *Maybe XIV*), Bruce Owen, Lawrie Smith and the rest of *Scoundrel*'s crew watched the video replays.

The decision was made an hour before the awards ceremony. Once again *St Francis IX* had lost the trophy by the skin of her teeth and ended up 4th overall. *Scoundrel* took the top honours with *Notorious* and *Joe Cool* in 2nd and 3rd.

'He didn't deserve to win. He is a professional and should know better', said young Benjamin de Rothschild, referring to Cayard, the outspoken sailmaker from North Sails whose summer's sailing had already taken in the 12-metre Worlds, Maxi Worlds and San Francisco Big Boat Series. De Rothschild's concerns were shared by other sailors in this true-blue corinthian class. The Bruce Owen/Lawrie Smith combination was only accepted since both had been extremely active in the class over a number of years and had helped its revival in Britain and Europe. Moreover, Smith – a 12-metre veteran – did not steer, merely calling tactics for *Scoundrel*'s owner.

Even in 1987, the question of professionalism was a strong issue in a class which prides itself in being one of the last high-profile, world class amateur fleets. An Olympic class until it was dropped in 1952, the 6-metres have never been looked upon warmly by those who make their living from the sport. It was the first class ever to disqualify a yachtsman (Swiss designer

Opposite page: **Scoundrel's crew (with Lawrie Smith in visor, left) relax in front of the elegant Seawanahaka Corinthian YC.**

6-METRE WORLD CHAMPIONSHIPS

Louis Noverraz) for not qualifying as an amateur. Those yachtsmen who received the Sixes after their virtual demise in the 1950s were in many instances the relatives of early class champions and they sought to retain 6-metre sailing as a gentleman's sport.

For example, Benjamin de Rothschild was perpetuating his father's line of *Gitanas*. Swedes Sven and Christopher Salen sailed *Maybe XIV*, a descendant of the legendary champion Sven Salen's Six. American Harry Morgan sailed a Six, just as his grandmother and grandfather had done at Seawanahaka decades earlier. Even Paul Cayard had family ties with the class, being Pelle Petterson's son-in-law. So the 1987 World Cup took on an intimate atmosphere as only a 6-metre event can do. Crews threw small dinner and cocktail parties for each other in the lovely villas and carriage houses they had rented for the week, and Seawanahaka members opened their homes to accommodate the visitors. Two families actually moved aboard their yachts for a fortnight.

The Seawanahaka Corinthian YC had been very much the home of American 6-metre sailing and in the 1920s and '30s produced a series of world champions. The club was founded in 1877 on what current commodore Larry Glenn referred to as 'the corinthian principle of yachtsmen preparing and racing their own boats'. In reality, Glenn was probably one of the few skippers at the regatta who had adhered to that principle.

While many of the crews racing in the Worlds were family (wives, sons and brothers) and most strictly amateurs, the cloud of professionalism cast its long shadow over events. Two

Swedish yachts had to change their names for the World Cup and, on other yachts, paid hands worked late into the evening as the owners and sailing crew dressed for dinner. The syndicate approach, espoused by their big sisters, the Twelves, had filtered down (the owners of *St Francis* and *Thisbe* watched from tenders), and necessarily so. While the costs of a Six still make them accessible to private owners, the amount of work necessary to campaign and maintain these highly technical toys, combined with the logistics of shipping the boat around the US and European circuit, has required paid help.

Yet, as class president Glenn Foster put it, 'The allure of a 6-metre is that it is a personal yacht. An owner can choose his design, create his own deck layout, work with a sailmaker and intricately know and love his own boat. And he still gets to sail.'

Foster and the majority of other officers and owners chose to curtail the route which would have taken the Sixes down the path of the Twelves by making them far too technical and expensive for private money to fund. True, the 6-metre has always been a development class: Sven Salen developed the Genoa jib back in 1927 and pioneered the parachute spinnaker; Olin Stephens first tank-tested the 6-metre *Goose*; and the origins of rod rigging, cold moulding and even modern race courses lie in the class's past. Nevertheless, it was felt that parameters of development had to be set.

Meetings during the week ruled that gennikers (which had made their appearance on *Thisbe* and the Australian *Port Douglas*) were permitted but that riblets were not. The latter dealt

Guy Gurney

an axe blow to the symbiotic design relationship between the Sixes and Twelves which had grown strong over the past four years.

Even designers who had based the Twelves on Sixes and *vice versa* welcomed the break. Ian Howlett, whose winged keels on *Battlecry*, the Petterson-designed *Thisbe* and *St Kitts* were direct offshoots of his work with *White Crusader*, praised the decision. 'To have allowed new appendages like the *USA* canard could have killed the class. The 6-metre rule is a brilliant one. Right now, any yacht, no matter how old, can be significantly modified by affixing a new keel. They are not throwaway boats and therein lies their beauty.'

Canadian designer Bruce Kirby agreed: 'It was nice to use the Sixes and Twelves to leapfrog design concepts but I'll keep designing Sixes because it is a fun rule. Like other metre boats, the rule allows plenty of different alterations but you only get tiny speed changes.' Howlett admitted that only one-tenth of a knot speed differences existed between his hull of *St Kitts* (generally considered to be the fastest new boat) and the 1933 classic entry *Fun*.

For both Kirby and Howlett it was a frustrating regatta. The Canadian's sole entry and only cold-moulded yacht in the series, *Capriccio*, was showing good speed with her new 1987 keel when she was dismasted half-way through. 'I had been trying new ideas and put on slightly shorter wings for this series. It was horrible to see two years of research go down the drain and I still don't know where she stands', Kirby lamented. 'Worse,' he added, 'when someone like Cayard sails the way he did, taking fliers and then

Peter Norlin's Six was renamed *Joe Cool* for a championship which jealously guards its amateur non-sponsored status.

With high reserves of stability, Sixes set a cloud of sail.

Phillip Walwyn's *St Kitts*, an Ian Howlett design, was considered most promising of the new boats.

Guy Gurney

moving ahead, you don't know whether his boat is fast or he is a tactical genius.'

Howlett had a slightly better gauge to go by, although his newest pride, *St Kitts*, had been designed for an inexperienced crew (Caribbean hotelier and multihull sailor Philip Walwyn) and sailed only seven times before the regatta. Yet the day Howlett was aboard the boat, banana yellow from deck to wingtip, she took the gun. *Thisbe* and *Battlecry* (an '83 boat with an '87 keel) also won races in the moderately windy conditions and they finished 5th and 6th overall.

The only other designer to use wings was Ron Holland, but he was not there to see his new keels perform on the

Petterson-designed *Scoundrel* and Grobety's *Gitana Jr*. Yet on *Scoundrel* the swept-back wings he developed for *KZ-7* appeared to enhance the year-old design; *Gitana Jr* proved faster than the other Grobety yacht, *Beep Beep*, sailed by Philippe Durr, in spite of 35 mm having to be cut off the top of the keel to measure-in.

Only the Swedes remained adamant on the no-wings theory and their results supported them with Pelle Petterson's *St Francis* so nearly winning. Peter Norlin also came away with strong conclusions concerning his new designs, which placed 2nd and 3rd. 'I am definitely against wings on these boats,' said the blond Swede, whose earlier design, *Klorina*, had had her

wings clipped, 'and I am against trim tabs as well.' In a revolutionary move, Norlin eliminated the trim tab on the two yachts. 'We balance them with the sails instead. It forces us to sail with more precision.' And would trim tabs be eliminated on Twelves? 'Perhaps,' answered Norlin, 'although that won't work as well on a winged keel.'

So, divorced from the Twelves, the Sixes have been saved to go their own way. While the designers were left guessing at the end of the series they will at least be able to watch their ideas bear fruit, for both Norlin and Howlett admitted to some new commissions.

'It's nice to see this class grow,' smiled Howlett, 'and not just for commercial reasons. It is a wonderful

class with wonderful people who take pride in their yachts', he continued, as he prepared to race in the follow-up Seawanahaka Cup, a revived match race series. 'There's emotion and nationalism about this class. I would love to see the British–American Team Trophy revived as well.'

And if *St Francis IX*'s crew wants a chance to take revenge, perhaps it will be.

Lisa Gosselin is an Associate Editor of the respected American journal Yachting.

6-METRE WORLD CHAMPIONSHIP

Britannia Sailing had eighty racing starts in the 1987 Channel racing season. Twelve were in the Fastnet. All the crews were amateurs learning to race. Yet our Channel Handicap results were pretty impressive.

1st JOG Cherbourg, 1st JOG Schroder Trophy, 1st, 2nd and 3rd in JOG Round the Island, 2nd, 3rd and 4th in the RORC Channel race, 2nd and 3rd in the RORC Morgan Cup and then 6th in class 4 IOR in the Fastnet. That was after being RORC Production Boat of the Year in 1986 along with 2nd overall in RORC and JOG Channel Handicap.

In 1985 Britannia Sailing were JOG Champions and RORC runners up after holding the RORC Championship in 1984.

All this makes Britannia Sailing the only sailing school to consider if you want to win.

BRITANNIA
SAILING
Britain's leading racing sailing school
Shamrock Quay, Northam, Southampton. Tel: (0703) 335496

LEARN
TO RACE
TO WIN

Though *Côte d'Or* (below) may not have the pace
of the newer big multihulls, skipper Eric
Tabarly is still the best-known sailor in the
class.

Below right: Sailing highly strung multihulls is not
without anxious moments.

Multihull Racing in 1987

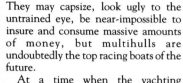

by JAMES BOYD

They may capsize, look ugly to the untrained eye, be near-impossible to insure and consume massive amounts of money, but multihulls are undoubtedly the top racing boats of the future.

At a time when the yachting fraternity worldwide is gradually getting used to professional yacht racing and the difficulties it presents when put alongside amateur yachting and its establishment, in France multihull racers have been playing the sponsor-boat-media triangle with varying degrees of success for several years now. The system there is becoming quite refined; no longer the unknown quantity of previous years. As the burly Devonian skipper of Britain's largest racing catamaran, *Novanet Elite*, Peter Phillips, half-jokingly explains: 'on the multihull circuit we make up our own rules'.

There is now a whole-hearted drive towards better media/spectator involvement which was this year displayed by the increased professionalism of the top TAG Round Europe teams and a revision to the structure of Formula 40 Grand Prix for this, the class's second season, now avoiding offshore races such as the MultiFigaro and putting the emphasis on the more easily accessible inshore courses.

So the concrete is hardening at the core of multihull racing in France and this is beginning to spur more international interest. In New Zealand *Lion New Zealand*'s skipper Peter Blake has mounted the massive Steinlager Challenge, a three-boat programme which kicks off with a David Alan-Williams-designed 60 ft trimaran which he will

be racing in the 1988 Round Australia Race (see separate chapter).

One aspect of multihull racing which is finding increasing importance due to the media focus on an individual boat and sponsor is record breaking. At the same time as the early-season Formula 40 Grand Prix in Brest Philippe Monnet arrived at the end of an arduous singlehanded around the world trip, and the Peyron brothers, Bruno and Loic, finished a two-boat singlehanded battle across the Atlantic in their catamarans *Ericsson* and the zebra-striped *Lada Poch* respectively. All three reached the port in France's north-western extremity with records under their belts.

The 28-year-old, curly-haired Monnet was racing the rather aged 75 ft (22.8 m) trimaran *Kriter Brut de Brut* (ex-*Jacques Ribourel*) and was out to break the 169-day record for the fastest multihull circumnavigation set in 1974 by the late and legendary Alain Colas in *Manureva*. Monnet smashed Colas's record by 40 days, setting a new record of 129 days and 19 hours and 27 minutes. However, he had been forced into Cape Town for 67 hours to make repairs to his forestay, costing him the 'non-stop' title. During his 27,000-mile trek, Monnet narrowly escaped with his life when he fell from half-way up his blue trimaran's mast and only managed to save himself by grabbing a spinnaker halyard on his way deckwards, causing him severe rope burns. Later, *en route* to Cape Horn, *Kriter* was swamped by a huge wave which left the radio disabled for a long period.

Monnet claimed that for the entire journey he never slept for more than 90 minutes at a time. He survived on a

specially prepared diet which included such exotic, if dehydrated, dishes as Poulet Catalane and Sauté de Porc au Capres, meticulously planned for him by the Department of Nutrition and Physiology in Dijon.

Meanwhile, the elder brothers of the transatlantic windsurfer Stéphane Peyron had set off from Ambrose Light, New York, on 7 April in an attempt to better the long-standing time of 12 days 4 hours and 1 minute, set in 1902 by Charlie Barr in the schooner *Atlantic*. The elder brother, Bruno, completed his solo transatlantic crossing first in the larger 75 ft (22.8 m) *Ericsson* in a new single-handed record time of 11 days 46 minutes and 36 seconds. Loic arrived twelve hours later in the shorter 54 ft (16.4 m) Irens-designed multihull.

A record which is frequently having time shaved off it is the fully crewed version of the Peyrons' record. Last year, on her way back from winning the Carlsberg two-handed transatlantic race, the 85 ft (25.9 m) catamaran *Royale* reduced the fully crewed transatlantic record to an amazing 7 days 21 hours and 5 minutes. On 12 June at 18.02 the Route de Rhum winner, *Fleury Michon VIII* and her renowned skipper Philippe Poupon passed Ambrose Light *en route* for the Lizard. On her fifth day at sea the 75 ft (22.8 m) Nigel Irens-designed trimaran covered 520 miles at an average of 21.7 knots, breaking Mike Birch's record set during the 1984 Quebec–St Malo in another Irens design, the 80 ft (24.3 m) catamaran *Formule TAG*. They were advised by their tactician, Jean-Yves Bernot, to take a more southerly course than the rhumb line,

MULTIHULL RACING IN 1987

Biscuits Cantreau III, Jean le Cam's new Formula 40 trimaran, is sailed catamaran-style with just the leeward float immersed and proved to be the boat to beat.

passing just north of the Azores, and *Fleury* reached the Lizard in 7 days 12 hours and 50 minutes at an average of 410 miles per day at 17.3 knots.

Within British waters the most popular record to attempt recently has been for sailing around Ireland. Such is the envy of the Irish yacht clubs of their French counterparts that it is believed that a Round Ireland Race may well be in the pipeline. The record is currently held by Peter Phillips's catamaran *Novanet Elite* with a time of 2 days 22 hours and 16 seconds.

With Olivier de Kersauson's attempt (departing November 1987) on Monnet's record in the 75 ft (22.8 m) trimaran *Poulain* still to come, it is most likely that we shall soon see the romantic target of round the world in 80 days actually achieved.

The most significant developments have been made in the high-flying world of the Formula 40s, however.

Formula 40 Lesson One: don't be fooled by all that was said at the outset of the class in the beginning of 1986. The design restrictions (weight, beam, length and sail area) have clearly had a minuscule effect on restricting costs. Besides, it is the cost of running the boats and keeping them competitive that gobbles up the most money, not their construction. A team which can afford new sails each race and have sufficient back-up virtually to rebuild an entire boat overnight, if need be, is a team which will be in the running for first place. Major sponsorship is essential if you're to win.

At the end of 1986 one French skipper was quoted as saying 'the MultiFigaro gave birth to Formula 40, but Formula 40 will be the death of the MultiFigaro'. The MultiFigaro was the culmination of the Formula 40s' first season and was a three-leg offshore race between Brest and La Rochelle, with

shorter inshore Grands Prix between legs. Although Californian Randy Smyth, the eventual first winner of the International Formula 40 Championships, treated it rather like a scaled-up version of the popular Worrell 1000 race (a long-distance race for dinghy catamarans up the east coast of the USA), it was apparent that the class was not suited as an inshore/offshore compromise and, from the media and spectator point of view, would benefit from being restricted to inshore day-race courses. Accordingly, the format of each Grand Prix in 1987 was one six- to eight-hour long 'offshore' race and three inshore races, each of two to three hours' duration.

This change was reflected in the new designs which arrived on the circuit at Brest over Easter along with numerous features which appeared on the boats during the 1986 season. For the catamarans, which represented the majority, these were ten in number.

(1) Lower volume hulls, in the case of the Nigel Irens and Gino Morelli designs, with less buoyancy aft than their previous 40s, to help curb the nose-diving tendency experienced on reaches.

(2) Lighter and stiffer hulls, due to their lower volume and more advanced construction. This was most noticeable in the Morelli designs. In 1986 *The Smyth Team* weighed in at 4520 lb (2050 kg), some 551 lb (250 kg) over the minimum weight. His 1987 design, *Richmond*, was built entirely in carbon/epoxy, weighed only 3461 lb (1570 kg) and had to have lead added to bring her up to the 3970 lb (1800 kg) minimum weight.

(3) Twin cockpits, one in each hull, with duplicate sail controls. This was noticed very early on in the first season as it is vital for the trim of these boats

that the crew can be on the windward hull, forward when beating and aft when reaching.

(4) Wider beam for added stability.

(5) Demountability. With two Grands Prix on Lakes Geneva and Garda in the second half of the season it was necessary that all the boats should be able to be disassembled for containerisation or road haulage.

(6) Rotating wingmasts. The rules state that masts should be made from standard aluminium extrusions. For 1987 the popular Francespar mast was superseded by a Marechal mast with hydraulic spreaders and Kevlar flaps on its trailing edge. The Morelli boats were the only exceptions, using the new American Hallspar mast, which is lighter in section than its French counterpart.

(7) Una-rigs. As Smyth put it 'all catamarans with restricted sail area have gone this way'. *The Smyth Team* and Serge Madec's *Jet 40* began the trend for this, with the tiny 96 ft² (9 m²) self-tacking storm jib which the rules demand and which in fact helps the catamarans to tack.

(8) Hydraulic mainsheets. There are currently two schools of thought, one in favour as it allows greater mainsheet tension, and one against it in preference of speed of handling.

(9) Long bowsprits extending forward from the foot of the mast and from which the asymmetric spinnakers and jibs are tacked.

(10) Higher aspect rigs for greater power within the restricted sail area.

These points apply to the 1987 season catamarans and were taken to the extreme in the Jean-Marie Finot designs, based upon ideas by the champion, Smyth. Two of these designs, Patrick Elies' *Chaffoteaux et Maury* and Yves le Bouvier's *Lessives*

The Formula 40 *Amtec* (left) illustrates that multihull sailing is like standing in front of a fire hydrant.

Olivier de Kersauson's *Poulain* (above) is reduced to a silhouette in one of the early-season French races at La Rochelle.

MULTIHULL RACING IN 1987

Philippe Monnet took *Kriter Brut de Brut* around the world single-handed to set a new time for a solo multihull circumnavigation.

Swedish car makers Saab have entered the world of sponsored multihull racing with the former *Ker Cadalac II* sailed by François Boucher.

Blanco which were racing at the first Grand Prix at Brest, also had the innovative feature of forward rudders and aft daggerboards, another Smyth idea which he believed would speed up|tacking.|Both were built by CDK Composites at Port la Fôret, which is more well known for the *Biscuits Cantreau* trimarans.

Marc van Peteghem and Vincent Lauriot Prevost's development of the *Biscuits Cantreau* theme was equally radical: a beamy trimaran with three rudders and hulls of virtually equal proportions (see Top Ten).

As in 1986, the first Grand Prix of the season was held at Brest over the Easter weekend. There were only twelve boats racing, which was slightly disappointing as for the MultiFigaro there had been over twenty and of these only four were still competing.

The race in the Rade de Brest was entirely dominated by the Irens-designed catamarans *Data General*, skippered by Pierre le Maout (one of the forefathers of Formula 40), and Poupon's latest *Fleury Michon 40*. It

was like two races within one, *Data* and *Fleury* streets ahead of the competition which generally seemed to have fallen into what in America might be termed 'first race situation gear failure'.

Le Maout and Poupon won two Grands Prix each and it was a close battle between them. The former narrowly came out on top because he won the offshore race, but the differences between the two boats were slight. *Data General* had a larger roach to her main than *Fleury* and canted daggerboards with unusual scoops at their tips, whereas *Fleury*'s boards were of the more normal vertical kind. The canted boards seemed to have the edge and it was quite noticeable that when going to weather, *Data*'s boards were giving more lift.

At the second Grand Prix at Cherbourg the fleet had increased to 19 with the addition of three of the four British Formula 40s, including the new Phil Morrison-designed *Business Design Group*. Known as *Rebel* when she was without a sponsor, *Business Design Group* was meticulously built by Spud

Rowsell in Exmouth from strip planked cedar, with Proctor spars and beams. Her weight of 4188 lb (1900 kg) was quite respectable, but she, like her other British 40s, unfortunately fell foul of Formula 40 Rule One by lacking sufficient funding, which was not helped by her dismasting in the first race.

The wind was gusting up to 50 knots and *Data General* also lost her mast. *Biscuits Cantreau*, however, after a disappointing race at Brest due to her late launching, thundered around that first inshore course at Cherbourg to dispute any contention that trimarans are merely light-weather machines by finishing an incredible 24 minutes ahead of the Loic Pajot's Joubert/Nivelt-designed *Cahier Clairefontaine* in the two-hour race.

Starting just outside Cherbourg's massive harbour wall, the 'offshore' course was the first race for Randy Smyth's new catamaran *Renaulac*. Sister ship to *Chaffoteaux* and *Lessives Blanco* with forward rudders, *Renaulac* had the additional oddities of a rig

without a boom or a bowsprit, as well as a tiller that pointed the 'wrong way' from the top of the rudderstock and aft over the main beam. Smyth's helming position was thus more or less at the centre of the hull, an advantage for positioning crew weight. Yet all these well thought-out features were outweighed by a major error somewhere along the line which left *Renaulac* in the slings at Cherbourg weighing 4585 lb (2080 kg), 66 lb (30 kg) heavier than his previous boat *The Smyth Team*. *Renaulac* gracefully retired from the offshore race with rigging problems, but returned the following day only to dismast as she went through her first tack.

The offshore race was won by *Biscuits Cantreau* again, but with a new rig the next day it was *Data General* who returned with a vengeance, winning the final two inshore races with ease.

Rerigged at the next Grand Prix further east along the coast at Boulogne, Smyth's Hallspar mast again sprang overboard. Smyth believes it was due to the colossal loadings on the lightweight mast imposed by three sets of hydraulics, two for the spreaders and one for the mainsheet. Another, equally plausible suggestion was that it was the absence of a boom which was the root of the problem.

The Grand Prix was sailed mostly in Force 3–4 winds and was once again won by Le Maout's white catamaran *Data General*. One of the best performances in the race was from Loic Peyron who had chartered Serge Madec's season-old *Jet 40 Multiplast*, fitted it with a new Marechal mast and managed to finish 4th, racing with backing from his *Lada Poch* sponsor.

The Southampton Grand Prix offered more of a multihull extravaganza with the Confederation Life National Championships at the same time for the smaller micro-multihulls. Winner of the micros on elapsed time was an excellent new catamaran built at Gweek on the Helston River called the Firebird 26. She was designed by the chief structural engineer for British Aerospace, Martyn Smyth, who in the past has been the engineer behind many of Nigel Irens' most successful designs, including *Formule TAG* and *Apricot*. Smyth has also taken on the

François Richard

MULTIHULL RACING IN 1987

THE FAMOUS GROUSE
COUNTRY OF ORIGIN - SCOTLAND NOTED FOR
ITS CHARACTER AND DISTINGUISHED APPEARANCE

Quality in an age of change.

Chaffoteaux **crossed the narrow line between control and wipe-out at the Brest Grand Prix.**

Février

role of designer in conjunction with Barry Noble for Tony Bullimore's new *Apricot* trimaran which is intended for the 1988 Carlsberg Singlehanded Transatlantic Race.

Conditions were lighter for the races around the Solent and this really put *Biscuits Cantreau* in her element, although there was a tough battle between her and the Irens cats. During the Round the Island Race the next day she proved her exceptional upwind light weather ability on the beat out to the Needles, but was overtaken around St Catherines by both Irens boats. Fortune was smiling on *Biscuits* and her skipper Jean le Cam, as *Data* and *Fleury* were stuck in a wind hole short of the Forts and *Biscuits* was able to find wind inshore of them.

After a navigational error on the final inshore course which cost them the last race, *Biscuits* went on to win an additional race, the Chaffoteaux et Maury Challenge, up and down Southampton Water, to win the Grand Prix in convincing fashion.

The strong wind at the fifth Grand Prix, at Nieuwpoort, Belgium, blew some new life into the results table. Helming *The White Team* (ex-*The Smyth Team*) was the British Tornado ace Robert White. Equipped with a new set of Hood Spectra sails earlier in the season, he finished the offshore race 5th, a respectable performance bearing in mind her 551 lb (250 kg) weight disadvantage. The Grand Prix was sponsored by Belgian cigarette manufacturer Richmond, who feature their own superb Morelli-designed catamaran, skippered by Philippe Hanin, in their advertising campaign. The whole of Nieuwpoort seemed ablaze in their orange banners.

Once again, though, the Grand Prix belonged to *Data General*, even though she was rammed on the startline of the second inshore race by the previous *Biscuits Cantreau*, now skippered by 22-year-old Roland Jourdain and renamed *CDK le Media de la Mer* complete with a blinding metallic purple paint scheme.

Although there was some doubt as to

exactly who was organising Formula 40 early in 1987 (was it the Fédération Français de Voile or the International Formula 40 Association?), at the sixth Grand Prix, at Lake Geneva, a new International Formula 40 committee was formally established. It comprised five skippers, two members of the FFV, one member of the FIV (the Italian National Authority), a race organiser, a sponsor and a member of the United States Yacht Racing Union and the International Yacht Racing Union, which now recognises the class officially. This will give the Formula 40 circuit the firm foundation it requires if generous sponsors are to treat it seriously. Already there are Grands Prix planned for Sydney and Perth either side of Christmas, with another for San Francisco some time in 1988 – it looks as if the new committee was established in the nick of time.

The inland lake Grands Prix at Geneva and Garda suffered from very light winds which allowed Jean le Cam's *Biscuits Cantreau* trimaran to leave the catamarans for dead. After

the Grand Prix at Lake Garda, Pierre le Maout and *Data General* had lost their lead in the championship table to *Biscuits* and Poupon's *Fleury Michon*, who with monotonous regularity had come 2nd in all the Grands Prix.

By the time of the Sete Grand Prix, *Biscuits Cantreau*, *Fleury Michon* and *Data General* headed the table, all three boats within a point of each other. *Biscuits* went on to win the final Grands Prix at Sete, Barcelona, and Monaco. Even though her wins were less emphatic than in earlier series, it was enough to make Jean le Cam the international Formula 40 Champion.

James Boyd's special interest is the multihull arena. He has followed closely the multihull circuit both in Europe and overseas and his reports have appeared in many magazines.

MULTIHULL RACING IN 1987

Daniel Forster

Kos

Main picture: **Porto Cervo's 12-metre dock is the best in the world and played host to the world's finest Twelves.**

Right: **David Barnes collects the trophy for** *KZ-7*'s win from the Aga Khan.

Far right: **Masakazu Kobayashi exchanges burgees with Commodante Gianfranco Alberini of the Yacht Club Costa Smeralda at the sensational Japanese party.**

S A I L I N G   Y E A R

12-Metre World Championship

by KEITH WHEATLEY

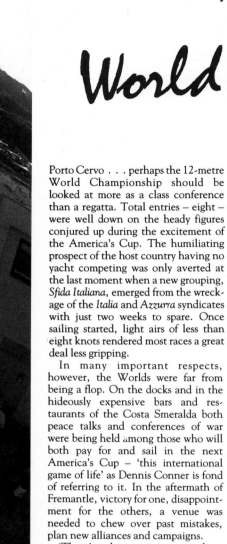

Porto Cervo . . . perhaps the 12-metre World Championship should be looked at more as a class conference than a regatta. Total entries – eight – were well down on the heady figures conjured up during the excitement of the America's Cup. The humiliating prospect of the host country having no yacht competing was only averted at the last moment when a new grouping, *Sfida Italiana*, emerged from the wreckage of the *Italia* and *Azzurra* syndicates with just two weeks to spare. Once sailing started, light airs of less than eight knots rendered most races a great deal less gripping.

In many important respects, however, the Worlds were far from being a flop. On the docks and in the hideously expensive bars and restaurants of the Costa Smeralda both peace talks and conferences of war were being held among those who will both pay for and sail in the next America's Cup – 'this international game of life' as Dennis Conner is fond of referring to it. In the aftermath of Fremantle, victory for one, disappointment for the others, a venue was needed to chew over past mistakes, plan new alliances and campaigns.

'There's a lot more going on here than just sailing', said John 'Chink' Longley, operations manager for the Bond syndicate. His Cup experience is virtually unparalleled in the modern era, having sailed his first campaign with Bond on *Southern Cross* in 1974. 'Most of the major players have come to Porto Cervo', he continued. 'There have been a lot of confidential discussions. People are positioning themselves. Other people are working out combinations of personnel.'

Longley himself was working for the most interesting newcomers to the 12-metre scene. During the final weeks of Fremantle, the Japanese property tycoon Masakazu Kobayashi purchased the Bond group lock, stock and genoas. *Australia III* was given a new livery and renamed *Bengal* for her entry in the Worlds under the flag of the Bengal Bay Club, the yachting and social club development that Kobayashi is establishing on the ruggedly beautiful coast south of Tokyo.

During the first week of the regatta he threw a party that made the syndicate's claim of a US$50 million campaign for the 1991 Cup seem credible, if not understated. Twelve Japanese chefs were flown in from Paris. Plans to airfreight the food direct from Tokyo had to be abandoned in the face of EEC agricultural regulations. A barrel of sake plus a full troupe of Kabake entertainers did make the 15-hour flight from Japan for a party estimated to have cost a cool US$100,000.

His yacht finished 2nd in the competition which made it all worthwhile for Mr Kobayashi. 'This syndicate wants credibility and I think they got that with the way the boat performed', said one of the Australian advisers who will continue to work with the Japanese. Colin Beashel helmed the boat, with Italian sailor Lorenzo Bortolotti as tactician. Plans to have Masakazu Kobayashi's right-hand man, Sam Amao, aboard as navigator did not materialise, although a Japanese grinder was there on the handles throughout the fleet race preliminaries which established the seedings for the match race finals.

New Zealand's *KZ-7* was the eventual winner and a popular one at that. The Kiwis had put up such a tremendous battle in Fremantle that there was a distinct, if inarticulate, desire to see them win some sort of trophy aboard the glassfibre Twelve. When it came, victory was finely balanced and the best-of-three final match against *Bengal* was ultimately decided in the protest room.

KZ-7 had won the first of the final races, beating *Bengal* easily. Colin Beashel badly misjudged his time-on-distance reckoning as *Bengal* ran into the startline and he opted to gybe round and sail back 50 yards to secure the committee boat end of the line. In doing so he arrived 18 seconds after the gun and *KZ-7* never lost the lead she had been handed, crossing the finish line 55 seconds ahead of the 1986 World Champion.

The second race was sailed in fresher breezes of around 16 knots and went to *KZ-7* by just over two minutes. *Bengal*, however, lodged a protest over a pre-start luffing incident and won back the race. Possibly David Barnes, the young Kiwi helmsman who had replaced Chris Dickson at *KZ-7*'s wheel at the behest of syndicate chief Michael Fay, had been getting overconfident, for on the next day he and his Californian tactician were more cautious and the start went to *Bengal*. The Australian/Japanese yacht led all the way around the track but was protested in the approach to a leeward mark for sailing below a proper course. It was the last buoy before the final beat to line and Barnes had chopped a 1m

57s lead to just 11s when the incident occurred.

The jury deliberated for five hours. *Bengal*'s crew celebrated – prematurely. Kay Beashel, newly wed to Colin, was furious with them and refused to leave her apartment until the protest was won or lost. Her choice was the wise one for in the end it was Barnes and his crew who were toasting their championship win.

In the New Zealand camp there was some mystification prior to the Worlds that wonder-boy helmsman Chris Dickson had been sacked. Until the finals of the Louis Vuitton challengers series in Fremantle his record had been stupendous. Losing to Dennis Conner in the challenger finals was no disgrace. 'Thirteen years beat thirteen months', was how Dickson put it at his parting press conference. Yet Dickson found himself in the cold while his *KZ-5* understudy, David Barnes, went to Sardinia and collected the laurels.

Bad blood existed between Michael Fay and Dickson. It was an open secret in Fremantle that the two men – so dependent on one another's talents – were barely on speaking terms. During the Sardinia World Championship Dickson gave a television interview back in New Zealand and made the somewhat rash prediction that he would never drive another Kiwi 12-metre whilst Michael Fay headed the syndicate. He implied that his demotion was the end result of Fay, merchant banker and principal investor in the 1987 New Zealand challenge, paying off personal scores.

Not surprisingly Fay denied this. He did it with a convincing argument. 'In late-1985 when we began our 12-metre campaign Chris was the only NZ sailor with serious match-racing experience. He was literally the only one we could go to, but as a businessman I don't like dealing with monopoly suppliers', explained Fay. By the time the next Cup rumbles round he wants to be in a position to choose from at least three or four Kiwi helmsman with international match-racing experience. 'Whatever the personal relationship between myself and Chris I can guarantee that if he is the best guy to drive the boat in '91, I'll hire him', said Fay.

It was an unsatisfactory regatta for the British. *White Crusader* had been brought from Fremantle to Sardinia and renamed *White Horse*, in honour of her principal sponsor. The yacht's livery was the most blatantly commercial of any competitor, with white

Carlo Borlenghi

The Yacht Club Costa Smeralda hosted the series and a number of parties. Their gracious club house overlooked the harbour at Porto Cervo and the visiting yachts.

Light airs plagued many of the races. Here Phil Crebbin coaxes *White Horse* over the Mediterranean slop.

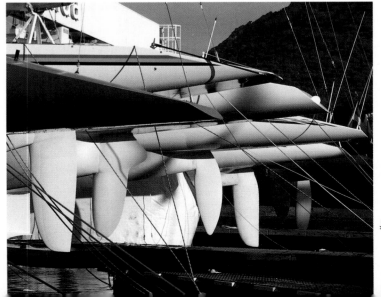

Kos

Hanging up to dry (left to right): *Entertainer, KZ-7, Bengal, Steak n' Kidney* and *White Horse*.

146

horses and whisky slogans adorning the previously severe white hull. Syndicate chairman, Graham Walker, was candid that one goal in Sardinia was to push the advertising relaxations of IYRU Rule 26 to the limits. With 1991 promising to be the most expensive America's Cup ever held, no commercial avenue can be left untested.

Phil Crebbin, technical director in Fremantle and longtime sailing companion of Harold Cudmore, was named skipper for the Worlds, with Derek Clark as tactician. Clark had recently left the *Kookaburra* syndicate where he served in the afterguard throughout the Fremantle campaign. He and Crebbin had sailed together in the Olympics, but it was a curious alliance since Clark had already contracted to work as technical director for the Blue Arrow challenge for the 1991 America's Cup. This had been put together by Chris Law and Peter de Savary.

In the fleet racing section of the regatta *White Horse* showed good boat speed but too often poor starts let the crew down. The hull had been fitted with the 3M friction-reducing riblets made de rigueur by Dennis Conner and *Stars & Stripes*. In addition, the plastic riblets were coated with a special low-friction paint developed in Sweden and unique to the British. Finishing in 5th place in the points table, the *White Horse* chiefs decided that the problems lay with the sailing team.

Harold Cudmore, fresh from a successful series of Admiral's Cup trials aboard *Indulgence*, came to Sardinia as tactician. Clark was 'let go', as the Victorians used to say of chambermaids who proved to be a difficulty. It made little difference to the results on the water since *White Horse* had qualified for the toughest semi-final group, containing *KZ-7* and *Kookaburra II*. Both boats beat the British entry and, to add insult to injury, so did the little-regarded *Sfida Italiana*.

Graham Walker had made the point before the regatta that, for technical and developmental reasons, the team had been keen to bring the radical David Hollom boat C2 to Sardinia. However, the need for immediate and medium-term sponsorship and team visibility swung the choice towards the proven ability of *White Horse*, the yacht that had been narrowly pipped for a Fremantle semi-finals place by *French Kiss*. For whatever reasons, the chosen yacht did not deliver the goods.

Meanwhile, on the waterfront, representatives from the two new British syndicates for 1991 were active. Chris Law was there for the Blue Arrow team, which is to be based in Falmouth, and Lawrie Smith represented the Smith/Howlett/Melrose consortium which seemed to have secured the initial backing of Richard Branson and the Virgin empire. In the British camp there was much talk of who had been offered jobs and who hadn't, but both Law and Smith were adamant that at this stage they were in the business of hiring designers and computer specialists, not grinders and trimmers. 'All I'm telling the sailors is: keep fit, don't get married, don't get Aids', joked Law, who says he has the expectation, but not the guarantee, of helming the Blue Arrow 12-metre.

After the egalitarian clumsiness of Fremantle, the European way of doing things came as a nasty shock to some of the crews. Down Under, sportsmen are gods, whereas in the Old World – particularly somewhere like Porto Cervo – a higher regard tends to be paid to the multi-millionaire owners and syndicate chairmen, watching the racing from luxury charter yachts. There were exceptions. Crewmen from *Australia III/Bengal* found themselves better off than ever before in their lives. The spartan Bond regime of bed, board and A$15 a day was replaced by showers of Yen and consequent ability to pick and choose among the waterfront restaurants. For most crew members from other syndicates, however, the regatta was a lesson in how little beer you can drink if it costs £2 a bottle.

Another entourage travelling in style was the one accompanying Dennis Conner. He brought 55 people on the personnel list for Dennis Conner Sports Inc. and another dozen or so for Dennis Conner Sports Television. It was Conner's first regatta since he won the America's Cup and an acute indication of how far the big helmsman had gone in turning sailing from a sport increasingly funded by business into a corporate endeavour that involves water.

Conner told everyone within earshot that it was costing US$1m to campaign *Stars & Stripes* in Sardinia – and that he was signing the cheques. Sail America had declined to enter the Worlds and DC had chartered the boat from them. He found his own sponsors in Ford, Pepsi, Merrill Lynch and Merit cigarettes. Even on the balmiest of race days, it was noticeable how *Stars & Stripes* flew heavyweight sponsor's spinnakers while the opposition, usually a good way in front, used gossamer-thin kites.

'I'm not here making a million dollars but my company has the potential to be enormously successful', said Conner as he organised his crew for a dockside poster-signing session. 'The opportunities for companies to merchandise their product is huge and will sell product in large quantities. People have done a good job merchandising their product through other upscale sports. Why not with yachting?'

Conner now talks 'Adspeak' like a man possessed. Where once he would wear down an inquisitor with minutiae about the previous day's tacking duel or his battles with Tom Blackaller, the great helmsman has now discovered

Business. In the period between retrieving the Auld Mug and the Worlds he had been hugely in demand by the US advertising industry, graced the cover of *Time* magazine, and done a tour of sixteen cities pushing his Cup book, *Comeback*, up on to the bestseller lists. A representative of the US publishers was in Sardinia, and while the book had done nothing like as well as John Bertrand's volume *Born to Win*, sales were regarded as excellent for a yachting book.

While Conner certainly failed to provide entertainment on the water – could he be blamed for bringing *Stars & Stripes* to a regatta where the weather would certainly not favour the heaviest of yachts? – on some of the key issues off the water he was dynamite. The most important was probably the decision of the International 12-metre Class Association technical committee to allow moveable wings on the next generation of Twelves.

John Marshall, Conner's design chief, and Malin Burnham, chairman of the *Stars & Stripes* syndicate, were instrumental in pushing the radical changes through the committee, but that did not stop DC laying into the implications of moveable wings. 'I have a concern that sailors are going to be playing this game of life for the satisfaction of designers and constructors', he complained. 'If this is still a sport then I think the guys out there on the water should have some substantial say in the final result. We're getting to be a smaller and smaller part of the whole thing.'

Conner's concern was not just an abstract one that the boats themselves will become too high-tech for the sailors to have any fun. Moveable wings and forward trim-tabs will mean a move into aircraft technology and add significantly to the already frightening cost of a 1991 Cup campaign. 'We're talking about boats alone that will cost five to ten million dollars to build with all their hydraulics and computers', Conner fulminated. 'I've been out there with the begging bowl and I know how hard it is to raise money. I'm concerned that the people running the 12-metre class don't seem to have any concern how high the budgets go.'

Even setting aside the issue of money, the current rules require 12-metre yachts to be designed and

12-METRE WORLD CHAMPIONSHIP

Sfida Italiana sailed with a crew culled from the Azzurra and Italia syndicates to ensure an Italian yacht would compete in the championships.

created in their country of origin. If moveable wings become the norm then countries like Denmark, Canada, Australia and Spain, which are without major aerospace industries, could be effectively debarred from the competition. 'You need quite a bit of money and science to develop things like moveable wings', said legendary Swedish Cup helmsman Pelle Petterson after the technical meeting. 'It's a move in favour of the big nations with a lot of scientific resources and not in the interests of a country like Sweden.'

On the other hand, nations don't come much smaller or more remote than New Zealand, but Kiwi syndicate chairman and backer Michael Fay is enthusiastic for the 12-metre class to embrace Star Wars technology. 'The wilder the better', exclaimed Fay. 'People don't watch the America's Cup because it's a safe little race sailed in safe little boats. The whole event is extreme and expensive and I don't see anything wrong with that. No-one has to play if they don't want to.'

At the same time that the class was deciding to throw itself into ever more expensive research programmes, a consensus emerged in the 12-metre association that it would be better not to hold a World Championship in 1988 – owing to lack of new boats and financial strength. Dreams of a Grand Prix-style circus for the Twelves with two or three events per year and an elite of career skippers seemed as far away as ever once Porto Cervo was over and done with. All eyes were on the next America's Cup.

Keith Wheatley has been a journalist since graduating in Law. He has reported for television and written columns for the London Evening Standard *and* Sunday Telegraph. *He moved to Fremantle in 1985 to write a book on the build-up to the Cup (*America's Cup: The Inside Story*) and covered events in Fremantle for* The Times, Sunday Times, Financial Times, Time Magazine *and* Melbourne Age. *He is now yachting correspondent of the* Sunday Times.

12-METRE WORLD CHAMPIONSHIP

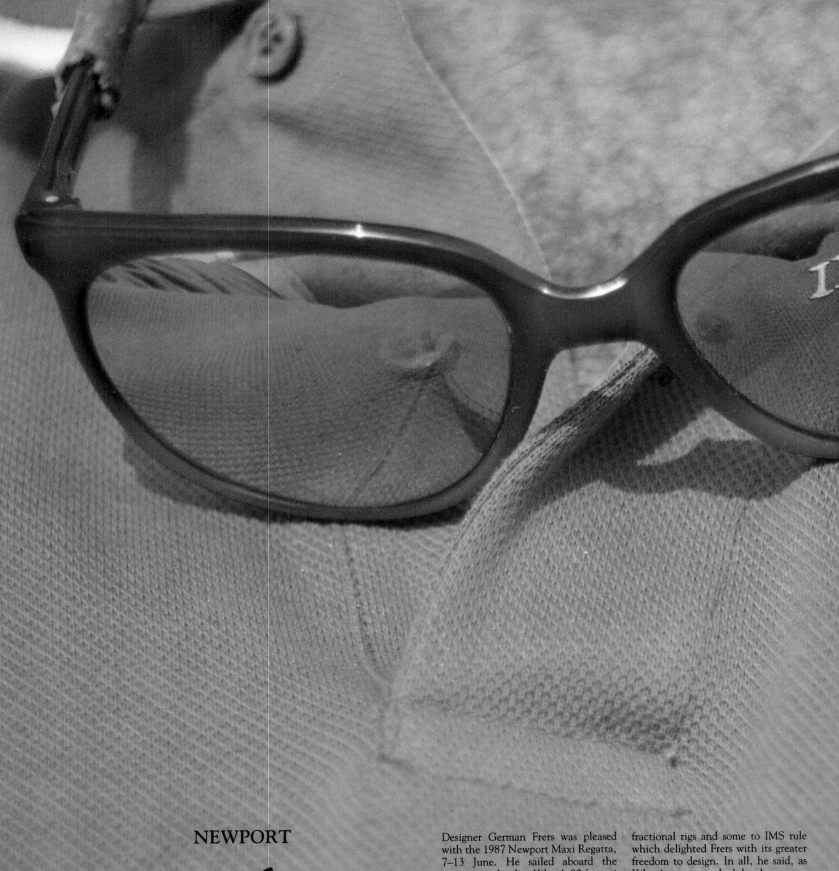

NEWPORT

Maxi Series

by GAIL SCOTT SLEEMAN

Designer German Frers was pleased with the 1987 Newport Maxi Regatta, 7–13 June. He sailed aboard the winning yacht, Jim Kilroy's 80 ft maxi *Kialoa V*, from his own drawing board. At the end of the regatta, *Kialoa* seemed well on her way to winning the International Class A Yacht Association (ICAYA) 1987 World Championship. The powerful yacht placed 1-6-1-3-1 in Newport, which provided the venue for the first half of the championship.

But then, Frers had a better than 80 per cent chance to have a winning design. All but two of the nine maxis racing the Newport regatta were Frers' designs. In addition, elsewhere five Frers maxis were taking shape in boatyards around the world, three with

fractional rigs and some to IMS rule which delighted Frers with its greater freedom to design. In all, he said, as Kilroy's crew uncorked the champagne after the last race, since 1979 he had designed 21 maxis, 'all different, all to different owner specifications.

'The secret,' he said, smiling, 'is no secret. It's hard work and knowledge and some inspiration.'

The two non-Frers maxis each raced in one of the two divisions at the regatta. Maxi-maxis, rating 70 ft IOR or close to it, raced Division I (the Blue Division, as it was titled), apparently in an effort to avoid qualifying the value of the yachts by size. Among them was the Gilles Vaton-designed *Milene V*, owned by Albert Mirlesse of Geneva, Switzerland, which did not

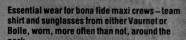

Essential wear for bona fide maxi crews – team shirt and sunglasses from either Vaurnet or Bolle, worn, more often than not, around the neck.

do well. In the process of being converted to a stripped-out round-the-buoys maxi, the yacht competed with an all-new crew, a new rudder and bulb keel, but less-than-new sails. Her last place was a disappointment to Vaton although the crew anticipated tuning and testing before the second half of the Worlds in September. Making up the remainder of the Blue Division boats were Bill Koch's *Matador*, George Coumantaros's formerly unbeatable *Boomerang*, Huey Long's *Ondine VII*, and Jim Kilroy's *Kialoa V*, the latter sporting a new keel and rudder, which, when combined with reballasting, enabled the once-tender maxi to outpoint the fleet.

Among the four mini-maxis (rated around 62.42) of the Yellow Division,

Sparkman & Stephens's *Obsession* fared far better than *Milene V*. *Obsession*, which is for sale as owner Stephen Nichols of Palm Beach attempts to curb his appetite for yachting competition, placed 2nd in the division. That put her behind the Frers-designed *Il Moro di Venezia II*, owned by Raoul Gardini of Ravenna, Italy, but ahead of sister ship *Emeraude*, owned by Jacques Dewailly of Villeneuve d'Ascq, France, and Charles Robertson's new (Frers) *Cannonball*, which was being finished as she pounded around the buoys in the often heavy-air regatta.

The fleet was scored overall as well as by division and competed for two individual race trophies and division match racing trophies. The awards

were the BMW Cups in the first race (won by *Kialoa* and *Il Moro*); the Mayor of Newport Trophies in Race Three, the distance race (won by *Kialoa* and *Obsession*); 1st in division (won by *Kialoa* and *Il Moro*); 1st in fleet overall (*Kialoa*); and 1st in division in the Rolex Match Race Series sailed the day following the regatta (won by *Ondine VII* and *Emeraude*).

The yachts were closely matched in their divisions, in contrast to the 1986 Newport maxi regatta when the newly launched *Kialoa* suffered from an experimental Dutch keel with trim tabs – 'not my design', Frers pointed out at the time. This time, however, it was *Matador* whose new keel worked less than perfectly, notably when working to windward in the strong

wind and channel currents in the first race.

Koch, a tall, quiet-mannered man who holds three graduate degrees from MIT, declined to name the designer. 'It's radical,' he said of the keel, 'but there are no wings attached. It is not as wide as the previous keel, more high aspect. It was great in tank testing, but in actual size it's side-slipping', he conceded.

By common consent, *Ondine* appeared to be the most powerful of the group, but problems dogged the year-old yacht, including tangling with one of the New England's omnipresent lobster pot lines in the first race. At the start of the distance race, *Ondine*'s recently repaired mast began to sway ominously. Huey Long and his helms-

man son, Russell, retired *Ondine* to retune. During the match racing, Huey Long was gashed by a flying batten. *Ondine* continued racing while crew member Dr Candi McCulloch tended the wound, but, said Russell, 'I lost concentration'.

With reasonably close boat speed in the fleet, tactical decisions and crew work made the difference.

In Race One, clockwise around Conanicut Island from a start off Goat Island, local knowledge sent many of the fleet into light air off Castle Hill to avoid the tide. *Kialoa*, with America's Cup-winning tactician Tom Whidden calling tactics, chose a better breeze to the west of the channel and rounded Brenton Reef tower first with a lead she

held for the rest of the race.

Boomerang, with L.J. Edgcomb and Robbie Haines assisting Coumantaros on tactics, won the start and was first at the windward mark in the second race, an Olympic triangle. *Ondine* then drove by her on the reaches, only to stall with a spinnaker wrap. *Kialoa* passed *Ondine* as the crew of the pale-blue boat struggled with the wrap, but at the last leeward mark of the race *Kialoa*'s spinnaker halyard jammed. The footloose spinnaker whipped out, throwing crew Merrick Pratt into the water.

'We didn't miss him at first', Whidden teased Pratt after the race. Recovering Pratt cost *Kialoa* five minutes and five places – time enough

for *Ondine* to recover 1st place.

In the 98-mile distance race, *Kialoa* overtook early leaders *Matador* (with Gary Jobson 'coaching') and *Boomerang*, after the two lead yachts tangled in a tacking duel that ended with a glancing collision and a disqualification for *Boomerang*.

Ondine was off to a fast start in the fourth race and led all the way around the 24.7-mile Olympic course.

Kialoa was in her element in the last stormy race. The fleet bucked strong southerly winds and confused ocean seas from Goat Island, south to Brenton Tower, where they turned and raced downwind to the top of Conanicut Island and back again. The wind moderated as the fleet ran north up the

channel, but *Kialoa* made the most of the start and tooth-rattling beat to the Tower and on the return beat to the finish sailed away from the fleet with her greater sail-carrying power.

During the match races on the day after completion of the fleet racing, ICAYA tried a new system for dealing with protests. The competing pairs were each followed by a jury boat with two judges aboard. The judges rendered instant decisions in disputes in an adaptation of the one-design 720° rule. Infringing yachts exonerated themselves by completing two 360° turns before proceeding. Not everyone was happy with the process but ICAYA president Coumantaros expected the class would continue to experiment

Sharon Green

Franco Pace

with the system.

'I'm encouraged by the growth in the class', said silver-haired real estate magnate Kilroy at the end of the regatta. (Kilroy was one of the founders of ICAYA when it was formed in Cowes in 1979). Coumantaros explained: 'We are a group of owners who built big boats and who decided to race together as a class. We are members of a sailing club.' Those words, however, draw a veil over the $750,000 annual cost needed to campaign a boat in this class.

Kilroy classified the present ICAYA competitive level as 'excellent'. 'I prefer this very aggressive active sport', he said, speaking for himself, but, perhaps also for the owner group as a

whole. 'I'm a participant. I drive my own boats . . . The sport is complex', he added. 'It's much more than administering 26 people [in the crew]. All of the planning and organisation I find challenging.'

Whether the class will continue to include Newport in its world-ranging schedule may now be in question. One of the city's attractions has been its deep water facilities, adjacent to other Newport pleasures. But the Williams & Manchester yard, where half of the 1987 fleet docked, has been sold for condominium development and the only other surviving working boatyard on Newport's condominium-walled waterfront is Newport Offshore, which seems destined to go the same way.

Main picture: **George Coumantaros's** *Boomerang* **was previously the boat to beat. Now she is herself outclassed by newer boats.**

Huey Long's *Ondine VII* (above) **was considered by many to be the fastest of the current maxi fleet. Inconsistent scores stopped her dominating her rivals.**

Gail Sleeman is a freelance photographer and journalist based in Connecticut. Among the journals she contributes to is Sail.

MAXI SERIES

PORTO CERVO MAXI SERIES

by PATRICK SMART

Even the new slimline, low-freeboard maxis dwarf the sailors who tame them. This is *Kialoa*'s crew preparing to peel spinnakers.

Generation gap: the new fractionally-rigged *Il Moro* (right) displays the latest in German Frers' design concepts. She leads the 1983-vintage *Boomerang* (main picture).

MAXI SERIES

On 2 September many of the sport's top players got the second half of the Maxi Worlds underway. They came to Porto Cervo to push nine boats around three Olympic-style courses, a 30-miler through the islands off the north-eastern Sardinia coast and a so-called long race of some 70 miles.

It could have been called the German Frers maxi show, as the circus packed its bags from the Newport series and travelled to the Mediterranean for a brief series in Palma before resuming the International Class A Yacht Association's World Championship. The show finished off the season with an extra series in Monaco and St Tropez where crews and owners unwound from the more serious Porto Cervo regatta.

While *Obsession* and *Cannonball* did not cross the Atlantic for the Mediterranean event, the fleet was boosted by Herbert Dahm's *Inspiration* and the debut of the radical *Il Moro di Venezia III*. Raoul Gardini's new boat succeeded his 70-footer which had done so well in the Newport series. More significantly, the new, bigger *Il Moro* is the first of a new generation of fractionally-rigged boats and she beat her rivals straight after her launch in the Palma series. In the Copa del Rey she was 1st overall with an impressive three wins from four races.

Newcomer to Class A sailing was Gianni Varasi, owner of the appropriately named *Othello*, a sister ship to *Emeraude*, formerly known as *Il Moro di Venezia II*.

When the fleet arrived in Porto

Cervo, everything was set for a good series: the boats were ready and the 'rock stars' had arrived. The only thing that looked capable of marring the prospects for the series was the good breeze which had been blowing for days already – often the kiss of death in the Med. Fortunately, it was never light for the duration of a race.

The first race started in 10 knots and proved to be the closest of the series. *Il Moro* had the best start, hitting the line on starboard at speed, sailed the first beat well, which turned into a one-tack leg, to reach the weather mark ahead. The next two legs were a run and jib reach, a parade in which *Kialoa V*, disadvantaged by her lack of waterline length, was trapped in 4th place. At the leeward mark *Boomerang*

split tacks with *Il Moro*, having rounded in 2nd place. Working the left-hand side of the course, *Boomerang* found a good header, tacked on it and rounded the second weather mark just ahead of *Il Moro*.

But *Boomerang's* elation was short-lived, for a crewman had fallen overboard during the spinnaker hoist. Luck was on the side of the big, midnight-blue boat, for her spinnaker turtle sausage had not opened properly which enabled the crew to keep the chute hoisted but not broken out while the boat was gybed round so the man could be picked up. *Boomerang* lost only two places in the incident.

On the third beat, *Kialoa* sailed in clear air and showed her mettle, with her good stability and ideal sail area for

strong upwind speed. She led the fleet at the top mark and held on until the finish, *Il Moro* chasing in hot pursuit.

Jim Kilroy won the race with *Kialoa* on corrected time, but *Emeraude* – with Dennis Conner aboard for the series – was 2nd, and *Il Moro*, in the hands of Paul Cayard, 3rd.

Similar conditions held for the second race; Conner guided *Emeraude* home to a fleet win ahead of *Il Moro* with *Othello* 3rd. But *Kialoa's* 4th enabled her to cling on to the championship lead.

The distance race got underway with a one-mile beat, in 12 knots of wind, followed by an 18-mile run which saw *Boomerang*, *Il Moro* and *Ondine* head out to sea while *Matador*, *Kialoa*, *Emeraude* and *Othello* worked along the

shore. The offshore pack lost out when they were becalmed off Porto Rotondo and rounded the next mark 10 minutes behind the leaders who were beating onwards towards Bonifacio on the southern tip of Corsica. With the wind rising to 20 knots, *Matador* and *Kialoa* had an exciting tacking duel through the islands before running home.

The final part of the course required the boats to turn past a small mark just off Porto Cervo to give a short beat into the line. When the leaders arrived however, the light on the buoy was out and neither *Matador* nor *Kialoa* rounded it before finishing.

Controversy ensued. When *Kialoa* checked by radio to see if the race committee had taken her time she was told that she had not finished cor-

Kos

rectly. *Matador* overheard this and both boats turned around, found the buoy and finished correctly. *Il Moro* was quick to lodge a protest, claiming that the boats had received outside assistance.

The expectation among the crews was that *Kialoa* and *Matador* would be penalised, so there was surprise – and a little anger – when the Jury announced the next day that the two were not being penalised. In fact, they were awarded 12 minutes redress for time spent looking for the mark.

In the third and final triangle *Emeraude* sailed a very good race in mostly light air to win a minute and a half ahead of *Il Moro* on corrected time. At the start, Dennis Conner took *Emeraude* to leeward of *Matador*,

Ondine and *Kialoa*, forcing them all over the line early. *Boomerang* led for the first three legs and headed right after rounding the bottom mark but was soon passed by *Il Moro*, which seemed to have a good edge in boat speed.

At the next mark, all the boats gybe-set their spinnakers with the smaller *Emeraude* and *Othello* executing normal bear-away sets. They got out to the right of the course and made out like bandits. *Othello* gybed back earlier than *Emeraude* to consolidate her gain and found she'd lost her advantage. *Il Moro* pulled herself back to 2nd in the last two legs having slipped to 3rd, while *Kialoa* ended up with a 6th and *Ondine* had her best result of the series with a 3rd.

At this stage, Jim Kilroy and *Kialoa V* had the World Championship sewn up, with a 12-point advantage over 2nd-placed *Matador*. Kilroy did not need to do the last race but, in typical *Kialoa* fashion, the white maxi not only sailed but she also beat *Il Moro* by 55 seconds to win. *Kialoa* led from the start, with *Il Moro* close behind but never able to overtake. The 35-knot breeze held for most of the race. It did back down a little, though not before a halyard winch let go on *Boomerang*, forcing her to retire with an injured crewman. A special mention should go to Herbert Dahm's Ron Holland-designed, fully fitted-out cruising maxi *Inspiration* which could not compete in this last race. She sailed doggedly in all the others despite being way out of

touch with the rest of the fleet.

Kialoa's win secured the overall ICAYA World Championship though she had to share the Rolex Cup for the Porto Cervo series as she was tied on points with *Emeraude*.

As is now common in ICAYA events, the fleet racing was rounded off with a quick match race series. *Ondine*, *Kialoa*, *Boomerang* and *Matador* went out in 25-knot winds for their races, with *Matador* beating arch-rival *Boomerang* and *Kialoa* dispensing with *Ondine* to make for a close final.

Matador's tactician, Gary Jobson, put the boat on the startline slightly ahead and to leeward of *Kialoa*. Tom Whidden responded with his much-used and highly successful tactic of shooting *Kialoa* right up to gain

valuable ground to windward and clear air. Within a few minutes, *Kialoa* demonstrated the advantage of her superior stability. While *Matador* feathered her mainsail and heeled excessively in the puffs, *Kialoa* was able to stay on her feet with sails driving. She soon climbed out to weather and ahead, where she remained all the way to the finish.

While the owners, 'rock stars' and other crews flew home for a short respite, the permanent crews headed north to Monaco where the Moët et Chandon Maxi Cup was staged. After the crucial points series in Porto Cervo, this was a much more relaxed affair. Ashore, the owners were entertained to dinner in the presence of Their Highnesses Prince Rainier and

Prince Albert in the super-smart Hotel de Paris, while even the crews were given a champagne reception and candlelight dinner in the Sporting Club's remarkable Salle d'Etoiles.

Light air plagued the triangle race in Monaco and it was even softer for the feeder race to St Tropez – just two and a half knots at the start. Despite the course being shortened off Cannes, the purpose of the race was served by delivering the maxi roadshow to the tiny port of St Tropez. Despite being one of the most popular of the super-chic towns on the Côte d'Azur, the former fishing port has not been spoilt by high-rise building. Indeed, the maxis towered comfortably above the quayside cafés and rambling buildings of the town behind. Few buildings

came up to second spreader level.

While the four races were taken seriously, the social side ashore was anything but. The water-fights embraced the innocent pastis-sipping spectators in the bars, while the flash-bang firecrackers which were let off were only partially successful in drowning out the live music of the competing restaurants in the Place de Lys. And then there was the Miss Maxi competition, about which the least said the better. Suffice it to say that those normally upstanding pillars of the international sailing community, Commodante Gianfranco Alberini and Harold Cudmore, took their judging of the Miss Maxi contestants most conscientiously.

It was the perfect antedote to a long,

tough and serious season of maxi sailing.

Patrick Smart sailed onboard Boomerang *and* Kialoa V *during the 1987 season.*

Raoul Gardini is as pleased as a maxi owner with two wheels. His new fractionally-rigged *Il Moro di Venezia III* **showed good potential** (main picture).

Above: **Harold Cudmore gets to grips with judging the spaghetti section of the Miss Maxi competition at St Tropez.**

MAXI SERIES

Cowes, 1–9 August

SANDHURST

Cowes Week

by STUART WOODS

A helicopter's eye view of the Royal Yacht
Squadron. The Squadron line is the fulcrum of
Cowes Week racing.

HRH Prince Philip (white cap) was joined by
ex-King Constantine of Greece (peaked cap)
aboard Sir Owen Aisher's *Yeoman XXVI* for
some early Cowes Week racing.

Cowes Week starts, officially, with the start of the Channel Race, on Friday evening, but each year there is some subtle point at which a spiritual beginning of the regatta is made. Two years ago, when the maxi racing and then the Swan Regatta were piled up ahead of the event, Sandhurst Cowes Week seemed to last a month. This year, it seemed not to begin until the time of the first Champagne Mumm Admiral's Cup race, but to anyone who attended the balls of the three major yacht clubs on successive nights, as I did, the week still seemed a month long.

The hangover is as much a part of the regatta as the sparkle of the sun on the water or the boom of a Squadron cannon, and to confirm this, one has only to venture into Ancasta Marina or the High Street before noon to see the puffy faces and dazed expressions of people who are about to sail 30 miles up and down the Solent, kept going only by the adrenalin-producing, hyper-electric, alcoholic buzz that is Cowes Week.

There are certain constants that tie one Cowes Week to the next and to the one before: hundreds of yachts in dozens of classes race each other around the buoys (sometimes even around the Island), each day; from ten in the morning until two in the afternoon, a race starts every five minutes; each evening there is at least one major cocktail party to attend, and many minor ones; on three nights (four in an Admiral's Cup year) there are full-bore, black-tie balls, starting at 10.0 p.m. and ending with dawn's early light; and on Friday night there are fireworks. But to rely on these events for a description of Cowes Week

is inadequate, for when three or four thousand yachtsmen, accompanied by another ten thousand of their wives, girlfriends (sometimes both), children, in-laws and various other hangers-on all congregate in a Victorian village on the Isle of Wight's north shore, something synergistic happens that can be felt in the earth, sniffed on the breeze, and heard in the hum of voices and the slapping of steel halyards against aluminium masts. It is *Cowes Week*, by God, and there is nothing else anywhere that is remotely like it.

In this year of the Champagne Mumm Admiral's Cup, Cowes Week switched on in the hour or so before the 42 yachts representing 14 countries left their berths for the first race. There was more than just excitement, there was anxiety, even raw fear vibrating in the air as diesels were started and warps slipped. Quietly, the crews made their way down to the starting line beyond Osborne Bay, only to suffer two hours of postponements before enough of a breeze came up to make a start. Anti-climax is a part of Cowes Week, too.

The Danes came out of the first inshore race ahead on points, only to be overtaken as the Brits thundered through in the Channel Race to take the lead, with Harold Cudmore on Graham Walker's *Indulgence* overcoming a poor start and hours of weed on the prop to rise from 31st to 8th place. They held their lead through the next two inshore races, only to slip behind the Kiwis in Christchurch Bay in the last race. The Fastnet, as is often the case in Admiral's Cup racing, could be the determining factor, but merely confirmed the Kiwis as the new holders of the Cup.

But the Admiral's Cup is only a dollop of cream on the huge gateau of racing that is Cowes Week. The Sigmas, the Contessas, the Darings and X-Boats, the dozens of classes sailed by thousands of Corinthians, make up the main body of events. The same faces are out there each year – Ernie Juer, Tim Herring, Bob Fisher, Peter Nicholson, Chris Dunning, Sandy Woodward, Robin Aisher – all those who, even if they are not sailing for Britain, sail for pure pleasure.

There was, as always, a royal presence in Cowes. On Friday evening, HRH Prince Philip came ashore at the Squadron steps to be greeted by ex-King Constantine of Greece and the best Cowes Week weather in years. The Royal Yacht, *Britannia*, was being refitted in Plymouth, but the Royal Navy guard ship was there, anyway. It was an open secret that the royals were staying at The Prospect, the late Sir Max Aitken's comfortable home built inside the old Ratsey & Lapthorn sail loft. Royalty-watchers were thrilled by the sight of the ex-King and the Prince strolling down the High Street towards their berth aboard Sir Owen Aisher's *Yeoman XXVI* or his son's *Yeoman XXVII*.

That wasn't the only ogling that got done during the week, either. The girls, as always, were delectable, and an ancient Chelsea Pensioner, resplendent in scarlet tunic and medals, could be seen parked on a bench in the middle of the village, leering at the passing parade.

The social whirl began, as always, on Monday night, with the Royal Yacht Squadron Ball, still the hottest ticket in town and the subject of much speculation on the part of those who

don't go. The Royal Corinthian Ball came on Tuesday, followed by the Royal London, on Wednesday. (Perhaps some day the Corinthian will move their ball to Friday and give everyone a bit of respite between events). On Thursday, the Champagne Mumm Admiral's Cup Ball happened at Northwood House, the only non-club ball during the week.

The major cocktail parties were, as always, the Royal Ocean Racing Club's, on the Squadron lawn, the Royal Naval Sailing Association's, in the John Powers' back garden, overlooking the marina, and the parties thrown by the various Admiral's Cup teams. The America's Cup reared its head, too, with a bash hosted by Admiral Sir Ian Easton and Graham Walker in the artefact-filled dining hall at the Prospect of Cowes, now a museum. Peter de Savary was seen to arrive at the door, then go into earnest discussion with New Zealand banker Michael Fay, Chris Whitty of the Virgin Group and Graham Walker. A party maybe, but an opportunity to discuss business too. De Savary's *Blue Arrow* (*Victory '82* with her new sponsor's paint job) was plying the Solent, joined later in the week by Harold Cudmore on *White Crusader* as the rival America's Cup groups vied for publicity.

The private parties abounded, too. Bob Fisher won honours for originality when he plugged the cockpit drains on his yacht, *Barracuda of Tarrant*, and filled the well with rum punch (and maybe a couple of old Topsiders). The various terraces at Osborne Court overflowed, and Laura Aitken Mallet threw her annual fireworks night bash at The Prospect.

Finishing at Cowes involves threading through
moored visitors, be they Royal Navy guardship
or Edwardian motor yacht.

SANDHURST COWES WEEK

A classic view of the Cowes waterfront as passers-by watch the Swallows starting from the Squadron line just by the Parade.

But if much was the same at Cowes Week, change was afoot, too. The old Groves & Guttridge Marina has been bought by Ancasta, the yacht broking and new boat marketing group, and a general tarting-up has begun. Most of the old sheds on the sites were razed (but not the huge and ugly main shed), the chandlery was closed and divided into several smaller, smarter shops and galleries, and a new arrangement of marquees – pubs, restaurants and hospitality suites – went into effect. Nobody seems to know exactly what to expect from Ancasta in their takeover, but major redevelopment is clearly the plan. A lot of people would like to see the main shed make way for a sort of yachting village, à la Newport, but there are fears that if the shed does go,

it might be replaced by something taller and uglier. The marina is right at the heart of Cowes and Cowes Week, and we can only hope that future changes on the site are made with due regard for the character of the the town and the sensibilities of the marina's customers and neighbours.

The marina, whatever its ownership, continued to be every bit as much a social centre as any of the Cowes yacht clubs, especially for the young and the visitors. It would be interesting to survey the Admiral's Cup teams and learn exactly how many people constitute a retinue for a single yacht. In the absence of hard facts, let us guess. There will be a crew of ten or so. Add a wife or girlfriend (or both) for half of them, four or five shore crew

and half a dozen warm bodies from the sponsors, and you have maybe 25 or 30 per yacht? Multiply that by 42 and plop them down at the temporary pubs and restaurants in the marina, surrounded by the year-round berth holders, a gaggle of equipment manufacturers and a great many yachting journalists, all drinking incessantly with both hands, and you have one hell of a crowd of people milling around the marina, awash in Swan Lager and Pimm's. The Mumm champagne would be saved for when the sun goes down.

The question of sponsorship for yachting has been answered, ringingly, in the affirmative, and the results were everywhere at Cowes Week. The shipping container, previously a status symbol afforded only by the maxis, is

now a fact of life, and Ancasta had to figure out what to do with the things. The problem was niftily solved by stacking a row of them on top of another, building a sort of deck of scaffolding to service the upper ones. Inside these steel boxes one could find almost anything in the way of tools, from a simple hand drill to a lathe. Inside the containers, tea was often taken, and on top of them, leggy sunbathers pared down onlookers' former notions of the minimum size possible for a bikini.

Chartered Admiral's Cuppers' names had been hastily changed from the private to the commercial, with appellations like *Irish Independent* and *Jameson Whiskey* replacing the traditional ones. Heights of commercialism

The Sparkman & Stephens-designed *Stormy Weather* came back to Cowes after a refit. It was from Cowes that she started the 1935 Fastnet Race from which she emerged the winner.

Beken of Cowes

The X1-Designs, of pre-First World War origin, are always one of the numerically strongest classes at Cowes, competing for their annual championship.

The traditional finale to Cowes Week is the Friday night fireworks display, each year seemingly bigger, better and louder than the last.

SANDHURST COWES WEEK

Racing, even keelboats as elegant as Dragons, is not always unremitting pleasure.

Kos

(and simplicity) were achieved by the Australian team, which named its yachts *Swan Premium I*, *Swan Premium II* and *Swan Premium III*. They became a familiar sight, sailing abreast into the harbour, flying identical black spinnakers bearing the name of their sponsor, Swan Lager. There seem to be only two ways in which the display of sponsors' names can be further employed: one is to turn actual racing sails into billboards; the other is to turn yachts' hulls into multiple billboards, in the manner of racing cars, plastering them with dozens of product names used on board – Lewmar! North! Sparcraft! Durex!

Fireworks night is, of course, the highlight of every Cowes Week, making even the start of the Fastnet the following morning seem anticlimactic. This year's Friday night was no exception, with the crowd, once again, counting out the thrilling explosions of light and sound. Ideally, one should borrow a child with whom to witness the spectacle and this is not hard, since so many adults become children again when the fireworks start. This Cowes Week, there was something different. In the past many people on boats have used the fireworks display as an excuse to set off their out-of-date parachute flares, but last year, one was fired horizontally, and a yachtsman was struck in the chest and died. This year, there was a firm ban on flares, with notice given in clubs and the yachting press, and the Cowes Harbourmaster and the police launch, *Ashburton*, were

on hand for enforcement. Some pride may be taken by all that not a single flare was fired, and everyone survived. One hopes this will be a permanent condition.

Cowes Week ended, as it always does in an Admiral's Cup year, with the start of the Fastnet. The crowds gathered, under the first leaden skies of the week, on the Parade and on the Royal London terrace and on the Squadron Lawn to watch the thrashing about that precedes the greatest of all ocean races. The start was postponed for twenty minutes to give the no-doubt apprehensive captain of a container ship time to plough through the middle of the fleet, then they were off, the smaller classes first, followed shortly by the larger boats. Baron

Edmund de Rothschild's *Gitana* and Marvin Green's *Nirvana*, the only two maxis racing, gave the crowds a particular thrill, then the Admiral's Cuppers did their final dance and plunged across the Squadron Line. Soon, they were gone to all but the few enthusiasts who raced in their cars past Yarmouth to watch the fleet sail through the Narrows and into the Channel.

The marina emptied, the hydrofoils and ferries filled, and those of us left sipped one last Pimm's and began the long task of resting up for next year's Cowes Week.

Stuart Woods is an author who divides his time between Atlanta, Georgia, and Cowes. He is a member of the New York YC and the Royal Yacht Squadron.

RODEO one ton cup

The RODEO crew has been testing RODEO's maritime collection under regatta conditions for three years.

The yachts at the starting line for the RODEO one ton cup '87 naturally included RODEO. She was the only boat to be sailed by an all-female crew.
The 12 RODEO girls proved themselves to be not only sailors worthy of respect, but also charming hostesses. The RODEO lay day in particular, with its entertaining programme, provided all those taking part in the regatta with a needed rest from the hard days of sailing.

Roger Lean-Vercoe

CHAMPAGNE MUMM

Admiral's Cup

by TIM JEFFERY

To most eyes, Christchurch Bay is a rather pleasant place on England's South Coast. To the east lie the chalk cliffs of the Isle of Wight running out to the Needles. To the north are the shores of Barton, Christchurch and Bournemouth with their rows of retirement homes, while to the south and west lies little else but sea.

It is also a good place for a yacht race and in 1987 it was where the most decisive battles of the Champagne Mumm Admiral's Cup were staged. The offshore Channel and Fastnet Races may have counted for more points but in Christchurch Bay German hopes to win the Cup for a record third successive time were dashed; British expectations of winning it back simply expired; and the Kiwi plan to grab the Cup for the first time ran its course smoothly.

The Kiwis won by beating the Germans at their own game: they came into the series the best prepared of the 13 nations, their three boats enjoying good but not exceptional speed, and their crews were confident they could sail percentage series in minimising risks and maximising points-winning places. It all worked out, to give the Kiwis their first win of the AC in seven attempts, crowning their successes on race courses all round the world in all manner of classes.

For the Germans, Christchurch Bay became something of a graveyard for their masterplan, though to everyone's surprise the wounds were self-inflicted. The fourth weather mark of the third inshore race was their undoing. *Diva* was the big boat of their team; her launch just three weeks before the trials edged out the fancied *Pinta* and *Rubin* X from the team. Willi Illbrück

took *Pinta* off into the Austrian team as he had done for the previous two series. With some irony then, *Diva's* helmsman, Bernie Beilken, found his way to the layline for the mark blocked by *Pinta*, in addition to *Original Beckmann* from Denmark and *Marisa Konica* from Italy. Beilken tried to tack under the line of the starboard tack boats and squeeze up to the mark but failed.

The Germans' self-destruct attitude reappeared minutes later when *Saudade* headed into the same mark with a clutch of one tonners. She underestimated the tide which was taking yachts down onto the mark and she touched it, but in rerounding it she managed to balk others including Alan Gray's Farr 40 *Jamarella* sailing for England. Helmsman Rodney Pattisson pulled off a Houdiniesque feat of threading *Jamarella* through the seemingly insufficient gap left between *Saudade* and the mark. But by then the damage was done, for the Germans were penalised by the jury that evening. *Diva* moved back from 16th to 24th and *Saudade* fell from 26th to 43rd.

The seeds of the German failure were sown before the series. *Diva*, for instance, surprised many by making the team when she had spent such a short time in the water. If she beat the fully worked-up *Rubin* X and *Pinta* so easily, had the Judel & Vrolijk big boats got enough speed? Fast or slow, *Diva* arrived in England after spending a night on the sands off Heligoland in the North Sea (she had picked up debris in her propeller while negotiating a narrow channel) which had put her keel out of true. Despite straightening the keel with hydraulic jacks, there was no time to get it 100 per cent before the series began.

Ancasta Marina, home of the series, was busy with crews, supporters and spectators throughout the event.

ADMIRAL'S CUP

Franco Pace

To add to the Germans' problems, an illness affected Berend Beilken in the first race of the CMAC, sailed in the Solent, which meant that Achim Griese had to be flown in to take the helm. Griese may be a top sailor, but he was completely new to the boat and it didn't work out.

As for *Saudade*, she had spent the early months of 1987 tuning up off Palma, Mallorca. This gave her great light-air speed but the 15 to 20 knot winds of the AC were a new experience. The same could be said of the Germans' other one tonner, *Container*, a new style of boat from the Hanseatic duo of Rolf Vrolijk and Freidrich Judel. Her crew, which included Vrolijk as tactician, were happy with their speed until they hit unfamiliar conditions. The German trials were sailed mainly in winds of 5 to 10 and 25 to 30 knots, and it took *Container*'s crew until the third AC race to achieve optimum VMG numbers in the middle ranges. Apparently helmsman Gerd Eirmann had a liking for plenty of weather helm but this was putting the keel on the limit of its optimum. The crew eventually found that easing the running backstay depowered the rig, got the keel working better and made VMG jump three-tenths.

'We didn't have an inherent speed problem with our boats or lack preparation', explained Rolf Vrolijk. 'Our problems were experience. The conditions in England were not normal and on *Container* our helmsman had no international experience. We are still amateurs in Germany and it shows. We have normal jobs to go to and when we reach a peak with our boats we forget about the basics. Sailing as amateurs doesn't work any more in competition

Kos

Randy Short's Reichel/Pugh 45 *Sidewinder* was the top inshore yacht of the series.

this intense.'

The same could be said for the British. Apart from the likes of Lawrie Smith and Rodney Pattisson who masterminded *Jamarella*'s campaign, Harold Cudmore who skippered Graham Walker's *Indulgence*, and Neil Graham who trimmed *Juno*'s mainsheet, the remainder of the crews were largely genuine amateurs. However, this is not the reason why the British failed to win, for their boats were certainly good enough and they had spent many hours on the water in practice and in trials.

More than anything else it was the old British problem of turning three crews and their skippers into a single fighting unit where the Cup comes first and individual honours are secondary. It was not until the Fastnet Race that firm orders from team manager Stuart Quarrie and captain Graham Walker were laid down about marking the opposition. By then it was too late, for Britain was lying second behind the Kiwis and needed to make up 22 places in one race.

Before that, the Kiwis had been able to sail as they pleased. 'We couldn't believe it when all three British boats went to the right-hand corner on the first beat of the second race in Christchurch Bay', said *Kiwi*'s skipper Peter Walker.

In Plymouth, when the British had to explain their loss they did not disguise their shortcomings. Alan Gray admitted: 'We had been trialling in Christchurch Bay and therefore we all thought we could win the race individually. It was a coincidence we all went right for although we had frequent briefings there were no team tactics.' Team captain Graham Walker

The Farr one tonner *Swan Premium II* sets her black-and-yellow spinnaker against a dark sea.

ADMIRAL'S CUP

THE CHAMPAGNE MUMM ADMIRAL'S CUP.

No Excuse To Go Overboard With The Bubbly.

MUMM CORDON ROUGE. THE CHAMPAGNE THAT'S TOO GOOD TO WASTE.

Bert Dolk's *Pro-Motion V* from Holland beats upwind against a backdrop of smaller boats during the 3rd Inshore Race held in Christchurch Bay.

Mayurca from Spain, a Gonzales-designed one tonner, leads the pack around the gybe mark in the 3rd Inshore Race *(top)*.

The Judel/Vrolijk one tonner **Container** beats into the confused seas of Hurst Narrows during the Channel Race *(bottom)*.

dismayed many with his very honest assessment: 'I don't think we raced this AC as a team. We had good rapport this time but not the discipline of the Kiwis.'

So why were the Kiwis so good? First, they were prepared. Manager Don Brooke said in Plymouth after the Fastnet finale: 'We believe we won the Cup 24 months ago', for the Kiwis had taken counsel from everyone who had ever sailed for New Zealand and they had held regular meetings at the Royal NZ Yacht Squadron.

Second, they enjoyed better back-up than they had in previous series, bringing with them their own forecaster, sailmaker (John Clinton from *KZ-7*) and coach (Olympic gold medallist Rod Davis). The Californian seems increasingly likely to play a pivotal role in Michael Fay's America's Cup plans. More importantly, he had the respect of the sailors so he was able to coach them hard, with the kid gloves off if necessary.

Third, Kiwi crews are now formidably good with most of the AC yachts enjoying afterguards who had notched impressive scores in Kenwood Cup, Southern Cross, Ton Cups and Admiral's Cup competition, together with shop floor crews with Whitbread Races and 12-metre campaigns behind them.

Finally, they had good boats. That didn't make them unique or overwhelmingly superior for it was only series top yacht *Propaganda*, sailed by Brad Butterworth and Peter Lester, that was demonstrably faster than her peers (upwind in medium to fresh conditions). Another Farr boat in the team was Peter Walker's 34 rater *Kiwi* and she proved to be the strong all-rounder he was seeking. The team's second one tonner was *Goldcorp*, the former *Mad Max* which had been extensively revamped and lightened by designer Laurie Davidson and her skipper Tom Dodson.

The Races

1st Inshore Race, Solent

By the time the crews left the marina, they would have had long enough to note how Ancasta's ownership had transformed the traditional home of the series. At last, the marina was properly dredged, the shower facilities upgraded and space provided for shipping containers, complete with spare gear and sails. Decked out with all manner of bars, for both food and

drink, as well as live entertainment, Ancasta Marina looked like the home of a big-time event. The crowds proved it. On the first Saturday of the series it was jumping: 15,000 people crowded into the assorted marquees, leaving Cowes High Street comparatively quiet.

It was quiet on the water, too. A postponement greeted the fleet assembled in the eastern Solent. Eventually a 6 to 10 knot north-easterly permitted a start for a race which both began and ended with a beat and a committee boat line. Gone it seems are the parking lots at Egypt Point as the fleet bunches on the approach to a finish line off the Royal Yacht Squadron.

The 24-mile course gave competitors a pretty good route, given the constraints of the Solent itself. Of the teams expected to do well, only the Danes lived up to their billing. Their Niels Jeppeson-designed and built boats, the X 1-Tons *Stockbroker Lief Jensen* and *Andelsbanken*, and the X 2-Ton *Original Beckmann Pletfjerner* (it's a stain remover), excelled in the light air and flat water. The X 1-Tons have always been strong in these conditions; their big hulls are pushed hard in terms of rating with bumps and distortions but it permits lofty sail plans. Indeed, to see *Andelsbanken* alongside *Juno* was a revelation. *Juno* is very much of the small, easily driven hull school, topped off by a moderate sail plan. That said, it was still a surprise to see her rig end two feet under that of the X 1-Ton.

But the Danes had their moment of glory for they topped the leaderboard after this race (just as they had done in 1985) with *Original Beckmann* taking best corrected time backed up by *Andelsbanken* at 20th and *Stockbroker* at 23rd.

The Kiwis threw some observers off the scent with *Goldcorp* being over the line at the start and having to struggle in the wash of inconsiderate spectator and TV boats.

But *Indulgence* will be remembered best for taking a flier well into the race when she was lying 9th on corrected time. She chose to split from the pack who were hugging the mainland shore and head out into the foul tide on a spinnaker run to Kemps. Navigator David Arnold claimed the crew were looking for a freeing and freshening

ADMIRAL'S CUP

LAGER BEER AT ITS BEST.

wind, a premise plausible enough for *Container* to try the same tactic. But the wind died and backed and *Indulgence* slumped, along with hopes that the British could put together an error-free series.

Channel Race

Harold Cudmore, Eddie Owen and *Indulgence*'s top drawer crew drawn from the ranks of *Phoenix* and *White Crusader* redeemed themselves in the Channel Race.

The course for the 210-miler had been changed especially for the Admiral's Cuppers from the normal triangle with two long cross-Channel legs to a multi-leg course. The fleet headed out from Cowes, through Hurst Narrows, past the Needles to Poole Fairway, back east by the Isle of Wight before completing two small triangles and returning to the Solent to finish near Portsmouth.

The Royal Ocean Racing Club's thinking was that the new course would make the race less of a small boat benefit as the prevailing south-westerlies would give a good amount of beating. But, the grand plan fell flat in the face of westerlies which provided plenty of reaching, much to the delight of the one tonners.

Indulgence was in deep trouble when weed opened her propeller at night. The problem sorted out, the Daniel Andrieu-designed yacht showed what a great planing boat she is. Surfing back from the mid-Channel EC 2 buoy for the second time, *Indulgence* lifted up on to her bow wave, planing for two minutes at a time as helmsman Eddie Owen steered up the back of one wave and then down its face, *Indulgence*'s spinnaker staying firm all the time. It was like doing an ocean race on a surfboard. The yacht took 45 minutes out of the bigger, more powerful *Sidewinder*, the potent Reichel/Pugh design in the US team which was sailed superbly by John Bertrand.

Sidewinder's team-mate, *Blue Yankee*, a Judel/Vrolijk 43, was the last boat to finish when she came into Ancasta Marina in the early hours. She'd lost the bottom half of her rudder when the Speedwave blade had split open. Her crew under Steve Benjamin and Dave Ullman struggled to finish the race under trysail and No. 5 jib in order to keep some control of the yacht. Needless to say, Ullman said that ocean racers should day-race only after that experience.

One tonners filled the top 12 slots, apart from *Indulgence* at 8th. With *Juno* 7th and *Jamarella* squeezed into 2nd place by *Propaganda* and the closest of finishes, Britain took the lead on points.

2nd Inshore race, Christchurch Bay

This year two of the three inshores were in Christchurch Bay and 10 to 16 knot winds, strong sun and a sparkling sea made this international competition at its best.

With the wind off the hot, sandy heathland to the north of the Bay, pressure was very uneven for this race. But the Kiwis turned in such a strong performance to take 1st (*Propaganda*), 3rd (*Kiwi*) and 10th (*Goldcorp*) that they were looking like Cup winners in the making. *Propaganda*, alone in their team, showed that she had something special to lift her away from similarly rated yachts and that was exceptional upwind speed. Bruce Farr had tipped her performance more that way than he had with the reaching-orientated *Jamarella*, but the difference was quite startling.

Juno and *Jamarella* got pushed so wide at the first gybe mark that they never got back to the top of the one ton pack. Meanwhile, luckless *Ritec Poinciana*, a 1985 Briand one tonner sailing for the makeshift Belgian team, showed that Admiral's Cup sailors are not all star quality. Her crew managed

One tonners round the leeward mark in the course of a Christchurch Bay race. Britain's *Juno* (K-505) is to leeward of the pack.

Alan Gray stands on the quarter of his Farr one tonner *Jamarella* as Lawrie Smith (fair hair) conducts operations in Christchurch Bay.

to lasso the first leeward mark when they dropped the spinnaker and then lost a man overboard as they tried to sort out the mess. It gave Sunday afternoon drivers great heart.

3rd Inshore Race, Christchurch.

In the diaries of the crewmen from *Diva*, *Saudade* and *Juno*, this was Black Wednesday. Not only did the Germans hit the buoy, but *Juno* also managed to foul the French yacht *Centurion* (ironically, the old *Jade* and forebear of *Juno*) at the very same mark and earn a 20 per cent penalty.

In the Irish team it was all smiles, however, for their big boat, the Turkish-owned Castro 43 *Turkish Delight*, led the fleet on corrected for two-thirds of the race, only to fade slightly at the end. It was a good show in a boat steered by Mark Mansfield of Cork but with a strong Aussie connection in the shape of tactician Hugh Treharne and bowman Don McCraken from the 12-metre scene. But this was the only Irish performance of merit apart from *Irish Independent/Full Pelt*'s great Fastnet Race showing. With two Dubois one tonners, backing up *Delight*, a long trials series and good crews, the Irish were tipped as long-odds winners. But, like their rugby team, they failed as favourites. If they had been written off, the team might have pulled it off.

The biggest smile of all belonged to Gary Weisman, skipper of the Nelson/Marek 45 *Insatiable* which won the race. He won his weight in champagne (some four cases!). As one of only two masthead-rigged yachts in the entire fleet, *Insatiable* struck a blow for the American school of yacht design.

For the second time running, the Kiwis placed all three boats in the top ten with their one tonners breaking away from the pack. It had been a perfect display of the art of team racing.

ADMIRAL'S CUP

Bruno Troublé aboard *Xeryus* rounds the bleak Fastnet Rock ahead of Udo Schütz's *Container* from Germany.

Fastnet Race

Once again, this classic among races earned its competitors' respect. At 605 miles it requires three nights at sea, even in fast conditions; its course around the headlands of southern England provides plenty of tidal gates; and the turning marks (Lizard, Fastnet and Bishop Rock) are inspiring enough to satisfy.

But the lure of the great race was not enough for Belgium as *Val Maubuée*, a curious Guy Ribadeau-Dumas-designed 44 rater, and *CGI*, a sponsored French team reject, didn't bother to start.

Key period in the race was the leg from Land's End to the Rock for the wind swung from north-west round to the south. Those boats on the rhumb line sailed the shortest distance on a two-sail reach into the Rock, while those who had gone west looking for the shift, overdid it. Jo Richards, Tim Goodbody, Ed Dubois, Tom Power and the rest of *Pelt*'s crew found themselves conveniently sailing into the Rock on a wind angle of 160° and tacking out from it with an angle 210°. Being able to keep the boat moving fast on the rhumb line was a home water advantage, the Irish crewmen reckoned.

Pelt actually had the best corrected time but her win was hollow. Being a sponsored boat racing in the open division she was ineligible for the main Fastnet Race prize. That went to *Juno* instead.

And the Champagne Mumm Admiral's Cup belonged to the Kiwis. 'It was dedication which brought us this win,' said team manager Don Brooke, 'along with the support of three million people and sixty million sheep.'

It was a dedication which saw the Kiwis hold an alcohol-free team barbecue on the eve of the Fastnet. The boys made up for it later in Plymouth though . . .

Kaoru Soehata

ADMIRAL'S CUP

Tour de France

À LA VOILE

by GILLES MARTIN-RAGET

It all started as a flight of fancy about ten years ago. Bernard Decré, native of Nantes but Brêton by adoption, is one of those people who have wild ideas and then makes them happen. As he made his way around the yachting world spreading the news that he was going to organise a Tour de France yacht race with a fleet of identical production boats, all to be financed by local authorities, his listeners quietly agreed he must have gone mad. When he went on to say his aim was to train crew for the Admiral's Cup, they turned on their heels and went off to finish their beer elsewhere . . .

Today the Tour de France is an institution with a tremendous influence on cruiser-racing in France. In ten years 35,000 crew have passed through this great school of offshore racing. This unique event can be the avenue for a winning crew to go on to a career in sailing. A few years ago the first prize was a half tonner with a budget to race the boat during an entire season including two highlights: the Half Ton Cup and the *Figaro* Single-handed Race. Last year's prize was no less than *CGI*, the custom one tonner designed by Daniel Andrieu. Thus, Benoit Caignaert, winner in 1983 and 1st in Menton in 1986 in the Sélection production boat, called *Le Havre*, was able to skipper the one-off design *CGI* for the entire 1987 season. He was considered as a potential member of the French Admiral's Cup team, but lost his chance along with his rudder during a spectacular Chinese gybe in the de Guingand Bowl race, an important selection trial.

The Tour de France yacht race is a commercial company, with a staff of ten people, an annual turnover of

Sea and See

FF12m (US$2m or £1.2m), involving 1000 people and 350 vehicles which travel through France over a month-long period. This well-disciplined organisation moves 35 boats from the Atlantic to the Mediterranean in less than 24 hours. As the yachts clear the finishing line their masts are unstepped and the boats are lifted out of the water and loaded onto one of 35 lorries (almost all the boat transporters in the country are used), which immediately starts off for Cap d'Agde.

The success of Tour de France lies in the strength of its basic ideas. First, the boats are all of the same type. Whilst the production boats used for the first races (Ecûme de Mer) were not exactly thoroughbreds, those in the following years have grown: First 30 from Bénéteau came next, followed by Rush Régates from Jeanneau. An important turning-point was 1984, when Bernard Decré asked the Joubert/Nivelt office to design a true racing yacht suitable for the Tour de France. And so the Sélection was born. This monohull, built by Jeanneau, is not very stiff but it is lively and a good performer, and is now the most dominant French production boat. Over 60 boats were in the class national championships at Sète in September '86 and over 300 yachts have been built in four years. To maintain class integrity for the event, masts, sails (all from the same sailmaker) and basic racing equipment are all supplied with the boat, which is then chartered by the competitor from the owners, the Tour de France organisation.

The second strength of the Tour de France comes from its financial system. Over the years it became evident that local authorities not only had the

Despite its course around the coast of France, the Tour de France's short legs ensure that it is sailed like a round-the-buoys day race *(above)*.

The fleet of Jeanneau Sélections was decked out in the livery of its sponsor, Orangina, a soft drinks manufacturer.

Kodak co-sponsored the Tour de France. In a similar fashion to its namesake cycle race, the leading yacht after each leg was awarded a yellow spinnaker.

The evenly matched Jeanneau Sélections brought out the best in one-design racing, especially at the closely contested starts of each leg.

means to finance the crews, but their enthusiasm was such that they put together permanent crews for whole seasons with the sole aim of winning the Tour de France.

Crews now start their training very early in the year. The rules require at least 21 crew to sail in relays on each boat during the Tour de France. Skippers attend winter courses as well as participating in other events at the start of the season to prepare their crew.

Inevitably, standards continually improve. In 1987 *Sète*, the winning boat, was manned by crew members from *French Kiss*, just back from Fremantle. Bertrand Pacé and Pierre Mas, the two co-skippers, each had a Ton Cup victory under their belt: Bertrand won the Quarter Ton Cup in *Comte de Flandres*, and Pierre won the Half Ton Cup in 1984 at the helm of *Anteor*. One would expect them to be way above the others in what is really only a promotional event. But even this super-crew had a tough fight through to the last race to secure their victory.

The Tour de France is a sailing school with a comprehensive curriculum, as it puts young competitors through many stages. First there is the search for finance. To get good results today one needs a minimum budget of FFr400,000 (US$65,000 or £40,000) and it's usually no problem to find this figure either at the town or county hall. Next is organisation. Plans have to be made for a training programme, management of finance, choosing a crew, arranging a timetable, lodgings, food and transportation. This is no mean task, since the Tour de France is a travelling event and sound organisation of logistics is essential. Most crew have several support vehicles to provide a dry place to sleep and eat at each

stopover. There is no spare time ashore and the best organised will be the freshest at the next start.

Then there is the sport itself. The Sélection is very sensitive to tuning. Sails and equipment are identical, so those who go fastest must be the better sailors. Much of the Tour de France is sailed in fair weather offwind conditions, so the top boats in each leg are often the same. However, there are numerous traps along the coast of France. From the strong currents of the Channel past the rocks of Brittany to the heavy squalls of the Mistrale in the Mediterranean, it is essential to leave a safety margin to avoid even one bad result. At the same time, in the fleet of 35 identical boats with their 35 aggressive crews, there should always be a readiness to take calculated risks at the start and to keep well placed to avoid a reversal of positions which often happens in the unexpected situations brought about by the unpredictable winds of summer. Extreme tactical options must be rejected – these are never worthwhile in an event where points are totalled over twenty races. At last, on the final run along the crowded beaches of the Côte d'Azur it is especially essential to cover adversaries closely. In 1986 three boats had a close fight for the victory on the last leg: the first to finish would win the whole event . . . and a one tonner to compete in the 1987 Admiral's Cup trials.

The air is full of tension and fatigue. The 25 legs roll on at a rapid pace: Olympic triangles, day races, overnight races, with the longest race up to 150 miles. Skippers have to instil and maintain motivation amongst their crew for a whole month's racing and this is no easy matter, especially after the break when the boats are moved from the Atlantic to the Mediterra-

nean and crew members are lured away by the sirens lying on sunny beaches.

On its tenth anniversary, the Tour de France again made some major changes for 1987. After three years of good loyal service, the fleet of Sélections Royale was replaced by 35 bright new Sélections Orangina. Whilst changing to new boats and a new main sponsor, Bernard Decré took the opportunity to reduce the duration of the event. As a result, the already unremitting rhythm is accelerated. In 1987 there was a record number of competitors (35) and some outstanding crew. The yacht *Saint Tropez* had a charming skipper in the person of Florence Lebrun, recent ladies' 470 World Champion. Her entirely female crew drew a lot of attention. Also remarkable was the 'super-papys' crew of *ANEP Le temps retrouvé*, sailed by a group of pensioners. These dynamic 60-year-olds had a colossal budget of FF2m (US$330,000 or £200,000) and a tough series of trials to select the crew from their 600,000 members. Training ran for six months and included group psychology; their entire operation was efficiently promoted.

As in previous years, several foreign crews took part: four from Switzerland (*Lausanne*, *Genève*, *Bern*, *Haut-Léman*), one from Belgium (*Région Walonne*) and even one from America (*California*, skippered by James Skaug).

Two main factions take part in the fight for the yellow spinnaker awarded to the overall leader. Firstly, there are those who sail Sélections all year round and are now competing in their 10th Tour de Voile, such as Gilles le Coz (*Angers*), Hervé de Kergariou (*Le Havre*), Yannick Dupetit (*Pays de Vannes*) – winner in 1985 – and Jean-Paul Mouren (*Oyonnax Plastics Vallée*), who won in 1983. The second group comprises top-level young

helmsmen from dinghies and other class boats, including: *Sète* (Bertrand Pacé, Pierre Mas and some crew from *French Kiss*), *Grenoble* with Yannick Pollet (ex-420 World Champion), and Alan Feydensieu, former national champion of First Class 8 with his Mediterranean crew (*Haute Garonne*).

More than ever before, the 1987 Tour de France was a bitter fight, with the slightest mistake during the 1500 miles costing dearly. Winner of the practice and first races, *Sète*, lost her lead due to a slip-up during a race in the Channel. The new leader was *Brest*, and *Sète*'s crew took an even lower dive in overall results when they were disqualified following a protest. Not until the Mediterranean, ten races later, did the crew from *Sète* surface again. Having kept out of trouble, the *Le Havre* crew had been leading for a long time when the brilliance of Pierre Mas and Bertrand Pacé in the Olympic triangles and in the Mediterranean changed the position. The most spectacular race was off Marseilles, where the fleet was hurled along by a Mistrale of a good Force 7. There was no question of leaving spinnakers in their bags – the Sélection loves fast, hard, offwind conditions.

The keenness in this unique event, held in strictly controlled one-design boats, clearly shows that it is the best crews who win. And in the world of yachting, where it's often the richest, best-equipped or luckiest crew who win, this is quite a revolution.

Gilles Martin-Raget is a freelance photo-journalist based in Marseilles. He has also sailed in many top regattas both in France and overseas.

Translation by Susan Green.

TOUR DE FRANCE

TAG

Round Europe Race

by JAMES BOYD

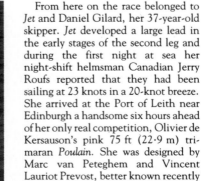

In 1985 Robin Knox-Johnston described the inaugural TAG Round Europe race as a war of attrition. In 1987 it was more of a slaughter, for the latest *Jet Services* catamaran demolished the opposition.

The TAG Round Europe is like many other French events in that it is the brainchild of an entrepreneur. It is an event specifically designed to take the heavily sponsored multihulls to venues dotted around Europe's coast. By and large, the traditional yachting centres such as Cowes or St Tropez are ignored: this is a travelling circus willing to go where local organisers are prepared to buy the show.

For the second race, Gérard Petipas planned the 3500-mile course in an anti-clockwise direction. It started in Den Haag in The Netherlands, running north to Scotland before heading south to the Mediterranean and the finish at San Remo in Italy.

Lessons have been learned since the last Round Europe. In that race two 75 ft (22·9 m) multihulls – Philippe Jeantot's *Credit Agricole II* and François Boucher's *Ker Cadelac II* – took the line honours, although both were shorter than the 85 ft (25·9 m) maximum length. Consequently, they suffered far fewer time-consuming breakages that slowed their larger rivals. As a result, at the beginning of 1987 ACIMO, the skippers' association, imposed a reduction on the size of Formula 1 to 75 ft (22·9 m), which, if it has had the temporary effect of cutting down the number of competing boats, has also cut down the carnage.

Lined up along the harbour wall in the port of Scheveningen at Den Haag (The Hague), home of famous boats

such as *Flyer* and *Philips Innovator*, with spectators by the busload·staring in awe at these 'greyhounds of the sea' and with the bells and shrieks of some far-off yodellers, the TAG fleet seemed prepared for the worst. Yet, before the race had even started there was an accident involving Louise Chambaz's 50 ft (15·2 m) trimaran *Women of Europe* which got rammed by a large fishing boat, crumpling her starboard aluminium outrigger and breaking the 'T'-foil off the port. The Canadian lady skipper was unable to make the start but managed to rejoin the race at the second stopover in Edinburgh.

As usual, there were several boats in the entry list who for the normal reasons of either not being ready or lacking sponsorship had failed to make the start. These included Christian Auge's 65 ft (19·8 m) proa *Fumée Noire*, and *Paca*, Paul Ayasse's new trimaran from the south of France, designed by Gilles Vaton, designer of Alain Gabbay's monster foiler *Charles Heidsieck*. Like Tabarly's *Côte d'Or II* trimaran, *Paca* uses Bruce foils but has no daggerboard. On *Côte d'Or* the foils also have hydraulically adjustable trim tabs.

With much pomp and due circumstance the start gun was fired by Jacques Delors, President of the EEC. As at the start of most of the eight legs there was a short warm-up 'Grand Prix' for the benefit of press and the land-based onlookers, with the boats racing close to the beach. The aim was part of the same drive towards making this more of a spectator sport that gave birth to the Formula 40 circuit. Off Scheveningen it was *Jet Services* which won the initial 20-mile circuit and led

the 14 multihulls away on the first 220-mile stage to Bremerhaven in West Germany.

The conditions were ideal and it was a very fast leg. First into the German port was the 25-year-old skipper of *Elf Aquitaine*, Jean Maurel, who had managed to average 20 knots in the cat. Apart from her original X-beams, *Elf* is now a very different beast to the one which Marc Pajot left behind to concentrate on his America's Cup campaign in *French Kiss*. She has, however, retained her unique balestrom rig, with a colossal one-piece rotating boom for her main and jib, along with her wingmast. After the *Royale* disaster in the Route de Rhum race last autumn, *Elf*'s rig is now the only one of such a size still in use.

The British Formula 2 entry, *Calor Challenge* (ex-*Exmouth Challenge/ Umupro Jardin*), skippered by Richard Tolkien, ran out of luck when she hit a sandbank on the way into Bremerhaven and with her skeg and rudder smashed, retired from the race.

Eric Tabarly, the strong and normally silent skipper of the Belgian trimaran *Côte d'Or II*, said that the start of the second leg to Edinburgh in Scotland was one of the most exciting moments in his long sailing career. To get to the open sea the competitors had a 20-mile spinnaker run down the Weser river, but what should have been a glorious start was turned into a fight for survival as the fleet was ravaged by a violent squall, which burst spinnakers like balloons after a party. Flat water and strong winds are ideal conditions for these boats and as *Jet Services* left the mouth of the river she was clocking over 30 knots.

From here on the race belonged to *Jet* and Daniel Gilard, her 37-year-old skipper. *Jet* developed a large lead in the early stages of the second leg and during the first night at sea her night-shift helmsman Canadian Jerry Roufs reported that they had been sailing at 23 knots in a 20-knot breeze. She arrived at the Port of Leith near Edinburgh a handsome six hours ahead of her only real competition, Olivier de Kersauson's pink 75 ft (22·9 m) trimaran *Poulain*. She was designed by Marc van Peteghem and Vincent Lauriot Prevost, better known recently for their revolutionary Formula 40 trimaran *Biscuits Cantreau*.

The story was much the same for the rest of the race, with *Jet* winning the

next five legs between the bleak drizzle of Edinburgh and the brilliant sunshine of Toulon. It wasn't until the final leg that the very light Mediterranean winds put the trimarans at an advantage over the cats. *Jet Services'* most staggering performance, though, was on the sixth leg from Vilamoura in Portugal to Barcelona in the south of Spain, politically the most important section as both countries have only recently joined the EEC.

The start from Vilamoura had again been very fast with *Côte d'Or II* thundering across the line 1st, and both she and *Jet* maintained speeds of around 27 knots for a long period. Going through the Straits of Gibraltar the gusty winds caused her to gybe

unexpectedly, breaking the top seven carbon-fibre battens in her costly North mainsail. *Jet's* Formula 40-style rig is most unusual for a maxi-multihull for it relies on its large mainsail for drive. Yet even with her main source of power tattered, *Jet* still somehow managed to win the leg, even though by this stage there was little doubt that they had the overall race in the bag.

The white-hulled *Jet* was designed by France's leading maxi-catamaran designer, Gilles Ollier, and was built entirely in carbon fibre. She cost about FF6,000,000 (£600,000). Certainly there is no doubting which boat is now the fastest in the world on a Force 5 reach, but after the Round Europe *Jet* still remained virtually untested going

to weather in a strong wind and a lumpy sea.

Gilard's team consists of some of the top names on the circuit. These include Yves Loday and Daniel Souben, two leading French Olympic sailors, Oliver Despaigne, who with the late Loic Caradec, won the Carlsberg Two-handed Transatlantic Race in 1986 onboard *Royale*, and Jerry Roufs and Gael de Kerangat from Mike Birch's *Formule TAG*. Another crew member, who was perhaps more instrumental than anyone in *Jet's* success was Jean-Yves Bernot, possibly the best navigator in France. He is also the creator of the MacSea computer navigation system, which before the TAG race was used on board *Fleury*

The TAG fleet attracted crowds in all the stopovers. This is Toulon, in the south of France.

Daniel Gilard's *Jet Services* (left) stormed to a fine win in Class 1.

TAG ROUND EUROPE RACE

Christian Février

With a squall blowing and the visibility closed right in, *Roger & Gallet*'s navigator checks the chart for sandbanks around Bremerhaven.

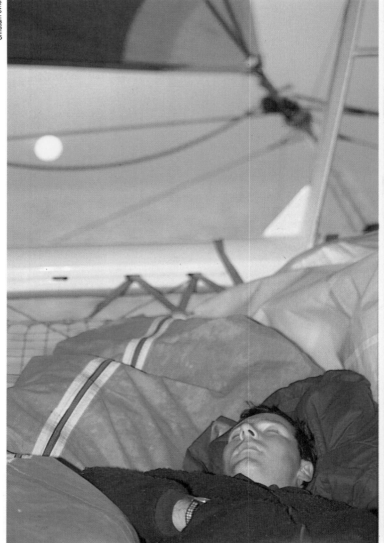

Even skippers have to get a nap. *Challenge Grundig*'s master, Thierry Canoni, snatches some sleep under the setting sun.

Christian Février

A foredeck hand's life is no drier on a multi than on a monohull. Here an *Ericsson* crewman changes the spinnaker guy with the pole end buried in the water.

TAG ROUND EUROPE RACE

Christian Février

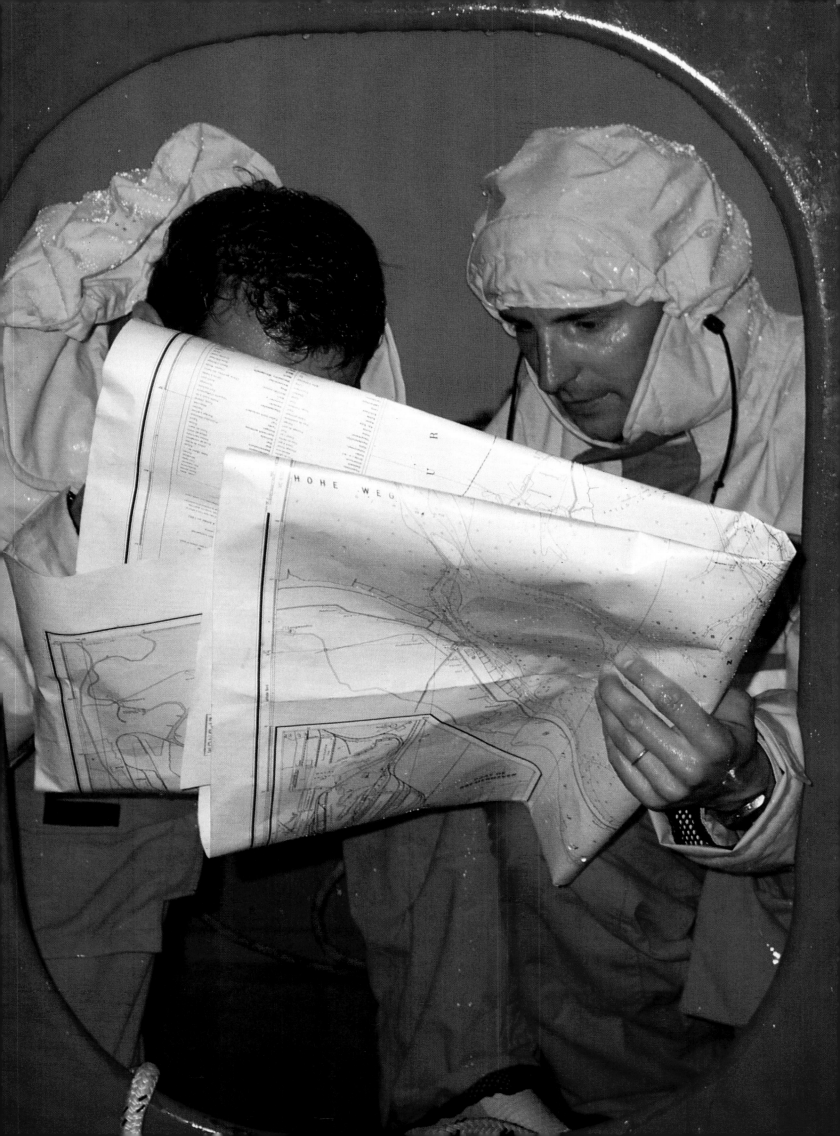

Race winner Daniel Gilard poses with his victor's silverware. Tragically, Gilard was lost overboard from *Jet Services* during the end-of-season La Boule–Dakar race.

Michon for her record-breaking transatlantic run and which is finding increasing popularity on many of the other top maxis.

Jet uses an NKE system to measure boat and wind information, which is connected to the Apple MacIntosh-based MacSea, along with her powerful Icom SSB/VHF radio and her Decca, Loran and satnav position locators. As the boat is sailing the computer can accumulate performance information from the NKE which is then plotted in polar curves and stored in its memory. In conjunction with these curves and the weather information received by telex via the SSB, it is possible for *Jet's* crew to make performance predictions and optimise routeing, alternatives of which are superimposed on the screen on electronic charts, developed by Informatique et Mer in France. Of course, like any computer system it is only as good as the information it is provided with, so if the weather forecast supplied by the Met. Office looks suspect then the system can still work from information provided from the NKE and the old technique of the navigator sticking his head out of the hatch and making a judgement himself. Bernot has been careful to make the system as simple as possible, so all functions are carried out by a mouse; as he says, 'I am a navigator and not a computer programmer'.

The Dublin stopover proved that the Irish Tourist Board had really done their homework. Quietly, multihull racing has become quite popular in Ireland, possibly a by-product of the renewed competition for the Round Ireland record. At the time of the race this was held by Peter Phillips in Britain's largest racing multihull, *Novanet Elite*, which retired from the race *en route* to Vilamoura from Lorient after hitting a log. The retired Exeter police sergeant, a well-known mischievous character on the circuit, has even appeared on the Gay Byrne TV show to give the race a boost. One of the girls from the tourist board commented that she had never seen so much traffic between Dublin and Dun Laoghaire, where the boats were moored, proving that the race does have a valid pan-European role.

The crowds were even thicker at the penultimate stopover at Toulon in the south of France. There they were

gathering even before *Jet's* triumphant arrival. After a few more competitors had docked a one-way system was set up on the pontoons so that spectators could get to see the boats and their heroes more closely. There was an extra air of anticipation as the great Tabarly arrived in 2nd place to go through the motions of cracking open the champagne and being reunited with his wife and child. The cameras whirred, the spectators waved their EEC flags with twelve gold stars on a blue background and a massive cheer went up.

The final, short 100-mile leg to San Remo past the sunny Côte d'Azur, was made more exciting by an aerobatic display by the 'Patrouille de France' team, and was won by the trimarans *Poulain* and Philippe Poupon's Route de Rhum-winning *Fleury Michon VIII*. The trimarans were followed by Bruno Peyron in the catamaran *Ericsson*, racing with the most international crew of the race. Two years earlier, *Ericsson* had won the race in a very different guise as Jeantot's *Credit Agricole II*.

The only disaster in the 1987 event occurred in one of its rare moments of bad weather whilst the fleet was off Cape Finistere. After a successful season in 1986 winning the two-handed Rouen–New York Liberty Race, Eric Loizeau's 75 ft (22·9 m) catamaran *Roger et Gallet* ended a less successful 1987 with a capsize. As the race was for the most part in winds of no greater than Force 5, Loizeau had been making use of the 40-knot gusts to gain some ground on the leaders. Sailing under masthead spinnaker and full mainsail at 25 knots, the maroon-and-gold cat was flying a hull when she was hit by a very powerful wave which pitchpoled her. One of the crew later said that her capsize seemed to be in slow motion, as her enormous mast and sails took their time to submerge. Her crew were unhurt and, after seven hours on the upturned hull, were rescued by a passing cargo ship.

Meanwhile, *Jet* had the bit between

her teeth. 'We were surfing down waves totally out of control', Jerry Roufs commented later. 'If it hadn't been for the preventers we would have done a Chinese gybe. We went down to main alone and were still doing 28 knots.'

In the smaller 60 ft class Formula 2, a late entry into the race, *Challenge Grundig*, François Forestier's old Lombard-designed catamaran *Lejaby Rasurel*, had managed to be 1st in class on every leg, emulating Tony Bullimore's performance with *Apricot* in 1985. Racing with Thierry Caroni, *Challenge Grundig's* new skipper was Yvon Fauconnier, winner of the last OSTAR and a most sought-after navigator. Also along for the ride was popstar Francis Lalanne, the French version of Simon le Bon, and who at the time had a number one hit in the charts. He intended to write his next song about the TAG race.

Contented, if in last place, was Frank Jubelin in the only boat competing with a compact disc player and a microwave oven. *Kiamiloa*, a 65 ft (19·8 m) cruising catamaran also designed by Vaton (the *Charles Heidsieck* man), was built by CDK Composites, builders of *Poulain* and *Biscuits Cantreau*. She is owned by Frank Goddio, the grandson of Eric de Bisschop, who back in 1936 built his first catamaran, also called *Kiamiloa* and who pioneered the resurgence of the Polynesian cruising catamaran. None the less her successor looked incongruous among the stripped-out racing machines.

The prize-giving in San Remo was the typical affair with all the local and some not so local dignitaries. Both Gilard and Caoni were presented with the appropriate cheques for 10,000 ECUs (European Currency Units) for their class wins and an extra 1500 for Gilard for an overall win, bringing his total prize money for the race up to 19,000 ECUs.

The TAG race with its European political aspect and its numerous stopovers is a unique, if lengthy race, lasting over a month. From a European point of view it was, perhaps, too dominated by the French, as both the German and Finnish entries were unable to make the start. But then the French are the foremost multihull nation in Europe.

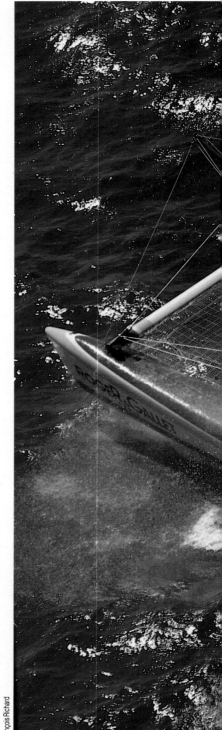

Roger et Gallet's race came to a very abrupt end when she capsized off Cape Finistère whilst piling on the power in an attempt to catch up with fleet leaders.

Côte d'Or, with a full head of steam up, clocks
25 knots.

Christian Février

La Nioulargue

by GILLES MARTIN-RAGET

Main picture: *Aile Blanche* powers upwind, her crew revelling in the fresh going.

It was seven years ago that the idea of a race from St Tropez to the La Nioulargue buoy was conceived. Like so many yacht races, the idea for this was born in a bar.

While enjoying the local Provençal wine those two pillars of Tropezienne society, Jean Lorrain, skipper of the old 12-metre *Ikra*, and Dick Jayson, owner of the Swan 44 *Pride*, made a bet. Whoever lost the race out to La Nioulargue, which marks a shoal off the Bay of Pampelonne, would pick up the bill for a victory dinner after the race. *Ikra*, owned by the Alpine car designer Jean Redelé, won the private race and so La Nioulargue was born.

It was the original spontaneity which set the mould for La Nioulargue to grow into a full-blown series which has become so popular that an entry limit of 200 boats has had to be set.

After all, who would have thought that a 12-metre and a fully fitted cruising boat could have a decent race? The protagonists were not actually much concerned about that. Dick Jayson was considering returning to his native Florida when he saw *Ikra* sailing into Saint Tropez. *Ikra*, the one-time *Kurrewa* British Twelve built in 1966 as a sister ship for *Sovereign*, could not have been more different from *Pride*. But Jayson swore that his cruising boat, whose amenities included an ice-maker, could beat a purpose-built race boat, even one getting long in the tooth.

The challenge was simple (even if *Ikra*'s skipper had to comb the deserted streets to find a crew): sail from the Tour du Portalet which stands sentinel on the St Tropez harbour wall, around La Nioulargue and back to the finish off the beach near the Club 55.

Patrice de Colmont, owner of Club 55, which is located on one of St Tropez's most popular beaches, realised the potential of the race, especially as it had taken place after the end of the busy July and August season. The following year he opened up the event to other yachts, with *Pride* and *Ikra* having to share their private race with a dozen boats including the Frers maxi *Helisara* belonging to German maestro Herbert von Karajan. Dick Jayson extracted revenge by winning, but the *Ikra–Pride* private rivalry was broken forever when 65 yachts turned up in 1983.

The reason for this rapid growth can be attributed to the exceptional setting

of this former fishing port. By the end of September, the summer tourists have thinned out and the sailors can enjoy themselves in the countless bars and restaurants which line the harbour and narrow streets. It is a great place for sailors to talk sailing.

The relaxed atmosphere makes La Nioulargue more like a European version of Antigua Sailing Week. The principal aim is to have fun, and people enjoy the more relaxed style of sailing as a consequence. There are no world championships or points series decided at St Tropez, so the serious racers can unwind at the end of the season.

While *Helisara* was a local boat, Patrice de Colmont and his fellow revellers thought it would be a good idea to attract a few more of the maxis to St Tropez. They headed off to Porto Cervo in 1982, loaded with bottles of local rosé wine and a bag of T-shirts. Late for their meeting with the maxi owners, they were confronted by the impeccably dressed owners who did not seem to see the funny side of the St Tropez way of doing business . . . Undeterred, de Colmont organised a dockside wine tasting before the start of the following day's racing. Bill Whitehouse-Vaux, owner of *Mistress Quickly*, was intrigued and promised to take a look at what was on offer. A year later, he turned up in St Tropez.

That made the other maxi owners sit up and take note. This year, 11 of them brought their big boats to St Tropez for the Moët et Chandon Maxi Cup. Not only was the event a big success but it was the largest gathering of maxis yet seen (see separate chapter on the maxis).

But variety is what La Nioulargue is all about. Within the overall programme there are races for all manner of craft. Around 50 traditional boats were drawn to the event this year including some of the world's most beautiful yachts: *Orion*, *Puritan*, *Shenandoah* and *Gloria*. There were also 15 Swans, including Dick Jayson's black 44 *Pride* (he's still not made it back to Florida), some 60 IOR boats including French Admiral's Cuppers *Corum* and *Xeryus*, a couple of old 12-metres (*Ikra* and *France III*), a few 8-metres which are popular in Cannes, and a handful of charter yachts *en route* from the Med to their winter season in the Caribbean.

Then there were the exceptional boats, such as *Phocea*, the giant four-masted 72 m yacht which began

Nordwind is now a successful charter yacht.
She was built originally for Hermann Göring.

Swell autumn conditions as a Swan rounds a mark off St Tropez.

life in 1976 as Alain Colas's *Club Méditerranée* and which has now been transformed into a super-luxury private yacht by industrialist Bernard Tapie. The multihulls present included the former *Charles Heidsieck* maxi foiler and Philippe Monnet's *Kriter Brut de Brut* in which he circumnavigated the world single-handed.

They made an incredible gathering. What event, anywhere, can boast such an interesting and diverse fleet of yachts?

The success is even more remarkable when you consider that, going against all trends (in France at least), Patrice de Colmont and the International Yacht Club de Pampelonne decided to apply Rule 26.2. In keeping with the spirit of the regatta, Bruno Troublé changed the name of his Givenchy-sponsored yacht from *Xeryus* to *X et ryus* and then proceeded to have T-shirts made showing both the new name and the rule which forced it.

A typical day at the Nioulargue usually begins with breakfast at Senequier's, the most frequented café in the port. There the crews sit, wearing their prized Nioulargue T-shirts, enjoying a coffee and brioche. They try to work out the day's programme while recovering from the excesses of the night before.

Fortunately, the starts don't take place before midday, when the guns are fired from the Portalet tower on the harbour wall and boom around the amphitheatre-like port. But the day really begins in earnest at aperitif time. A drink in the cockpit is usually followed by another ashore in any one of the numerous street cafés, then wine in the restaurant and a digestif back down at the quay. The Nioulargue regime is a tough one.

That is very much the spirit of the event, though. Only one thing matters; don't take it too seriously. Rather, you should enjoy the racing, take in the last of the summer and revel in the spectacle of it all. There should be more events like it!

Gilles Martin-Raget is a freelance photo-journalist supplying material to many French journals. He is also a top sailor, having been involved in French 12-metre campaigns.

Olympic Classes

by ROGER LEAN-VERCOE

Roger Lean-Vercoe

Carlo Borlenghi

In Pusan, Korea, at 11.0 a.m. on 29 September 1988, Olympic gold medals are due to be presented to winning crews in the eight Olympic classes. Not only will each crew have triumphed in the seven physically and mentally fatiguing races of this regatta, but they will also have won an even tougher battle to be selected for their national team in the first place.

For many years before this culmination of their efforts they will, without exception, have invested countless hours and more money than they care to contemplate on the achievement of this goal. Some of the medallists will tell you that one Olympic campaign is enough; for others this quest for Gold is their main occupation; and some of them will have already stood on the Olympic rostrum. In whichever category they fall, these dedicated few are at the peak of a sailing speciality that is often regarded by less competitive sailors as an insignificant part of the sport. Nevertheless, it quietly attracts an exceptionally large following at its lower levels, not solely for its Olympian rewards (a goal that is too distant for many) but the thrill of competing in the premier small boat class.

This year, in celebration of its 100th anniversary, the Kieler Yacht Club in Germany organised an event which comprised either the World or European Championship for each of the eight Olympic classes. Such was the

demand to compete that restrictions had to be placed on the size of national teams, but even so a total of 900 dinghies, sailboards and keelboats, crewed by 1542 competitors from 42 nations, sailed in this week-long event. By this gauge, Olympic racing can scarcely be called insignificant!

After intensive competition at regattas in Europe and throughout the world during the 1987 season, the British Olympic sailing team joined those of 25 other nations in Pusan for the Olympic Practice regatta, a dress-rehearsal for sailors as well as organisers that took place exactly one year before the main event. In line with many other nations and for reasons of finance, Britain did not compete in the two keelboat events (Solings and Stars), yet none the less brought home gold medals in three out of the six remaining classes – an amazing achievement.

There has often been intense rivalry between classes in order to gain or retain Olympic status, a battle that is sometimes swayed by political and business pressures. Today, however, there is relative stability in the Olympic fleet with seven different types of craft, one of which is raced in separate divisions for men and women. Largest of these classes is the three-man keelboat, the Soling, designed by Jan Linge of Norway. At 26 ft 9 in. (8.1 m) overall and with 233 ft² (21 m²) of sail

area, it is a class that has been raced in the Games since 1972.

The leadership in this class, which produces very level racing, has recently been divided between the East Germans and the Americans, with the 1986 Worlds going to John Kostecki of the USA. This year's light and flukey series in Kiel was won by East German Helmar Nauck. The contest will now remain a draw until the 1988 session begins, as the East Germans (together with several other nations) did not send a Soling team to Pusan. This latest event was again won by Kostecki, sailing a Canadian-built Abbott hull with sails developed by Kostecki himself, a North sailmaker. Jesper Bank of Denmark finished 2nd, and Sweden's Lennart Persson came 3rd. US chances for a 1988 medal look particularly high, with top helmsmen such as Dave Curtis and Kevin Mahaney pushing Kostecki constantly. In contrast, British hopes in this class, which is not being actively raced in UK waters, look slim for the next Games, especially as top helmsman Chris Law remains occupied with preparations for the America's Cup.

The oldest design of yacht still racing at the Olympics is the Star, a two-man keelboat with an LOA of 22 ft 8 in. (6.9 m) that carries a disproportionately large sail area. Designed in 1911, it was first raced in the 1932 Olympics and has done so

Far left: **Opening ceremony of the Pusan pre-Olympic regatta. The South Koreans were keen to impress their international visitors.**

Kieler Woche provided the biggest Olympic fleets of the year.

Strong tides and fresh breezes made Pusan conditions tough going.

The Star is the oldest of the Olympic classes (*right*), but the racing is very close.

Far right: Britain's Cathy Foster (right) sailed in the 1984 Olympic regatta before the 470 class was split into separate fleets for men and women. She hopes to make it two Olympics in a row with new crew Jackie Patton.

ever since, except for 1976 when it was replaced temporarily with the Tempest. In this long history the Americans have always been at the front of the fleet and this remains the case today. The European Championships in Kiel were won convincingly by Vince Brun and Hugo Schreiner, past World Champions and Bacardi Cup winners, whilst the 1987 World Championships in Chicago were won by another US team, Ed Adams and Tom Olsen. The latter were amongst a relatively small Star fleet that raced in the varied conditions at Pusan this year, an event which they won with a mixture of North, Sobstadt, Shore and Fritz sails in their Foley-built hull. Their boat is a real veteran having had 12 previous owners! Although the depth of talent in the US fleet means that this crew may not be the one to represent the States in Pusan next year, one thing is almost a certainty – the Gold will go to whoever gets selected for the US team.

Apart from the single-handed dinghy, which first intruded into an all-keelboat Olympics in 1920, dinghy racing is a relatively new development in the Olympic scene, with the first two-man dinghy, the 12 m² Sharpie, being introduced as late as 1956. This unexciting craft was replaced in 1960 by the Flying Dutchman that is still raced today.

Two more classes, the Tornado catamaran and the 470 dinghy, were added in 1976, whilst the sailboard was introduced for the 1984 Los Angeles Games. Largest and fastest of these is the Tornado, with an LOA of 20 ft (6.1 m) and a beam of 10 ft (3 m). Its 235 ft² (21 m²) of sail can propel those lightweight craft at over 20 knots. The current World Champions are the Hagara brothers from Austria who won four out of five races in the windless Worlds at Kiel. This was perhaps a flash in the pan as they were unable to do better than 13th overall in the windier conditions at the Olympic Practice regatta in Pusan, with their best result a 7th in the moderate sea breeze of the last race. Pusan was won by Michael Faou and Yvon Quernec of France, whilst American ex-FD sailors Gary Knapp and Cam Lewis took 2nd place and Roland Gaebler and Hans-Jürgen Pfohe from West Germany 3rd.

There were some notable absences from Pusan, however, not least of these being ex-World Champion Randy Smyth from the USA, attempting to defend his Formula 40 crown, and

Chris Cairns from Australia, another ex-World Champion and bronze medallist who was 2nd in this year's Worlds. There should be some dramatic competition next year when these crews join in the fray. In the past, Britain has excelled in this class, with Reg White and, later, his son Rob not only showing the world how to win, but also building the winning boats. Rob White, sailing with Jeremy Newman, won the 1986 Worlds held in Bermuda, but is at present off the pace affected by severe rig problems.

The Flying Dutchman, with 36 years of development behind it, is probably the most sophisticated of all the Olympic classes and certainly a particularly exciting dinghy. That little extra performance needed to win races comes from a maze of control lines allowing every aspect of the sensitive rig to be adjusted. In recent years, composite construction technology has given the Americans an edge, helping Jonathan McKee and Mike Buchan to their gold medal in '84. This lead has been eroded, however, and the class is wide open today. Sergei Borodinov of the USSR won Kiel Week, Luis Doreste from Spain (the 1984 470 class gold medallist) took the World title, whilst Jørg Bojsen-Muller from Denmark won the Pusan event. The only name to appear in the top three in more than one of these events was J.B. Braun of the USA, sailing with Bill Kenney, who scored a 3rd both in Kiel and Pusan. Britain's hopes in the class are represented by Roger Yeoman/Nick Burgin and Will Henderson/Andy Bowers who are pushing the current top British crew, Jon Turner and Pete Allam. A top place has been in sight on a couple of occasions for Turner and Allam, particularly at Pusan, but it has been snatched away by misfortune.

Having taken Golds in both the men's and women's 470 class at the Pusan Olympic Practice regatta, Britain looks like being the nation to beat in this 15 ft 6 in. trapeze dinghy. Both crews have considerable experience in the class, and Cathy Foster was selected as the British 470 helmsman for the Los Angeles Games before the class was sexually segregated. At that time she scorned the idea of racing in the proposed 'Women Only' class, but has none the less given it a try, teaming up with 6 ft blonde amazon Jackie Patton at the beginning of 1987.

Winning has certainly not been easy, and at times, with results like a

33rd in the Worlds, it looked as if it might not come at all. Korea was the turning point. After an 18th in the first race they won three of the remaining races and added two 4ths and a 5th to take the series by a big margin. This outstanding success, coupled with Cathy's previous experience, must now put them amongst the front runners for a medal. Their rivals include several US crews, particularly Lisa Niece (2nd at Pusan) and Pease Hearndon (2nd at the Kiel Worlds), who remain a continuing challenge.

Cathy Foster's crew at the Los Angeles Games was naturalised New Zealander Pete Newlands, who has

now teamed up with Bruce Banks's sailmaker Nigel Buckley, and this pair took the Men's 470 Gold at Pusan. Perhaps it was familiarity with tidal sailing that enabled them to perform well on this strongly tidal course. Or, maybe they were better able to interpret the changeable weather patterns than crews from more settled climates, but there is no doubt that they had excellent boat speed, winning one race and taking 3rd in three others. Jodok Wicki from Switzerland, who took 2nd place overall, won two of the races, as did Peter Evans from New Zealand who finished 6th. These crews, whilst undoubtedly fast, were not able to

Carlo Borlenghi

Roger Lean-Vercoe

maintain the same enviable consistency as Buckley and Newman. This is a tough class in which to race and is certainly not one that encourages predictions, but Britain has a team in the top group once more, something not seen since the mid to late '70s.

In the Finn class, a solidly constructed single-hander that is most suited to heavyweight sailors, Britain's youthful Stuart Childerley has been dominant for the whole of 1987. Apart from the World Championships, which, sailed in light and fickle zephyrs, were considered by many to be a lottery, Childerley won just about everything that there was to win,

including the European Championships and the Pusan Olympic Practice regatta in which he sailed his new Vanguard hull for the first time. In this class, though, performance prior to the Games themselves is a less reliable indicator, as for the Olympic regatta competitors are supplied with dinghies rather than allowed to bring their own. This can be a chancy business, especially if the issued craft are not equal in performance. The Olympic Finns made in Korea by Hyundi were constructed under the supervision of Bungy Taylor, a boatbuilder who in the past has served the British Olympic team.

Amongst Childerley's closest rivals, the very experienced Russian allrounder Oleg Khopersky must rank top after this year's victory in Kiel Week, whilst Spaniard José Doreste, who won the lightweight World Championship, is particularly quick in these conditions. In addition to these two are plenty of possible winners, including Denmark's Lasse Hjortnæs, Sweden's Stig Westergaard and two Americans, Scott McLeod and Brian Ledbetter, all of whom have a good chance.

Newest of the Olympic classes, and smallest in size and price, is the revolution of the Eighties – the sailboard. The Windglider, a one-

design class, was adopted for the Los Angeles Games, but such was the rapid development of the sport that in the three years between selection and the event itself the class was obsolete. To avoid a recurrence of this, the Division II development class was selected for the 1988 Olympics with the provision that a specific design would be nominated a year before the event itself and that the boards would be provided by the host nation.

A Lechner design with a North sail was finally chosen by the International Yacht Racing Union after much lobbying and debate. But by the end of 1987, the Lechner was still not generally available, much to the dismay of the competitors who needed them for practice. Without doubt, the French must be considered favourites in this class, but they were also in this position before the last Games and yet they failed to win a medal of any colour.

Division II racing is divided into weight categories for non-Olympic events (there is no such division for the Games) and competitors sail different board designs, so it is difficult to make a realistic assessment of likely candidates for gold medals. Nevertheless, some names automatically float to the top. Foremost amongst these is Robert Nagy from France, a four-time World Champion and winner of Pusan '87, and Scott Steele of the USA, 2nd in Pusan and the silver medallist from the LA Games. Beneath them is a host of names whose fortunes will rise and fall with the wind: Michel Quintin and Eric Belot from France, Sweden's Jonas Davidson, and Thomas Foyen from Norway, to name but a few.

The road to Olympic selection is beset with difficulties, although Britain's chief coach is more than happy with progress so far.

As for the Games themselves, IYRU president Peter Tallberg liked what he saw in South Korea. 'The sailing facilities provided by the Koreans at Pusan are the best I have seen', he declared. And, despite the unrest which has affected the country throughout 1987, it seems unlikely that the 1988 Games will suffer the politically inspired boycotts which hit the previous Games in Moscow and Los Angeles. If that optimism is correct, Pusan will host the largest sailing Olympics ever.

OLYMPIC CLASSES

Kieler Woche & Kiel Worlds

by ERIK von KRAUSE

Kiel hosted by far the biggest sailing event in the world in 1987 – 4000 sailors from 43 nations sailing 1850 boats in 23 different classes.

It was a special year, for the Kieler Yacht Club had been founded 100 years earlier and it received many presents and centenary congratulations. But the biggest present of all had been organised by the club itself. On the last day of Kiel Week, 28 June, a solemn ceremony opened a second event which is so far unique in sailing: the Kiel Worlds.

Here, for the first time, five World Championships and two European Championships were contested simultaneously in each of the Olympic classes. Some said it was better than the Olympics themselves, especially as countries were not limited to one entry per class as happens with the Games' regatta.

The birthday party continued late into the summer, for in late August/early September the Kieler Yacht Club hosted the One Ton Cup, the premier level rating IOR class which attracted many top boats from the Champagne Mumm Admiral's Cup.

So why did Kiel indulge in such a summer-long party of sailing? In 1871 this Baltic seaport became the home of the German Imperial fleet and ten years later enjoyed its first yacht race, spawned by sailors spending their free time afloat. In 1882, 20 yachts competed in assorted races, and so Kieler Woche was born.

A couple of enterprising officers founded the Marine Regatta Verein on 12 February 1887, the origins of the KYC. In contrast to the situation in England at the time, the German Imperial family's interest in yachtng

was limited to the Princes Heinrich and Friedrich Karl, who were enthusiastic competitors.

All that changed when Emperor Wilhelm II succeeded to the throne. In 1891 he became the first commodore of the fledgling club and, in his honour, the Regatta Verein became the Kaiserlicher YC. Wilhelm's patronage worked the same magic for Kiel as had the British royal family's patronage of Cowes. Indeed, the Kaiser's yachts, such as *Meteor*, frequently attended both regattas.

The First World War ended that patronage although initially Hitler's National Socialists allowed the club's name to remain. After the 1936 Olympic Games, however, the name was deemed to have outlived its political usefulness and it was merged with all the other German sailing organisations into the Yacht Club von Deutschland.

At the end of the Second World War, the British played a hand in shaping the club's future for they allowed it to revert to its KYC initials, although Kieler was substituted for Kaiserlicher.

In its centenary year, the KYC is Germany's second-largest club, counting some 1250 members and 600 yachts. Along with two other clubs it organises the annual Kiel Week regatta and it played a key role when the 1972 Olympic regatta was hosted by the city.

For more than fifty years, one-design classes have played a major role in Kiel Week, with the elite of the Olympic class sailors in particular making it an important focus of their year's programme. There are no fewer than six Olympic courses laid out in Kiel Bight – and that still leaves room for the

YPS/Peter Neumann

Far left: **120 Finns made the Kieler Woche event one of the toughest of the year. Sadly for the class, lack of wind spoiled the following week's World Championship.**

Above: **Crews from all over the world braved showers during the grand opening parade which got the Kiel Worlds underway. Here, the Soling 'fleet' passes through.**

YPS/Peter Neumann

Right: **West Germans Karl Gilhaus and Georg Liebecke were among the 92 flying men in the Tornado class.**

ferries and cargo vessels entering Kiel or the canal to the North Sea. Even with six courses, the 1987 Kieler Woche was no less congested for the one-design classes than in previous years.

For many sailors, the early start and late return from the most seaward courses is part of the Kiel regime. So is sharing the course with some 200 boats in a mixture of classes. For instance, the venerable and lovely Dragons raced with the flighty 505 dinghies, even more flighty Tornado cats and popular H-Boat cruisers. The Flying Dutchmen, Solings and Stars shared a course and so did the 420s and the singlehanders – Laser, OK and Europe.

Five keel boat classes (the J-24, Yngling, Sprinta Sport, Kielzuvogel and Folkboat) used the same course, although at least the windsurfers (Division II and Mistral SSTs) only had each other to put up with. There were just two classes on the busiest course of them all, Course C, which was the battleground for some 300 Finn and 470 dinghies.

While the small boats sailed around their ten 10–17-mile courses, coping with the Bight's slight tide and very shifty winds, the offshore racers had a very different programme.

Some 200 IOR boats turned up this year for the seven-race series which gives an excellent mix of courses. The first Saturday opens the proceedngs with the traditional Eel Race. From right outside the Club House, the fleet races some 30 miles to the small town of Eckernforde at which every yacht is presented with two smoked eels. Needless to say the first finishers get the best eels!

Normally such nourishment is

necessary for a 60–110-mile offshore race, but this year a short course was set to allow crews to return to Kiel for Tuesday's big parade by all participants from Schillksee to the city of Kiel. Olympic courses filled the rest of the big boat racing schedule.

Usually the IOR boats come just from Germany, Denmark, Sweden and Norway. This year, however, a few one tonners from further afield came to practise in preparation for the One Ton Cup. *Vento* from Spain was one, a Tony Castro-designed one tonner sailed by John Kolius.

Like many big sailing events today, Kiel Week is fuelled by sponsors' money. Daimler-Benz plays a leading role, not just with cash but with an efficient car service too. The area between the nine boat basins at Kiel-Schillksee and the apartments behind is closed to all traffic except for the Mercedes fleet during Kiel Week. They tow the boats and trailers to and from the cranes at the beginning and end of the regatta while cars and buses run a wide-ranging service for competitors.

Electrical giant Siemens assisted with the computer results service while Lufthansa and Champagne Mumm were co-sponsors. So too was Hanseboot (the Hamburg International Boat Show) who hosted evening activities in the Vaasa Hall. Each night more than a thousand sailors came to watch video action of the day's racing and get into some equally serious drinking, eating and dancing. Each class had its own night at the Vaasa Hall.

But even with these sponsors the economic health of Kieler Woche is not in the best shape. As ever, the German Navy supports the KYC but

KIELER WOCHE/KIEL WORLDS

the Defence Ministry asks for more money – to cover overtime and fuel – while the budget becomes increasingly stretched. Indeed, the Navy's bill accounted for much of the 500,000 DM (£167,000) costs remaining after sponsors' money had been used. All that is quite apart from the provisions offered *gratis* such as the press centre and all the harbour facilities.

There was another spectacular present among the myriad gifts: the Tall Ships Parade prior to the start of the Cutty Sark Tall Ships race. More than a hundred of them mustered in Kiel, spending a few days before they departed for their race in the Baltic. A staggering crowd of 300,000 lined the shore to see the old timers and the more modern Tall Ships sail out of Kiel Fiord.

Yet Kieler Woche has always been rather more than a regatta. Ashore, sport, theatre, music, dancing, games and art are all staged, with the festival atmosphere running all along the shore from the ferry docks to the old 1936 Olympic harbour, and from the very centre of the old city to the market place. The event draws in people from all over northern Germany in their thousands as well as visitors from overseas.

But, to return to the sailing, the most outstanding success of Kieler Woche was the fifth successive victory in the 470 class by brothers Wolfgang and Joachim Hunger. This year, they were pushed hard by another German crew, Huttermann and Korte, with both crews going into the last race with

the same points tally after their worst result had been discarded. The reigning champions showed their best form to triumph in the finale and win the 108-strong class.

East Germans Schumann and Flach took the honours in the Soling Class with three firsts, a distinction also achieved in the Tornado class by Australians Cairns and Forbes. In the venerable Star class, the West Germans Griese and Marcour led the fleet until the fifth race but had to be content with 2nd overall behind the American crew of Adams and Olsen.

The Russian Oleg Khoperski dominated the singlehanded Finn class while his countrymen Borodinov and Surin did the same in the two-handed Flying Dutchman class. As for the women in the 470s, the Kiwis continued their recent run of success in this section with Galloway and Schearer recording a win. Perhaps the best individual performance in the entire event was that by the Italian Paco Wirz who posted a perfect 0.0 pts score in the windsurfer (light) division with the heavy division taken by Thomas Muller of West Germany.

Oddly, Kieler Woche was not that important in terms of results. Those crews who came to compete used it very much as a practice for the Worlds which followed. Many took the opportunity to test new boats and sails, and to optimise their performance in Kiel conditions.

The Kiel Worlds themselves got off to a very damp start, 2000 competitors from 38 nations braving the heavy

showers of the opening ceremony to find that the regatta that followed was spoiled by little or no wind. Luck played a large role in determining the titles up for grabs. With wind shifts of 100 degrees or more and large areas of suffocating calm, the Worlds were little more than a game of poker played on a giant scale out in Kiel Fiord.

Whatever the conditions, one subject seemed to be very important among the competitors: weight, especially among the Star and Soling fleets. Some sort of record was set by the Dutchman Vandenberg (who, with Steven Bakker, was the champion going into the Kiel Worlds) at some 300 lb (135 kg). Also among the Big Men was Australian Matthew Percy, who was the middleman in Jamie Wilmot's Soling, reputed to have been able to pack one of *Australia IV's* big genoas in 90 seconds and still be able to bring it up on deck singlehanded. Just as in offshore racers, heavy crews mean more stability, which in turn means more speed.

Another topic of considerable debate was that of outside assistance. Advice to competitors whilst competing is clearly illegal, yet the frequencies used by race officials to transmit results back to the computer centre were regularly found filled with coaching advice in all languages. Some of the sailors were seen using small VHF radios while racing. Nevertheless, proving they were being used for illegal purposes, as opposed to monitoring the race committee's radio traffic for instance, was impossible. Winning is what

every competitor strives for, but it appears that, for some sailors today, sportsmanship takes the back seat.

Even if the conditions conspired to make the results of the Kiel Worlds a poor form guide to those preparing for next year's Olympic regatta, there were some stunning performances none the less.

Take the Doreste family from Spain, for instance. José Luis ended up as Finn World Champion; Luis, the FD World Champion; and the youngest brother, Manuel, a creditable 15th in the FDs – a fast family! Then there were the West German girls Meyer and Adlkofer who won the women's 470 Worlds, with Susanne Meyer sailing with one leg in plaster. Her leg became increasingly painful as sea water had got trapped between the flesh and its cast.

Despite the less-than-ideal conditions I would like to leave the final word to American Star boat sailor and World Champion Vince Brun. With his crew Hugo Schreiner, Brun took line honours three tmes in the Star fleet on his way to adding the European title to his collection. He concluded: 'Kiel is just great. It is a Mecca of yachting. Such a big regatta that is so well organised is something I have never experienced before.'

Brun, and many others, will be back in 1988.

Erik von Krause is an editor with the leading West German magazine Die Yacht. *He is also a top offshore navigator and has competed in the last four* Champagne Mumm Admiral's Cups.

The big 470 fleet was split into separate divisions for the men and women.

Among the keelboats sailing in Kieler Woche
were the van de Stadt-designed Sprinta Sports.

KIELER WOCHE/KIEL WORLDS

**Folke Larsen won the Quarter Ton Cup in his
Tony Castro-designed MG 26, *McDonald's*.**

Ton Cups

by W.M. NIXON

Notwithstanding the unfortunate rumours concerning Prince Hamlet, one had always tended to think of the Danes as a happy-go-lucky, unsolemn people. Until, that is, one met Folke Larsen. Mr Larsen had been pursuing the Quarter Ton World title with dogged determination for at least three years. Mr Larsen is not into smiling. But even he managed a slight display of pleasure when, on the sunlit waters off Cork on Tuesday, 1 September, he finally achieved his ambition.

Folke Larsen's somewhat gloomy view of life had been in no way improved by his experience in the 1986 Quarter Ton Cup in his own home waters. Racing a Tony Castro-designed MG 26 called *Whopper*, he appeared to have won the event but for a disqualification – a query over navigation lights – and two years of effort seemed to have been wasted.

But Mr Larsen is nothing if not determined. He gathered himself again for 1987, getting a very sophisticated hyper-light MG 26 specially built in England by Steve Etheridge, and moving his sponsorship meanwhile within the fast food world with the new boat being *McDonald's*.

Then off he went to Crosshaven in Southern Ireland, where the Royal Cork Yacht Club were preparing a superb regatta with all the calm expertise which you can build up over 267 years of existence.

Into this relaxed atmosphere came Mr Larsen with *McDonald's* to remind everyone that official ORC World Championships are a very serious business. The greatest obstacle to his ambition was a little boat whose campaign contrasted very strongly with his own. Owned by Justin and Lynda Burke of the National YC on Dublin Bay, and skippered by Gordon Maguire of Howth, *Quest* had been designed in the Rob Humphreys office under the special attention of Marcus Hutchinson, and had been built relatively low-tech and economically by Stuart Deas of Wiz Boats in Bristol.

She's had some fun on the way to Cork, having dominated her class in the McEwan's Scottish Series in early summer, become overall champion of ISORA Week, and swept the board in class at Sandhurst Cowes Week. For the Quarter Ton Worlds, she became *Innovation Group Quest*, sponsored by an advertising agency.

Each of the world level rating championships has its own special atmosphere and the quarter ton level still seems to be the one at which new crews and designers and builders can begin to prove themselves seriously for the bigger stuff. But there are plenty of adherents, too, who simply like this size of boat, and so the fleet of 23 which gathered at Cork for the big event included a mixture of old stagers, rising stars and hired killers.

In the midst of all this, the *McDonald's* campaign was outstandingly determined. In addition to being 880 lb (400 kg) lighter than any other contender, the Larsen boat also brought in the talents of Poul Jensen. Winning an Olympic Gold Medal in either the Soling or the Star class would be a good training for the three Olympic races of the Quarter Ton Worlds. Mr Jensen has done both . . .

Even so, with a windshift towards the end of the first Olympic course, neither of the hot shots took the gun, which went to the Scottish entry *Senator Incitatus* (Caligula's horse), an attractive boat remarkable for being designed, finished and skippered by Jim MacIlwraith. But while *McDonald's* had slipped from the lead to 3rd through the shift, *Innovation Group Quest* dropped back to 6th.

However, the long offshore race next day (Wednesday 26 August) changed things somewhat, a near gale from the north at the start dismasting *Incitatus*, while the rigours of a 110-mile course in a small boat showed that even Poul Jensen can't helm for ever. Although *McDonald's* was nine minutes ahead after a planing run out to the offshore mark 30 miles at sea, the tough beat back saw *IG Quest* take a lead which she didn't afterwards lose, finishing some five minutes ahead of the Danes, with the next boat, clarinet ace Jean Ramon's *MNEF*, getting 3rd for France half an hour astern.

A hyper-light day of Olympic coursing on Saturday 29 August had the Danes winning again, and as *MNEF* took 2nd with *Quest* 3rd, the gap between the two leaders widened once more. However, the Irish boat then showed her enjoyment of offshore racing by taking the 78-mile offshore race in a brisk easterly, the lead being 2m 14s from *McDonald's*.

This meant that the outcome of the final race (an Olympic course) would decide which of the two top contenders would become the new World Champion, as *Innovation Group Quest's* weakness in the inshore racing had been more than offset by the higher points awarded for offshore success, and both had to be more than ten places behind MNEF.

It was clear that everything would hinge on *Quest's* ability to increase her lead sufficiently on the first four legs in order to offset the advantage the lighter Danes would have on the dead run. She got ahead as planned in a moderate northerly which disobligingly softened on the run. Just 300 metres from the leeward mark, *McDonald's* slipped through, and on the beat, though the breeze came to life again, Poul Jensen refused to be drawn into a tacking duel. By keeping a loose cover on *Quest's* wild flyer away to the west, he actually finished 7th, but *Quest* was 11th as the rest of the fleet streaked up the beat with the gun being taken by *Drakkar Noir* (Anthony O'Leary) of the host club.

It was quite a moment for Tony Castro's MG 26 design, which also took the Production Boat prize through Trevor Halliwell's *Mad Gamble* from Northern Ireland placing 9th in the overall listings. Nevertheless, while the new and deserved World Champion *McDonald's* must surely be the ultimate development of the MG 26 design, one had the feeling the *Quest* story was only beginning.

W.M. Nixon is editor of the Irish yachting magazine Afloat *and a contributor to newspapers and many other magazines including* Yachting World.

ONE TON CUP

by ERIK von KRAUSE

Of the 34 yachts competing, just two were in contention for the title of 1987 World Champion one tonner. Right up until the final race, the third Olympic triangle, the One Ton Cup was a match between two Farr boats, *Fram X* and *Sirius IV*.

Neither boat had sailed in the Champagne Mumm Admiral's Cup earlier in August but each had been specially prepared for the level rating event.

With an excellent series of results in which a 5th was the worst, *Fram X* won the last race to secure the title. *Sirius IV* had needed to finish three places ahead of the Norwegian yacht to make the Cup hers, so she had to accept 2nd place, well ahead of the 3rd-placed yacht, *Monaco*.

Owned by Crown Prince Harald of Norway, *Fram X* was campaigned superbly. The boat had been built in New Zealand by Cookson Brothers and shipped to Norway in a ready-to-sail condition. Her crew tuned the yacht in several Baltic races before heading south to Kiel.

Sirius IV, on the other hand, was one of last year's yachts yet none the worse for that. She placed 2nd in the 1986 One Ton Cup in Palma and was considered very much the yardstick by which the new boats were judged, her 1987 Farr-designed successors included.

Owned and sailed by the Spanish Navy from their base in Palma, *Sirius IV* benefited from having as tactician Ib Ussing Andersen of Diamond Sails in Copenhagen. He has been instrumental in several recent Spanish sailing successes and is active in promoting Grand Prix racing in that country. There is a personal side to his involvement with Spanish efforts, for his wife is the daughter of the Spanish national sailing association's president.

Most of the other competitors had rushed to Kiel from Plymouth, where they had finished the Fastnet Race to round off the Admiral's Cup. Few of them, therefore, arrived in time to train in Kiel, to obtain new sails or even to have a break before the rigours of another tough series. The lack of a breathing space between two such important events can be no excuse for losing but neither is it entirely satisfactory.

The Kieler YC had little choice in the matter for it had been fully occupied with the Kieler Woche and Kiel Worlds during June and July. As

YPS/Peter Neumann

the dinghy and keelboat sailors had already discovered, Kiel is a demanding place to sail. Weather conditions are unpredictable, and the tides and currents of the western Baltic are difficult.

Of the five races, only the first Olympic triangle could be considered a fair one. A steady wind on the Stolergrund brought a short, steep sea but at least the windshifts were small, no more than 10 degrees. *Sirius IV* performed to expectations when she led around the course with the best Admiral's Cup boats in pursuit. Harold Cudmore, sailing Guillermo Cryns' Gonzales-designed *Mayurca*, protested successfully Udo Schütz's *Container* for a port and starboard incident. Elsewhere, *Container*'s sister ship, *New Yorker* (ex-*Outsider*), retired with a mast failure, as did 1986 champion *Andelstanken*. The German all-girl crew on *Rodeo* pulled out minutes after the start with a damaged forestay.

Despite not being a pre-series favourite, *Fram X* attracted interest by taking a 2nd behind *Sirius IV* and ahead of *Mayurca*. In 4th place was *Andelsbanken*, a new epoxy version of the X One Ton design which had won in 1986 as *Andelstanken*. The old crew under helmsman Jens Christensen and tactician Henrik Soderlund had moved over to the new boat, sponsored by the Danish bank of the same name. In 1986 they had changed the name of her predecessor to *Andelstanken* as a thin disguise to fulfil the requirements of Rule 26.2 and, confusingly, the new Italian owners of the 'old' boat had retained this name.

The 380-mile offshore race was a demanding event. A 32-mile starboard tack beat took the fleet into Denmark's Lillebelt, followed by a reach along the island of Arø with a square run in fresh conditions to Gedser. Britain's Eddie Warden-Owen led for the most part on the Andrieu-designed *Monaco* with Alan Gray's *Jamarella* close behind. But those who really enjoyed the run were the German *Saudade* (ex-*Rubin IX*) and the French *Centurion-Musclor* (ex-*Jade*).

The race continued with a 55-mile close reach to the north-east and the Kullagrund lighthouse off the Swedish coast. The remainder of the course took yachts off on another run before a beat back around Gedser and the Fehmarnbelt mark some 30 miles from the finish. As is the way of ocean races, it wasn't that straightforward. Minutes after the yachts had started tacking back to Kullagrund, a light, 30-degree wind shift split the fleet. The few who tacked onto starboard after the light got the shift right and were given a big advantage. The remainder tried to recover by tacking close inshore but lost yet more time avoiding large areas of fish traps. And, as a final *coup de grâce*, the wind died altogether when the fleet was just half a mile from the finish line at Kiel. *Fram X* was first home, trailed by *Sirius IV* 30 minutes behind. Most of the fleet struggled home four to six hours later.

If this put the crews in poor humour then the second Olympic triangle did absolutely nothing to improve matters. To many it must have seemed a bad joke. The first leg saw a 40-degree wind shift while the second beat coincided with a 90-degree shift. Yet, despite all this, *Fram X* came through to take 2nd behind another Farr design (also from Spain), *Ramel Dos*.

Unsatisfactory conditions prevailed for the short offshore, too, its start delayed by the absence of wind and the prevalence of fog. When it did get underway the course was the same as the opening part of the long race. Fifty miles from the finish the wind died again and clocked right round the compass. *Sirius IV* made it to the line in 1st place ahead of *Monaco* and *Jamarella*. Once again, *Fram X* showed she could rise to the top, no matter what the conditions, by taking 5th.

After two nights at sea and a finish in the early morning, the competitors were pleased when the committee delayed the start of the final race due at 11.0 a.m. The sailors were not so

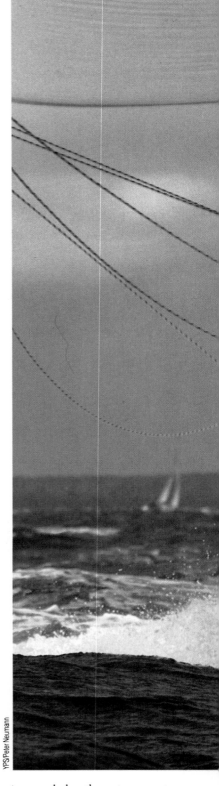

YPS/Peter Neumann

impressed when the postponement was just an hour long and the race turned out to be plagued by shifts as large as 80-degrees, favouring one half of the fleet and then the other. Some areas had no wind at all.

As an example of the great Kiel lottery game, played for high stakes, *Fram X* lay 18th at the first weather mark, whilst *Sirius IV* was well ahead in 1st place and looking as if she had secured the championship. But then the Norwegian yacht got a private wind, literally. She was the only one in the fleet to set a spinnaker and sailed to leeward of all of the 17 yachts ahead, rounding the gybe mark 10 minutes in front of *Sirius IV*. Despite the best efforts of the Spanish/Danish combina-

tion aboard *Sirius IV*, they could do no better than hold on to 2nd for the race, and the championship.

Were frustrations afloat not enough, then the entire Cup was plagued by accusations of cheating. These were not the usual claims of moving sail bags to the weather side but involved much more sophisticated forms of shifting ballast. It was alleged that the German/Japanese Judel/Vrolijk-designed *I-Punkt* had moved 200 litres of water ballast during the Admiral's Cup to boost her stability upwind, and was doing the same at Kiel. On boarding *I-Punkt* to investigate, the International Jury at the One Ton Cup (under Jean-Louis Fabry of France) discovered a two-way bilge pump.

I-Punkt's water tanks were removed to have their contents checked for salt traces but none were found. No evidence was forthcoming from her crew either, despite being questioned one by one. The jury even tried to catch out any cheaters by calling for a last-minute postponement of the short offshore race and sending inspectors aboard yachts with question marks against them. But, again, no proof of cheating was found.

Nevertheless, the series threw up so many questions about cheating that it has to be hoped the national and international authorities can develop realistic and enforceable means of cleaning up the sport in time for next year's Grand Prix events.

The first sign of this came when the RORC took action to have the Admiral's Cup jury reconvened. They took evidence from Thomas Friese and three of *I-Punkt*'s crewmen, and subsequently disqualified the yacht from the Admiral's Cup. The German national authority, the DSV, followed this up by banning Friese from racing in West German waters.

Crown Prince Harald of Norway sailed a remarkably consistent series in *Fram X* despite the flukey conditions at Kiel.

TON CUPS

La Rochelle, 2–14 July
HALF TON CUP

by MARK HEELEY

La Rochelle was a busy place in July. Whilst the 30 entries to the Half Ton Cup did not add significantly to the number of bodies, the tenth summer pop festival certainly did.

Bona fide 1960s hippies arrived *en masse* and set up camp (literally) in, on and around the historic harbour entrance. The audience for this five day and night spectacle came from every corner of Europe, doubtless annoying the countless pickpockets who found themselves having to make frequent trips to the bureau de change. Whilst the common denominator of this cosmopolitan audience was the backpack, that of the music was simply volume. Each of the five separate music stages, which theoretically went live in sequential manner, seemed intent on being remembered as the loudest at the festival. This jarringly competitive element was certainly not on the original agenda but reached its own rather suitable crescendo when La Rochelle literally and metaphorically blew its own fuse. Starved of electrical power, it became its dark and serene self again.

Meanwhile, the Port des Minimes marina immediately adjacent to the old harbour was being used as the location for the half tonners.

The overlying tone of this championship was one of practicality and efficiency. Any brief illusion of a romantic French event was rapidly dispelled by the omnipresent sponsorship and extensive pre-regatta training, with team managers, doctors and coaches almost outnumbering the crews. The French team were clearly intent on winning again what they now consider their own championship.

Rating and measurement verification was handled in a thorough manner but was not without its problems for some competitors. Under the watchful eye of an intelligent-looking man armed with files, clipboards and a portable VHF (immediately dubbed 'le coach'), the French boats had no queries and so were able to return immediately to the job of tuning. Many other boats, however, found the rating judges less easy to satisfy. The slab-sided Joubert/Nivelt designs suffered particularly on the bumps and hollows rule, necessitating copious use of filler and elbow grease. Difficulty was also experienced in reproducing inclination results that might have been obtained two years before on a wet day near a fresh water outlet. The officials' attitude was, quite rightly, far

from *laissez faire*, which led to many eleventh-hour headaches and the Japanese, amongst others, having to load lead into one of their boats.

The first race day got under way in hot, sunny and almost windless conditions. The boats motored out to the racing area, pursued by a spectator fleet which in numbers was genuinely worthy of the phrase 'convoi exceptionel'.

The first Olympic race started on time in five knots of true wind, which rose to barely eight knots at the finish. In smooth water the fleet split left and right, with a 15-degree persistent shift giving the left-hand boats a substantial advantage on approaching the first mark. The Italian *Stern* (Cecarelli 1987) was first round, pursued by *Salora* (Andrieu 1987), who was 2nd overall in 1986, and *Catch Up* (Judel/Vrolijk). In this keyed-up fleet, place changing was difficult; the consistency of the wind direction, which saw barely a murmur of a shift after the first beat, compounded the problem. *Catch Up* was the eventual winner by 25 seconds from *Stern* who accepted a 30 per cent penalty for a collision with *Pinky* (Nissen 1987). Whilst the owner of *Pinky* wore a worried look as he inspected the largely superficial damage to his beautiful, if delicate machine, it was nothing compared to the expression on the face of 'le coach', whose personal and national pride had taken more than a small dent with just one boat in the top ten.

The race committee set one of the shorter courses for the long offshore in full anticipation of light airs, taking the fleet 197 miles around the La Rochelle coast. The race was far from a purely light-airs competition, for the wind periodically filled in to give 15 knots true. The final leg was a downwind slide away from five knots of true wind and saw *EJP3* (Andrieu 1985) surprisingly fail to cover the fleet and lose her 12-minute lead to finish 7th. French boats dominated the race and, with six in the top ten, the spirit of bonhomie returned to the home camp. Conveniently for the French, only three top-ten finishers were repeating their first-race performance, so there was plenty to play for.

True form at last became apparent in the second Olympic race when the top crews squeezed their boats to the front again. *Tom Bombadil* (Joubert/Nivelt 1984) was first round, four seconds ahead of *René Chateau Video* (Andrieu 1983) and *La Concorde* (Berret 1986).

In superb sailing conditions these three took turns to lead around the course, with *La Concorde* the eventual winner.

In the short offshore race, *Silva* (ex-*Cofica*, Berret 1984) showed her double World Champion form by leading the fleet around all but one mark of the 125-mile course. Several boats lost their chance to challenge for overall honours on the very light-air last leg, including *Pinky* who dropped from 2nd to 9th. *Stern*, however, again looked quick in the lighter stuff, pulling up from 10th at the penultimate mark to finish a useful 3rd. *Chateau Video* had another good result at 2nd, and as the only consistent performer she went into an overall lead . . . to the not inconsiderable

relief of 'le coach'.

Chateau Video knew that 10th or better would secure her the title, whereas *Stern*, *Salora*, *EJP3* or *La Concorde* would have to win to have any chance. After three recalls in 14 knots of wind, *Salora* picked the shifts to round first from *Ville de Toulon* (ex-*Freelance*, Briand 1983) and the British *Insatiable* (Andrieu 1985), each within one boat length of the other. *Chateau Video* could only manage 12th at the first mark, but her well-drilled crew showed their mettle as they climbed impressively to finish 5th in the race and 1st overall. *Ville de Toulon* scrapped hard to win from *Salora* (top Olympic course boat) and *EJP3*.

The winner, *René Chateau Video*, is

René Chateau Video won the Half Ton Cup this year, having narrowly missed the title in 1984 as *EJP 2*.

the Andrieu-designed yacht that, as *EJP2*, so nearly won the Worlds in Scotland in 1984. Since then, further speed has been developed as a result of some intensive work by her designer. The sight of a 1983 design winning this year's Worlds might suggest a lack of competition, but this was not the case. Quite simply, with the present stability of the IOR rule, the half ton design concept (which was by far the most developed of the level rating classes in 1984) has remained constant. Thus, a 1986/87 Andrieu design is remarkably similar to a 1983 sister and, indeed, when asked directly and 'off the record', several designers can promise no more speed from a 1987 design. Although this does allow for advances

in construction techniques, it is of less significance in a half tonner than a larger one tonner.

This is all essentially good news for the sailors, as boats of 1983 vintage onwards have categorically proved themselves to be as competitive as the latest 1987 creations.

One of the 1987 boats was *Pinky*, a development of *Portuguese Connection/ Flyer*, who placed 2nd in 1985 and 3rd in 1986. She had been immaculately built by Speedwave and had shown form by beating most of the French triallists at La Trinité in May. Her progressive design included all running rigging lines being led under the coachroof in Dubois one tonner style, a bulb keel and a high-tech three-

spreader rig. Steered by the prolific Ruddi Magg of Speedwave/Denninger & Maile fame, she never quite had the necessary speed and agility to recover from some indifferent starts.

Australian David Birkhill chartered the Briand-designed *Passion 4* (a 1986 boat) and brought together the same crew which had won the Quarter Ton Cup in 1986. Despite the talented crew, *Passion 4* failed to impress and found it hard to stay with the front runners as the wind went lighter.

With ten of his designs in the fleet, Daniel Andrieu was the best-represented designer. Better still, five of them finished in the top ten, including the winner. Whilst no one boat had a clear boat speed advantage,

the Andrieu designs seemed to be the best all-rounders. In a series where overtaking was notoriously difficult, a good start and consistent speed were at a premium. *René Chateau Video's* advantage in this respect was complemented by a particularly strong offshore performance.

Once again, the French won the individual prize and the team prize, making 'le coach' a very happy man indeed as he turned his attention to Poole in England for the 1988 event.

Mark Heeley campaigned his own half tonner Insatiable *both at La Rochelle and throughout the Solent-based championships.*

THREE-QUARTER TON CUP

by WILLY MOONS

Nieuwpoort literally means Newport and as a yachting centre the Belgian town is as famous in its own way as its more illustrious American namesake.

Belgium may be one of the more modest sailing nations but the KYCN club had already staged the 1984 Quarter Ton Cup before this year's event and has been granted the right to stage the 1991 One Ton Cup too.

As Ton Cups go, this was not a particularly competitive field in terms of new boats or size of the fleet. Only 15 of them lined up on 19 August for the series, the 1986 winner *Indulgence* among them. No longer British owned, this Daniel Andrieu-designed yacht was sailing under the Italian flag and had high hopes of retaining her title.

The only other one-offs in the fleet which threatened to trouble her were the Philippe Briand-designed *Prudential Bache* (ex-*Dear Pablo*) and the Stephen Jones-designed *Fiona of Burnham* (ex-*Lion*). According to the form book, *Indulgence*'s Italian skipper, Vittorio Codecasa, should have had only the Flemish waters to master, but, like the last seven Three-Quarter Ton Cups, the Nieuwpoort series became a battle between the production X-Yachts and Dehler db types.

Competition between the Danish Niels Jeppesen-designed and built X 3/4 Tonners and the Dutch/German van de Stadt-designed and Dehler-built db2s has been going on since the 1982 Cup in La Trinité sur Mer. But as far as Dehler are concerned it looks as if the new db3 revisions have not kept pace with their arch-rivals.

The superiority of the early db1s (in 1981 they took the first five places in Helsinki) and the db2 in which Carl Dehler himself won the 1984 Kiel championship ahead of two sister ships has been eclipsed by the Danish boats.

As early as 1982 the X 3/4 Tonner's forerunner, the X-102 *Lille Du*, beat the db1s in Spain at Denia. The same happened in 1985 at Marstrand, Sweden, when *Green Piece* took the title. And the X 3/4 Tonner *Front Runner* finished 3rd in 1986 at Torquay when the production boats came up against serious competition from custom one-offs (*Indulgence* and the Humphreys-designed *Decasol*) at last.

Few eyebrows were raised at Nieuwpoort, therefore, when seven X 3/4 Tonners and three db3s turned up. Along with the rest of the fleet they raced in all manner of conditions, from mirror-like seas which saw yachts kedging in the tide to a full gale in the short offshore race which ended in retirement for five yachts plus damage to two masts and a boom.

The first 24-mile Olympic race was shortened due to light air but was won by the Belgian X boat *Salamander*. Local knowledge seemed to be the key for this host country victory as navigator Jacky Rogge (a former Finn champion and vice-president of the Belgian Olympic Committee) took *Salamander* in 7th place out to sea, around the parked leaders, where she found a private breeze to take the lead.

The long offshore race was shortened prior to the start simply by deleting the first and last marks from the course to bring the distance down from 240 miles to 190. But the course change caught out a few navigators because they failed to cancel the last buoy's waypoint from their Decca sets. After a long and trying race in light airs, they sent their yachts off on a needless 24-mile leg only to come to the line and finish incorrectly from the wrong direction.

Indulgence had led at every mark and she was the first to sail the wrong course, followed by *Prudential Bache* and *Temeraire* from Belgium. The winner of the race was 1987 Dutch X 3/4 Ton *Jelfi-X*, sailed by Pieter Carels, who crossed the line six hours after *Indulgence*. The latter's error put her out of the running just as surely as it did for *Prudential Bache*.

Indulgence made up for her mistake in a small way by sailing a faultless third race, the second Olympic triangle. As

Eveline

before, she led the whole way round ahead of 2nd-placed *Ramasjang* from Denmark. *Ramasjang*'s consistency, in the hands of skipper Steen Anderson, ensured that she went into the series' lead.

Ironically, lack of wind delayed the start of the short offshore race and when it got going, it still took competitors one hour to sail the mile to the first mark. There they kedged to hold station against a foul running tide which threatened to take them back to the startline.

Those who prayed for wind certainly got it. By the time *Prudential Bache* rounded the second mark in the lead, the wind had come through, a Force 6-7 north-westerly which built into a Force 8 gale. The Dutch *X-treem* and the Royal Air Force's *Wings of Cowley* from England pulled out because of the weather and crew injuries, but worse was to come. Series leader *Ramasjang* was dismasted when her backstay failed and the German *Zwiebel* headed for Nieuwpoort with a broken boom.

Race leader *Prudential Bache* was put under pressure by *Indulgence* who threatened her as night fell, only to retire when her mast collapsed without warning. Eventually *Jelfi-X* placed 2nd behind *Prudential Bache* to stake her claim to the series.

In the final Olympic triangle *Jelfi-X* was almost sure to win the Cup if she could finish near the top . . . which she did with a 3rd place. There was a good local scrap among Belgian boats for 2nd place. A win by *Prudential Bache*, who enjoyed the north-westerly Force 6 conditions, made sure of her runner's-up slot, while yet another mast, the third in the championships, fell from the Dutch db1 *Matjas*.

Whatever the depth of the competition, the series certainly did not lack interest.

Willy Moons is a Belgian journalist who works for De Standard.

Three-quarter Ton World Champion *Jelfi-X* is seen with *Prudential Bache* at the start of the short offshore race.

TON CUPS

Centomiglia

by PAULO VENANZANGELI

As the largest of the Italian lakes, Garda is virtually an inland sea. It separates two of the most industrial regions of the country, Lombardy and Venice, and, with such large centres of population close by, it has always been an important sailing centre.

Garda is also a major destination for foreign tourists, particularly Germans, who appreciate the warm hospitality of the inhabitants and the beauty of the surroundings.

Each little town along the shore has its own harbour, protected against the sometimes strong winds. These winds attract the boardsailors, particularly to the northern part of the lake near Torbole. There the local wind, the Peler, can turn the morning surface of the lake white as it blasts down from the Alps.

While the north is narrow and surrounded by vertical rock faces, the southern part is more open. Like most of the Alpine lakes which were created in the Ice Age, the more open parts of the lake in the south make for more shifty and unpredictable winds.

Garda, then, has always had a strong sailing tradition and its varied winds have brought a consequent variety in yachting from the fiercely competitive to the gentle recreational.

The Centomiglia began 37 years ago near Brescia, a town where the famous Mille Miglia motor race was founded. While that was a thousand-mile race, the yacht race required competitors to sail just 100 miles. Every September all the Garda boats would meet at Gargnano on the lake's western bank for what was initially more of an adventure under sail than a yacht race. The classes were divided quite simply by waterline length and a huge variety of

yachts have competed over the years. In 1951 the winner was the 6-metre *Airone*. In 1964 the late president of the International Yacht Racing Union, Beppe Croce, won in the 5.5-metre *Manuela VI*. America's Cup sailor Flavio Scala won in 1966 in a Star boat, and in 1971 Giorgio Falck narrowly won in his Class 1 ocean racer *Guia*.

But what the simple length rule did not anticipate was that not only would boats be built especially for the race but in time they would be some of the most extraordinary monohulls afloat. The Class Libera boats have evolved slowly from 1972 to their present spectacular state complete with sitting-out platforms, trapeze racks, towering fractional rigs which can set masthead spinnakers and the most advanced composite construction. They have won the race every year since 1972 and have been likened to the 18 ft skiffs of Sydney Harbour. There is one important difference, however: the biggest Class Libera Garda racers are as long as 42 ft (13 m).

The spectacle of these overblown dinghies brings out the crowds both to stare at their praying-mantis forms ashore when they arrive on road trailers and to enjoy the man-versus-machine struggle afloat. Such is the local importance of the event that the twisty lakeside roads become blocked and the towns, with their narrow streets, pretty squares and promenades, are choked with the public. The talk is all about sailing, with most reckoning they are a second Pelaschier.

The early-morning start, necessary to complete the 100-mile course, does not seem to put off the crowds. In fact, the sight of the sun rising from behind

Though the Libera boats grab the headlines, the Centomiglia is open to all manner of conventional boats.

CENTOMIGLIA

When it goes wrong . . . *Liberini*'s crew fail to right their Lake Garda racer.

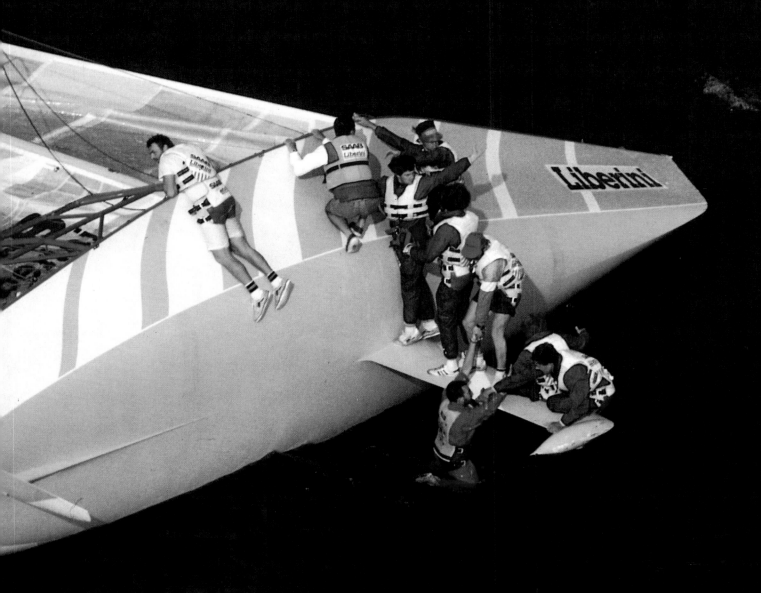

Right: **Among the big spectator fleet are the traditional Lake Garda paddle-steamers.**

Below: ***Cassiopea II*'s crew enjoy the Garda scenery from their vantage point.**

Carlo Borlenghi

Mt Baldo and warming up the colours of the lake is an added attraction. But even a 5.30 a.m. alarm is not sufficient to get all the competitors ready in time. Congestion in the little harbours means that some crews miss their starts and the early-morning light winds give little scope to catch up.

This year's innovation was not in the Class Libera but in the rest of the 180-strong fleet, which is made up of IOR classes, one-designs such as the Soling, J-24 and Sprinta Sport, and the cruiser classes. It was the new Beppe Croce Trophy for the best time by a non-Libera boat, put up in honour of the two-time winner of the race.

The trophy was to mark Croce's long association with the sport in general and the Centomiglia in particular. President of both the IYRU and the Italian national authority, the FIV, Croce had once said of the race: 'All regattas make news and, with time, their own history. But very few can add a fairy tale, called the Centomiglia, to this news and history.'

The lake's cyclic winds force competitors to tackle heavy air during the morning as they beat north past Campione, Malcesine and Limone to complete a short sausage before they turn south for the long leg from Capo Reamol right down to Desenzano, finally heading north once more to the finish off Gargnano. As the breeze eases in the afternoon, it swings round

to the south as the new Ora wind establishes itself. While the big Libera boats finish fairly smartly, the slower cruising boats struggle to find wind on the shores and to avoid each other as they bunch at the buoys in the gathering dusk. Much of the fleet finishes at night, navigation lights showing, though not too late to join the post-race celebrations.

As for the Libera boats, when they turn downwind they are able to set their colossal spinnakers skiff-style using poles launched through, or just above, the stem. With their fully battened mainsails, these boats can touch 25 knots, such is the combined effect of their staggering power/weight ratios and their ability to use live ballast to keep them on their feet.

The Libera boats are what the crowds and photographers come to see, the boats frequently in danger of collision in the mêlée of craft which include the traditional Garda paddle steamers, customs launches near the Italian/Swiss border and all manner of small motor boats. When the Libera crews get it right, it is a fine display of synchronised sailing with ten men moving in and out of the trapeze wires as helmsman, throttle man (the mainsheet trimmer) and the rest of the crew keep the boat upright in the changing breeze. When it goes wrong it is even more spectacular, with crewmen not coming in off the trapeze quick enough

in the tacks getting an involuntary ducking. A poorly anticipated gust can, and often does, overwhelm the boat.

Whatever the class of boat, the changing breeze strength and direction makes the Centomiglia a tough race for finding the wind which is so strongly affected by the surrounding hills and gullies. Gears have to be shifted constantly so that rigs have the right sail combination and trim.

Winner of the race was *Lillo*. Skipper Andrea Damiani had already won last year's race and he managed to claw back the lead from *Ines*. Early on in the race a particularly savage Peler gust had capsized three boats, causing one to retire with mast damage.

Only one boat headed *Lillo* home and that was the smaller *Uragan Italsat* sailing the shorter course. Her time of 10h 05m 22s got her home 22 minutes ahead of *Lillo* and the other Libera greyhounds, winning the Beppe Croce Trophy. Among the hares, the slowest boat around the course was the German *Surlej Express* which managed a pedestrian 16h 50m 50s.

But for many, competing in the Centomiglia is a goal in itself.

Paulo Venanzangeli is a journalist and photographer with the Italian journal Nautica, *where he is responsible for race event coverage.*

When it goes according to plan . . . *Grifo* was one of the first of the new skiff-style Garda racers complete with flared topsides, racks and trapezes.

Carlo Borlenghi

CENTOMIGLIA

British Summertime

by PETER JOHNSON

The Royal Ocean Racing Club, with its headquarters in the very centre of London, organised no less than 18 offshore courses in 1987. Though it sometimes runs races as far away as the China Sea, the current year showed only one in foreign waters, the Caribbean race from Gran Canaria to Barbados in late November. No other organisation in the world carries such a season-long programme offshore and there is no comparable club or association in any other country.

This heavy programme was maintained in 1987 against a continuing fall in the number of International Offshore Rule boats both in Britain and Europe and certainly in the USA. From a peak in Britain of around 1800 in 1975, the total of valid rating certificates had fallen to about 950 in the current year. However, the number of boats rated under the newer Channel Handicap System (CHS) has risen considerably to 1600 from none at all three years ago, and there is now an additional class for them in RORC races. The 1987 season saw 21 boats competing in five or more events, though considerably more in just one or two.

As ever, there was continued support from Dutch and French-owned yachts, which figured well in the prize lists. Several races finished in ports of those countries. Other nationalities were also represented in the lists of starters, especially in the Channel and Fastnet races, apart from the Admiral's Cup entries. Being a Fastnet year, the entry lists were swollen, not only because of that race and its effect on bringing boats to British waters, but also because the Fastnet entry qualification (which has been in force since 1979) demands each competitor complete at least two RORC races in the same season, with the skipper and at least half the Fastnet crew on board.

Despite all this, the number of starters in the Fastnet, just under 200, was the lowest since 1969, which is just before the IOR was introduced. Another regular event, the Morgan Cup, held every year in mid-June, also had its smallest entry list since the start of the IOR; indeed, if the 19 CHS entries were not counted the number was very low indeed.

For several years, the Solent clubs have organised day racing on most weekends when there is no RORC race and such events comprise the Solent Points Championship (SPC). The last two years have witnessed a dramatic

fall in the number of entries and 1987 saw no reversal of this trend. About 40 boats have been regular starters in the six classes, but Class 1 has really only been used as Admiral's Cup trials, so that one SPC weekend in mid-September produced a total of just 12 starters. The organisers have split the series into an 'early' and 'late' points, to fit in with individual sailing programmes. It would seem advisable now for the clubs to revert to running the various races on an individual basis, for most of the events existed before the SPC was instigated. By contrast, Sunday morning series in the autumn, run from Hamble and Lymington, get consistently good support; so do specific events, such as the annual Cowes–Deauville, reported below, and, of

course, the Island Sailing Club's Round the Island race.

The races

The 605-mile Fastnet was a light to moderate affair in 1987. Only 10 per cent of the fleet retired, in comparison to 65 per cent in 1985. Of the starters, 20 per cent were Admiral's Cup yachts. The only maxi in the race, *Nirvana* (Marvin Green, US), already held the Fastnet elapsed time record and was first to finish in 74h 7m 25s, but dropped to 22nd in class on corrected time. Her compatriot, *Sidewinder*, a very attractive 35 rater (Randy Short, US), won the class, after finishing seven and a half hours later. The winner of the Fastnet Cup was Michael

Peacock's *Juno*, rating at 30.5 and designed by Rob Humphreys, while just five seconds behind her on corrected time was *Jamarella* (Alan Gray), whose rating exceeded *Juno*'s by just 0.04 ft (using the new IOR system which allots hundredths of a foot). *Jamarella* actually finished two and a half minutes ahead. *Propaganda* (Adrian Burr, NZ) was a minute ahead of both. Such timings may not be uncommon now, but they are still remarkable for a race of such length and boats of different design, albeit to the same rating. Modern navigational aids and computers do tend to give tacticians the same solutions.

For sponsored boats the RORC has an 'Open class' now and, in this, *Irish Independent/Full Pelt* had the best time in the fleet, but she was not eligible for the traditional prizes. *Jamarella* was designed by Bruce Farr and *Pelt* by Ed Dubois.

Fastnet conditions were not untypical, with a beat all the way from Cowes to west of the Longships. There were many windshifts to be worked and spring tides to cause hard thinking at Portland, Start Point and Lizard. Despite a westerly filling in for the reach out to Fastnet Rock, it did not pay to hold up to the west, for those that did found themselves on a slack run near the Irish coast, while those who kept a little to the north and east fetched into the Rock. The only blow occurred on the Tuesday with some 12 hours of winds up to 35 knots, drizzle, bad visibility and some confused seas over the Labadie Bank. For the smaller classes, the race ended with light air along the Cornish coast, fog at the Scillies and boats under light spinnakers finishing in tight bunches.

By contrast, the early races were windy and sometimes cold. The traditional opener for the Cervantes Trophy on 2 May was won by *Jamarella* at an average speed of 8.4 knots over the 140-mile course. This was mainly due to a Force 7 northerly which made the last leg from Poole Fairway to Cherbourg inner harbour very fast (after a Spithead–EC2–Poole leg). The Loujaine Cup, two weeks later, was a triangle in the Channel taking in the Nab Tower, Needles Fairway buoy,

RORC Class 1 Champion was Graham Walker's Andrieu 44 *Indulgence*.

BRITISH SUMMERTIME

Jacobite (centre), an Oyster 41, had yet another successful RORC season.

Tom and Vicky Jackson's *Sunstone* (below) had another great year offshore for a 'golden oldie'.

EC1 buoy and Nab again, starting and finishing in Spithead. The course was only 130 miles and, again, it was a quick race, despite moderate winds. The new *Indulgence* (Graham Walker), designed by Andrieu and built in France by B&B, averaged 8.1 knots. More than one-third of the starters were CHS class.

The De Guingand Bowl, from Lymington to Torbay and back to Spithead, was a buster with a steady Force 8 for much of the time and a proportion of broken masts, a broken rudder (which involved calling out the lifeboat) and retirements for other reasons including a man overboard and a crew injury. For a period off the Devon coast, the westerly involved beating into Force 9 and 55 per cent of the fleet did well to finish. Although *Indulgence* was the winner, a remarkable feat was that of *Barracuda of Tarrant* (Bob Fisher), sailed by the RORC Vice Commodore and AC selectors. She had a faster time than all except *Indulgence*, surfing back from Torbay under spinnaker and finishing a long way ahead of any other CHS boat. Designed as definitely 'non-IOR' by Tony Castro, she has twin rudders.

The North Sea race is mainly a Dutch affair these days and was won by *Caiman* (Gerrit Jeelof, NL); the Morgan Cup was largely sailed in fog, was very tidal and ended in light air. Light weather also dogged the Cowes to St Malo race, which this year went direct from the Needles to Casquets and had 197 starters, 96 of them CHS and 21 in the IOR being Sigma 33 OODs. Best corrected time in IOR was by the three-quarter tonner *Jane Bottomley* (Robert Bottomley), designed by Rob Humphreys. A traditional Channel race course has for some years been abandoned and this year appeared to have been designed for the media, rather than the competitors, with no less than four legs between EC2 and the Nab–Owers area. It was not well supported outside the Admiral's Cup, partly because it clashed with the first weekend of Cowes Week. The irony was that the vintage *Clarionet*, built as a RORC rule one tonner to Sparkman & Stephens designs (J. Breakell), was overall winner.

At the end of the season, the RORC ran three cross-Channel races, each less than 110 miles, which attracted varying support.

Boats of the season

The RORC runs a points system which gives awards to boats and clubs based on their performance over the season. With Harold Cudmore in charge of *Indulgence*, she had a clear lead in Class I, followed by *Caiman*. In Class II, where the one tonners are to be found, the order was *Jamarella*, with Rodney Pattisson and Lawrie Smith sailing her, *Juno*, and then *Junon* (A. Faure), a French one tonner. Class III is one area where current Ton Cup boats are excluded, although it contains the 'old one tonners', which started out at around 27.5 ft IOR. *Asterix* (Willy Walcharts, B), having won the class in both the Cowes–St Malo and Fastnet, was points leader. She is a Contessa 35, designed by Doug Peterson in the early 70s, carries a low rating, but is also sailed with determination. She was followed by two consistent boats, *Jacobite* (Stephen James), a 1984 Stephen Jones design, and *Highwayman* (Sir Peter Johnson), a 1981 Rob Humphreys design. Following them closely were *Xara* (David Barham), *Geronimo* (Alan Curtis) – both Swans – *Rakau* (Gérard Louyot, F) and

Pentagram (Lord Burnham). All these boats sailed at least six RORC courses. One is driven to the conclusion that a few boats do a lot of mileage and many boats not so much, in this class and in offshore racing generally.

Two very old boats were 1st and 2nd in Class IV, despite the presence of three-quarter tonners. *Sunstone* (Mr and Mrs T. Jackson) completed an amazing eight RORC races and won the class by a large margin. She was followed by *Clarionet*. Successes by boats of more than a dozen years old reached into Class V, where *Trocar* (Duncan Munro-Kerr, a RORC Rear-Commodore) was winner, beating the very modern half tonner *Stradivarius* (William Borel, F). The latter rescued a man overboard from another yacht early in the season before being herself nearly wrecked on the Lizard rocks in the Fastnet, though fortunately salvaged by lifeboat – but scoring no big Fastnet points!

Solent Points and Channel races

The best-supported SPC races were just before Cowes Week, when foreign AC entries used the races for working up. The classes are different from

Yachting World

Rick Tomlinson

1987 and future pattern

The increasingly high standard of racing, sponsorship of and advertising by leading boats, and the specialisation of Grand Prix ocean racer design has given unprecedented racing and spectacle. It does mean that cruiser-racers (racers, say, on which people live and can also cruise) are excluded from such competition and particularly from certain classes – for instance, Class II RORC and Class 1 SPC. For the first time in its existence, the RORC has two rules and is toying with a third. The IOR, while giving the close results mentioned above, is increasingly being seen as a Grand Prix rule. Channel Handicap, on the other hand, seems likely to attract increasing support and if the boats rating to it in any race are disparate, then more classes can be contrived, using both size and rating bands and also types, such as light or moderate displacement. The latter will deal with the boats with wing keels, double rudders or very light displacement which are new and fast but barred from IOR. Clubs will need to transfer some of their trophies to the class, since the top awards, for historical reasons, are usually presented to IOR winners of poorly supported classes. The third rule comes from the USA in the form of the International Measurement System (IMS) and is unlikely to be used for measurement in Britain until the RORC or other clubs give races under it. Its use is expensive and its time allowance system is complicated and may not be suitable for tidal waters, but it does exist. In 1987, three British boats were certified to it!

Whatever the rules, the fact remains that there are hundreds of boats which continue to prove able at sea in all weather and the support of offshore racing, rising or falling from year to year, is a main feature of sailing enthusiasm in British waters.

Top left: **Bob Fisher's Castro-designed** ***Barracuda of Tarrant*** **was an enthusiastic and successful Channel Handicap campaigner.**

Ernest Juer's Humphreys 50 ***Blizzard*** *(centre left)* **contested the British Admiral's Cup trials and RORC races.**

Left: ***Amanda Kulu***, **a de Ridder-designed High Tension 36, proved that well-sailed 10-year-old boats can still put up good performances.**

BRITISH SUMMERTIME

RORC, with, for instance, RORC III and IV both being in Class 2. Thus *Indulgence* was best in Class 1, which includes all AC boats and those of similar and greater size, whilst in the early points *Jane Bottomley* won Class 2. Half tonners comprise Class 3 and *Insatiable* (J. Bibby and M. Heeley), an older but well-refitted Briand boat, won five out of eight races. Class 4 seldom had less than five starters and the small CHS class, 6, was virtually unsupported.

If the CHS class does not support SPC, it certainly turns out on established cross-Channel fixtures. The Cowes to Deauville (run by two Solent clubs and the Deauville YC) was celebrating its 25th anniversary and had a CHS fleet of 64 yachts, with 24 IOR and 27 Sigma 33s. This 100-mile race ran out of wind on its last ten miles, a characteristic of a number of 1987 races in the Channel. A successful series was the attractive Semaine des Minquiers, or 'Channel Week', held with, and immediately after, the Cowes to St Malo. It consisted of four offshore races between Brittany ports; the IOR class was won by *X-Com* (Pierre Merlivat, F), an AC triallist.

227

Alan Gray's Farr one tonner not only topped
Class II but was RORC Yacht of the Year too.

Burnham Week

by BOB FISHER

Burnham Week always leaves many memories, as its regulars will testify. However, 1987 was particularly memorable, with its highlight being the third win in a row for Tim and Cathy Herring's *Backlash* in the Town Cup. The trophy is the bigger offshore boats' culminating race in the Week and the Herrings' feat is something never performed before.

The Week is not all about big boats. In fact, the opposite is the case, for there are local classes which make up the largest numbers and probably gain the greatest enjoyment, for this is their great week too – an end-of-season championship and get-together with scores to be settled and fun to be had.

But what a week it was. Aeolus had deserted the Crouch until the final Saturday, and tidal gates consequently dominated the racing. There are those who consider the racing to be secondary to the main event at Burnham and, for certain, the parties were well up to the usual standard.

Glamour still surrounds the 'big' class at Burnham and inevitably a few make the passage from the South Coast to take part in what was, traditionally, *the* end-of-season regatta. Between the Wars, professional hands used to be paid off and yachts laid up after Burnham Week, but there is little cause for either these days. Even though support among the bigger boats has fallen away in recent years, the regatta remains a major point in the yachting calendar.

The arrival on the Crouch of Graham Walker's Andrieu 44, *Indulgence* – fresh from her exertions in the British Admiral's Cup team, in the hands of local sparmaker and the boat's regular mainsheet trimmer, John Boyce – triggered the expectation of the majority that she would win as she pleased. Certainly, her early form gave every indication that this would be so.

Indulgence took the Houghton Cup, the East Anglian Offshore event which begins the Week, and then went on to win the next two (the second of them by 12½ minutes) and it seemed that the prophets had got it right. Her most poignant win was also her biggest, for it was the Paul Flemming Memorial Straight Glass Trophy. There were many of Paul's friends among the star-studded crew of *Indulgence*, several of them it, should be said, nursing sore heads following Alastair and Stewart Munro's Shorts & Wellies party. There were some on the Herrings' boat, too, but then *Backlash* lived up to her name:

the silver-hulled Julian Everitt-designed 43-footer, complete with novel forward canard and strut and bulb keel held off every one of *Indulgence*'s challenges in the fourth race to beat her home and, more importantly for the Week's points, put five other boats between them on corrected time.

The change had some other dramatic effects, with Stan Page's Sigma 36, skippered by Dick Lonton, taking a 2nd place to begin her assault on the mid-week trophy. Her next three results sandwiched a 6th between two wins, and she was easily the best, gaining her cup. *Backlash* kept on beating *Indulgence* by the odd place, so when she claimed her two-second win in the Town Cup, she was able to take the trophy for the Week's points.

To the uninitiated, racing at Burnham appears to consist of little more than a charge up and down the River Crouch with a wander among the sandbanks offered in the name of variety; they are the sort who receive their come-uppance at the hands of the local sailors. It is no longer, as Willie Hornby-Steer used to lead the Royal Corinthian One-design sailors in song, 'Holliwell, Roach and Home'. There are now many more buoys (most of them named after nearby farms) around which to race. One of the locals who dealt out a great deal of punishment was Dick Pitcher. At the helm of David Geaves's Stephen Jones-designed three-quarter tonner *Fiona*, Pitcher was only twice pushed into 2nd place. His skilful handling of boat and conditions was an example to the younger competitors.

Another of the more mature brigade to have a week to remember was Terry Wade, whose Dragon *Avalanche* scored

three wins in a twenty-strong fleet. His most significant success came on the Thursday when Wade also celebrated his 60th birthday. The entire class gathered around *Avalanche* at the ten-minute gun to sing their congratulations. On the other hand, Wade will also remember how he threw away the Week's points trophy to Mike Patten in *Union Jack* by rounding the last mark in the final race the wrong way and losing nine places as a result.

Another of those who seem to have raced in Burnham Week since time immemorial is Murray Prior, perhaps the town's best-known boatbuilder. This year he sailed in those most local of boats, the Stellas, and won seemingly as he pleased. His most commanding win came on the Wednesday when, with one of Sonny Cole's granddaughters in his crew, he won by 22 minutes. Those with long memories may recall Sonny winning every race in the original Stella, Dicky Bird's *La Vie en Rose*, and the family connection with the lovely Kim Holman-designed yachts persists.

What the Stella began, the Squib continued: a Burnham boat that went on to enjoy much wider success, eventually becoming a National class.

Fresh from his win at the national championship, Jonathan Tucker took the Oliver Lee-designed class apart during the Week and was only twice edged out of the winning berth.

The best performance, rewarded by the Premium Liferaft's Champion's Bell, was that of *Nab III*, a Meridian 24 in Class 8. The class is one for heavy displacement yachts under 29 ft (8.8 m) LOA where the likes of Folkboats were much in evidence.

Burnham Week also extended its welcome to dinghies, Cadets, Lasers, Larks, GP 14s, Wayfarers and Ospreys enjoying class racing while two handicap classes took care of the rest. Bob Shaw cashed in with *Two Bob Bit* in the Ospreys, winning both the Week and the weekend's trophies, while Ian Montague's 505 *Magic Rabbit* hopped in to take the two-man dinghy handicap class.

But it is perhaps the more indigenous local classes which make Burnham Week what it is. The Royal Corinthian and Royal Burnham One-Designs provide much of the colour while the Estuary One-Designs sail round from Southend-on-Sea for their week's racing. Top of the Estuaries was *Requiem for Woodwind*, which was only once out of breath for 1st place.

Above left: **David Gieves's Jones-designed three-quarter tonner *Fiona*.**

The Robber quarter tonner *T-Leaf* (above) chases a sister ship at Burnham.

Bob Fisher's work in writing, photographing and broadcasting about yachting has taken him to all corners of the globe. But, as an East Coast man, he enjoys returning to his home waters' best-known annual regatta.

BRITISH SUMMERTIME

JOG Season

by BRIAN GOULDER

JOG, or, more precisely, the Junior Offshore Group, was founded in the winter of 1950/51 by a number of people not convinced that the Royal Ocean Racing Club requirement of 24 ft (7.3 m) on the LWL was essential for a yacht to go offshore safely in all reasonable weather.

The moving spirit behind this was Patrick Ellam, whose engaging habit it had been to sail across the English Channel in a sliding seat canoe. He commissioned Jack Laurent-Giles, the leading yacht designer of the day, to design a little boat 19 ft 8 in. (6.0 m) LOA and then convinced John Illingworth, Commodore of the RORC, of the soundness of the idea. The yacht, *Sopranino*, was then allowed, unofficially, to take part in the 1950 Plymouth–Santander race, with Tony Needham as crew. She arrived only a few hours after the last of the 'proper' fleet and, the story has it, Patrick and Anthony then stepped ashore in full yachting rig. Patrick's canoe was called *Theta* and so the Group's burgee became a white theta on a blue ground. *Sopranino* went on to cross the Atlantic with Patrick and Colin Mudie, who had been responsible for her detail drawings, and a classic book resulted.

The group continued to sail these very small yachts for some twenty years until, one suspects, some of the founding fathers sought a little extra comfort and speed, both of which demanded an increase in size. The present fleet would be quite unrecognisable to the 1950 pioneers, for although small yachts are still encouraged, the bulk of those sailing are in the medium range – for example, Impala 28s, Contessa 32s, Sigma 33s and 36s, even Sigma 41s. Not all are one-designs either, for there are also typical three-quarter, half and quarter tonners, of which some are modern and some a trifle long in the tooth, though well-maintained and with encouraging handicaps.

However, the race programme itself has hardly changed (certainly not in principle) since the earliest days. With one exception, JOG avoids the classic pattern of offshore racing in the Channel – a 200-mile slog finishing at the starting place. A typical JOG race starts from Cowes on a Friday evening from the somewhat domestic line at the bottom of Bob Lloyd's garden and then directs the competitors to a pleasant port in France or the Channel Islands in time for dinner on Saturday night, returning ready for Sunday

evening at home and back to work on Monday morning. The actual distance sailed is thus between 150 and 200 miles, but with an interlude of a good dinner and most of a night of undisturbed sleep to ease the pain.

The numbers of JOG starters have increased considerably, if erratically, for some years, with numbers from 1979 running as follows: 201, 296, 264, 371, 384, 476, 383 (a major race cancelled due to bad weather), 523 and this year a new record of 604. There appear to be three obvious reasons for this increase: the greater availability of sound, seaworthy yachts, fast enough to thrill and built well enough not to fall apart; the appearance of the offshore one-designs, a concept which JOG encouraged from the very first; and the arrival of the Channel Handicap System, as an alternative to IOR, another development enthusiastically supported by JOG and which now provides nearly half the total starters.

These reasons, allied to the popularity of the type of racing offered by JOG, are further reinforced by the deliberate JOG philosophy of trying to keep the fun in racing. A low profile, entirely amateur approach is maintained; so with no individual sponsorship, no big names and no big egos to support, a friendly yet very competitive atmosphere prevails, supported by a number of convivial dinners which arrange themselves in French and Channel Island restaurants.

Nor should it be forgotten that the skills of racing offshore have to be learnt by experience and JOG prides itself now on the seamanship of its members, accumulated slowly over the years. New crews are recruited and taught by the older hands and the available pool of crew expands. This is actively encouraged by JOG and, with each set of Sailing Instructions, we issue a list of crew available for that particular race, so that the minimum time is wasted by owners who would otherwise have to work from crew registers, necessarily out of date.

That, then, is the background to the 1987 JOG season. The weather dominated this year as always, providing gales (twice), fog (once) and calm patches (innumerable), but all could be counted as almost ideal weekends; so, apart from the incurable optimists, people enjoyed a typical English Channel summer.

Several new yachts appeared regularly. Michael Moss and John Lawrence disposed of their Grinde and

bought a Sigma 362 with a David Thomas-designed winged keel. Immediately, they moved up from cheerful last, or thereabouts, to somewhere near the top of the CHS Class 8 table. One or two Formula 28s continued to brave the offshore scene, notably *Pinocchio* (who has so many owners that they have to hide behind a cloak of anonymity as 'Team 10'), the rest deciding that the yacht was at her best inshore. Most, however, were old friends of JOG with, thankfully, no high-tech miracles of modern science and no rigs held up by the sleight of hand of the sometime-derided running backstay handler. The one-designs dominated by sheer numbers, mainly Sigma 33s and 36s and Contessa 32s, but one of the original OODs selected by Sir Peter Johnson's committee about 12 years ago, the OOD 34, continues to send a small but enthusiastic and highly competent fleet offshore.

Fashion is a fickle creature and the Impala 28s which have for years turned out with JOG have now largely left the scene and are forming the backbone of one-design fleets elsewhere in the country. One looks somewhere for a successor and wonders why the Laser 28 has not sold better; certainly, the one example which races with JOG, *Leda* (David Brown) has been highly successful despite her rather unsympathetic CHS handicap.

There were 54 different yachts in IOR Class 3–4, 26 in IOR Class 5–7, 70 in CHS Class 8 and 36 in CHS Class 9: 186 in all, averaging between three and four starts each. There have been traditionally two short, daylight races; one at the beginning and one at the end of the season. These were always SONCs (Southsea–Owers–Nab–Cowes) but a combination of factors conspired against the old course. The growth of Portsmouth as a commercial port rendered the Southsea starting line quite impracticable, it was recognised that the Owers Lanby (former light vessel) provided a disastrous tidal gate, and finally JOG operations were transferred to the Secretary's house overlooking Gurnard buoy off Egypt Point. Now the two short races are run with the tidal stream, either round the Nab Tower or out into Christchurch Bay, or even all round the Island.

This year, in an effort to encourage owners to dip their toes into the offshore scene, two other daylight races were run, one to Brighton and one to Poole, via the back of the

Island. The two 'easy' races were sailed in winds of Force 6 or more, the Brighton race provided a screaming spinnaker run all the way and only the Poole race, sailed in a fine sailing breeze and brilliant sunshine, was likely to convince the potential recruit that offshore racing should not carry a government health warning.

Another innovation for 1987 was a daylight race to Cherbourg on Good Friday, the intention being to avoid the biting cold of the middle watch and to enjoy a pleasant sail in the Easter sunshine. Naturally, there was thick fog and drizzle!

The race to St Vaast was supported by a clearing banks contingent and produced 74 entries. Strong winds on the nose, both forecast and actual, reduced the ranks sadly and the race went to the bigger yachts, most capable of crashing on into the considerable seas. The Fecamp race met a similar fate and, with strong (even gale force) westerlies forecast, the finishing line was switched to Le Havre where entry is safe in any weather and state of tide. Two of the new Westerly Storm 33s distinguished themselves and we hope to see many more of them in future.

The race of the year was, as it has been ever since it was inaugurated, the NM Schroder Channel Race, Cowes–St Peter Port, which is supported by Schroder (now with an Australian accent as NM Schroder) and the States of Guernsey. Yet another JOG record was broken with 127 starters, all intent on reaching the finishing line in time for a memorably hospitable reception. Kedging was the skill most in demand as the wind fell very light; most people finished legitimately but the less patient resorted to the 'iron tops'l'. This did not affect the prizegiving luncheon held in Castle Cornet in brilliant sunshine and which was quite unforgettable.

The JOG points system is an ingenious one: devised by Rex Turner, of *Riot* and Brookes & Gatehouse fame, it involves logarithm scales, weighted points and a complex system of discards. It seems to have the undisputed advantage of throwing up the worthy winners, and this year *Jane Bottomley* (Humphreys 33, Robert Bottomley and Peter Bentley) stayed just clear of *Scorpio* (Humphreys 30, Paul Gatrill) in the IOR classes and *Talisman* (Sigma 41, Michael Stephens), the winner of the CHS classes, provided a complete contrast in size to the runner-up, *Blondie* (Bolero, Robin Lawton).

Sir Maurice Laing's three-quarter tonner *Bathsheba* was a regular JOG competitor.

Yachting World

Right: **Robert Bottomley's Humphreys three-quarter tonner** *Jane Bottomley* (ex-*Decasol*) **gave up the Grand Prix circuits for more relaxed – and successful – JOG racing.**

The Heeley/Bibby team had a very successful year of Solent races in their Andrieu half tonner, *Insatiable* (below).

Rick Tomlinson

Brian Goulder is secretary of the Junior Offshore Group as well as of a number of class associations, such as the Sigma 33 and J-24.

BRITISH SUMMERTIME

McEwan's Scottish Series

by BOB CAMPBELL

Though we may still have a small problem remembering that the Scottish Series is now called the McEwan's not the Tomatin, the formula and appeal of this early-season event remain undiminished.

This was the 13th time the event had been held and 176 yachts arrived in the Clyde, to make the Scottish Series the biggest keelboat event in Britain outside Cowes Week. That 76 of the yachts came from beyond the Clyde says much about the drawing power of the May Bank Holiday regatta.

After all, it was a heady brew for any sailor, especially when sponsors McEwan's endeared themselves to the competitors by laying on daily free hospitality. The venue was Tarbert, a small and virtually land-locked fishing port located half-way down the Mull of Kintyre, which acts as the point of departure for the Olympic courses in Loch Fyne and the destination of the three feeder races from Gourock (Clyde), Bangor (Belfast Lough) and Dun Laoghaire (Dublin Bay).

The long overnight feeder races were plagued this year by light airs to such an extent that those struggling up the North Channel from the Dun Laoghaire start were arbitrarily deemed to have finished when the finish-line crew decided at 2.0 a.m. that a second night without sleep was not on. Between these feeder races and the three Olympic type courses was a long inshore race.

Sailed on the Sunday, it was the best race of the '87 series, with the fleet beating out of Loch Fyne towards Mull to sail one or two triangles depending on their class. Nevertheless, the Olympic courses were still as enjoyable as ever. Good plain-sail breezes and busy courses where all classes shared the same weather mark made Loch Fyne a spectacular place for yachting, especially when the sun brought the green hills, dotted with rhododendrons, alive in broad bands of colour.

Winner of the McEwan's Trophy for the yacht judged to have put up the best performance was Alan Fitton's Rob Humphreys-designed three-quarter tonner *Scenario Act II*. Very much a family yacht, with sons Stuart and Anthony as key members of her crew, *Scenario* has enjoyed steady success in Irish Sea races, Cowes Week and previous Scottish Series since her launch in 1983. But for the '87 season Alan Fitton gave her a complete revamp with new sails from Mike Relling and new keel, propeller and spar combination to update her speed/rating. It seemed to do the trick, for *Scenario*'s well-accustomed crew kept her near the front throughout. She won the high points scoring feeder race from Gourock (which is loaded more favourably than the Bangor and Dun Laoghaire races as more yachts take part), and then strung together four 2nds in the other races.

This year, *Scenario*'s efforts were a little overshadowed by the Irish Admiral's Cuppers who were using the Scottish Series as part of their trials. Though numbers were down in the IOR classes, the battle royal between the Dubois-designed *Jameson Whiskey* and Briand-designed *Local Hero IV* one tonners in Class 1 added real zest to the series. It's not often that the latest

full-on, no-expense-spared IOR custom boats make forays to the Clyde, so Richard Burrows's *Jameson Whiskey* attracted a lot of interest. She was, however, beaten by *Local Hero*, a 1985 boat owned by Scottish estate agent Geoff Howison and chartered to Seamus Gallagher and Frank Hughes for the Irish trials. The stiff competition between the two boats was such that they sailed away from the rest of the fleet, including the lovely varnished Holland 51 *Born Free*, although she was able to salvage her pride by finishing ahead of *Local Hero* in one race. That said, her margin was just 21 seconds.

While *Scenario* was the most consistent in IOR Class 2, two other boats shared the honours for the inshore races but without matching *Scenario's* consistency. They were *Scenario's* close sister ship, *Countdown*, now called *Showdown* having passed into Geoff Semple's ownership, and the Dehler db2 *Rhett Butler*, sailed by Clyde offshore stalwarts Murray Findlay and Jonathon Anderson.

A good turn-out in IOR Class 3 was expected but did not materialise. Interest was focused on the new Humphreys quarter tonner *Quest*, sailed by Marcus Hutchinson from the design office, and Jim McIlraith's self-designed, built and campaigned *Senator Incitatus*. Like McIlraith's earlier own one-off, *Caligula*, *Senator* came to the Scottish Series rating well above her target; nevertheless, she and *Quest* each won two races on corrected time as a preliminary skirmish for the later Quarter Ton Cup in Cork.

But the bulk of the Scottish Series fleet was made up of the cruiser classes sailing under the Clyde Yacht Clubs' Association handicap system and the one-design Sonatas and Sigma 33s, who had their own starts. Hotelier Alan Milton (of *Pepsi* fame) was top of the Sigma pile and Donald McLaren's *Footnote* took the honours in the more competitive Sonata fleet.

With two-thirds of the fleet in the cruiser classes, it's not surprising that there were some strong performances. Alan Poole of MG Yachts returned to his home waters from his new base on the Hamble to win Cruiser A in one of his new Castro-designed MG335s. Another production boat, the super-comfortable van de Stadt-designed Trintella 42 *Salamander*, took Cruiser C honours, while that most longlived of racing designs, Peter Norlin's Scampi type, took Cruiser D in the shape of Nick Wright's *Itch*.

By way of contrast to the Ulster 7-metre cruiser-racer *Norella* which took Cruiser D, the boats in Cruiser E were of a distinctly sporty hue. The Bénéteau First Class 8 *Decision* was the winner, having seen off a crop of Boleroes and a Laser 28 sailed by Nick Stratton (the man who used to sell the Bolero besides sailing his own rather well). In fact, Stratton could have won his class in the Farr-designed Laser 28 but for an early start in the opening race which spoiled his impressive subsequent record of three 1sts and a 3rd. Perhaps he will make amends next year. The Scottish Series is one that draws people back time after time.

Bob Campbell is a freelance writer. He has sailed in five Scottish Series.

Far left: **The Scottish Series begins with a number of feeder races from different locations. This is the Gourock start.**

Centre: **Dubois one tonner *Jameson Whiskey* chases *Local Hero IV* in Loch Fyne.**

Tarbert on the Mull of Kintyre – idyllic setting for the Scottish Series *(top).*

BRITISH SUMMERTIME

Irish Sea Season

by W.M. NIXON

Whatever fate may hold in store for the IOR in the rest of the world, the news is that it is alive and well and doing very nicely, thank you, in the Irish Sea. Under the benign administration of the Irish Sea Offshore Racing Association, that handy stretch of water between England, Wales and Ireland once again provided interesting courses from 72 miles to 140 miles in length on seven weekends. In all, some 78 different boats took part in the overall championship.

The term 'different boats' is used advisedly, as the ISORA fleet is astonishing in its variety. Daddy of them all is Stewart Morris's 1962-vintage 35 ft (10.6 m) Kim Holman-designed sloop *Grenade*, which continues to race successfully out of Abersoch against a fleet which also includes former Admiral's Cuppers up to very recent vintage, an excellent group of three-quarter tonners, and a good sprinkling of offshore racers from the 1970s.

Of course, not all the boats listed in the championship tables took part in every race. The average turn-out ranged between 35 and 50, with numbers thrusting towards the 70 mark for the mid-season RORC Race which was also the feeder event for ISORA Week. That sailfest, staged by the National Yacht Club in Dun Laoghaire (12 – 18 July), was a particular delight, providing good summer sailing and including a neat sponsorship from Furstenberg lager and Visa credit card (the services of the latter enabling ample consumption of the former!).

The season-long programme began in traditional manner on Saturday 23 May with the Holyhead–Wicklow race, a crisp north-easterly seeing Nobby Reilly's Humphreys 44 *Comanche Raider* setting the pace. Formerly *Marionette* of 1985 vintage, and made notably handsome by a stylish new paint job, *Raider* zoomed away towards the western horizon on the long run to the turn at the Kish lighthouse. Unfortunately, her speed took her into a light patch which didn't affect others, and then, to add insult to injury, another flat patch towards the finish off the Wicklow pierheads was circumvented by Tony Vernon's 1985 Davidson 40 *Canterbury*, which duly took line honours. The overall win, however, went to the Hill family's SJ 35 *Banga Wanga*, making a good start at defending the overall championship won in 1986.

One week later, the course was Dun Laoghaire–Carlingford Buoy–Holyhead for a longer race which started in a fresh to strong south-westerly. This gave an interesting close fetch from the turn to the finish, fast sailing and invited intriguing tactical decisions. Although *Comanche Raider* made no mistake about the line honours this time, and although the three-quarter tonners had themselves a great old ding-dong, it was Urban Taylor's Humphreys 37 *Megalopolis* (= the ultimate urban centre) which got everything right to win overall.

Race 3, from Pwllheli round the Codling and into Howth, was an 80-miler of sunshine and light breezes starting on Saturday 13 June. *Comanche Raider* had lost her stick in Howth YC's gale-swept Lambay Race the weekend before, so it was *Canterbury* which set the pace, gamely chased by Roy Dickson's 1977 Holland veteran *Imp*, and at the end the Vernon boat took line honours and the overall win as well.

Thus, with three different overall winners the points position was satisfyingly open for the mid-programme event, 80 miles from Holyhead down to the Codling Lanby and then up to the finish at Howth. And this spread of scores continued, for in difficult conditions with everything from calm to Force 6 there was yet another overall winner, Liam Shanahan's Dehler db2S *Lightning*.

New ingredients were added with the large-entry feeder race from Pwllheli to Dun Laoghaire and ISORA Week itself. Although Denis Doyle's handsome 1981 Frers 51 *Moonduster* strode away into a line honours win, it was one of the smallest boats in the fleet, the new Humphreys quarter tonner *Quest* (Justin & Lynda Burke), which took the overall prize. Rob Humphreys' larger design, *Comanche Raider*, happened to be last overall after getting stuck in a tidal gate!

ISORA Week (an inshore regatta within the overall offshore programme) was an agreeable mixture of moderately serious racing over the good courses which the Dublin area's wide selection of marks provides, combined with some very dedicated socialising. On some days it looked like being a Rob Humphreys festival, with *Comanche Raider* setting the pace in Division A1, Alan Fitton's *Scenario Act II* making the running in the three-quarter tonners, Alan Barton's MG 30 *Glider II* leading the half tonners, and little *Quest* leading the quarter tonners and the fleet overall. In the end, it was only *Quest* which kept her placing to be a popular overall winner, Division A1 going to Roy Dickson's *Imp*, and the fiercely raced three-quarter tonners being led in by Chris Haworth's oversize former half tonner *Beat and Run*, a 1982 Lars Bergstrom design.

The traditional mid-season lull saw the more dedicated heading south either for Cowes Week or the Fastnet Race, and in some cases for both. In Cowes Week, *Canterbury* and Ciaran Foley's much-travelled Oyster 43 *Storm Bird* took silverware home to the Irish Sea, as also did *Quest*, while the Fastnet saw *Imp* taking the Philip Whitehead Cup for the Restricted Division exactly ten years after she'd been the overall winner of the race when she was the star of the USA Admiral's Cup team.

Back home, two of the Cowes Week stars resumed the contest on Friday 14 August with the Holyhead–Rockabill–Dun Laoghaire race, and good old *Storm Bird* got it right in a difficult beat across the Channel to take line honours from a possibly rather surprised *Canterbury*, which however continued her progress towards the overall title by placing 2nd overall.

This progress was brought to a successful conclusion in the final ISORA event, the 110-mile Pwllheli–Rockabill–Howth race on 29 August, where *Canterbury* got herself clear away by going outside Bardsey Island rather than dicing with its ultra-strong tides, and she was never headed thereafter. She took line honours and the overall win, and moved into the champion's slot with *Lightning* taking 2nd place in the points table.

Interestingly enough, with one of those twists of class racing within large fleets, *Canterbury* was the overall winner, yet her class, Division A1, was topped by *Megalopolis*. However, *Lightning* was on top in Division A2, while the smaller boats of Division B saw Neville Maguire's veteran Shamrock half tonner *Demelza* finishing the season strongly to win from *Grenade*, pace-setter *Glider II* having to be content with 3rd. Neville Maguire is father of Gordon Maguire, helmsman of *Quest*. ISORA racing is very much a family business.

Winkie Nixon is Ireland's best-known yachting writer. He edits Ireland Afloat *and is a regular contributor to* Yachting World.

Canterbury (above) **was a member of the 1985 Kiwi Admiral's Cup team and is enjoying a second career in Irish hands.**

Comanche Raider, **the former** *Marionette,* **was the new scratch boat for the '87 season Irish Sea circuit.**

Bob Hobby

BRITISH SUMMERTIME

POWDER BYRNE

ORIGINAL SKIING

AT Powder Byrne we specialise in providing skiing holidays in catered chalets and hotels which are tailor made to suit our clients, whatever their level of skiing ability. The choice of skiing holidays available is enormous with all the large tour operators promising the best packages but what you WON'T get from them is the genuine old fashioned personal service that is a Powder Byrne hallmark.

For the 1988 season we've created a wider-than-ever range of options. It includes:

Powder Byrne Junior Club – bring your children and we'll look after them

Beginners' Weeks – a programme designed to give the beginner the best possible introduction to the sport

Introduction to Powder Skiing – how to ski off-piste, taught by an expert Swiss instructor

Powder Fun 10,000 – concentrated powder skiing with an expert local guide

Ski Touring – ski-trekking through the high Alps

Weekend skiing – the perfect winter break

Two-centre holidays

Anydate departures

The Ultimate Week – A Five Star holiday with a difference

If you'd like to know more about ORIGINAL SKIING please telephone 01-223 0601 to receive our full brochure.

TELEPHONE FOR OUR BROCHURE
01-223 0601

Powder Byrne are one of the first companies to receive the backing of the Young Entrepreneurs Fund

PHONE FOR OUR BROCHURE 01-223 0601

Results

Atlantic Race for Cruisers

Pos.	Name	Skipper	Design	Nat.	Elapsed time			Corrected time			Fleet pos.
Yachting World Trophy for the first yacht to arrive in Barbados											
	Running Cloud	Larry Pollock	54 ft D. Flint tri	US	13d	22h	04m	21d	08h	27m	
Jimmy Cornell Trophy for best overall performance on handicap											
	Molla III	Kari Hynninen	Helmsman 30	SF	9d	15h	48m	16d	07h	35m	
Class A (Over 50 ft/15m): Prime Minister of Barbados Trophy											
1	Albatros	Manfred Kerstan	Swan 61	D	14d	16h	07m	23d	07h	52m	93
2	Moonshadow	Michael Gluck	Deerfoot 62	US	14d	03h	22m	23d	15h	25m	112
3	Cuquita	Conrad Flower	Vagabond 47	GB	20d	03h	19m	24d	01h	05m	124
Class B (45-50 ft/13.7-15 m): Barbados Minister of Tourism Trophy											
1	Rainbowsea	Hans Seidel	Contest 48	D	16d	18h	40m	21d	14h	01m	53
2	Soliea	Bob Steen	Kerney 48	IRL	18d	03h	27m	21d	15h	29m	55
3	Airwave	Tim Aitken	Centurion 47	GB	15d	10h	54m	22d	00h	33m	62
Class C (40-45 ft/12.2-13.7 m): Barbados Port Authority Trophy											
1	Flamingo	Hanspeter v. Allmen	Calypso 43	CH	19d	10h	59m	18d	07h	54m	2
2	Josephine	G. Luken Elvers	Trintella IV	NL	18d	07h	57m	18d	20h	16m	6
3	Shearwater	Mugs Davock	Rhodes 41	US	18d	09h	07m	19d	21h	40m	18
Class D (35-40 ft/10.6-12.2 m): Gran Canaria Trophy											
1	Mursejler	Leif Hansen	Engholm 36	DK	19d	00h	28m	18d	15h	47m	3
2	Taube	Dietrich Theder	Najad 39	D	19d	03h	46m	19d	09h	45m	10
3	Snow-Bunting	Roland Boissevain	Sweden 38	GB	16d	15h	36m	19d	17h	32m	16
Class E (30-35 ft/9-10.6 m): Die Yacht Magazine Trophy											
1	Molla III	Kari Hynninen	Helmsman 30	SF	19d	15h	48m	16d	07h	35m	1
2	Apogee	George Smith	Southern Cross 31	US	20d	23h	31m	19d	00h	41m	7
3	Takara	Paul Carlson	Marken 30	US	23d	03h	31m	19d	08h	25m	9
Class F (Under 30 ft/9 m): Adlard Coles Trophy											
1	Alfa	Erkki Lempiainen	Accent 26	SF	18d	19h	21m	18d	19h	48m	4
2	Andani	Tim Wright	Elizabethan 29	GB	22d	14h	50m	18d	20h	11m	5
3	Rebecca	Klaus Zoels	Bandholm 27	D	23d	00h	10m	19d	13h	21m	12
Multihulls: Multihull International Trophy											
1	Twinsum	Andrew Worby	Heavenly Twins 26	GB	22d	19h	18m	19d	04h	49m	8
2	Guzzledown	Nigel Lennard	Oceanic 30	GB	23d	22h	43m	21d	02h	19m	42
3	Running Cloud	Larry Pollock	D. Flint tri 54	US	13d	22h	04m	21d	08h	27m	49
Line Honours											
A	Moonshadow	Michael Gluck	Deerfoot 62	US	14d	03h	22m				
B	Airwave	Tim Aitken	Centurion 47	GB	15d	10h	54m				
C	Aquarion	Pål Stiansen	Centurion 42	N	15d	11h	14m				
D	Snow Bunting	Roland Boissevain	Sweden 38	GB	16d	05h	13m				
E	Desire	Stuart Feinblatt	Dehler 34	US	17d	07h	42m				
F	Alfa	Erkki Lempiainen	Accent 26	SF	18d	19h	21m				
MH	Running Cloud	Larry Pollock	D. Flint tri 54	US	13d	22h	04m				

1st skipper over 60: *Kimper* (Jørgen Lorenzen, DK), Puzzle 39, 18d 01h 06m. **1st competitors under 16:** *Bagheera* (Andy Copeland, CDN), First 38, 17d 04h 13m (Duncan 10, Colin 8, Jamie 3). **1st single-hander:** *Sweet Dreams* (Noelle Corbett, GB), Moody 33, 21d 22h 33m. **Cruising World Trophy for 1st couple on handicap:** *Apogee* (George Smith and Janet Murphy, US), Southern Cross 31, 20d 23h 31m (corr. 19d 00h 41m). **Youngest competitor:** Alex Plummer of *Bounder* (NZ, 3 months). **Oldest competitor:** David Ward of *Seannine* (US, 71). **Oldest boat:** *Godnok* (Dag Egeberg, N), 59 ft Nyhavn Berger, built 1913. **Last arrival:** *Dunkers* (David Shipton, GB), Achilles 24, 33d 05h 00m.

IN ASSOCIATION WITH
YACHTING WORLD

America's Cup

Elimination & Cup Record Oct 1986–Feb 1987

Stars & Stripes

	Competed against	Series	Race day	Result	Delta
1	Italia I-7	Round robin 1	01	won	5:49
2	Azzurra I-10	Round robin 1	02	won	3:19
3	Eagle US-60	Round robin 1	03	won	3:00
4	White Crusader K-24	Round robin 1	04	won	1:16
5	USA US-61	Round robin 1	05	won	0:06
6	Challenge France F-8	Round robin 1	06	won	4:42
7	America II US-46	Round robin 1	08	def	0:33
8	Courageous IV US-26	Round robin 1	09	won	
9	Canada II KC-2	Round robin 1	10	won	2:19
10	New Zealand KZ-7	Round robin 1	11	won	0:49
11	French Kiss F-7	Round robin 1	12	won	3:40
12	Heart of America US-51	Round robin 1	13	won	3:07
13	USA US-61	Round robin 2	01	def	0:39
14	New Zealand KZ-7	Round robin 2	02	def	0:58
15	Challenge France F-8	Round robin 2	03	won	4:51
1	Heart of America US-51	Round robin 2	04	won	4:50
2	Italia I-7	Round robin 2	05	won	5:15
3	Eagle US-60	Round robin 2	06	won	6:29
4	French Kiss F-7	Round robin 2	07	won	2:34
5	Azzurra I-10	Round robin 2	08	won	0:37
6	White Crusader K-24	Round robin 2	09	def	2:18
7	Canada II KC-2	Round robin 2	10	def	0:29
8	America II US-46	Round robin 2	11	won	1:31
9	Canada II KC-2	Round robin 3	01	won	3:46
10	America II US-46	Round robin 3	02	won	13:04
11	New Zealand K-Z7	Round robin 3	03	def	0:32
12	Challenge France F-8	Round robin 3	04	won	10:48
13	Heart of America US-51	Round robin 3	05	won	1:32
14	USA US-61	Round robin 3	06	def	0:42
15	Eagle US-60	Round robin 3	07	won	10:11
1	French Kiss F-7	Round robin 3	08	won	2:07
2	Italia I-7	Round robin 3	09	won	3:37
3	Azzurra I-10	Round robin 3	10	won	4:11
4	White Crusader K-24	Round robin 3	11	won	4:12
5	USA US-61	Semi-finals	01	won	0:10
6	USA US-61	Semi-finals	02	won	3:02
7	USA US-61	Semi-finals	03	won	2:23
8	USA US-61	Semi-finals	04	won	0:43
9	New Zealand KZ-7	Final	01	won	1:20
10	New Zealand KZ-7	Final	02	won	1:36
11	New Zealand KZ-7	Final	03	def	0:38
12	New Zealand KZ-7	Final	04	won	3:38
13	New Zealand KZ-7	Final	05	won	1:29
14	Kookaburra III KA-15	America's Cup	01	won	1:41
15	Kookaburra III KA-15	America's Cup	02	won	1:10
16	Kookaburra III KA-15	America's Cup	03	won	1:46
15	Kookaburra III KA-15	America's Cup	04	won	1:59

Kookaburra III

	Competed against	Series	Race day	Result	Delta
1	Steak 'n Kidney KA-14	A	01	won	4:03
2	Australia IV KA-16	A	02	won	0:43
3	Australia III KA-9	A	03	won	4:30
4	Kookaburra II KA-12	A	04	won	0:02
5	South Australia KA-8	A	05	won	6:43
6	Australia IV KA-16	A	06	def	0:36
7	Australia III KA-9	A	07	won	1:58
8	Kookaburra II KA-12	A	08	won	0:06
9	South Australia KA-8	A	09	won	6:05
10	Steak 'n Kidney KA-14	A	10	won	
11	Steak 'n Kidney KA-14	B	01	won	4:00
12	South Australia KA-8	B	02	won	2:25
13	Kookaburra II KA-12	B	03	won	1:34
14	Australia IV KA-16	B	04	won	3:18
15	Australia III KA-9	B	05	won	2:01
1	Kookaburra II KA-12	B	06	won	0:04
2	Australia IV KA-16	B	07	won	0:02
3	Australia III KA-9	B	08	won	2:07
4	South Australia KA-8	B	09	won	1:09
5	Steak 'n Kidney KA-14	B	10	won	3:18
6	Kookaburra II KA-12	C	01	won	0:32
7	Australia IV KA-16	C	03	def	0:50
8	Steak 'n Kidney KA-14	C	04	won	1:52
9	South Australia KA-8	C	05	won	
10	Kookaburra II KA-12	C	06	won	0:26
11	Australia IV KA-16	C	07	won	
12	Steak 'n Kidney KA-14	C	08	won	0:26
13	Kookaburra II KA-12	C	09	def	0:36
14	Australia IV KA-16	C	10	def	0:14
15	Steak 'n Kidney KA-14	C	11	won	2:54
1	Kookaburra II KA-12	D	01	def	0:12
2	Australia IV KA-16	D	02	def	0:12
3	Steak 'n Kidney KA-14	D	03	won	2:06
4	Kookaburra II KA-12	D	04	def	0:50
5	Australia IV KA-16	D	05	won	0:17
6	Steak 'n Kidney KA-14	D	06	def	0:39
7	Kookaburra II KA-12	D	07	won	8:57
8	Australia IV KA-16	D	09	won	0:24
9	Australia IV KA-16	E	01	dsq	0:29
10	Australia IV KA-16	E	02	won	1:34
11	Australia IV KA-16	E	03	won	0:46
12	Australia IV KA-16	E	04	won	2:06
13	Australia IV KA-16	E	05	won	1:13
14	Australia IV KA-16	E	06	won	0:55
15	Stars & Stripes US-55	America's Cup	01	def	1:41
16	Stars & Stripes US-55	America's Cup	02	def	1:10
17	Stars & Stripes US-55	America's Cup	03	def	1:46
18	Stars & Stripes US-55	America's Cup	04	def	1:59

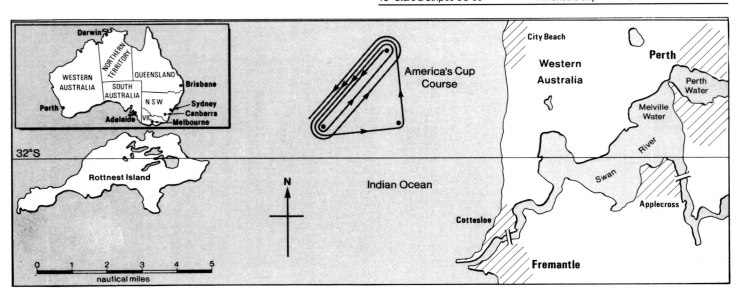

	Elapsed time	Leg gain	Leg speed	Average speed	Elapsed time	Leg gain	Leg speed	Average speed	Delta

Race Day 1, 31 January 1987

Kookaburra III (left) / *Stars & Stripes* (right)

	Elapsed time	Leg gain	Leg speed	Average speed	Elapsed time	Leg gain	Leg speed	Average speed	Delta
Line	0:04				0:04				0:00
Leg 1	35:54		6.90	6.89	34:39	1:15	7.15	7.13	1:15
Leg 2	59:17		8.34	7.46	57:57	5	8.37	7.63	1:20
Leg 3	1:33:26	39	7.24	7.38	1:32:45		7.10	7.43	0:41
Leg 4	1:51:06		7.81	7.45	1:49:52	33	8.06	7.53	1:14
Leg 5	2:05:23		9.66	7.70	2:04:08	1	9.67	7.78	1:15
Leg 6	2:34:52		8.38	7.83	2:33:35	2	8.39	7.90	1:17
Leg 7	3:01:46		7.25	7.74	2:59:46	43	7.45	7.83	2:00
Finish	3:30:30	19	8.60	7.86	3:28:49		8.51	7.92	1:41

Start time: 13:30:00; **course length:** 24.10 nm; **wind speed:** 8–18 knots 165–225°.

Race Day 2, 1 February 1987

Stars & Stripes (left) / *Kookaburra III* (right)

	Elapsed time	Leg gain	Leg speed	Average speed	Elapsed time	Leg gain	Leg speed	Average speed	Delta
Line	0:04				0:01	3			0:03
Line 1	30:17	15	8.18	8.16	30:29		8.11	8.11	0:12
Line 2	49:38	17	10.08	8.91	50:07		9.93	8.82	0:29
Line 3	1:19:48	45	8.19	8.64	1:21:02		8.00	8.51	1:14
Line 4	1:32:12	8	11.13	8.97	1:33:34		11.01	8.84	1:22
Line 5	1:44:17		11.42	9.26	1:45:34		11.50	9.14	1:17
Line 6	2:14:31	6	8.18	9.01	2:15:54		8.15	8.92	1:23
Line 7	2:32:43		10.71	9.22	2:33:51	15	10.86	9.15	1:08
Finish	3:02:23	2	8.33	9.07	3:03:33		8.32	9.02	1:10

Start time: 13:10:00; **course length:** 24.10 nm; **wind speed:** 22–23 knots 195°.

Race Day 3, 2 February 1987

Kookaburra III (left) / *Stars & Stripes* (right)

	Elapsed time	Leg gain	Leg speed	Average speed	Elapsed time	Leg gain	Leg speed	Average speed	Delta
Line	0:04				0:04				0:00
Leg 1	30:15		8.19	8.17	30:00	15	8.26	8.24	0:15
Leg 2	52:53		8.62	8.36	51:56	42	8.89	8.51	0:57
Leg 3	1:22:27		8.36	8.36	1:21:06	24	8.48	8.50	1:21
Leg 4	1:36:18		9.96	9.59	1:34:47	10	10.09	8.73	1:31
Leg 5	1:49:10	2	10.32	8.00	1:48:11		10.30	8.92	1:29
Leg 6	2:20:15		8.08	8.65	2:18:26	20	8.17	8.76	1:49
Leg 7	2:41:29	8	9.18	8.72	2:39:48		9.13	8.81	1:41
Finish	3:11:46		8.16	8.63	3:10:00	5	8.19	8.71	1:46

Start time: 13:10:00; **course length:** 24.10 nm; **wind speed:** 12–18 knots 210°.

Race Day 4, 4 February 1987

Stars & Stripes (left) / *Kookaburra III* (right)

	Elapsed time	Leg gain	Leg speed	Average speed	Elapsed time	Leg gain	Leg speed	Average speed	Delta
Line	0:03	5			0:08				0:05
Leg 1	29:45	21	8.32	8.31	30:11		8.23	8.19	0:26
Leg 2	50:17		9.50	8.79	50:39	4	9.53	8.73	0:22
Leg 3	1:20:03	20	8.30	8.61	1:20:45		8.21	8.54	0:42
Leg 4	1:32:59	7	10.67	8.90	1:33:46		10.57	8.82	0:49
Leg 5	1:46:39		10.10	9.05	1:47:27	1	10.11	8.98	0:48
Leg 6	2:16:14	23	8.36	8.90	2:17:25		8.25	8.90	1:11
Leg 7	2:37:47	5	9.05	8.92	2:39:03		9.01	8.85	1:16
Finish	3:05:55	43	8.79	8.90	3:07:54		8.57	8.81	1:59

Start time: 13:10:00; **course length:** 24.10 nm; **wind speed:** 16–20 knots 210–220°.

Kookaburra III

Owner	Taskforce '87
Syndicate chairman	Kevin Parry
Skipper	Iain Murray
Yacht club	Royal Perth YC
Sail no.	KA 15
Designers	Iain Murray, Alan Payne, John Swarbrick
Builder	Parry Boatbuilders
Spar	Sparcraft
Winches	Lewmar
Sails	North (in house); designer: Howie Marion
Electronics	Ockam, Digital
Crew	
Skipper	Iain Murray
Navigator	Ian Burns
Tactician	Derek Clark
Starboard trimmer	Paul Westlake
Port trimmer	Glen Bourke
Mainsheet and starting helmsman	Peter Gilmour
Mastman	Greg Cavill
Sewer	Tony Bellingham
Bowman	Don McCracken
Grinders	(from) Rick Goodrich, Daren Bracewell, Anthony Rice

Stars & Stripes

Owner	Sail America Foundation
Syndicate chairman	Malin Burnham
Skipper	Dennis Conner
Yacht club	San Diego YC
Sail no.	US 55
Designers	Britton Chance Jnr, Bruce Nelson, David Pedrick
Builder	Derecktor
Spar	Sparcraft
Winches	Lewmar
Sails	Sobstad, North and in-house WBG; designer: Tom Whidden
Electronics	Ockam, Digital
Crew	
Skipper	Dennis Conner
Navigator	Peter Isler
Tactician	Tom Whidden
Starboard trimmer	Adam Ostenfeld
Port trimmer	Bill Trenkle
Mastman	John Barnitt
Sewer	Jay Brown
Bowman	Scott Vogel
Grinders	(from) James Kavle, Kyle Smith, Henry Childers

Swan California Regatta

Class A
1 *Trumpeter* (E. Townsend, Swan 46), 3·50 pts; **2** *Troubadour* (J. Diepenbrock, Swan 46), 11·00; **3** *Bandit* (K. Jaffe, Swan 46), 12·00; **4** *Ms Blu* (H. Thomassen, Swan 59), 16·00; **5** *Lady Godiva* (V. Fargo, Swan 57), 21·00.

Class B
1 *No Illusion* (E. McDowell, Swan 44), 6·75 pts; **2** *Sea Star* (J. Camp, Swan 42), 23·00; **3** *Toboggan* (P. Queyrel, Swan 42), 23·00; **4** *Zeus* (V. Fowler, Swan 391), 23·00; **5** *Cygnet* (L. Freeman, Swan 391), 36·00.

Class C
1 *Lohengrin* (T. Wolfe, Swan 51), 2·25 pts; **2** *Cygnus* (N. Cobbs, Swan 41), 7·00.

Overall winner: *Trumpeter* (Ernie Townsend, Swan 46).
Rolls-Royce Prix d'Elegance: *Bandit* (Kevin Jaffe, Swan 46).
Ruffino Vintage Trophy (oldest Swan): *Panther* (Chris Warner 1971, Swan 48).

Swan European Regatta

Standard Division One
1 *Elan* (H. Baum), 134 pts; **2** *Chastenet* (N. Brick), 132; **3** *Mariposa II of Hamble* (J.C. Silveira), 130; **4** *Crackerjack IX* (K.M. Miller), 126; **5** *Shadow Of A Dream* (S.K. Knowles), 126; **6** *Gregal* (J.P. Peche), 120; **7** *Beija Flor* (S. Clarke & M. Lamy), 104; **8** *Red Otter* (R. Kenny), 100; **9** *Wet 'n Wilde* (A.H. Wilde), 94; **10** *Snowgoose* (G. Meredith), 84; **11** *Pingvin V* (L. Schwabe), 80; **12** *Silveren Swaen* (P.H.J. Bakker), 70; **13** *Delnic* (L. Rousselin), 70; **14** *Sarabande V* (B. Diethelm), 56; **15** *Desperado* (R. Loftus), 50; **16** *International* (D. Boyer), 48; **17** *Quadra* (K. Ruiter), 46; **18** *Yellowdrama IV* (S. Matthews), 44; **19** *Kyla* (L. Warry), 40; **20** *Lady Forrester II* (I. Sorrell), 26.

Standard Division Two
1 *Moustique* (M.D. Spear), 130 pts; **2** *Finndabar of Howth* (J.P. Jameson), 124; **3** *Amadea of Wayde* (M.J. Atkin), 120; **4** *Pavlova II* (F.G. Walker), 116; **5** *Cecille* (G. Radley), 108; **6** *Eclipse 80* (M.J. Leadbetter), 102; **7** *Xara* (D.C. Barham), 94; **8** *Bypass* (G. Howe), 88; **9** *Fringale* (J.P. Scheins), 80; **10** *King of Hearts* (C.R. King), 74; 11 *Geronimo* (A. Curtis), 74; **12** *Carte Blanche* (J.D. Tetley), 62; **13** *Kuutar* (A.M. Newton & J.G. Hancock), 44; **14** *Adfin's Flight* (G.D. Adams), 44; **15** *Spica* (R. Kroon), 36; **16** *Calypso* (W. Michalski), 34; **17** *Swan of the South* (M. Owen & J. Hollamby), 22; **18** *Star Swan* (W. Smout), 8.

Modified Division
1 *Stratus* (D. Smith), 22 pts; **2** *Flying Neleb* (F. Garcia-German), 18; **3** *Jezabel* (Msr Crepeau), 8.

Combined Standard Divisions
1 *Elan* (H. Baum), 264 pts; **2** *Chastenet* (N. Brick), 262; **3** *Moustique* (M.D. Spear), 256; **4** *Mariposa II of Hamble* (J.C. Silveira), 254; **5** *Shadow Of A Dream* (S.K. Knowles), 250; **5** *Finndabar of Howth* (J.P. Jameson), 248; **7** *Crackerjack IX* (K.M. Miller), 248; **8** *Gregal* (J.P. Peche), 234; **9** *Amadea of Wayde* (M.J. Atkin), 232; **10** *Beija Flor* (S. Clarke & M. Lamy), 208; **11** *Pavlova II* (F.G. Walker), 206; **12** *Red Otter* (R. Kenny), 204; **13** *Cecille* (G. Radley), 198; **14** *Eclipse 80*·(M.J. Leadbetter), 196; **15** *Wet 'n Wilde* (A.H. Wilde), 194; **16** *Bypass* (G. Howe), 168; **17** *Xara* (D.C. Barham), 168; **18** *Pingvin V* (L. Schwabe), 168; **19** *Snowgoose* (G. Meredith), 162; **20** *Silveren Swaen* (P.H.J. Bakker), 152; **21** *Delnic* (L. Rousselin), 146; **22** *Fringale* (J.P. Scheins), 138; **23** *Geronimo* (A. Curtis), 138; **24** *Sarabande V* (B. Diethelm), 124; **25** *Desperado* (R. Loftus), 122; **26** *King of Hearts* (C.R. King), 118; **27** *International* (D. Boyer), 114; **28** *Quadra* (K. Ruiter), 102; **29** *Kyla* (L. Warry), 98; **30** *Carte Blanche* (J.D. Tetley), 96; **31** *Yellowdrama IV* (S. Matthews), 96; **32** *Adfin's Flight* (G.D. Adams), 78; **33** *Lady Forrester II* (I. Sorrell), 66.

US Offshore

Southern Racing Ocean Conference

Pos.	Yacht name	Skipper	Design/LOA	Rating	Fleet pos.
Class 1 IOR					
1	*Kialoa V*	J. Kilroy	Frers 79	69.45	7
2	*Boomerang*	G. Coumantaros	Frers 80	69.36	5
3	*Matador*	W. Koch	Frers 81	69.62	6
4	*Obsession*	S. Nichols	S&S 70	62.42	18
5	*Rooftop*	P. Fehlmann	Farr 80	68.76	19
6	*Il Moro di Venezia II*	D. Conner & R. Gardini	Frers 72	62.11	25
7	*Ondine VII*	H. Long	Frers 80	70.01	29
8	*Winterhawk*	H. Day	Farr 68	62.49	32
9	*Milene*	A.A. Mirlesse	Vaton 80	69.90	34
10	*Saga*	G. Walet & D. Geyer	Nelson/Marek 68	69.56	36
Class 2 IOR					
1	*Infinity*	J. Thompson	Nelson/Marek 50	40.13	3
2	*Leading Edge*	E. Mondry	Joubert/Nivelt 50	40.03	15
3	*Fujimo*	J. Schostak	Frers 50	40.15	12
4	*Pioneer*	T. Wilson	Vallicelli 50	39.40	16
5	*Nitissima*	J. Uznis & G. Uznis	Frers 50	40.01	10
6	*Abracadabra*	L. Lemak & J. Andrews	Nelson/Marek 50	40.43	17
7	*Locura*	R. Vadia & G. de Guardiola	Soverel 50	40.61	21
8	*Gem*	W. Ziegler	Nelson/Marek 49	38.76	27
9	*Windquest*	R. DeVos	Frers 50	40.02	28
10	*Carat VI*	W. Forss	Frers 50	39.99	22
11	*Merrythought*	J. King	Frers 50	40.54	30
Class 3 IMS					
1	*Lunatic*	C. Walsh Jnr	Frers 45	502.30	2
2	*Pied Piper*	D. Jennings	Peterson 42	510.90	4
3	*Wassail III*	J. Ashbaugh	Frers 47	508.10	6
4	*Stainless*	R. Evelyn	Evelyn 42	490.20	11
5	*Rambunctious*	S. Robertson	Olsen 40	494.90	12
6	*Diane*	R. Schwartz	Peterson 48	486.50	16
7	*Chiquita*	R. Ripley	Nelson/Marek 44	498.20	19
8	*XL*	M. Flanagan	Olsen 40	496.10	20
Class 4 IOR					
1	*Sprint*	J. Stevens	Joubert/Nivelt 42	32.95	1
2	*Advantage*	J. McBride	Farr 43	33.64	2
3	*Blue Yankee*	R. Towse	Judel/Vrolijk 43	33.94	4
4	*Midtown*	J. Blain	Joubert/Nivelt 43	33.23	11
5	*Insatiable*	F. Krehbiel	Nelson/Marek 45	35.21	24
6	*Sidewinder*	R. Short	Reichel/Pugh 45	35.18	23
7	*Mandrake*	D. Marlow	Dubois 43	32.00	26
Class 5 IOR					
1	*Bodacious*	W. Coolidge	Farr 41	30.60	8
2	*Ragtime*	J. Georges & C. Ulmer	Nelson/Marek 40	30.58	13
3	*J. Knife*	J. Greenberg	Johnstone 41	30.13	31
4	*Arête*	C. Shumway	Jones 42	31.15	33
Class 6 IMS					
1	*Regardless*	R. Lynds	Holland 40	530.70	1
2	*Man-O-War*	S. Duttenhoffer	Johnstone 35	529.30	3
3	*Pirate Twin*	J. Loveless Jnr	Schumacher 37	521.20	5
4	*Epatant*	E. Holland	Holland 40	538.90	7
5	*Once Upon a Time*	P. Alexander	Schumacher 37	525.60	8
6	*Thunder*	M. Hartung	Frers 42	527.50	10
7	*Robin*	E. Hood	Hood 36	570.10	9
8	*Aggressor*	T. Kent	Soverel 37	523.30	13
9	*Jubilation*	N. Emery	Cook 41	522.90	14
10	*Gin*	A. Davies	Farr 40	525.80	15
11	*Kicks*	P. Hartleb	Johnstone 35	533.80	17
12	*Irish Rover*	W. McCormick	Frers 33	559.30	18
Class 7 IOR					
1	*Kathryn*	J. Hughes	van de Stadt 34	24.54	9
2	*Picante*	D. Parravano	van de Stadt 34	24.58	14
3	*Pipe Dream*	S. Piper	Jeppesen 33	24.46	20
4	*Hot Tub*	W. Terry	Farr 36	28.34	35

San Francisco Big Boat Series

Pos.	Yacht name	Owner	Design/LOA	Points
St Francis Perpetual Trophy				
1	Mongoose	P. Simonson	Santa Cruz 70	3.75
2	Citius	B. Wilson	Santa Cruz 70	14.00
3	Hotel California	J. Wintersteen	Santa Cruz 70	15.00
City of San Francisco Perpetual Trophy				
1	Earl of Mar	K. Erskine	Santa Cruz 50	7.25
2	Hana Ho	R. Croker	Santa Cruz 50	12.50
3	Allure	C. Jacobson	Santa Cruz 50	20.00
4	Racy II	L. Taylor	Santa Cruz 50	23.00
5	Elusive	R. Vollmeer	Santa Cruz 50	23.00
Atlantic Perpetual Trophy				
1	Jubilation	J. James	Frers 54	5.00
2	Blade Runner	W. Twist	Reichel/Pugh 47	13.75
3	Locura	G. de Guardiola	Soverel 50	17.00
4	Carat IV	W. Forss	Frers 51	22.00
5	Fujimo	J. Schostak	Frers 50	25.00
Keefe–Kilborn Trophy				
1	Insatiable	F. Krehbiel/D. Tank	Nelson/Marek 45	12.50
2	Quintessence	D. Hughes	Reichel/Pugh 43	17.75
3	Sidewinder	R. Short	Reichel/Pugh 45	18.50
4	Camouflage	A. Schultz	Frers 45	22.00
5	Jano	M. & R. Kahn	Frers 43	23.00
Rheem Perpetual Trophy				
1	Pendragon III	J. MacLaurin	Davidson 40	7.25
2	Pacific Sundance	A. Morgenstern	Farr 40	9.50
3	Coyote	I. Loube	Bénéteau 40	18.00
4	Skedaddle	L. Otterson	Reichel/Pugh 40	25.00
5	Bondi Tram	P. Stocker	Frers 41	25.00

Brenton Reef Series

Pos.	Yacht name	Owner	Design/LOA	Points
1	Insatiable	F. Krehbiel/D. Tank	Nelson/Marek 45	90.0
2	Sidewinder	R. Short	Reichel/Pugh 45	88.0
3	Tuff Enuff Texas Style	C. Vaughan	Bénéteau 40	82.0
4	Blue Yankee	B. Towse	Judel/Vrolijk 43	71.0
5	Regardless	W. Corcoran	Nelson/Marek 39	68.0
6	Skye Hie	B. McLeod	Judel/Vrolijk 40	63.0
7	Leverage	S. Lover	Tripp 40	61.0
8	Slip, Sliding Away	D. Marlow	Graham & Schlagater 39	60.0
9	Full Tilt Boogie	B. Kelly	Joubert/Nivelt 39	45.0
10	Mad Max	R. Johnstone	J-41	35.5
11	Amazing Potato	P. Comfort	Joubert/Nivelt 40	20.0
12	Fiddler	A. van Liew	Peterson 42	3.0

Caribbean

Miami–Montego Bay Race

IMS Class: 1 Scaramouche of Warwick (B. Baer), 4d 07h 46m 01s; **2** Eclipse (D. Polak), 5d 02h 26m 18s. **PHRF Class: 1** Ugly Duckling (G. Sharpe), 4d 14h 27m 37s; **2** Iroquois (J. de Lisser), 4d 14h 27m 37s; **3** Nueva Vida (D. Sherron), 5d 08h 44m 07s; **4** Spranzie (L. Stewart), 5d 08h 45m 18s; **5** Willoway (T. Berry) 6d 03h 08m 49s. **Overall prize** (the Johnnie Walker Cup): Scaramouche of Warwick.

Rolex Cup Regatta

Class A Racing PHRF: 1 Stuart Little; **2** Titan IV; **3** Jalpari; **4** Rising Star; **5** Celtic; **6** Immigrant. **Class B Racing PHRF: 1** Piolin; **2** Campechano; **3** Extasis; **4** Pipedream; **5** Windwalker; **6** Flako. **Class C Racing PHRF: 1** Eclipse; **2** Hot Pursuit; **3** Uncle Sam; **4** Alligator; **5** Barbarian; **6** Reckless. **Class D Racing PHRF: 1** Humbug; **2** Cold Beer; **3** Sassy Lady; **4** Carolo; **5** Aventura; **6** Annick 11. **Class E Cruising PHRF: 1** Acadia; **2** Red Fever; **3** Blue Charm; **4** Cabrite; **5** Cat Lady; **6** Wings. **Class F Cruising PHRF: 1** Guanahani; **2** Finally; **3** Dai Sei; **4** Guinivere; **5** Attorante; **6** Posh. **Class G Racing IOR: 1** Immigrant; **2** Rising Star; **3** Colt.

Antigua Sailing Week

Racing Class Overall: 1 Titan IV; **2** Immigrant; **3** Reverie. **Racing Class 1: 1** Mistress Quickly; **2** Kialoa IV; **3** Eclipse. **B Division:** Mistress Quickly. **Racing Class 2: 1** Titan IV; **2** Immigrant; **3** Connie D. **B Division:** Troon. **Racing Class 3: 1** Reverie; **2** Cold Beer; **3** Uncle Sam. **B: Division:** Cold Beer. **Best Performance Cruiser Classes: 1** Sur; **2** Curlew; **3** Alphida. **Cruising Class 1: 1** Sur; **2** Rhoobarb; **3** Odin. **B Division:** Decoy. **Cruising Class 2: 1** Alphida; **2** Sara; **3** Acadia. **B Division:** Sara. **Cruising Class 3: 1** Curlew; **2** Ziggurat; **3** Galatea of Tortola. **B Division:** Curlew.

CORT Overall Series

Fleet 1 Racing: 1 Hot Pursuit (John Foster); **2** Uncle Sam (Sam Laing); **3** Campechano (Eric Tulla); **4** Piolin (Klaus Rehring); **5** Titan IV (Tom Hill). **Fleet 2 Cruising: 1** Acadia (Burt Keenan); **2** Dai Sei (Cliff Campbell).

ICAYA Maxi World Championship

Newport Series
1 Kialoa V (J. Kilroy), 11.25; **2** Matador (W. Koch), 19.00; **3** Ondine VII (S.A. Long), 23.50; **4** Boomerang (G. Coumantaros), 24.00; **5** Il Moro di Venezia III (R. Gardini), 26.00; **6** Cannonball (C. Robertson), 28.00; **7** Obsession (S. Nichols), 28.00; **8** Emeraude (J. Dewailly), 30.00; **9** Milène V (A. Mirlesse), 41.00.

Porto Cervo Series
1= Kialoa V and Emeraude, 13.50; **3** Il Moro di Venezia III, 14.00; **4** Matador, 19.75; **5** Ondine VII, 22.00; **6** Othello (G. Verassi), 23.00.

Overall
1 Kialoa V, 24.75; **2** Matador, 38.75; **3** Il Moro di Venezia III, 40.00; **4** Emeraude, 43.50; **5** Ondine VII, 45.50; **6** Boomerang, 59.00.

CHAMPAGNE MUMM
ADMIRAL'S CUP 1987

Individual Yachts

Pos.	Yacht name	Designer	Builder	Sails	Mast	Year	LOA	Rat.	Points
1	Propaganda	Farr	Cookson	North	Sparcraft	1986	12.1	30.59	527
2	Jamarella	Farr	Bushe	Shore	Sparcraft	1987	12.1	30.54	497
3	Original Beckmann Pletfjerner	Jeppesen	X-Yachts	Carlsson/Diamond	Sparcraft	1986	13.5	34.51	457
4	Sidewinder	Reichel/Pugh	Esprit	North	Sparcraft	1986	13.6	34.99	452
5	Irish Independent/Full Pelt	Dubois	Hutton	Banks	Sparcraft	1987	12.2	30.49	427
6	Goldcorp	Davidson	Spriggins	North	MSF	1985	12.2	30.58	425
7	Kiwi	Farr	Franklin	North	Sparcraft	1986	13.2	34.47	413
8	Indulgence	Andrieu	B & B	Banks	Sparcraft	1987	13.3	34.52	393
9=	Juno	Humphreys	Thompson	North	Sparcraft	1987	12.0	30.50	391
9=	Swan Premium II	Farr	McConaghy	Fraser	Yachtmasts	1987	12.2	30.55	391
11	Container	Judel/Vrolijk	Schütz	North	Sparcraft	1986	12.0	30.52	388
12	Pinta	Judel/Vrolijk	Schütz	Ulmer/Kolius	Sparcraft	1986	13.2	34.21	387
13	Swan Premium III	Farr	McConaghy	North	Zapspar	1986	13.2	34.31	365
14	Swan Premium I	Dubois	Jago	Hood	Sparcraft	1987	12.2	30.55	349
15	Centurion-Musclor	Humphreys	Thompson	Elvström	Proctor	1985	12.0	30.45	347
16	Saudade	Judel/Vrolijk	Schütz	Diamond	Reckmann	1986	12.0	30.55	344
17	Turkish Delight	Castro	Raisedale	Banks	Sparcraft	1985	12.9	34.21	336
18	Insatiable	Nelson/Marek	Goetz	North	Sparcraft	1986	13.7	35.18	299
19	Corum	Briand	Bénéteau	AMG	Sparcraft	1987	13.2	34.59	298
20	Mayurca	Gonzalez	Barracuda	Banks	Sparcraft	1986	11.9	30.54	293
21	I-Punkt*	Judel/Vrolijk	Schütz	Sobstad	Sparcraft	1987	12.0	30.50	292
22	Vento	Castro	Schect	Ulmer/Kolius	Sparcraft	1986	11.9	30.54	282
23	Xeryus	Berret/Finot/Fauroux	Bénéteau	North	Sparcraft	1985	12.0	30.21	281
24	Jameson Whiskey	Dubois	Vision	McWilliam	Sparcraft	1987	17.2	30.55	275
25	Mandrake-Krizia	Briand	Schütz	North	Sparcraft	1987	13.3	34.60	274
26	Diva	Judel/Vrolijk	Magg	North	Magg	1987	13.4	34.42	270
27	Andelsbanken	Jeppesen	X-Yachts	Diamond	Sparace	1987	12.1	30.55	261
28	Marisa-Konica	Brenta	Nautica C4	North	Proctor	1987	12.5	34.88	255
29	Mean Machine	Farr	Hutton	Relling	Sparcraft	1987	12.1	30.55	239
30	C.G.I.	Andrieu	Jeanneau	Technique Voile	Sparcraft	1987	12.0	30.47	237
31	Stockbroker Leif Jensen & Co	Jeppesen	X-Yachts	Diamond	Sparace	1987	12.1	30.55	229
32	Blue Yankee	Judel/Vrolijk	Wiggers	Ullman	Sparcraft	1986	13.3	34.20	221
33	Caiman	Judel/Vrolijk	Standfast	Ulmer/Kolius	Sparcraft	1986	13.3	34.68	213
34	Royal Blue	Briand	Batbyggarna	Diamond	Sparcraft	1987	15.1	40.00	202
35	Pro-Motion V	Frers	Bénéteau	North	Hallspars	1986	15.2	39.81	188
36	Civic	Norlin	Vibramat	Gran	Sparcraft	1985	12.2	30.19	172
37	Anquin's Too	Joubert/Nivelt	Bianca	Diamond	Sparcraft	1985	13.3	34.22	157
38	Eurocard	Norlin	Bosovarvet	North	Sparcraft	1985	12.2	30.54	120
39	Merope	Vallicelli	Nautica C4	Ulmer/Kolius	Sparcraft	1986	12.1	30.55	102
40	Ritec Poinciana	Briand	Standfast	North	Francespar	1985	12.0	30.47	80
41	Port du Crouesty	Berret	Bénéteau	Technique Voile	Z Spar	1987	12.0	30.38	76
42	R.E.F. Val Maubuée	Dumas	Maas	Technique Voile	Sparcraft	1987	13.8	34.59	28

Note: * I-Punkt was disqualified subsequent to a hearing by the International Jury.

Teams after 5 races

Pos.	Team	Sail no.	Yacht name	Skipper/Owner	Rat.	R.1	R.2	R.3	R.4	R.5	Total
1	New Zealand	KZ-296	Goldcorp	R. Dodson/M. Canning	30.58	18	111	66	70	160	425
		KZ-6161	Propaganda	B. Woolley/A. Burr	30.59	48	126	84	74	195	527
		KZ-6191	Kiwi	P. Walker/Admiral's Cup C	34.47	70	72	80	76	115	413
				Total		136	309	230	220	470	**1365**
2	United Kingdom	K-180	Jamarella	R. Pattisson/A. Gray	30.54	58	123	78	38	200	497
		K-505	Juno	A. Hurst/M. Peacock	30.50	24	108	54	0	205	391
		K-919	Indulgence	H. Cudmore/G. Walker	34.52	54	105	72	72	90	393
				Total		136	336	204	110	495	**1281**
3	Australia	KA-2-SM	Swan Premium I	L. Abrahams/L. Abrahams	30.55	30	96	24	14	185	349
		KA-3000	Swan Premium III	I. Murray/P. Kurts	34.31	78	21	68	78	120	365
		KA-4000	Swan Premium II	G. Appleby/G. Appleby	30.55	36	102	70	48	135	391
				Total		144	219	162	140	440	**1105**
4	Ireland	IR-1780	Jameson Whiskey	R. Burrows/B. Butkus	30.55	10	99	16	0	150	275
		K-1036	Turkish Delight	M. Mansfield/H. Bezman	34.21	62	42	52	80	100	336
		K-243	Irish Independent/Full Pelt	T. Power/S. Fein	30.49	60	84	49	24	210	427
				Total		132	225	117	104	460	**1038**
5	Germany	G-1909	Container	G. Eiermann/U. Schütz	30.52	8	117	49	44	170	388
		G-1919	Saudade	U. Mares/A. Buell	30.55	44	87	38	0	175	344
		G-2994	Diva	B. Beilken/P. Westphal-Langlogh	34.42	0	90	62	38	80	270
				Total		52	294	149	82	425	**1002**
6	USA	US-18968	Sidewinder	J. Bertrand/R. Short	34.99	80	69	76	82	145	452
		US-41110	Blue Yankee	S. Benjamin/R. Towse	34.20	6	3	57	50	105	221
		US-41241	Insatiable	G. Weisman/Krehbiel/Tank/Lee	35.18	74	39	42	84	60	299
				Total		160	111	175	216	310	**972**
7	Denmark	D-1211	Original Beckmann Pletfjerner	I. U-Anderson/P. Jespersen	34.51	84	93	57	68	155	457
		D-1215	Andelsbanken	P. Kampmann/V. Greulich	30.55	46	66	36	28	85	261
		D-1226	Stockbroker Leif Jensen & Co	J. Host/J. Host	30.55	40	60	34	0	95	229
				Total		170	219	127	96	335	**947**
8	France	F-9070	Xeryus	B. Trouble/Co-Yacht	30.21	12	33	24	32	180	281
		F-9247	Centurion-Musclor	L. Delage/J. Dick	30.45	42	81	16	18	190	347
		F-9287	Corum	P. Briand/Bénéteau	34.59	72	45	64	62	55	298
				Total		126	159	104	112	425	**926**
9	Austria	G-3417	Pinta	W. Illbruck/W. Illbruck	34.21	68	63	60	56	140	387
		H-61	Ritec Poinciana	J. Bouscholte/T. Vinke	30.47	26	24	6	4	20	80
		J-3063	I-Punkt*	H. Raudaschl/T. Friese	30.50	28	120	82	12	50	292
				Total		122	207	148	72	210	**759**
10	Spain	E-2525	Anquin's Too	U. Costa/A. Quinteiro	34.22	0	15	26	46	70	157
		E-2747	Mayurca	P. Zendrera/G. Cryns	30.54	8	114	20	36	115	293
		K-2772	Vento	J. Abascal/M. Fernandez	30.54	32	78	22	20	130	282
				Total		40	207	68	102	315	**732**
11	Holland	H-189	Mean Machine	P. de Ridder/P. de Ridder	30.55	14	54	46	0	125	239
		H-36	Caiman	G. Jeelof/G. Jeelof	34.68	66	18	44	40	45	213
		H-96	Pro-Motion V	B. Dolk/B. Dolk	39.81	82	0	8	58	40	188
				Total		162	72	98	98	210	**640**
12	Italy	I-10790	Merope	M. Tumiati/ Marina Militare	30.55	38	3	10	26	25	102
		I-11001	Marisa-Konica	U. Lucarelli/U. Lucarelli	34.68	76	30	74	60	15	255
		I-11023	Mandrake-Krizia	G. Carriero/G. Carriero	34.60	56	51	28	64	75	274
				Total		170	84	112	150	115	**631**
13	Sweden	S-10010	Royal Blue	G. Ekdahl/R. Gustafson	40.00	64	9	18	66	45	202
		S-9121	Civic	J. Norrman/J. Norrman	30.19	16	75	4	42	35	172
		S-9171	Eurocard	B. Sall/B. Sall	30.54	36	36	12	6	30	120
				Total		116	120	34	114	110	**494**
14	Belgium	F-9213	C.G.I.	B. Caignaert/Tour Voile	30.47	34	57	14	22	110	237
		F-9229	R.E.F. Val Maubuée	G. Ribadeau Dumas/J. Dumone	34.59	2	12	4	8	2	28
		F-9230	Port du Crouesty	C. Facque/Crouesty	30.38	22	48	2	2	2	76
				Total		58	117	20	32	114	**341**

Note: *After I-Punkt's disqualification her score was struck out. Austria dropped to 13th place.

BOC Challenge, 1986–87

Leg times and running elapsed times by class. All times in days, hours minutes and seconds; placement in class in parenthesis. Times include all penalties and adjustments.

Yacht and skipper	Leg I time (Place)					Leg II time (Place) / Total I, II					Leg III time (Place) / Total I-III					Leg IV time (Place) / Final total				
Class I																				
Credit Agricole III	42	16	57	35	(2)	28	12	52	43	(2)	36	17	46	53	(1)	26	05	46	45	(3)
Philippe Jeantot (France)						71	05	50	18	(1)	107	23	37	11	(1)	134	05	23	56	(1)
Ecureuil d'Aquitaine	46	08	04	22	(5)	28	07	13	22	(1)	36	21	15	45	(2)	26	05	02	37	(2)
Titouan Lamazou (France)						74	15	17	44	(2)	111	12	33	29	(2)	137	17	36	06	(2)
UAP-Pour Médecins sans Frontières	47	16	44	50	(6)	31	04	55	25	(3)	40	09	54	18	(3)	27	03	23	37	(7)
Jean-Yves Terlain (France)						78	21	40	15	(5)	119	07	34	33	(3)	146	10	58	10	(3)
Biscuits Lu	43	05·	58	43	(3)	33	01	01	14	(5)	43	23	52	00	(4)	26	05	59	37	(4)
Guy Bernadin (USA)						76	06	59	57	(3)	120	06	51	57	(4)	146	12	51	34	(4)
Tuna Marine	42	01	10	36	(1)	35	04	16	20	(8)	44	01	56	44	(5)	26	00	50	20	(1)
John Martin (South Africa)						77	05	26	56	(4)	121	07	23	40	(5)	147	08	14	00	(5)
Triple M/Spirit of Sydney	51	03	20	30	(8)	32	11	41	54	(4)	46	18	43	23	(7)	26	06	17	51	(5)
Ian Kiernan (Australia)						83	15	02	24	(7)	130	09	45	47	(6)	156	16	03	38	(6)
Stabilo Boss	50	17	39	48	(7)	40	18	09	43	(9)	45	23	10	31	(6)	26	10	42	54	(6)
Bertie Reed (South Africa)						91	11	49	31	(9)	137	11	00	02	(7)	163	21	42	56	(7)
Legend Securities	51	17	20	20	(9)	34	14	23	25	(6)	51	08	56	20	(8)	27	06	25	17	(8)
David White (USA)						86	07	43	45	(8)	137	16	40	05	(8)	164	23	05	22	(8)
Class II																				
Airco Distributor	47	15	30	30	(2)	34	16	03	52	(1)	47	03	00	00	(2)	28	01	10	22	(2)
Mike Plant (USA)						82	07	34	22	(1)	129	10	34	22	(1)	157	11	44	44	(1)
Let's Go	51	11	16	55	(3)	36	17	43	52	(3)	45	21	56	09	(1)	26	21	10	20	(1)
Jean-Luc van den Heede (France)						88	05	00	47	(2)	134	02	56	56	(2)	161	00	07	16	(2)
Belmont Finland	52	11	36	29	(5)	36	09	34	11	(2)	51	10	42	20	(4)	28	01	28	13	(3)
Harry Harkimo (Finland)						88	21	10	40	(3)	140	07	53	00	(3)	168	09	21	13	(3)
American Flag	52	12	13	17	(6)	38	09	43	25	(5)	51	08	39	57	(3)	29	13	21	39	(4)
Hal Roth (USA)						90	21	56	42	(5)	142	06	36	39	(4)	171	19	58	18	(4)
Declaration of Independence	51	11	34	15	(4)	38	10	42	00	(6)	51	11	25	58	(5)	30	20	58	50	(7)
Richard Konkolski (USA)						89	22	16	15	(4)	141	09	42	13	(4)	172	06	41	03	(5)
Lone Star	54	10	59	30	(8)	38	09	02	20	(4)	52	08	42	24	(6)	30	09	39	38	(6)
Mark Schrader (USA)						92	20	01	50	(6)	145	04	44	14	(6)	175	14	23	52	(6)
Colt by Rettig	53	18	55	22	(7)	39	18	27	32	(7)	52	09	28	46	(7)	29	19	10	59	(5)
Pentti Salmi (Finland)						93	13	22	54	(7)	145	22	51	40	(7)	175	18	02	39	(7)
Joseph Young	55	00	23	52	(9)	39	23	49	40	(8)	92	11	27	38	(8)	37	02	14	14	(8)
John Hughes (Canada)						95	00	13	32	(8)	187	11	41	10	(8)	224	13	55	24	(8)

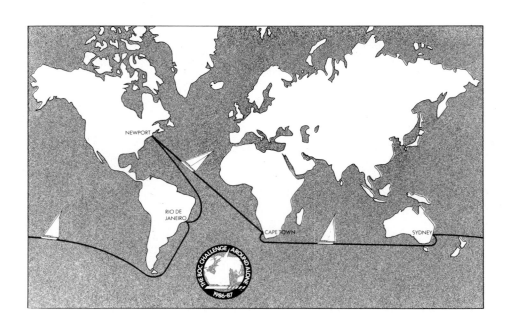

Ton Cups

Rodeo One Ton Cup

Pos.	Sail no.	Yacht name	Designer	Builder	Club	City	1	2	3	4	5	Points
1	N-7000	Fram X	Farr	Cookson	KNS	Oslo	2	1	2	5	1	213.75
2	E-2586	Sirius IV	Farr	Barracuda	CNRA	Palma de Mallorca	1	2	8	2	2	209.75
3	MO-1989	Monaco	Andrieu	Jeanneau	YCM	Monte Carlo	6	9	4	1	8	190.38
4	D-1215	Andelsbanken	Jeppesen	X-Yachts	KDY	Lyngby	4	6	3	9	22	173.00
5	E-2747	Mayurca	Gonzalez	Barracuda	RCNP	Palma de Mallorca	3	5	20	14	10	163.50
6	K-180	Jamarella	Farr	Bushe	RORC	London	8	17	5	3	3	158.00*
7	D-1199	Antic	Jeppesen	X-Yachts	KDY	Harlev J	15	14	9	8	7	156.50
8	H-189	Mean Machine	Farr	Hutton	WSV MS	Wassenaar	26	4	12	10	16	150.50
9	J-3063	I-Punkt†	Judel/Vrolijk	Schütz	HSC	Hamburg	5	8	10	20	20	146.50
10	K-505	Juno	Humphreys	Thompson	RORC	London	18	10	30	6	6	144.50
11	G-1909	Container	Judel/Vrolijk	Schütz	YCS	Selters	24	3	32	13	5	141.00
12	I-11100	Bonifati	Jeppesen	X-Yachts	CVB	Rome	20	19	6	7	17	136.00
13	E-2611	Ramel	Farr	Barracuda	RCNB	Barcelona	13	11	1	23	23	134.25
14	I-11101	Andelstanken	Jeppesen	X-Yachts	CVN	Rome	DNF	13	7	17	11	124.00
15	F-9247	Centurion-Musclor	Humphreys	Thompson		Nice	12	16	18	27	13	112.00
16	D-1226	Stockbroker	Jeppesen	X-Yachts	KDY	Charlottenlund	11	18	28	15	18	112.00
17	I-10790	Merope	Vallicelli	Nautica	SVMM	Rome	24	17	33	12	12	106.50
18	K-2772	Vento	Castro	Schecht	NYC	Harlem CT	19	15	23	24	14	105.50
19	F-9250	Diamant Bleu	Joubert/Nivelt	Gib Sea		Treflaouenan	29	20	11	18	15	105.50
20	S-9444	Ragnarrök	Ängermark	Team Ragnarrök	GKSS	Kungsbacka	21	21	14	19	24	98.00
21	I-10900	Brava I.Copains	Vallicelli	Green Marine	YCCS	Rome	14	27	34	16	4	97.50
22	BL-1375	Victoria	João Carlos Goes		ICS	São Paulo	17	25	19	11	32	93.00
23	S-9189	Happy Hour	Andrieu	Elephant Boatyard	GKSS	Helsingborg	26	30	22	4	26	87.50
24	G-1919	Saudade	Judel/Vrolijk	Schütz	NRV	Hamburg II	10	23	29	29	21	78.00
25	G-2929	New Yorker	Judel/Vrolijk	Schütz	KYC	Kiel I	DNF	30	16	22	9	77.50
26	N-6959	Hewlett-Packard	Andrieu	Thompson	KNS	Oslo 3	33	24	13	21	25	67.00
27	K-512	Blue Diamond	Finot Group	Bénéteau	RORC	London	25	28	15	25	28	66.00
28	F-9230	Port du Crouesty	Andrieu	Jeanneau	CNC	Sarzeau	35	22	31	26	19	59.50
29	N-6530	Conte o.Florence	Jeppesen	X-Yachts	KNS	Skarer	23	29	24	31	DNC	42.00
30	G-136	Rodeo	Judel/Vrolijk	Schütz	KYC	Düsseldorf	DNF	26	26	32	29	38.50
31	D-1155	Sweetheart o.Svendborg			SSS	Svendborg	28	DNF	27	28	27	35.50
32	F-9300	Ellora V	Finot	Bénéteau	SRR	Paris	30	DNF	21	30	30	33.50
33	D-1218	Cirkeline II	Frers	Bénéteau	KDY	Odense Nord	DNF	DNF	25	33	31	20.00
34	BL-898	Carro Chefe	Farr	Barracuda	ICAB	Rio de Janeiro	27	DNF	DNC	DNC	DNC	13.00

Notes: * Penalised 2×30 pts because of full fuel container.
† I-Punkt was subsequently disqualified.

Three-Quarter Ton Cup

Pos.	Yacht name	Skipper	Flag	Designer	Points
1	Jelfi-X	P.J. Carels	NL	Jeppesen	82.50
2	Salamander	R. Tanghe	B	Jeppesen	68.75
3	Yamaha	D. Leeten	B	Jeppesen	68.50
4	Glade Vanvidd	K. Oestmark	N	Jeppesen	64.00
5	Prudential Bache	J. Migom	B	Briand	63.12
6	Escapade	P. Heerema	NL	Jeppesen	57.00
7	Ramasjang	S. Anderson	DK	Jeppesen	54.50
8	Matjas	P. de Kort	NL	Jeppesen	52.50
9	Profilen	T. Blixt	S	Norlin	49.50
10	Fiona of Burnham	D. Geaves	GB	Jones	47.00
11	Temeraire	C. Lejeune	B	van de Stadt	31.00
12	Zwiebel	R. Jenner	D	van de Stadt	29.50
13	Indulgence	V. Codecasa	I	Andrieu	28.75
14	Wings of Cowley	J.L. Best	GB	Jones	24.50
15	X-treem	C. Walder	NL	Jeppesen	22.50

Heineken Quarter Ton Cup

Pos.	Name	Skipper	Nat.	Design	Year	Points
1	McDonald's	F. Larson	DK	MG 26 Special	1987	125·25
2	Innovation Group Quest	J. & L. Burke	IRL	Humphreys	1987	120·38
3	MNEF	J. Ramon	F	Fauroux	1986	114·00
4	Phoenix 2	L. Bankson	GB	Weguelin	1987	105·00
5	Madchen	H. Dietrich	D	Judel/Vrolijk	1986	104·50
6	Drakkar Noir	A. O'Leary, C. Love & N. Kenefick	IRL	MG 26 Special	1985	101·75

Production Boat Prize: Mad Gamble (T. Halliwell, NI), MG 26.

Half Ton Cup

1 René Chateau Video (P. Pasco), 13-3-3-2-5, 152 pts.
2 EJP3 (N. Duizend), 11-7-6-6-3, 139.
3 Stern (L. Baldissera), 10-6-11-3-12, 132.50.
4 Salora (A. Bonsdorf), 5-16-5-4-2, 132.
5 La Concorde (J. Pahun), 8-8-1-14-6, 130.25.
6 Catch Up (K. Saalmann), 1-10-13-8-7, 129.25.
7 Ville de Toulon (S. Destremau), 10-14-4-7-1, 128.75;
8 Home Kit (P. Massu), 14-5-12-5-11, 127.50; 9 Normerel
(A. Liardet), 18-2-7-12-10, 125; 10 Armour Nautic (F.
Lamiot), 16-1-15-13-8, 122; 11 Tom Bombadil (J. Money),
6-13-2-10-17, 116; 12 Passion 4 (D. Birkill), 3-9-14-11-16,
114.50; 13 Pinky (R. Magg), 12-4-9-9-RTD, 112.50;
14 Silva (K. Olofsson), 25-19-17-1-18, 82.875; 15 Fidelia
(H. Funakoshi), 7-12-21-18-21, 82; 16 Harmony 87 (P.
Dyer), 4-20-8-19-23, 78.50; 17 Ballerine (P. Surkeyn),
17-21-16-15-14, 70.50; 18 Paola Sei (A. Rivolta), 9-Disq-
23-16-4, 66; 19 3M Electronique (E. Blanchard), 22-11-18-
25-19, 63.50; 20 Seihako (H. Hitoshi), 15-23-19-17-25,
51.50; 21 Insatiable (Bibby/Heeley), 23-24-20-23-9, 47.50;
22 Picksou 2 (C. Berhault), 19-17-25-26-20, 45; 23 Fore
Shore (M. Ohlson), 24-25-26-20-15, 37; 24 Pairo Cuatro
(Friere/Friere), 21-27-24-21-21, 28.50; 25 Rock n Roll (M.
Achtenhagen), 20-RTD-23-24-24, 25.00; 26 Spirit (Spark/
Saward), 26-18-27-27-22, 24.50; 27 Lemandja (T. Sanchez), 27-26-22-22-26, 22.

Olympic Classes

12-Metre
World Championship

Olympic Practice Regatta, Pusan

Pos.	Crew	Country	Results	Points
Star				
1	E. Adams/T. Olsen	US	2-1-1-6-11-2	17.7
2	G. Gorla/A. Peraboni	I	1-PMS-5-2-7-1	26.0
3	M. Johannsen/M. Hansson	S	3-4-2-8-2-PMS	33.7
4	S. Gould/G. Sieck	US	5-2-10-4-1-10	37.0
5	A. Jensen/M. Mikkelsen	DK	7-3-7-3-6-6	47.8
Division II Sailboards				
1	R. Nagy	F	8-6-1-1-6-Disq-1	37.4
2	S. Steele	US	1-14-10-2-15-1-6	50.7
3	T. Foyen	N	21-1-6-11-1-13-4	55.7
4	E. Belot	F	2-4-3-13-7-5-18	58.7
5	H. Ling	S	4-13-5-10-4-Disq-2	64.0
British placings: 16 S. Goody (5-18-16-18-21-9-16), 117.0 pts; **18** W. Banham (6-20-9-25-19-11-Rtd), 125.7 pts.				
Flying Dutchmen				
1	J. Bojsen-Muller/C. Grenborg	DK	4-PMS-1-6-1-2	22.7
2	Y. Sela/E. Amir	ISR	10-1-2-1-6-11	30.7
3	G. Braun/W. Kenney	US	1-4-3-3-7-14	32.4
4	H. Koening/H. Schelling	NL	2-3-4-5-20-5	36.7
5	J. Turner/P. Allam	GB	3-10-12-2-17-3	48.4
Other British placings: 15 R. Yeoman/N. Burgin (14-11-15-10-12-15), 92.0 pts.				
470 Men				
1	N. Buckley/P. Newlands	GB	1-3-13-3-3-6-9	43.8
2	J. Wicki/A. Frey	CH	3-PMS-1-10-8-1-20	61.7
3	M. Lundgren/U. Lagneus	S	11-4-20-7-7-6-3	68.4
4	P. von Koskull/J. von Koskull	SF	22-16-2-11-4-DNF-4	86.0
5	T. Janka/N. Korte	D	4-9-12-5-9-DNF-14	86.0
Other British placings: 18 A. Stead/A. Hemmings (7-PMS-14-8-16-Rtd-11), 126.0 pts.				
470 Women				
1	C. Foster/J. Patton	GB	18-4-4-1-1-5-1	26.0
2	L. Niece/P. Raymond	US	2-11-1-14-3-4-8	47.7
3	L. Egnot/J. Egnot	NZ	3-17-2-3-DNC-1-7	50.4
4	B. & A. Lemstrom	SF	4-1-6-2-8-DNF-12	54.7
5	C. & A. Alexandersson	S	5-16-3-10-6-2-5	56.4
Other British placings: 10 K. Hedgecock/R. Rushall (15-2-14-4-19-PMS-9), 92.0 pts.				
Tornado				
1	M. Faou/Y. Quernec	F	10-3-1-6-1	17.4
2	G. Knapp/C. Steinfeld	US	3-1-5-3-13	21.4
3	R. Gaebler/H-J. Pfohe	D	Rtd-2-4-4-2	22.0
4	J. van Ek/H. Lambrieux	NL	1-4-9-2-DNC	26.0
5	R. Sellers/C. Timms	NZ	2-8-14-1-10	33.0
British placings: R. White/J. Newman (17-12-19-13-DNC), 85.0 pts; I. Gray/M. Bishop (20-22-24-22-DNF) 112.0 pts.				
Soling				
1	Kostecki/Bayliss/Billingham	US	1-6-5-1-2	13.0
2	Bank/Mathiasen/Secher	DK	6-2-10-4-1	22.7
3	Persson/Wallin/Oberg	S	2-5-4-3-4	24.7
4	Shaiduko/Poliakov/Kanov	USSR	Disq-1-1-6-9	26.7
5	Jungblut/Kroger/Bartel	D	12-4-6-2-5	32.7
Finn				
1	S. Childerley	GB	21-1-6-1-4-2	22.7
2	S. Westergaard	DK	7-PMS-2-9-3-1	36.7
3	S. MacLeod	US	3-5-3-7-5-3	37.1
4	B. Ledbetter	US	6-3-13-14-1-14	56.4
5	L. Crispin	GB	13-4-8-2-12-9	58.0

Semi Finals

Day 1

Division 1

KZ-7 beat *Kookaburra II*		0:33
Sfida Italiana beat *White Horse*		0:53

Division 2

Bengal beat *Stars & Stripes*		6:25
Entertainer 12 beat *Steak 'n Kidney*		2:48

Day 2

Division 1

Kookaburra II beat *White Horse*		6:57
KZ-7 beat *Sfida Italiana*		2:12

Division 2

Bengal beat *Entertainer 12*		7:00
Steak 'n Kidney beat *Stars & Stripes*		8:02

Day 3

Division 1

KZ-7 beat *White Horse*		5:18
Kookaburra II beat *Sfida Italiana*		5:10

Division 2

Entertainer 12 beat *Stars & Stripes*		3:18
Bengal beat *Steak 'n Kidney*		2:32

Yacht name	Skipper	D1	D2	D3	Total
Division 1					
KZ-7	D. Barnes	1	1	1	3
Kookaburra II	P. Gilmour	0	1	1	2
Sfida Italiana	M. Pelaschier	1	0	0	1
White Horse	P. Crebbin	0	0	0	0
Division 2					
Bengal	C. Beashel	1	1	1	3
Entertainer 12	P. Petterson	1	0	1	2
Steak 'n Kidney	P. Thompson	0	1	Disq	1
Stars & Stripes	D. Conner	0	0	0	0

Finals

Day 1	*KZ-7* beat *Bengal*		00:53
Day 2	*Bengal* beat *KZ-7*		Disq
Day 3	*KZ-7* beat *Bengal*		Disq

6-Metre
World Championship

Pos.	Yacht name	Skipper	Designer	Year	Results	Points
1	Scoundrel	B. Owen	Petterson	1986*	4-5-8-2-3-3	17.00
2	Notorious	J. Sundelier	Norlin	1986	7-7-2-1-2-8	18.75
3	Joe Cool	P. Norlin	Norlin	1986	2-3-9-4-6-4	19.00
4	St Francis IX	P. Cayard	Petterson	1985	1-2-3-7-7-24	19.75
5	Thisbe	P. Bateman	Petterson	1987	3-8-6-8-24-1	25.75
6	Battlecry	J. Prentice	Howlett	1983*	5-6-1-14-8-9	28.75
7	Maybe XII	C.G. Piehl	Norlin	1978	19-1-5-5-10-14	34.75
8	St Kitts	P. Walwyn	Howlett	1987	12-24-4-6-1-12	34.75
9	Beep-Beep	P. Durr	Grobety	1986	8-16-11-9-4-6	38.00
10	Maybe XIV	C. Salen	Petterson	1987	11-12-7-13-12-2	44.00

11 *Gitana*, 50.3 pts; **12** *OMX* 51; **13** *Klorina*, 53; **14** *Chinook*, 55; **15** *Port Douglas*, 62; **16** *Capriccio*, 73; **17** *Nivola*, 73;
18 *Steverino*, 74; **19** *Gredelin*, 87; **20** *Tempest*, 94; **21** *Sachem*, 97; **22** *Fun*, 97; **23** *Conga*, 105.
* More recent keel additions.

Kieler Woche

Dragon: 1 M. & M. Glas & H. Herwig (D); **2** A. Haubold, M. Klemmt & A. Milkowski (D); **3** W. Rappel, M. Lipp & W. Rappel (D).
Europe: 1 H. Jacobsson (S); **2** T. Johansson (S); **3** N. Sletten (N).
Finn: 1 O. Khoperski (USSR); **2** S.J. MacLeod (US); **3** O. Müller von Blumencron (D).
Finn: 1 C. Bergström & P. Hallberg (S); **2** P. Lecrit & P. Serane (F); **3** A. Petersson & R. Isby (S).
FD: 1 S. Borodinov & O. Surin (USSR); **2** F. McLaughlin & J. Millen (CAN); **3** J.B. Braun & W. Kenney (US).
470 Men/Mixed fleet A: 1 W. & J. Hunger (D); **2** L. Hüttermann & N. Körte (D); **3** P. Evans & S. Mander (NZ).
470 Women: 1 F. Galloway & J. Schearer (NZ); **2** B. & A. Lemström (SF); **3** L. & J. Egnot (NZ).
420: 1 J. Olbrysch & M. Stock (D); **2** W. Sanchez Diez & B. Dumortier (F); **3** T. & M. Eckardt (D).
H-Boat 1 J. & M. Seppae (SF); **2** N. Springer & G. Frund (D); **3** T. Andersen & J. Seier (DK).
Laser: 1 S. Warkalla (D); **2** J. Dettmann (D); **3** S. Schuur (NL).
OK: 1 D. Josefsson (S); **2** K. Hitz (D); **3** M. von Zimmermann (D).
Soling: 1 J. Schümann, T. Flach & B. Jäkel (DDR); **2** T. Jungell, M. Mannström & S. Harima (SF); **3** J. Kostecki, R. Billingham & W. Baylis (US).
Star: 1 E. Adams & T. Olsen (US); **2** A. Griese & M. Marcour (D); **3** H. Vogt & U. Seeberger (D).
Tornado: 1 C. Cairns & J. Forbes (AUS); **2** M. Faou & Y. Quernec (F); **3** G. Zuccoli & L. Santella (I).
Division II Windsurfer, Heavy Division: 1 P. Wirz (I); **2** S. Vidakovic (YU); **3** C. Meyer (D).
Division II Windsurfer, Light Division: 1 T. Müller (D); **2** M. Gebhardt (US); **3** E. Bellini (E).
Division II Windsurfer, Women: 1 H. Burger (YU); **2** C. Maia (BR); **3** K. Snellenbörg (US).
Flying Dutchman: 1 L. Doreste & A. Serra (E) 71.7 pts; **2** S. Borodinov & V. Budantsev (USSR) 72; **3** M. Weiser & F. Weiser (D) 74.1.
470 Men: 1 B. Hoeft & F. Bier (DDR) 40; **2** P. Dali & G. Cojana (I) 45.7; **3** P. Evans & S. Mander (NZ) 50.
470 Women: 1 S. Meyer & K. Adkofer (D) 25.4; **2** P. Hearndon & C. Goff (US) 36; **3** S. Theel & S. Preuss (DDR) 52.
Finn: 1 J.L. Doreste (E) 19.7; **2** L. Hjortnæs (DK) 61; **3** B. Ledbetter (US) 83.
Soling: 1 H. Nauck, N. Hellriegel & S. Diederling (DDR) 87; **2** J. Kostecki, B. Billingham & W. Baylis (US) 89; **3** G. Shaiduko, S. Kanov & N. Poliakov (USSR) 91.
Tornado: 1 A. Hagara & R. Hagara (A) 0; **2** C. Cairns & J. Forbes (AUS) 11.7; **3** G. Zuccoli & L. Santella (I) 31.4.
Star: 1 V. Brun & H. Schreiner (US) 48; **2** M. Reynolds & H. Haenel (US) 60; **3** H. Raudaschl & X. Buxkandl (A) 69.7.
Division II Heavyweights: 1 C. Muzellec (F) 42.7; **2** J.L. Lochus (F) 55; **3** G. Kendler (A) 80.7.
Division II Women: 1 J. Horgen (N) 8.7; **2** V. Capart (F) 42.7; **3** J. Söderström (S) 43.7.

La Nioulargue

Nioulargue Grand Prix IOR/CHS

Class A: 1 Iorana (D. Wolfgang), 122.88; **2** Bewitched (M. Iblez), 105.88; **3** Ikra (J. Rédelé), 102.23. **Class 1: 1** BabaCorum (P. Briand), 63.26; **2** Mandrake (G. Carriero), 44.13; **3** Noonmark (R. Fenhalls), 43.5. **Class 2: 1** Numéro 1 (B. Caignaert), 68.39; **2** X et Ryus (B. Troublé), 53; **3** Junon (A. Faure), 53. **Class 3-4-5: 1** Aqua vit (Tournis/Laurent), 69.88; **2** Christina Bella (J.M. Guennart), 67.13; **3** Odin (O. Vattine), 64.75. **Class CHS A: 1** Bleu Marine (G. Cornou), 321.76; **2** Liberty (R. Estoppey), 301.88; **3** Gibtune V (R. Téolier), 293. **Class CHS B: 1** Excalibure (F. Quaranta), 238.63; **2** Papillon (B. Lambart), 226.38; **3** Abricotine (H. Manier), 211.88.

Voiliers de tradition, Club 55 Cup

Class A: 1 Aile Blanche (M. Edelman); **2** Atalante (J.D. Englefield Horn); **3** Puritan. **Class B: 1** Eugenia V (E. de Sérini); **2** Gael (P. Coussens); **3** Hygie (Simonetti/Costa). **Class C–D: 1** Pantaya (B. Vidal); **2** Aile Blanche (D. Gulik); **3** Childe (E. Fay).

Monotypes Selection: 1 Orléans loiret (J. Couturier); **2** Saint Tropez (P. Novara); **3** Ville d'Arcachon (X. Husson).

Swan: 1 Liberty (R. Estoppey); **2** Wassilissa; **3** Formosa (B. Savage).

Coupe performance Tuffier associés: 1 Z3333 (P. Fehlmann); **2** X et Ryus (B. Troublé); **3** Pride (D. Jason).

Trophée IOR Bénéteau: BabaCorum (P. Briand).
Coupe de la Ville de Saint Tropez: Z3333 (P. Felhmann).
Triangle IOR Corum: Divirona V (T. Tuffier).

Moët et Chandon Maxi Cup

1 Kialoa V (J. Kilroy) 7.5; **2** Matador (W. Koch), 10.75; **3** Ondine VII (H. Long), 11; **4** Othello (G. Verassi), 15; **5** Emeraude (J. Dewailly), 20.75; **6** Divirona V (T. Tuffier) 27; **7** Gitana VIII (E. de Rothschild), 29; **8** Milène V (A. Mirlesse), 30; **9** Z3333 (P. Fehlmann), 32; **10** Midnight Sun, 36; **11** Inspiration (H. Dahm), 44.

Trophée Byblos (match racing)
Blue division: 1 Kialoa V; **2** Matador; **3** Ondine VII; **4**= Divirona; **4**= Z3333. **Yellow division: 1** Emeraude; **2** Othello; **3** Gitana VIII.

Centomiglia

Class Libera A: 1 Lillo (A. Damiani), 10h 27m 54s; **2** Ines-Sangiacomo (B. Fezzardi), 10h 39m 10s; **3** Farrneticante-Liber (L. Lievi), 12h 05m 08s. **Class Libera B: 1** Haumdacha Zwoa (F. Huber), 11h 02m 25s; **2** Azzar-Sesto Senso (O. Tonoli), 12h 08m 40s; **3** Arrow (A. Salcher), 12h 20m 35s. **Class Libera C: 1** Sirius (R. Knusel), 14h 23m 00s; **2** Speedy (G. Muller), 14h 25m 30s. **Class Libera A–B: 1** Liberte (R. Weiser), 12h 17m 25s; **2** Xenophon (K. Fricke), 13h 55m 05s; **3** High-Tex (H.J. Kochi), 13h 56m 10s. **Class Libera Classic C: 1** Super Akros (R. Mai), 14h 19m 30s; **2** Hel (M. Decosterd), 14h 38m 53s; **3** Simsalabim (E. Steeg), 15h 12m 48s. **Class Asso 99: 1** Packone (M. Walter), 13h 25m 30s; **2** Fiasco (K. Werndl), 13h 26m 30s; **3** Fatti Nostri (I. Rossi), 13h 32m 25s. **Cruiser Class A: 1** Uragen-Italsat (R. Pattiston), 10h 15m 32s; **2** Wagner (M. Lavazza), 12h 34m 51s; **3** El Midi (F. Schon), 13h 08m 45s. **Cruiser Class B: 1** Skorpion II (R. Benamati), 13h 22m 50s; **2** Elena (G. Gallina), 13h 23m 40s; **3** Wahoo (V. Vemagi), 13h 29m 45s. **Cruiser Class C: 1** Gonfi Gonfi (E. Dal Cero), 12h 08m 22s; **2** Signorsi' (G. Filippini), 12h 34m 22s; **3** Latus (A. Nalin), 13h 27m 00s. **Cruiser Class D: 1** Pucciola (R. Spata), 13h 25m 45s; **2** Frivola (L. Pusterla), 13h 28m 15s; **3** Sans Surprise (M. Pagani), 13h 33m 00s. **Cruiser Class E: 1** Tumi Turbi (V. Festa), 13h 45m 40s; **2** Deffardo (G. Stabiuni), 14h 01m 30s; **3** Malu' 7 (M. Valle), 14h 01m 30s. **Soling: 1** Caprice (F. Piz), 14h 03m 15s; **2** Trutel 3 (A. Manenti), 14h 05m 30s; **3** Alligator (S. Feltrinelli), 14h 25m 55s. **Sprinta Sport: 1** Duckanterl (F. Morzinsky), 14h 02m 45s; **2** Gipy (J. Lechner), 14h 04m 20s; **3** Charivari (H. Frenzer), 14h 10m 30s. **J-24: 1** Jab (F. Albarelli), 13h 47m 45s; **2** Jack Rabbit (G. Bonaventura), 14h 02m 50s; **3** Lariosauro (L. Cappa), 14h 16m 22s. **Fun: 1** Baffun (G. Curami), 13h 45m 40s; **2** Fun King (E. Giambarda), 13h 51m 38s; **3** Mediatel 1 (E. Zambiasi), 13h 55m 20s. **Etchell 22: 1** Manuela VII (F. Battiti), 13h 32m 05s; **2** Violetta VII (A. Lanza), 13h 55m 20s; **3** Viceversa (S. Sintschnig), 13h 46m 50s. **IOR Class IV–V: 1** Ziza (P. Barziza), 10h 29m 08s; **2** Controcorrente (V. Pighi), 10h 35m 11s; **3** Kismet (S. Leporati), 10h 51m 10s. **IOR Class VI: 1** Carnaro XII (D. Tuchtan), 10h 41m 49s; **2** Sula (R. Zanca), 10h 42m 35s; **3** Snorza e Sbrighis (P. Busnello), 10h 44m 01s. **IOR Class VII: 1** Fragola (R. Moreschini), 10h 20m 01s; **2** Pettirosso (L. Terragni), 11h 16m 18s.

Tour de France

à la Voile

Pos.	No.	Yacht name	Points
1	35	Sète Languedoc Roussillon	1064·00
2	31	Haute Garonne Conseil General	963·00
3	10	Le Havre	917·50
4	23	Genève	911·50
5	9	Angers	896·00
6	25	Saumur Brut	871·00
7	32	Orleans Loiret	870·00
8	6	Dauphine Grenoble	850·50
9	14	Pays de Vannes	838.00
10	11	Brest	835.00
11	28	Chartres Eure et Loir	826·50
12	20	Nantes	825.00
13	34	Haut Léman	800·50
14	1	Oyonnax Plastics Vallée	797.00
15	16	Cherbourg Nord Cotentin Entreprises	789·50
16	33	Ville d'Arcachon	765·50
17	27	Douarnenez	734·00
18	29	Finistère Baie d'Audierne	733·50
19	24	Lannion Développement	726·00
20	5	Gers-Conflans	715·00
21	22	Côtes du Nord Bretagne	706·50
22	12	Lausanne Ville Olympique	705·50
23	13	Lanveoc Poulmic École Navale	689·00
24	30	Bern	662·50
25	2	Vendée Puy du Fou	659·50
26	8	Saône et Loire Vins du Maconnais	648·50
27	15	Marennes Oleron	636·00
28	21	Dunkerque	618·50
29	19	Saint Nazaire	612·00
30	18	Saint Tropez	570·00
31	4	Ville de Garches	518·00
32	26	California	483·50
33	3	Région Wallonne	471·50
34	7	Palaiseau Polytechnique	453·00
35	17	Rueil Malmaison	448·50

Overall Results

Formula 1

	Yacht name	Skipper	Points
1	Jet Services	D. Gilard	13.7
2	Poulain	O. de Kersauson	45.7
3	Elf Aquitaine	J. Maurel	48.4
4	Ericsson	B. Peyron	63.8
5	Côte d'Or II	E. Tabarly	74.8
6	Fleury Michon VIII	P. Poupon	75.1
7	Roger et Gallet	E. Loizeau	117.7
8	Jean Stalaven	B. de Broc/D. Marsaudon	124.0
9	Novanet Elite	P. Phillips	139.0
10	Kiamiloa	F. Jubelin	141.0

Formula 2

	Yacht name	Skipper	Points
1	Challenge Grundig	T. Caroni	0
2	Picardie-Agri Obtentions	A. Petit-Etienne	24.0
3	Dupon Duran	P. Herold	50.2
4	Women of Europe	L. Chambaz	66.8
5	Calor Challenge	R. Tolkien	RTD

Leg Results

Pos.	Name	Skipper	Leg time	Tot. elap. time
Den Haag–Bremerhaven (220 miles)				
Formula 1				
1	Elf Aquitaine	J. Maurel	12h 14m 10s	
2	Poulain	O. de Kersauson	12h 20m 00s	
3	Jet Services	D. Gilard	12h 29m 00s	
Formula 2				
1	Challenge Grundig	T. Caroni	14h 55m 38s	
2	Picardie-Agri Obtentions	A. Petit-Etienne	18h 25m 50s	
Bremerhaven–Edinburgh (450 miles)				
Formula 1				
1	Jet Services	D. Gilard	38h 48m 28s	51h 17m 28s
2	Poulain	O. de Kersauson	44h 43m 28s	57h 03m 28s
3	Côte d'Or II	E. Tabarly	46h 07m 59s	58h 00m 05s
Formula 2				
1	Challenge Grundig	T. Caroni	51h 27m 43s	66h 23m 21s
2	Picardie-Agri Obtentions	A. Petit-Etienne	61h 07m 12s	79h 33m 02s
Edinburgh–Dublin (650 miles)				
Formula 1				
1	Jet Services	D. Gilard	59h 41m 55s	110h 59m 23s
2	Elf Aquitaine	J. Maurel	60h 43m 18s	119h 16m 36s
3	Poulain	O. de Kersauson	62h 47m 06s	119h 50m 34s
Formula 2				
1	Challenge Grundig	T. Caroni	73h 31m 22s	139h 54m 43s
2	Picardie-Agri Obtentions	A. Petit-Etienne	89h 31m 10s	169h 04m 12s
Dublin–Lorient (405 miles)				
Formula 1				
1	Jet Services	D. Gilard	32h 39m 45s	143h 29m 08s
2	Elf Aquitaine	J. Maurel	34h 51m 10s	154h 07m 46s
3	Ericsson	B. Peyron	35h 52m 15s	160h 44m 18s
Formula 2				
1	Challenge Grundig	T. Caroni	38h 25m 54s	178h 20m 37s
2	Picardie-Agri Obtentions	A. Petit-Etienne	42h 17m 50s	211h 22m 02s
Lorient–Vilamoura (800 miles)				
Formula 1				
1	Jet Services	D. Gilard	60h 59m 15s	204h 28m 00s
2	Ericsson	B. Peyron	63h 30m 10s	224h 14m 28s
3	Fleury Michon VIII	P. Poupon	66h 57m 50s	227h 54m 01s
Formula 2				
1	Challenge Grundig	T. Caroni	75h 30m 50s	253h 51m 00s
2	Picardie-Agri Obtentions	A. Petit-Etienne	83h 40m 14s	295h 02m 16s
Vilamoura–Barcelona (700 miles)				
Formula 1				
1	Jet Services	D. Gilard	46h 08m 29s	250h 36m 29s
2	Poulain	O. de Kersauson	47h 29m 59s	271h 49m 59s
3	Elf Aquitaine	J. Maurel	49h 39m 41s	271h 21m 41s
Formula 2				
1	Challenge Grundig	T. Caroni	60h 57m 21s	314h 48m 21s
2	Picardie-Agri Obtentions	A. Petit-Etienne	63h 46m 39s	358h 48m 55s
Barcelona–Toulon (210 miles)				
Formula 1				
1	Jet Services	D. Gilard	28h 18m 28s	278h 54m 57s
2	Côte d'Or II	E. Tabarly	29h 07m 26s	317h 44m 38s
3	Elf Aquitaine	J. Maurel	29h 13m 55s	300h 35m 36s
Formula 2				
1	Challenge Grundig	T. Caroni	44h 44m 32s	359h 32m 53s
2	Picardie-Agri Obtentions	A. Petit-Etienne	44h 56m 16s	403h 45m 11s
Toulon–San Remo (100 miles)				
Formula 1				
1	Poulain	O. de Kersauson	13h 39m 10s	315h 45m 08s
2	Fleury Michon	P. Poupon	13h 47m 29s	329h 53m 38s
3	Ericsson	B. Peyron	14h 42m 45s	321h 21m 27s
Formula 2				
1	Challenge Grundig	T. Caroni	16h 44m 07s	376h 17m 00s
2	Picardie-Agri Obtentions	A. Petit-Etienne	21h 39m 30s	425h 24m 00s

International Formula 40

Pos.	Yacht name	Skipper	Results										Total
1	Biscuits Cantreau II	J. le Cam	0	9	2	9	4	9	9	9	9	9	69
2	Data General	P. le Maout	9	2	9	4	9	4	4	1	6	4	52
3	Fleury Michon VII	P. Poupon	6	6	6	6	6	6	6	0	4	6	48
4=	La Rochelle	J.F. Fountaine	0	1	0	2	2	3	0	2	3	0	14
4=	Region Nord Pas de Calais	A. Comyn	0	0	4	0	0	2	2	6	0	0	14
6	Renaulac	R. Smyth	0	0	0	3	0	0	1	0	0	1	12
7	CDKI/Le Media de la Mer	R. Jourdain	4	3	0	0	0	0	0	0	2	0	10
8	Chaffoteaux et Maury	P. Elies	3	0	1	0	0	0	0	3	1	0	7
9=	Cahiers Clairefontaine	L. Pajot	0	4	0	0	0	0	0	0	0	0	4
9=	Richmond III	P. Hanin	0	0	0	1	3	0	0	0	0	0	4
9=	Rochefort	P. Follenfant	0	0	0	0	0	1	3	0	0	0	4
12=	Lessives Blanco	Y. Lebouvier	1	0	0	0	0	0	0	0	0	2	3
12=	Louis Feraud		0	0	0	0	0	0	0	0	0	3	3
12=	Lada Poch	L. Peyron	0	0	3	0	0	0	0	0	0	0	3
15	Optique Beaumont	B. de Boc	2	0	0	0	0	0	0	0	0	0	2
16	The White Team	R. White	0	0	0	0	1	0	0	0	0	0	1

Did not score: Baby Cresci (C. Ricci); Collanti Avanzini (R. Vigano); Munego (P. Battaglia); Rubinettieria Cisal (G. Angiolani); La Nina (J. Lastra); Helly Hansen (T. Cooke); Business Design Group (S. Rowsell).

British Summertime

Junior Offshore Group

Race 1: Round the Island
IOR Class 3–4: 1 *Bathsheba* (Humphreys 34, Sir M. Laing); **2** *Gilue* (Sigma 33, M. Davis); **3** *Sigmatic II* (Sigma 33, D. Bonner). **IOR Class 5–7: 1** *Insatiable* (Andrieu 30, J. Bibby & M. Heeley); **2** *Double Plush* (HB31, M. Holdsworth); **3** *Scorpio* (Humphreys 30, P. Gatrill). **CHS Class 8: 1** *Boadicea* (Sigma 36, Britannia Sailing); **2** *Hope & Glory* (Sigma 36, Britannia); **3** *Baccarat* (Sadler 34, R.G. Smith). **CHS Class 9: 1** *Blondie* (Bolero, R. Lawton); **2** *British Tiger* (Contessa 32, B. & L. Reiske); **3** *Elan* (Eygthene 24, J. Bennet & M. Painter).

Race 2: Cowes to Cherbourg
IOR Class 3–4: 1 *Popje* (Sigma 33, T. Wormington); **2** *Jane Bottomley* (Humphreys 33, R. Bottomley & P. Bentley); **3** *Bathsheba*. **IOR Class 5–7: 1** *Scorpio*; **2** *Insatiable*; **3** *Pinocchio* (Formula 28, Team 10). **CHS Class 8: 1** *Boadicea*; **2** *Sorcerer* (Dehler 34S, G. Johnson & P. Bennett); **3** *British Bulldog* (Sigma 36, Britannia). **CHS Class 9: 1** *Binkie II* (Contessa 32, Mr & Mrs C. Wetherall); **2** *Emblem* (Contessa 32, P. Mead); **3** *Trader Jo* (Contessa 32, J. Gresham & N. Inchbald).

Race 3: Cowes to Brighton
IOR Class 3–4: 1 *Jane Bottomley*; **2** *Imperator* (Hustler 35, P. Waxman & P. King); **3** *Gilue*. **IOR Class 5–7: 1** *Scorpio*; **2** *Harmony 87* (Humphreys 30, P. Dyer); **3** *Rattler* (MG26, T. Pountain). **CHS Class 8: 1** *Nokomis* (Sigma 362, M. Moss & J. Laurence); **2** *Talisman* (Sigma 41, M. Stephens); **3** *Innovator* (Selection 37, J. Batt). **CHS Class 9: 1** *Zadig* (H Boat, T. Short); **2** *Blueshank* (Contessa 32, S. & A. Butler); **3** *Dafrida* (Carter 30, M. & M. Allum).

Race 4: Brighton to Cowes.
IOR Class 3–4: 1 *Jane Bottomley*; **2** *Imperator*; **3** *Bathsheba*. **IOR Class 5–7: 1** *Harmony 87*; **2** *Scorpio*; **3** *Double Plush*. **CHS Class 8: 1** *Nokomis*; **2** *Talisman*; **3** *Geronimo* (Swan 371, A. & W.M. Courtis).

Race 5: Cowes to Alderney
IOR Class 3–4: 1 *Bathsheba*; **2** *Ivory Moon* (Sigma 33, J. Yarrow); **3** *Jane Bottomley*. **IOR Class 5–7: 1** *Rattler*; **2** *Alchemist* (Dubois 30, M. Wynter & D. Bremner); **3** *Glissade* (HB 31, N. Towers). **CHS Class 8: 1** *Allamanda II* (OOD 34, M. Kilsby); **2** *Talisman*; **3** *Redcoat* (OOD 34, Army Sailing Assn). **CHS Class 9: 1** *Blondie*; **2** *British Tiger*; **3** *Elan*.

Race 6: Cowes to Deauville
IOR Class 3–4: 1 *Starfall II* (Sigma 33, G.A.W. Stocker & C.J.C. Campbell); **2** *Acrimony 2* (Sigma 33, S. Patterson & E. Logan); **3** *Hawk* (Sigma 33, R. Joppe). **IOR Class 5–7: 1** *Spirit* (Humphreys 30, M. Sparks & A. Saward); **2** *Min-o-Din* (Thomas 25, J. Humphries); **3** *Pinocchio*. **CHS Class 8: 1** *Talisman*; **2** *Jabberwock* (Sigma 36, P. Mousley); **3** *Geronimo*. **CHS Class 9: 1** *Emblem*; **2** *Moongirl* (Contessa 32, Mr & Mrs R. Burley); **3** *Blondie*.

Race 7: Cowes to St Vaast
IOR Class 3–4: 1 *Acrimony 2*; **2** *RamShackle* (MG RS-34, D. Grimes); **3** *Kamisado* (UFO 34, M. Green). **IOR Class 5–7: 1** *Hooligan* (Humphreys 30, E. Broadway & I. White); **2** *Alchemist 2*; **3** *Tamasin II* (Nicholson 30, R. Bishop). **CHS Class 8: 1** *Redcoat*; **2** *Talisman*; **3** *Nokomis*. **CHS Class 9: 1** *British Tiger*; **2** *Blueshank*; **3** *Blondie*.

Race 8: Channel Triangle
IOR Class 3–4: 1 *Jane Bottomley*; **2** *Bathsheba*. **IOR Class 5–7: 1** *Scorpio*; **2** *Catch* (Briand 26, J. Allenby); **3** *Smokey Bear* (Hustler 32, J. Lillie). **CHS Class 8: 1** *Talisman*; **2** *Saturday Slow* (Naja 30, G. Peck).

Race 9: Cowes to St Malo
IOR Class 3–4: 1 *Jane Bottomley*; **2** *Hawk*; **3** *Starfall II*. **IOR Class 5–7: 1** *Pinocchio*; **2** *Scorpio*; **3** *Glissade*. **CHS Class 8: 1** *Allamanda II*; **2** *Electron III* (Sigma 36, HMS Collingwood); **3** *Sorcery*. **CHS Class 9: 1** *British Tiger*; **2** *Binkie II*; **3** *Moongirl*.

Race 10: Cowes to Dartmouth
IOR Class 3–4: 1 *Bathsheba*; **2** *Akka II* (Sigma 33, R. Purkiss); **3** *Halcyone* (MG RS-34, NatWest Bank SC). **IOR Class 5–7: 1** *Scorpio*; **2** *Min-o-Din*; **3** *Bambi* (Impala 28, J. & L. Hill). **CHS Class 8: 1** *Pegasus II* (SHE 36, P. White); **2** *Maghda* (MG 335, M. Allum, J. Devey & N. Harper); **3** *Pipedreamer* (Ohlson 38, J. Metherall). **CHS Class 9: 1** *British Tiger*; **2** *Zadig*; **3** *Bumble* (Sadler 25, P. Chignell & A. Tomkins).

Race 11: NM Schroder Channel Race – Cowes to St Peter Port
CHS Class 3–4: 1 *Jane Bottomley*; **2** *Heart of Gold* (Dubois design, Capt. J. Parry, RN); **3** *Buckshot* (Sigma 33, R. Emberson & D. Every). **IOR Class 5–7: 1** *Scorpio*; **2** *Harlequin* (Jones 30, H. Sellars); **3** *Insatiable*. **CHS Class 0: 1** *Highwayman* (Humphreys 38, Sir P. Johnson); **2** *Talisman*; **3** *Arbitration* (Sigma 41, J.A. Gray). **CHS Class 8: 1** *True Brit* (Sigma 36, Britannia Sailing); **2** *Leda* (Laser 28, D. Brown); **3** *Xepha* (MG RS-34, Rank Xerox SA). **CHS Class 9: 1** *Blondie*; **2** *Zadig*; **3** *Emblem*.

Race 12: Cowes to Le Havre
IOR Class 3–4: 1 *Jane Bottomley*; **2** *Charisma* (Sigma 33, R. Craigie, R. Gregory & K. Dolling); **3** *Akka II*. **IOR Class 5–7: 1** *Glissade*; **2** *Scorpio*; **3** *Hooligan*. **CHS Class 8: 1** *Gunshot* (Storm 33, P. & C. Wallace & E. Nettleton); **2** *British Bulldog*; **3** *Storm Master* (Storm 33, C. Rennie & P. Pearce). **CHS Class 9: 1** *Blondie*.

Race 13: Cowes to Poole
IOR Class 3–4: 1 *Jane Bottomley*; **2** *Imperator*; **3** *Suspicion* (Sigma 33, G. & V. Trevelyan & I. Llewelyn). **IOR Class 5–7: 1** *Scorpio*; **2** *Harlequin*; **3** *Hooligan*. **CHS Class 8: 1** *Evening Mist* (Rival 41, S.R. Godwin); **2** *Baccarat*; **3** *Bleuet* (Fastnet 34, T. Moy). **CHS Class 9: 1** *Zadig*; **2** *Blondie*; **3** *British Tiger*.

Race 14: Spithead (provisional)
IOR Class 3–4: 1 *Jane Bottomley*; **2** *Imperator*; **3** *Paranoah* (Sigma 33, R. Granger). **IOR Class 5–7: 1** *Harlequin*; **2** *Alchemist*; **3** *Bullfrog* (Formula 28, M. Thorpe). **CHS Class 8: 1** *Nokomis*; **2** *Bleuet*; **3** *Leda*. **CHS Class 9: 1** *British Tiger*; **2** *Zadig*; **3** *Blondie*.

Overall (provisional)
IOR Class 3–4: 1 *Jane Bottomley*; **2** *Bathsheba*; **3** *Imperator*. **IOR Class 5–7: 1** *Scorpio*; **2** *Hooligan*; **3** *Glissade*. **CHS Class 8: 1** *Talisman*; **2** *Redcoat*; **3** *Nokomis*. **CHS Class 9: 1** *Blondie*; **2** *British Tiger*; **3** *Zadig*.

McEwan's Scottish Series

McEwan's Trophy: *Scenario Act II* (Humphreys three-quarter tonner, Alan Fitton).
IOR Class 1: 1 *Local Hero IV* (Briand one tonner, Howison/Gallagher/Hughes), 36.75 pts; **2** *Jameson Whiskey* (Dubois one tonner, R. Burrows), 36.125; **3** *Calvin B. Marshall* (Jeanneau one tonner, B. Allan). **IOR Class 2: 1** *Scenario Act II* (Humphreys three-quarter tonner, A. Fitton), 45.875; **2** *Rhett Butler* (db2, Anderson/Findlay), 36; **3** *Scarlet O'Jara* (SJ35, G. Smith), 31. **IOR Class 3: 1** *Quest* (Humphreys 25, J. Burke), 58.75; **2** *Senator Incitatus* (McIlraith 25, J. McIlraith), 56.125; **3** *Flash II* (Formula 28, B. Bullen), 52.75.
Cruiser Class A: 1 *Flair II* (MG335, J. McGregor/A. Poole), 137.375; **2** *Lingo* (J-29, I. Tiefenbrun/W. Mackay), 123.5; **3** *Bubblegum* (Contessa 43, I. Fyfe), 120.25. **Cruiser Class C: 1** *Salamander VII* (Trintella 42, J. Corson), 167.625; **2** *Shadowfax* (Verle 33, Mr & Mrs I. Campbell), 164.25; **3** *Moonlighter* (Contessa 33, B. Hunt), 157.5. **Cruiser Class D: 1** *Itch* (Scampi, N. Wright), 113.75; **2** *Norella* (7-metre cruiser-racer, G. Finlay), 110.125; **3** *Eau Vation* (Jeanneau Arcadia, D. Clark), 105.375. **Cruiser Class E: 1** *Decision* (First Class 8, C. Buchanan), 74.5; **2** *Morag Rho* (Bolero 25, B. McLean), 68.125; **3** *Wakajawaka* (J-24, T. Kershaw), 65. **Cruiser Class F: 1** *Igls* (Westerly Pembroke, J. Yuill), 142.375; **2** *Bridean* (Oyster 26, I. Downs), 138.25; **3** *Pippa III* (Ballad, G. Murray), 126.25.
Sonata: 1 *Footnote* (D. McLaren), 69; **2** *Red Hot Poker* (R. Pender/S. Pender), 62.75; **3** *Diana* (J. Hunt), 61. **Sigma 33: 1** *Pepsi* (A. Milton), 52.375; **2** *Sula of Arne* (J. Taggart), 43.25; **3** *Spooky* (G. Wolfenden), 35.75.

Irish Sea Offshore Racing Association

Overall Championship: 1 *Canterbury* (1985 Davidson 40, A.J. Vernon, South Caernarvon YC), 524.5 pts; **2** *Lightning* (1983 db2s, L. Shanahan, National YC), 510; **3** *Banga Wanga* (1985 SJ 35, Hill family, Holyhead SC), 479; **4** *Megalopolis* (1984 Humphreys 37, U. Taylor, HSC), 464.75; **5** *Checkmate* (1984 MG 34, J. Biggs, HSC), 461.5; **6** *Seren Wib* (1984 MG 34, W. Humphreys, Pwllheli SC), 448; **7** *Demelza* (1976 Club Shamrock, N. Maguire, Howth YC), 444; **8** *Grenade* (1962 Holman 35, H.S. Morris, SCYC), 433.25; **9** *Glider II* (1985 MG 30, A. Barton, SCYC), 424; **10** *Act of Defiance* (1986 Contessa 33, A.N. Hall, SCYC), 424. **Division A1: 1** *Megalopolis*, 461.5; **2** *Canterbury*, 451.75; **3** *Imp* (1977 Holland 40, R. Dickson, HYC), 434. **Division A2: 1** *Lightning*, 512.75; **2** *Banga Wanga*, 469; **3** *Seren Wib*, 467.5. **Division B: 1** *Demelza*, 485.25; **2** *Grenade*, 475.75; **3** *Glider II*, 464. **Club Championship:** Holyhead SC, 358.5; **2** South Caernarvon YC, 337; **3** Howth YC, 316; **4** National YC, 311.5; **5** Pwllheli SC, 269.5; **6** Royal Alfred YC, 218.

Cowes Week

1st Saturday
Royal Southampton YC Regatta
Queen's Cup Race

Class 1–Marchwood Cup: *Backlash* (T. & C. Herring). Class 2–Armitage Cup: *Excalibur* (M. Candellier). Queen's Cup overall winner: *Excalibur*. Class 3–Lorne Currie Cup: *Insatiable* (J. Bibby & M. Heeley). Class 4–Southampton Cup: *Quest* (J. & L. Burke). Class 5–Rear Commodore's Bell: *Panic Major* (D.J. Pitt). Class 6: *Sorcery* (R. Wigley). Class 7: *Blue Air* (R.E. Goddard). Sigma 33: *Sibilation* (P.C. Nicholson). Contessa 32–Saturday's Cup: *Mutiny* (M. Pattinson). Impala: *Kudu* (A. & C. Cox). J24–Pussar's Rum Trophy: *Little Eagle* (Aiglon College). Sonata: *Fruesli II* (R. & J. Eglin). SCOD: *Peter Baker* (A.V. Cherry). Darings–A.W. Barlow Cup: *Damsel* (T. Sheldon & J. Hungerford). Dragons–Commodore's Trophy: *Dragonfly* (E. Williams). Swallows–Captain's Prize: *Spindrift* (J. Upton & W. Knight). Redwings–1922 Cup: *Redstart* (J. Janson). Sunbeams: *Fay* (K. Webster & P. Clementson). Mermaids: *Zara* (R. & C. Dobbs). Flying 15–Michelmore Trophy: *Bullrush II* (J.A. Mander). Squibs–The Georgian Tray: *Phaedra* (M.H. Fawcett). XOD–Hiscock Cup: *Silhouette* (R. & T. Wallrock).

Sunday
Royal Thames Yacht Club

Class 1–Glazebrook Cup: *Monaco* (P. Morton & R. Stowe). Class 2–Morson Cup: *Oly* (V. Schröder). Class 3–Festival of Britain Cup: *Insatiable* (J. Bibby & M. Heeley). Class 4–Coupe Vase: *Quest* (J. & L. Burke). Class 5–Burt Cup: *Talisman* (M.J. Stephens). Class 6–Victory Cup: *Leda* (D. Brown & F. Bergman). Class 7–Williams Salver: *Rondo* (H. Walsh). Sigma 33–Champion Lauder Trophy: *Sibilation* (P.C. Nicholson). Contessa 32–Trophy Minema Bowl: *Tenacity* (M.A. Rich). Impala–Howard Cup: *Burhou* (C.S. King). J24–Prince of Wales Cup: *Popincotta VII* (W. Brogden). Sonata–Neal Junior Cup: *Cadenza* (J. Froy). Etchells–Southampton Corinthian's Cup: *Vixen* (F.M. O'Neill). Darings–Thornycroft Cup: *Darius* (T. Parr & C. Caws). Dragons–Solent Trophy: *Dragonfly* (E. Williams). Swallows–Thornycroft Cup: *Archon* (J. McCann & D. Palmer). Redwings–Thornycroft Cup: *Redstart* (J. Janson). Sunbeams–Ball Cup: *Fleury* (R. Dale). Mermaids–Edwards Trophy: *Zara* (R. & C. Dobbs). Flying 15–Holt Cup: *Bullrush II* (J.A. Mander). Squibs–Grog Tub: *Razzo Secondo* (J. Piddy). Victory–Victory for Eagle Trophy: *Nada* (I. & J. Andrews). XOD–Royal Thames YC Cup: *Heyday* (D. Bedford & L. Vincent).

Monday

Class 1–Sir Walter Preston Cup: *Xpanda* (P. Shiels). Class 2–Purdey Cup: *Jacobite* (S.L. James). Class 3–Muriel Gretton Cup: *Insatiable* (J. Bibby & M. Heeley). Class 4–Hyland Trophy: *Chipeau* (M. Cumberlege). Class 5–Dowson Trophy: *Oystercatcher 12* (R.B. Matthews). Class 6–Bones Trophy: *Sorcery* (R. Wigley). Class 7–Birkett Cup: *Skean Dhu* (A. McLelland). Sigma 33: *Somer's Isle* (R. Carrell). Contessa 32–Courtney Cup: *Cantilena* (S.M. Collyer). Impala: *La Camarguaise* (D.C. Johnson). J24–Pussar's Rum Trophy: *Sanjola IV* (J. Adams & E. Warwick). Sonatas: *Cadenza* (J. Froy). SCOD–Fremantle Salver: *Tuonela* (R.J. Harding). Etchell–Astrid Cup: *Fortitude* (E. Fort). Darings–Cayley Cup: *Loup Garou VIII* (J.B. Clark). Dragons–Celline Vase: *Dragonfly* (E. Williams). Swallows–Ratsey Cup: *Archon* (J. McCann & D. Palmer). Redwings–Redwing Cup: *Tarpon* (P.N. Samuelson & M. Andreae). Sunbeams–Royal London YC Salver: *Romany* (K. van der Klugt). Mermaids–Carritt Cup: *Bluebell* (C.R. Taylor & A. Graham). Flying 15–Fitzpatrick-Robertson Cup: *Bullrush II* (J.A. Mander). Squibs–Hewitt Trophy: *Super Kipper* (J.W. Mobbs). Victory: *Zest* (R. & S. Taylor). XOD–Grenfell Trophy: *Madcap* (R. Smith).

Tuesday
Royal Yacht Squadron Regatta

Class 1–Britannia Cup: *Monaco* (P. Morton & R. Stowe). Class 2–Bathsheba Trophy: *Liberty* (W. Haehnel). Class 3: *Insatiable* (J. Bibby & M. Heeley). Class 4: *Starborn II* (P.G. Dickson). Class 5: *French Mustard* (R.M. French). Class 6–British Telecom Trophy: *Highwayman* (Sir Peter Johnson). Class 7: *Monochrome* (C.M. Hurst). Sigma 33–Dunelm Trophy: *Sibilation* (P.C. Nicholson). Contessa 32–Pollock Trophy: *Cantilena* (S.M. Collyer). Impalas: *Bambi* (I.R. Botting). J24: *Gossip* (E.W. McLean). Sonatas: *Cadenza* (J. Froy). SCOD: *Macaroon* (J.C. Schinas). Etchells–Chisholm Cup: *Fortitude* (E. Fort). Darings: *Darius* (T.M. Parr & C. Caws). Dragons–Nainbyluxmore: *Dragonfly* (E. Williams). Swallows–Tomahawk Trophy: *Mistral* (Sir Walter Blount & A. Donaldson). Redwings–Brabazon Trophy: *Blue Jay* (J. Cleave). Sunbeams–Pera Messervy Trophy: *Fay* (K. Webster & P. Clementson). Mermaids: *Zara* (R. & C. Dobbs). Flying 15–Hayling Hull Trophy: *Yahoo* (A.G. Gardener). Squibs–Lapsang Tea Tray: *Satu* (Cdr R.L. Hewitt). Victory: *Blackbird* (R. Brown & N. Hill). XOD–Ark & Dove Cup: *Mystery* (M. & T. Martell & C. Wallace).

Wednesday

Class 1–Camrose Trophy: *Canterbury* (A.J. Vernon). Class 2–Creighton Trophy: *Amaryllis of Dart* (Britannia Royal Naval College). Class 3: *Fantasy* (D. Bishop). Class 4: *Quest* (J. & L. Burke). Class 5: *Marionette X* (C.A. Dunning). Class 6: *Electron III* (HMS Collingwood). Class 7: *Monochrome* (C.M. Hurst). Sigma 33–Nicholl Trophy: *Sabre* (J.N. & J.C. White). Contessa 32–Desmond Cheers Salver: *Tenacity* (M.A. Rich). Impala: *Kudu* (A. & C. Cox). J24–Jean Machine Trophy: *Judge Dredd* (D. & S. Levison). Sonatas: *Cadenza* (J. Froy). SCOD: *Macaroon* (J.C. Schinas). Etchells: *Aquaviva* (P.H. Chisholm). Darings–Williams-Freedman Cup: *Darius* (T.M. Parr & C. Caws). Dragons–Sir John Ward Trophy: *Dragonfly* (E. Williams). Swallows–Swift Prize: *Ptarmigan* (R.M. Fox & M. Clarke). Redwings–Andreae Salver: *Blue Jay* (J. Cleave). Sunbeams–Half Century Trophy: *Query* (J. Oldham). Mermaids–Swinburne Salver Trophy: *Zara* (R. & C. Dobbs). Flying 15–Alistair Miller Salver: *Gandalff* (T. Robinson). Squibs–Mary Rose Bowl: *Super Kipper* (J.W. Mobbs). Victory: *Shearwater* (Dr M.B. & I. Mead). XOD–Steele Pilcher Salver: *Mystery* (M. T. Martell & C. Wallace).

Thursday

Class 1–New York YC Challenge Cup: *Yeoman XXVII* (R.A. Aisher). Class 2–Vanity Challenge Cup: *Oly* (V. Schröder). Class 3–De Maas Challenge Cup: *Fantasy* (D. Bishop). Class 4: *Quest* (J. & L. Burke). Class 5: *Talisman* (M.J. Stephens). Class 6: *Gusto II* (A. & S. Hinton-Lever). Class 7: *Wavelength* (J. Cornish & Dr M. Green). Sigma 33: *Sibilation* (P.C. Nicholson). Contessa 32: *Roulette* (J. Matthews & B. Cowper). Impalas: *Bambi* (I.R. Botting). J24: *Sanjola IV* (J. Adams & E. Warwick). Sonatas: *Afterthought* (W. & S. Jacobs). SCOD: *Topkapi* (R. Wheeler). Etchells: *Fortitude* (E. Fort). Darings: *Doublet* (R.W. Syme & F. Gilbert). Dragons: *Fanfare* (Brig. P.H. Henson). Swallows: *Boomerang* (J. Buckwell & J. Prunty). Redwings: *Vera* (Dr P.D. & Miss S. Swinstead). Sunbeams: *Query* (J. Oldham). Mermaids: *Zara* (R. & C. Dobbs). Flying 15: *Morning Storm* (R. Simmonds). Squibs: *Satu* (Cmdr R.L. Hewitt). Victory: *Dunlin* (D. Penn). XOD: *Madcap* (R. Smith).

Friday

Class 1–Rocking Chair Challenge Trophy: *Yeoman XXVI* (Sir Owen Aisher). Class 2: *Liberty* (W. Haehnel). Class 3: *Insatiable* (J. Bibby & M. Heeley). Class 4–White Cup: *Quest* (J. & L. Burke). Class 5–Island Cup: *Secret Obsession* (G.L. Shaw). Class 6–Cowes Town Challenge Cup: *Sorcery* (R. Wigley). Class 7: *Goud Reinette* (R. Maller). Sigma 33: *Sigmatic II* (D.C. Bonner). Contessa 32: *Wight Rabbit* (P. Ralls). Impala: *Kudu* (A. & C. Cox). J24: *Gossip* (E.W. McLean). Sonatas: *Xantz* (M.H. Tennant). SCOD: *Macaroon* (J. Schinas). Etchells: *Fortitude* (E. Fort). Darings: *Duenna* (C. Prout & J. Green). Dragons: *Ganymede VI* (P. Wilson & A. Cassell). Swallows: *Archon* (J. McCann & D. Palmer). Redwings: *Blue Jay* (J. Cleave). Sunbeams: *Romany* (K. & D. van der Klugt). Mermaids: *Bluebell* (C. & R. Taylor & A. Graham). Flying 15: *Fflipinek* (J. Corby). Squibs: *Super Kipper* (J.W. Mobbs). Victory: *Steadfast* (B. Middleditch & P. Coit). XOD: *Mystery* (M. & T. Martell & C. Wallace).

2nd Saturday

Sigma 33: *Vogon II* (C.M. Smith). Etchells: *Shamal* (T. Herbert-Smith & M. Schicht). Darings: *Loup Garou VIII* (J.B. Clark). Dragons: *Fanfare* (Brig. P.H. Henson). Redwings: *Redstart* (J. Janson). Mermaids: *Zara* (R. & C. Dobbs). Squibs: *Mergus* (M.L. Goffe). Victory: *Zest* (K. & S. Taylor).

RORC ** Restricted Division boat*

Cervantes Trophy

Class 1: 1 *Giant Panda* (Porter/Morrell/Sheldon), 19h 33m 21s; **2** *Blizzard* (E. Juer), 17h 44m 49s; *No other finishers.* **Class 2: 1** *Jamarella* (A. Gray), 17h 04m 00s; **2** *Not awarded*; **3** *Griffin* (NSC), 18h 32m 12s; **4** *Top Gun* (C. Davis), 19h 14m 58s; ***** *Big Boots* (D.J. Saunders), 20h 18m 04s. **Class 3: 1** *Jacobite* (S. James), 18h 23m 13s; **2*** *Rakau* (G. Louyot), 18h 39m 10s; **3*** *Highwayman* (P. Johnson), 19h 01m 04s. **Class 4: 1** *Sunstone* (T.C.H. & V. d'E. Jackson), 18h 08m 43s; **2** *Olya IV* (M. Faure), 18h 44m 10s; **3** *Wings of Cowley* (RAFSA), 19h 19m 06s; ***** *Sigmatic II* (D.C. Bonner), 19h 50m 01s. **Class 5: 1** *Insatiable* (Bibby/Heeley), 18h 03m 56s; **2** *Not awarded*; **3*** *Hooligan* (Broadway/White), 20h 15m 36s; **4=** *Fletcher Lynd* (Leroux/Guernon/Champigneux), 20h 51m 03s; **4=*** *Counterpoise* (Met. Pol. SC), 18h 50m 45s (21h 30m 18s after 20 per cent penalty). **Restricted Division. Classes 1, 2 & 3: 1*** *Rakau* (G. Louyot) 18h 39m 10s; **2*** *Highwayman* (P. Johnson), 19h 01m 04s; **3*** *Big Boots* (D.J. Saunders), 20h 18m 04s. **Class 4: 1*** *Sigmatic II* (D.C. Bonner), 19h 50m 01s; **2*** *Beautiful Just* (D. Bates), 19h 59m 26s; **3*** *Somers Isle* (R. Carrell), 20h 13m 14s. **Class 5: 1*** *Hooligan* (Broadway/White), 20h 15m 36s; **2*** *Counterpoise* (Met. Pol. SC), 21h 30m 18s; *No other finishers.* **CHS: 1** *Barracuda of Tarrant* (R. Fisher), 18h 02m 34s; **2** *Phantom* (C. Hatton), 19h 53m 12s; **3** *Zapopan* (J. Stanton), 20h 27m 34s.

North Sea Race

Class 1: 1 *Caiman* (G. Jeelof), 29h 17m 49s; **2** *Promotion V* (B. Dolk), 29h 31m 10s; **3** *Formidable* (P. Vroon), 29h 32m 43s; ***** *Panta Rhei*, 31h 25m 38s. **Class 2: 1** *Mean Machine* (P. de Ridder), 29h 53m 47s; **2** *Poinciana* (T. Vinke), 30h 16m 31s; **3*** *Anne Mazurka* (E. Zande), 32h 02m 29s. **Class 3: 1** *Esperanza* (H. Kraan), 31h 41m 01s; **2*** *Samantha* (A. Duin), 31h 43m 54s; **3*** *Asterix* (W. Walscharts), 31h 48m 52s. **Class 4: 1** *Jelfi-X*, 30h 42m 20s; **2** *Fiona of Burnham* (D. Geaves), 30h 58m 45s; **3** *Escapade* (P. Heerema), 31h 09m 24s; ***** *Matjas* (P. de Kort), 31h 24m 47s. **Class 5: 1*** *Bright Spark* (D. Powell), 31h 28m 45s; **2*** *Courtesan* (C. Brown), 31h 35m 00s; **3*** *General Tapioca* (P. Pilate), 32h 10m 41s.

Loujaine Cup Race

Class 1: 1 *Indulgence* (G. Walker), 17h 19m 23s; **2** *Turkish Delight* (H. Bezman), 17h 21m 37s; **3** *Yeoman XXVI* (O.O. Aisher), 17h 35m 15s. **Class 2: 1** *Xpanda* (P. Shiels), 16h 59m 57s; **2*** *Big Boots* (D.J. Saunders), 18h 04m 13s; **3** *Griffin* (NSC), 18h 13m 30s. **Class 3: 1** *Jacobite* (S. James), 17h 18m 31s; **2** *Spartan* (R. Keeling), 17h 46m 07s; **3*** *Highwayman* (P. Johnson), 17h 53m 02s. **Classes 4 & 5: 1** *Insatiable* (Bibby/Heeley), 17h 53m 18s; **2** *Imperator* (P. Waxman), 18h 06m 43s; **3** *Sunstone* (T.C.H. & V. d'E. Jackson), 18h 08m 44s; ***** *Misty Star* (M.H. Corbin), 20h 14m 32s. **CHS: 1** *Impulse II* (E. Dragten), 19h 12m 55s; **2** *Barracuda of Tarrant* (R. Fisher), 19h 14m 41s; **3** *Houdini* (P.M. Lahaise), 19h 19m 42s. **Restricted Division. Classes 2, 3 & 4: 1*** *Highwayman* (P. Johnson), 17h 53m 02s; **2*** *Big Boots* (D.J. Saunders), 18h 04m 13s; **3*** *Flycatcher* (J.W. Roome), 18h 13m 22s.

De Guingand Bowl Race

Class 1: 1 *Indulgence* (G. Walker), 23h 40m 25s; **2** *Turkish Delight* (H. Bezman), 25h 06m 16s; **3** *Backlash* (T. & C. Herring), 25h 49m 02s. **Class 2: 1** *Jamarella* (A. Gray), 24h 08m 39s; **2** *Juno* (M. Peacock), 24h 40m 12s; **3** *Local Hero IV* (Gallagher/Howison), 24h 48m 18s; ***** *Stormbird* (C.P. Foley), 30h 17m 08s. **Class 2, Open Division: 1** *Jameson Whiskey* (R. Burrows), 24h 29m 00s; **2** *Port du Crouesty* (C. Faque), 24h 35m 22s; **3** *Diamand Bleu* (SNCY La Metairie), 24h 50m 11s. **Class 3: 1** *Jacobite* (S. James), 28h 24m 49s; **2*** *Highwayman* (P. Johnson), 28h 58m 15s; **3*** *Flycatcher* (J. Roome), 29h 02m 33s. **Class 4: 1** *Sunstone* (T.C.H. & V. d'E. Jackson), 27h 25m 12s; **2*** *Enchantress of Hamble* (BP YC), 34h 14m 47s; **3*** *Xepha* (C. Daunton), 36h 30m 22s. **Class 5: 1** *Stradivarius* (W. Borel), 31h 21m 00s; *No other finishers.* **CHS: 1** *Barracuda of Tarrant* (R. Fisher), 26h 18m 35s; **2** *Goose Green* (Britannia SC), 35h 50m 35s; **3** *Sigmadon* (Britannia SC), 37h 07m 32s. **Restricted Division. Classes 2 & 3: 1*** *Highwayman* (P. Johnson), 28h 58m 15s; **2*** *Flycatcher* (J. Roome), 29h 02m 33s; **3** *Stormbird* (C. Foley), 30h 17m 08s. **Class 4: 1*** *Enchantress of Hamble* (BPYC), 34h 14m 37s; **2*** *Xepha* (C. Daunton), 36h 30m 22s; *No other finishers*.

West Mersea–Zeebrugge Race
Class 3: 1* *Moustique* (M. Spear), 31h 54m 00s; **2*** *Asterix* (W. Walscharts), 32h 04m 57s; **3*** *Xara* (D. Barham), 33h 04m 02s. **Class 4: 1** *Fiona of Burnham* (D. Geaves), 30h 41m 35s; **2*** *Clarionet* (J. Breakell), 31h 07m 00s; **3*** *Speak-Easy* (D. & B. Watkinson), 31h 50m 07s. **Class 4: 1*** *Bright Spark* (D. Powell), 30h 39m 03s; **2** *Secrets* (R. Stewart), 31h 01m 03s; **3*** *Tchaika* (G. Anrys-Dufaye), 33h 00m 27s.

Morgan Cup Race
Class 1: 1 *Caiman* (G. Jeelof), 28h 09m 09s; **2** *Yeoman XXVI* (O.O. Aisher), 28h 25m 46s; **3** *Giant Panda* (Porter/Morrell/Sheldon), 28h 30m 17s. **Class 2: 1** *Jamarella* (A. Gray), 27h 04m 35s; **2** *Full Pelt* (S. Fein), 27h 05m 16s; **3** *Juno* (M. Peacock), 27h 06m 19s; * *Big Boots* (D. Saunders), 34h 03m 21s. **Class 3: 1** *Jacobite* (S. James), 27h 37m 54s; **2*** *Geronimo* (A. Curties), 28h 09m 51s; **3** *Flourish* (R. Hedger), 28h 45m 02s. **Class 4: 1** *Sunstone* (T.C.H. & V. d'E. Jackson), 28h 14m 59s; **2** *Imperator* (P. Waxman), 32h 03m 23s; **3*** *White Rooster* (J. Donegan), 32h 04m 34s. **Class 5: 1*** *Alchemist* (Wynter/Bremner), 47h 51m 44s; **2** *Stradivarius* (W. Borel), 48h 32m 49s; **3*** *Olivia Anne IV* (R. Hawkes), 49h 47m 26s. **CHS: 1** *Crackerjack IX* (K. Miller), 29h 52m 50s; **2** *Houdini* (P. Lahaise), 30h 55m 09s; **3** *Barracuda of Tarrant* (R. Fisher), 31h 11m 37s. **Restricted Division. Classes 2 & 3: 1*** *Geronimo* (A. Curties), 28h 09m 51s; **2*** *Rakau* (G. Louyot), 29h 23m 29s; **3*** *Big Boots* (D. Saunders), 34h 03m 21s. **Class 4: 1*** *White Rooster* (J. Donegan), 32h 04m 34s; **2*** *Excalibur* (Dumont/Candellier), 32h 05m 56s; **3*** *Magic Touch* (Horner/Medley), 46h 54m 38s. **Class 5: 1*** *Alchemist* (Wynter/Bremner), 47h 51m 44s; **2*** *Olivia Anne IV* (R. Hawkes), 49h 47m 26s; *No other finishers.*

Cowes–Dinard–St Malo Race
Class 1: 1 *Caiman* (G. Jeelof), 29h 09m 05s; **2** *Backlash* (T. & C. Herring), 29h 34m 05s; **3** *Alvine VIII* (H. Evans), 29h 40m 56s; * *Trilogy* (B. Rizzi), 30h 09m 13s. **Class 2: 1** *Clair de Lune* (B. Labey), 30h 13m 29s; **2** *Ouistreham* (J. Lachevre), 30h 21m 09s; **3*** *Big Boots* (D. Saunders), 30h 24m 42s. **Class 3: 1*** *Flycatcher* (J. Roome), 29h 43m 57s; **2*** *Asterix* (W. Walscharts), 29h 48m 06s; **3*** *Highwayman* (P. Johnson), 29h 48m 32s. **Class 4: 1** *Jane Bottomley* (R. Bottomley), 28h 46m 49s; **2** *Lion* (J. Cruette), 28h 46m 58s; **3*** *Morning Choup* (M. Milinaire), 28h 53m 19s. **Class 5: 1*** *Trocar* (Greville/Munro-Kerr), 28h 55m 24s; **2*** *Scorpio II* (P. Gatrill), 29h 14m 33s; **3** *Fletcher Lynd* (Leroux/Guernon/Champigneux), 29h 24m 48s. **Classes 6 & 7: 1*** *Hullabaloo* (A. Evans), 28h 53m 28s; **3=** *Pinocchio* (Team 10), 29h 01m 50s; **3=*** *Chipeau* (M. Cumberlege), 29h 52m 11s. **Open Division: 1** *X Com* (Coprupriete Tournesort), 28h 49m 03s; *No other finishers.* **CHS Class 1: 1** *Ossian X* (P. Ratzel), 30h 58m 57s; **2** *Crackerjack IX* (K. Miller), 31h 02m 04s; **3** *Option IV* (J. Desteux), 32h 09m 03s. **CHS Class 2: 1** *Quilla* (L. Thomas), 30h 35m 21s; **2** *Billy Bones* (O. Boudot), 30h 55m 40s; **3** *Serenite* (F. Chaplain), 31h 14m 29s. **CHS Class 3: 1** *Fior di Lecci* (A. Legros), 30h 18m 39s; **2** *Trotaralasoup* (R. Bourdin), 30h 41m 28s; **3** *Angimic III* (G. Gouronnec), 30h 58m 03s.

Irish Sea Race
Classes 1 & 2: 1* *Moonduster* (D. Doyle), 23h 49m 19s; **2*** *Imp* (R. Dickson), 24h 31m 13s; **3*** *Stormbird* (C. Foley), 24h 38m 39s. **Class 3: 1** *Megalopolis* (U. Taylor), 24h 17m 47s; **2*** *Tearaway* (Hughes/O'Reilly), 24h 28m 28s; **3*** *'Smagic of Lleyn* (C. Peters), 24h 36m 34s. **Class 4: 1*** *Merry Fiddler* (J. Butterfield), 23h 21m 00s; **2*** *Scenario* (A. Jones), 23h 29m 55s; **3*** *Tessanda III* (B. Pimlott), 23h 30m 49s. **Class 5: 1*** *Insoluble* (N. Thistleton), 23h 10m 47s; **2*** *Enigma* (T. Earls), 23h 13m 52s; **3** *Shearwater* (T. O'Reilly), 23h 16m 45s. **Restricted Division. Classes 1 & 2: 1*** *Moonduster* (D. Doyle), 23h 49m 19s; **2*** *Imp* (R. Dickson), 24h 31m 13s; **3*** *Stormbird* (C. Foley), 24h 38m 39s. **Class 3: 1*** *Tearaway* (Hughes/O'Reilly), 24h 28m 28s; **2*** *'Smagic of Lleyn* (C. Peters), 24h 36m 34s; **3*** *Blue Oyster* (B. Ord), 25h 16m 13s. **Class 4: 1*** *Merry Fiddler* (J. Butterfield), 23h 21m 00s; **2*** *Scenario* (A. Jones), 23h 29m 55s; **3*** *Tessanda III* (B. Pimlott), 23h 30m 49s. **Class 5: 1*** *Insoluble* (N. Thistleton), 23h 10m 47s; **2*** *Enigma* (T. Earls), 23h 13m 52s; **3*** *Crystal Clear* (P. Farrelly), 23h 20m 28s.

Channel Race
Classes A–I: 1 *Indulgence* (G. Walker), 31h 11m 38s; **2** *Diva* (P. Westphal-Langloh), 31h 20m 34s; **3** *Kiwi* (P. Walker), 31h 23m 55s. **Class 1, Open: 1** *Original Beckmann Pletfjerner* (P. Jesperson), 31h 20m 32s; **2** *Mandrake-Krizia* (G. Carriero), 31h 27m 08s; **3** *Corum* (Bénéteau/Corum), 31h 29m 16s. **Classes 1 & 2, Restricted: 1*** *Stormbird* (C. Foley), 31h 51m 15s; **2*** *Struntje* (Schafer/Havemann), 32h 30m 07s; **3*** *Tyfoon VI* (L. Dewulf), 32h 39m 37s. **Class 2, Division 1: 1** *Propaganda* (A. Burr), 30h 55m 34s; **2** *Jamarella* (A. Gray), 30h 55m 50s; **3** *Mayurca* (G. Cryns), 31h 06m 22s; * *Stormbird* (C. Foley), 31h 51m 15s. **Class 2, Open: 1** *I-Punkt* (T. Friese), 31h 02m 47s; **2** *Container* (V. Schütz), 31h 06m 20s; **3** *Goldcorp* (M. Canning), 31h 07m 30s. **Class 3, Division 1: 1*** *Asterix* (W. Walscharts), 31h 17m 32s; **2** *Jacobite* (S. James), 31h 33m 34s; **3*** *Rakau* (G. Louyot), 31h 49m 56s. **Class 3, Restricted: 1*** *Asterix* (W. Walscharts), 31h 17m 32s; **2*** *Xara* (D. Barham), 31h 12m 55s; **3*** *Rakau* (G. Louyot), 31h 49m 56s. **Class 4 Division 1: 1*** *Clarionet* (J. Breakell), 30h 03m 45s; **2** *Sunstone* (T.C.H. & V. d'E. Jackson), 30h 07m 48s; **3** *Liberty* (W. Haehnel), 30h 34m 09s. **Class 4, Restricted: 1*** *Clarionet* (J. Breakell), 30h 03m 45s; **2*** *Matjas* (P. de Kort), 30h 39m 44s; **3*** *Speak-Easy* (D. & B. Watkinson), 30h 51m 03s. **Class 5, Division 1: 1*** *Przeprazam* (F. Jungblut), 30h 10m 16s; **2** *Glider* (Barton/Morris), 30h 22m 48s; **3** *Stradivarius* (W. Borel), 30h 34m 05s. **Class 5, Restricted: 1*** *Przeprazam* (F. Jungblut), 30h 10m 16s; **2*** *Trocar* (D. Munro-Kerr), 30h 38m 42s; **3*** *Freyja* (E. Fries), 30h 39m 25s. **CHS: 1** *Quilla* (L. Thomas), 32h 05m 08s; **2** *Jay Jay* (Britannia SC), 33h 03m 31s; **3** *Goose Green* (Britannia SC), 33h 04m 55s.

Fastnet Race
Class 1: 1 *Sidewinder* (R. Short), 87h 14m 36s; **2** *Pinta* (W. Illbruck), 87h 19m 13s; **3** *Kiwi* (P. Walker), 87h 50m 04s. **Class 1, Open: 1** *Original Beckmann Pletfjerner* (P. Jesperson), 87h 07m 04s; **2** *Swan Premium III* (P. Kurts), 87h 48m 10s; **3** *Mandrake-Krizia* (G. Carriero), 89h 02m 47s. **Class 1, Restricted: 1*** *Struntje V* (Schafer/Havemann), 92h 15m 32s; **2*** *Moonduster* (D. Doyle), 96h 58m 16s; **3*** *Hamburg* (C. Frieling), 113h 30m 03s. **Class 2: 1** *Juno* (M. Peacock), 86h 35m 27s; **2** *Jamarella* (A. Gray), 86h 35m 32s; **3** *Propaganda* (A. Burr), 86h 37m 29s. **Class 2, Open: 1** *Irish Independent/Full Pelt* (S. Fein), 86h 33m 43s; **2** *Centurion-Musclor* (J. Dick), 86h 39m 00s; **3** *Swan Premium I* (L. Abrahams), 86h 44m 10s. **Class 2, Restricted: 1*** *Imp* (R. Dickson), 111h 16m 28s; **2*** *Norma* (H. Baum), 111h 30m 07s; **3*** *Big Boots* (D. Saunders), 111h 50m 34s. **Class 3: 1** *Asterix* (W. Walscharts), 106h 09m 27s; **2** *Veronier II* (C. Vroege), 106h 21m 45s; **3** *Xara* (D. Barham), 106h 47m 40s. **Class 3, Restricted: 1*** *Asterix* (W. Walscharts), 106h 09m 27s; **2*** *Veronier II* (C. Vroege), 106h 21m 45s; **3*** *Xara* (D. Barham), 106h 47m 40s. **Class 4: 1** *Sunstone* (T.C.H. & V. d'E. Jackson), 103h 17m 20s; **2** *Ivory Moon* (J. Yarrow), 103h 48m 48s; **3** *Clarionet* (J. Breakell), 103h 50m 06s. **Class 4, Restricted: 1*** *Clarionet* (J. Breakell), 103h 50m 06s; **2*** *High Spirits* (C. Gillard), 103h 54m 07s; **3*** *Somers Isle* (R. Carrell), 103h 57m 35s. **Class 5: 1*** *Olivia Anne IV* (R. Hawkes), 101h 18m 11s; **2*** *Trocar* (D. Munro-Kerr), 102h 14m 11s; **3** *Emblem* (P. Mead), 102h 23m 14s. **Class 5, Restricted: 1*** *Olivia Anne IV* (R. Hawkes), 101h 18m 11s; **2*** *Trocar* (D. Munro-Kerr), 102h 14m 11s; **3*** *Goud Reinette* (R. Maller), 102h 42m 14s.

Wolf Rock Race
1 *Panic Major* (R. Nickerson), 43h 31m 58s; **2** *Barracuda of Tarrant* (R. Fisher), 49h 51m 19s; **3** *Riot* (J. Turner), 53h 25m 37s.

Solent–Torquay Race
Classes 3, 4 & 5: 1 *Insatiable* (Bibby & Heeley), 18h 43m 52s; **2*** *Hullabaloo* (A. Evans), 19h 36m 56s; **3** *Sunstone* (T.C.H. & V. d'E. Jackson), 19h 42m 15s. **CHS: 1** *Amanda Kulu* (A. Porter), 22h 05m 02s; **2** *Mutine* (Cdr E. Morrison), 22h 57m 46s; **3** *Barracuda of Tarrant* (R. Fisher), 23h 22m 47s. **Restricted Division. Classes 3, 4 & 5: 1*** *Hullabaloo* (A. Evans), 19h 36m 56s; **2*** *Pentagram* (Lord Burnham), 21h 44m 51s; *No other finishers.*

Solent–Ouistreham Race
Class 1: 1 *Spartan* (R. Keeling), 19h 08m 07s; **2*** *Trilogy* (B. Rizzi), 19h 26m 53s; **3** *Giant Panda* (Porter/Morrell/Sheldon), 20h 07m 10s. **Class 2: 1*** *Manitou* (J. Merron), 19h 31m 59s; **2** *Sidewinder* (R. Short), 19h 47m 17s; **3** *Blue Saxon* (J. Burton), 19h 50m 48s. **Class 3: 1** *Jacobite* (S. James), 18h 35m 08s; **2** *Flourish* (R. Hedger), 19h 39m 15s; **3*** *Pentagram* (Lord Burnham), 20h 27m 18s. **Classes 4 & 5: 1** *Wings of Cowley* (RAFSA), 19h 55m 33s; **2** *Sunstone* (T.C.H. & V. d'E. Jackson), 20h 19m 25s; **3** *Smokey Bear* (Cyriax & Gale), 20h 28m 39s; * *Olivia Anne IV* (R. Hawkes), 20h 52m 00s. **CHS 1: 1** *Bobtail* (Britannia SC), 21h 09m 56s; **2** *Barracuda of Tarrant* (R. Fisher), 21h 49m 45s; **3** *Parhelion* (T.P. & Dr K. Waite), 22h 24m 13s. **CHS 2: 1** *Oblivion Ex* (C. Stow), 20h 53m 51s; **2** *Boadicea* (Britannia SC), 21h 46m 27s; **3** *Tirade* (J. Gibbons), 22h 46m 20s.

RORC OVERALL POINTS

RORC Yacht of the Year
Jamarella (A. Gray).

IOR   * *Position in Restricted Division*
Class I: 1 *Indulgence* (G. Walker, GB), 352 pts; **2** *Caiman* (G. Jeelof, NL), 335; **3** *Turkish Delight* (H. Bezman, GB), 323. **Class II: 1** *Jamarella* (A. Gray, GB), 388; **2** *Juno* (M. Peacock, GB), 372; **3** *Junon* (A. Faure, F), 307. **Class III: 1 (*1)** *Asterix* (W. Walscharts, B), 360; **2** *Jacobite* (S. James, GB), 325; **3 (*2)** *Highwayman* (P. Johnson, GB), 321. **Class IV: 1** *Sunstone* (V. Jackson, GB), 411; **2 (*1)** *Clarionet* (J. Breakell, GB), 360; **3** *Imperator* (P. Waxman, GB), 322. **Class V: 1 (*1)** *Trocar* (D. Munro-Kerr, GB), 357; **2 (*2)** *Olivia Anne IV* (R. Hawkes, GB), 275; **3** *Stradivarius* (W. Borel, F), 246.

Restricted Division
Class I: 1 *Tyfoon VI* (L. de Wulf, B); **2** *Moonduster* (D. Doyle, IRL); **3** *Spirit of Ramfish* (A. van Stolk, NL). **Class II: 1** *Big Boots* (D. Saunders, GB); **2** *Stormbird* (C. Foley, IRL); **3** *Imp* (R. Dickson, GB). **Class III: 3** *Xara* (D. Barham, GB). **Class IV: 2** *Speak-Easy* (D. Watkinson, GB); **3** *Magic Touch* (P. Homer, GB). **Class V: 3** *Counterpoise* (Met. Pol. SC, GB). **CHS: 1** *Barracuda* (R. Fisher, GB); **2** *Zapopan* (J. Stanton, GB); **3** *Aquadanca* (J. Oldland, GB).

SOLENT POINTS CHAMPIONSHIP

Early Series
Class 1 (IOR): 1 *Indulgence* (G. Walker, GB); **2** *Jamarella* (A. Gray, GB); **3** *Blazer* (Blazer Syndicate, GB). **Class 2 (IOR): 1** *Jane Bottomley* (R. Bottomley, GB); **2** *Bathsheba* (M. Laing, GB); **3** *White Gold III* (A. Miller, GB). **Class 3 (IOR): 1** *Insatiable* (J. Bibby, GB, & M. Heeley, GB); **2** *Bullfrog* (M. Thorpe, GB); **3** *Starlet* (J. Devine, GB). **Class 4 (IOR): 1** *Glass Onion* (R. Franklin, GB); **2** *Catch* (J. Allenby, GB); **3** *Quillet* (A. Dodd, GB, & D. Rider, GB). **Class 5 (CHS): 1** *Sun Beat* (W. Courtney, GB); **2** *Sea Biscuit* (H. Stafford, GB); **3** *Secret Obsession* (G. Shaw, GB). **Class 6 (CHS):** *No race.*

Late Series
Class 1 (IOR): 1 *Yeoman XXVI* (O.O. Aisher); *Jenny M* (R. Barker); **3** *Conspiracy* (Lethbridge & Partners). **Class 2 (IOR): 1** *White Gold III* (A. Miller); **2** *Bathsheba* (M. Laing); **3** *Pentagram* (Lord Burnham). **Class 3 (IOR): 1** *Insatiable* (J. Bibby/M. Heeley); **2** *Starlet* (J. Devine); **3** *Bullfrog* (M. Thorpe). **Class 4 (IOR): 1** *Catch* (J. Allenby); **2** *Rattler* (T. Pountain); **3** *Quillet* (A. Dodd/D. Rider). **Class 5 (CHS): 1** *Redcoat* (ASA); **2** *Barracuda* (R. Fisher); **3** *Impulse II* (E. Dragten). **Class 6 (CHS):** *No race.*

Australian & New Zealand Summertime

New Zealand

Admiral's Cup Final Selection Trials
Goldcorp (R. Dodson) 1-1-1-1-2-4-1; *Kiwi* (P. Walker) 5-2-2-4-1-1-2; *Propaganda* (B. Woolley) 2-3-3-3-3-3-4; *Fair Share* (D. Hogg) 3-4-5-2-5-2-5; *Swuzzlebubble VI* (I. Gibbs) 4-5-4-5-4-5-3.

Air Pacific Auckland–Suva Race
Line: *Satellite Spy* (M. Ross) 5d 19h 22m. **IOR: 1** *Dictator* (B. Petersen); **2** *Chick Chack* (S. Haslett); **3** *Domineer* (G. Roper). **PHRF overall: 1** *Foreign Exchange* (D. Nathan); **2** *Bon Accord* (B. Carmichael); **3** *Chinchilla* (W. Tomlinson). **A Division: 1** *Foreign Exchange*; **2** *Big Ruby* (L. Newhook); **3** *Chinchilla*. **B Division: 1** *Gemini Dream* (J. Peterson); **2** *Dictator*; **3** *Bon Accord*.

Avis Regatta
A Division: 1 *Party Pro* (G. Elliott); **2** *Witch Doctor* (R. Nalder); **3** *Satellite Spy* (M. Ross). **B Division: 1** *Head Office* (J. Davies); **2** *Warringa* (J. Foote); **3** *Cabaret* (R. Jones). **C Division: 1** *First Edition* (T. Taunt); **2** *Razzle Dazzle* (B. Heerdegen); **3** *Rainbow IV* (M. Ure). **D Division: 1** *Natasha* (B. Heron); **2** *Paramour* (B. Tantrum); **3** *Providence* (I. Bracey).

Bucklands Beach YC Auckland–Onerahi Race
Line, A Division: *Satellite Spy*. **B Division:** *River Rebel*. **C Division:** *Positive Touch*. **Two-handed:** *Big Ruby*. **Multihulls:** *Afterburner*. **Handicap, A Division: 1** *Domino II*; **2** *Transformer*; **3** *Satellite Spy*. **B Division: 1** *Maraquita*; **2** *Sergeant Pepper*; **3** *Quiet Fire*. **C Division: 1** *Promoter*; **2** *Wilparina*; **3** *Positive Touch*. **D Division: 1** *Cayucos*; **2** *Seventh Heaven*; **3** *Creme de la Creme*. **Multihulls: 1** *Demon Tricycle*; **2** *Falcon Forwards*; **3** *Twisted Sisters*.

Citizen Watch Match Racing Series
1 R. Davis (USA) 9 wins; **2** E. Warden-Owen (GB) 7 wins; **3=** P. Gilmour (AUS) and C. Dickson (NZ) 6 wins; **5** P. Isler (US) 5 wins; **6=** J. Shadden (US) and R. Royden (NZ) 4 wins; **8=** C. Packer (NZ) and M. Cookson (NZ) 2 wins; **10** K. Komatsu (J) 0 wins.

Continental Airlines Champion of Champions (sailed in Nolex 25s)
1 R. Davis (US) 23 pts; **2** T. Dodson (NZ) 24.2; **3** A. Ball (NZ) 33.4.

Dorlon Winter Series
Division 1, line: *Satellite Spy*. **Handicap: 1** *Witchdoctor*; **2** *Ranger*; **3** *Ponsonby Scow*. **Division 2, line:** *Big Ruby*. **Handicap: 1** *Big Ruby*; **2** *Clark Gable*; **3** *Force Eleven*. **Division 3 (Stewart 34), line:** *Prism*. **Handicap: 1** *Prism*; **2** *Pindaric*; **3** *Patrician*. **Division 4 (Ross 9.3), line:** *Recreation*. **Handicap: 1** *Pepe*; **2** *Sachtung*; **3** *Grunt Machine*. **Division 5, line:** *Tarara*. **Handicap: 1** *Stepping Stone*; **2** *Tarara*; **3** *Arbitrator*. **Division 6, line:** *Fleet Street*. **Handicap: 1** *Farrstrak*; **2** *Fleet Street*; **3** *Men At Work*. **Division 7, line:** *Rage*. **Handicap: 1** *Rage*. **2** *Convincible*; **3** *Clare Buoyant*. **Division 8 (Davidson 28), line:** *Freewheeling*. **Handicap: 1** *Thalassa*; **2** *Petty Theft*; **3** *Freewheeling*. **Division 9, line:** *Afterburner*. **Handicap 1** *Falcon Forwarders*; **2** *Wang*; **3** *Impulse*. **Division 10, line:** *E-Type II*. **Handicap: 1** *Space Runner*; **2** *E-Type II*; **3** *Manumea*. **Division 11, line:** *Hasslefree*. **Handicap: 1** *Dawnbreaker*; **2** *Hasslefree*; **3** *Bullwinkle*. **Division 12, (Reactor), line:** *Quita*. **Handicap: 1** *Toujours*; **2** *William Seagull*; **3** *Sassy*. **Division 13, line:** *Pelagos*. **Handicap: 1** *Torero*; **2** *Conquest II*; **3** *Undersided*. **Division 14 (Elliott 5.9), line:** *Fat City*. **Handicap: 1** *Fat City*; **2** *E-Type*; **3** *Whoop De Doo*. **Division 15 (Coronet), line:** *Caravel*. **Handicap: 1** *Nereid*; **2** *Chokito*; **3** *Caravel*. **Division 16, line:** *Crossfire*. **Handicap: 1** *Beach Loop*; **2=** *Fat Albert* and *Estelle*. **Division 17, line:** *Quip*. **Handicap: 1** *Rigmarole*; **2** *Tonic*; **3=** *Tui* and *Merlinder*. **Division 18, (Hobie 16), line:** *Hauraki Mark*. **Handicap: 1** *Dire Straits*; **2** *Elder*; **3** *Hauraki Mark*. **Division 19 (Prindle), line:** *Mr Fussy*. **Handicap: 1** *Fright-ning*; **2** *Catastrophe*; **3** *Mr Fussy*.

Epiglass Olympicsail Regatta
470: 1 P. Evans/S. Mander 6 pts; **2** G. Sowry/P. McNeil 14.7; **3** J. Bilger/I. Purdie 32.4. **Flying Dutchman: 1** M. Jones/G. Knowles 11 pts; **2** D. Mackay/L. Carter 14.7; **3** D. Barnes/B. Deegan 25.8. **Finn: 1** J. Irvine 16.7 pts; **2** L. Armit 28.1; **3** C. Monk 32. **Soling: 1** G. Gibson/Conroy/Guyver 8.7 pts; **2** P. Meo/Clark/Mark 12; **3** P. Shonk/Dickson/Sinclair 38.4. **Tornado: 1** B. Jones/A. Knowles 0 pts; **2** J. Thomson/M. Boswell 23; **3** T. Scott/C. Philpott 41.1. **Sailboard: 1** B. Kendall 0 pts; **2** N. Ball 20.7; **3** B. Trotter 36.7.

Epiglass/Richmond YC Wednesday Night Series (best 8 of 10 races)
A Division: 1 *Jenny G* 64.4 pts; **2** *Satellite Spy* 66.4; **3** *Clark Gable* 70.4. **B Division: 1** *Dollar Bill* 86.8 pts; **2** *Kon Tiki* 87.4; **3** *Windigo 88*. **C Division: 1** *Cayucos* 70.7 pts; **2** *Gatecrasher* 73.4; **3** *Vintago* 83.7. **D Division: 1** *Doughnut* 80.8 pts; **2** *Twiggy* 80.7; **3** *Hasslefree* 102.7. **E Division: 1** *Meltdown* 45.7 pts; **2** *The Pirate* 71.2; **3** *Legless* 78.8.

Macleay–Duff Auckland–Gisborne Race
Line: *Party Pro* (G. Elliott). **IOR: 1** *Witchdoctor* (R. Nalder); **2** *Fair Share* (D. Hogg); **3** *Barnstorm* (J. Hall). **PHRF: 1** *Satellite Spy* (M. Ross); **2** *Borderline* (D. Wade); **3** *Big Ruby* (L. Newhook).

Macleay–Duff Napier–Gisborne Race
Line: *Destination* (J. Bridgeman). **PHRF: 1** *Blood Vessel* (N. Page/T. Byrnes); **2** *Antigone* (R. Sheldrake); **3** *Actionaire* (P. Hobbs).

Macleay–Duff Wellington–Gisborne Race
Line: *Whispers II* (L. England) 2d 8h 12m 39s. **IOR: 1** *Whispers II*; **2** *Aztec* (B. Coleman); **3** *Nizam* (G. Hargreaves). **PHRF: 1** *Whispers II*; **2** *Aztec*; **3** *Machine Gun* (G. Butcher).

Malcolm Fowler Motors Auckland–Tauranga Race
Line: *Witchdoctor* (R. Nalder). **IOR: 1** *Razzle Dazzle* (R. Dickie); **2** *Berenice* (W. Mitchenson); **3** *Scoundrel* (A. Montague). **PHRF: 1** *Razzle Dazzle*; **2** *Kon Tiki* (J. Lavelle); **3** *Berenice*.

Royal Port Nicholson YC Cook Strait Race
Line: *Cotton Blossom* (D. Gold) 3h 44m 31s. **IOR: 1** *Nizam* (G. Hargreaves); **2** *Kinetic* (J. Moody); **3** *Aztec* (B. Coleman). **PHRF: 1** *Nirvana* (A. Macalister); **2** *Nizam*; **3** *Aztec*. **Club Handicap: 1** *Reflections* (K. Parker); **2** *Phortys* (J. Phorty); **3** *Nirvana*.

Russell BC Tall Ships Race
Line: *Tiree II* (B. Waldron). **Handicap: 1** *Tiree II*; **2** *Ginseng* (D. Scott); **3** *Rere Moana* (R.Hope-Lewis).

Wellington–Nelson Race
Line: *Party Pro* (G. Elliott) 18h 17m. **IOR: 1** *Aztec* (B. Coleman); **2** *Rhythm* (L. Evans); **3** *Kinetic* (B. Cardiff). **PHRF: 1** *Aztec*; **2** *Mint* (E. Fehsenfeld); **3** *Resolution Trader* (W. Rankin). **Club Handicap: 1** *Aztec*; **2** *Mint*; **3** *Party Pro*.

Australia

Dragon Worlds
1 *Nordjylloong* (V. Bandolowski, DK) 1-9-2-3-2-22-12, 44·7; **2** *Fiasco* (A. Lohmann, D) 5-2-28-5-3-Disq-1, 62·7; **3** *Maj Britt* (Stephen Boyes, AUS), 4-8-6-12-13-1-7, 64·7; **4** *Kirribilli II* (Geoff Morris, AUS) 11-10-9-31-8-5-2, 75·0; **5** *Hotspur* (Willy Packer, AUS) 6-5-17-Rtd-5-8-5, 78·7; **6** *Charisma* (Peter Bowman, AUS) 3-12-19-9-4-14-9, 80·7; **7** *Fascination* (David Wilson, AUS) 20-1-15-2-11-9-29, 82·0; **8** *St George* (Tony Bull, AUS) 16-18-4-6-14-2-19, 88·7; **9** *Joker* (Fred Imhoff, NL) 12-23-5-1-15-6-23, 89·7; **10** *Frange Benefit* (Bruce King, AUS) 8-3-32-21-7-4-16, 91·7.

Laser Worlds
1 S. Wallace (KA) 5-1-23-10-7-3, 25·75; **2** C. Pedersen (D) 11-46-8-3-1-14, 36·75; **3** P. Tanscheit (BR) 1-Disq-5-6-22-8, 41·75; **4** N. Alencastro (BR) 57-2-2-2-20-21, 47·00; **5** S. Cole (K) 23-43-3-4-9-12, 51·00; **6** G. Svensson (S) 2-3-10-8-33-52, 60·00; **7** B. Alm (S) 17-Pms-17-14-3-20, 71·00; **8** A. McClure (KA) 4-19-27-55-12-23, 85·00; **9** J. Penteado Bilho (BR) 16-3-37-1-40-29, 85·75; **10** M. Budd (K) 53-18-9-7-17-38, 89·00.

Moth Worlds
World Titles: 1 *Gladiator* (S. Shimeld, NSW) DNF-1-1-5-4-14-1, 38; **2** *Straycraft* (A. Cuddihy, NSW) 15-3-2-11-12-3-5, 59·4; **3** *Bunyip* (G. Hilton, WA) DNF-3-10-2-1-31-2, 64·7; **4** *Bruce the Boat* (R. LeFevre, NSW) DNF-2-4-16-6-4, 65·7; **5** *Relentless* (V. Tidy, WA), 1-9-43-1-2-48-3, 72·7; **6** *Ridjidij* (J. Cook, WA) 4-7-17-7-5-51-9, 82; **7** *Animul* (R. Angell, UK) 9-12-3-21-15-2-DNS, 89·7; **8** *Arpalfarpalfarpa Sprarpout* (P. Morrison, NSW) 10-6-6-9-14-17-10, 90·4; **9** *Wizard Glick* (J. Hilton, WA) 3-8-15-DNS-3-32-7, 97·4; **10** *Rampant* (A. Tidy, WA) 5-13-20-6-11-35-16, 105·7.

Admiral's Cup Trials
1 *Ronstan Ultimate Challenge*, Dubois 30·54, 6-3-4-6-3-4-3-2-2-3-2-1, 67·0; **2** *Sagacious V*, Farr 30·45, 4-4-5-2-DNF-5-4-1=-3-4-1-2, 65·661; **3** *Madeline's Daughter*, Farr 44, 34·34, 1-2-2-3-1-1-5-5-1-4-5, 65·326; **4** *Joint Venture*, Frers 30·55, 2-1-1-4-4-3-7-3-1-6-3-4, 57·695; **5** *Rosemount Wild Oats*, Farr 43, 33·41, 3-DNF-3-1-2-2-6-6-8-2-5-7, 51·660; **6** *Contractor*, Frers 34·44, 7-5-6-5-7-7-8-7-7-6-6, 28·663; **7** *Hitchhiker II*, 30·63 5-DNF-DNS-DNS-6-6-2-4-6-DNS-DNS-DNS, 27·332; **8** *Blue Max II*, Davidson 31·27, 8-DNF-7-7-5-8-5-8=-3-DNF-DNS-3, 24·665.

Hamilton Island Race Week
IOR Division: 1 *Indian Pacific* (J. Eyles) 6-1-2-5-1-4-1, 589; **2** *Witchcraft II* (B. Staples) 2-4-DNF-2-2-1-2, 588; **3** *Szechwan* (W. Johns) 1-3-5-1-7-6-4, 582; **4** *Ex-Tension* (T. Dunn) 5-2-3-3-5-3-12, 579; **5** *Sovereign* (B. Lewis) 4-11-1-4-8-2-8, 574; **6** *Bush Fire* (G. Bush) 3-7-4-10-4-7-3, 569; **7** *Di Hard* (R. Foot) 10-6-13-11-3-5-9, 556; **8** *Challenge II* (P. Rowsthorn) 9-8-6-13-9-8-7, 549; **9** *Castaway Enterprise* (E. Askew) 7-14-7-6-11-15-10, 545; **10** *Impeccable* (J. Walker) 12-9-10-12-10-13-6, 541. **Multihulls: 1** *Aurora* (P. Claringbold) 6-1-1-6-5-1, 589; **2** *Gold Rush* (G. Toomey) 3-5-4-3-1-3-3, 584; **3** *The Frog* (C. Hawkins) 2-6-2-7-4-1-4, 581; **4** *Gotcha Covered* (P. Leitner) 1-4-5-5-5-2-7, 579; **5** *Mad Dog* (K. Mitchell) 5-3-6-2-2-4-5, 579. **Performance Handicap: 1** *Farr Cical* (T. Kelly) 2-4-1-4-10-1-2, 588; **2** *Klinger* (M. Lowcock) 8-5-11-3-1-2-1, 582; **3** *Waterline* (D. Brook) 10-1-4-6-15-6-4, 570; **4** *Eric IV* (M. Munro) 4-2-3-9-9-7-13, 566; **5** *Imogene* (A. Seiffert) 1-12-8-11-13-3-6, 560; **6** *Welsh Dragon* (T. Hippisley) 5-15-6-5-5-10-10, 559; **7** *Akarana* (I. Hamilton) 7-6-10-7-8-8-5, 559; **8** *Kookaburra II* (R. Knott) 3-9-9-15-3-5-12, 556; **9** *Razoo* (D. Foster) 14-13-7-1-2-13, 551; **10** *Galatea* (F. Darbyshire) 6-14-12-8-7-14-3, 550. **Cruising: 1** *Allegro* (A. Young) 3-1-1-2-4-3-1, 592; **2** *Matelot of Mooloolah* (D. Seaborn 4-9-2-6-1-2-3, 583; **3** *Windborne* (N. Feros) 2-4-3-1-5-12-7, 579; **4** *The Thief of Time* (R. Darwen) DNF-7-5-7-2-1-2, 577; **5** *Nomad* (J. & A. Welk) 5-2-6-11-3-7-5, 572; **6** *Sam Jones* (N. Kerr/B. Peet) DNS-5-8-8-11-6-4, 558; **7** *Tanu* (P. Gibson) 9-8-11-9-8-4-6, 556; **8** *Gallivant* (A. Reid) 1-10-10-4-12-10-11, 555; **9** *Crackajack* (T. Cadell) 7-13-12-10-10-11-10, 540; **10** *Big Drak* (K. Gould) 6-12-13-15-9-9-DNS, 536.

AWA Sydney–Hobart 1986
Overall Handicap: 1 *Ex-Tension* (A. Dunn, NSW), Davidson 36, rating 27·5, corrected time 3d 1h 14m 30s; **2** *Impeccable* (J. Walker, NSW), Peterson 3/4, 24·2, 3d 1h 22m 52s; **3** *Southern Cross* (W. Gilbert, NSW), 3d 1h 41m 42s; **4** *Paladin* (C. Franklin, NSW), Farr 40, 30·4, 3d 0h 27m 38s; **5** *Szechwan* (W. Johns, NSW), Davidson One Tonner, 29·3, 3d 2h 33m 31s; **6** *Another Concubine* (J. Parker, NSW), Farr 40, 30·2, 3d 2h 44m 10s; **7** *Silver Minx* (G. Player, NSW), Farr 37, 27·9, 3d 2h 52m 16s; **8** *Hindsight II* (R. Griffin, NSW), Carter 30, 20·5, 3d 3h 11m 42s; **9** *Indian Pacific* (C. Jacobsen, Vic), Farr 40, 30·2, 3d 3h 16m 1s; **10** *Intrigue* (D. Calvert, Tas), Castro One Tonner, 30·3, 3d 3h 19m 45s. **Maxi division: 1** *Condor* (R. Bell, Bermuda), Holland, 70·0, 3d 3h 32m 2s; **2** *Windward Passage* (R. Muir, NSW), Gurney, 69·8, 3d 3h 50m 26s; **3** *Castaway Enterprise* (D. Taylor), Farr, 70·0, 3d 7h 12m 4s. **Division A: 1** *Challenge III* (L. Abrahams, Vic), Frers 43, 33·3, 3d 4h 35m 21s; **2** *Uptown Girl* (R. Winton, NSW), Peterson Two Tonner, 31·5, 3d 4h 49m 14s; **3** *Wild Oats* (R. Oatley, NSW), Farr 43, 33·4, 3d 5h 12m 9s. **Division B: 1** *Paladin*; **2** *Szechwan*; **3** *Another Concubine*. **Division C: 1** *Ex-Tension*; **2** *Southern Cross*; **3** *Silver Minx*. **Division D: 1** *Impeccable*; **2** *Hindsight II*; **3** *Singapore Girl* (P. Steingrad/G. Greenlaw, NSW), Davidson 34, 24·5, 3h 3d 49m 23s. **Line Honours: 1** *Condor*, elapsed time 2d 23h 26m 25s; **2** *Windward Passage*, 2d 23h 47m 54s; **3** *Castaway Enterprise*, 3d 2h 55m 8s.